Essays on the Political Economy of Africa

Essays on the Political Economy of Africa

*by Giovanni Arrighi
and John S. Saul*

Monthly Review Press
New York and London

Library of Congress Cataloging in Publication Data

Arrighi, Giovanni.
    Essays on the political economy of Africa.
    Includes bibliographical references.
    Contents: *Overviews:* Arrighi, G. and Saul, J. S.
Socialism and economic development in tropical Africa.
Arrighi, G. and Saul, J. S. Nationalism and revolution
in sub-Saharan Africa. [etc.]
    1. Africa, Sub-Saharan—Economic conditions.
2. Socialism in Sub-Saharan Africa. 3. Africa,
Sub-Saharan—Social conditions. I. Saul, John S. II. Title.
HC502.A73   330.9'67   72-81772   ISBN 0-85345-234-2

First Modern Reader Paperback Edition 1973
Third Printing

Monthly Review Press
62 West 14th Street, New York, N.Y. 10011
21 Theobalds Road, London WC1X 8SL

Manufactured in the United States of America

Contents

Preface

The essays collected in this volume, though they have been written over a period of some years and for a variety of forums and purposes, are held together as a more or less coherent whole by the common perspective which they evidence, a perspective nurtured by our experience during a number of years' residence in Africa. The first relevant dimension of this experience was a growing realization that our training in two of the established social sciences (economics and political science) was of only limited use in understanding the various transformations and problems we found to be present in Africa. This elicited an attempt to engage, with others, in the search for new methodologies capable of ordering and illuminating the data with which we were presented. The second relevant dimension was a growing awareness of the extent to which "structures of domination" (shaped by the interaction of contemporary imperialism with patterns of domestic class formation) were the most important variables affecting the prospects for African progress and development. This forced upon us the duty to assist in the search for novel and effective means whereby the anti-imperialist struggle could be waged.

These two dimensions coalesced in a conviction that one possible contribution to such a struggle would be to help in the development of theory and analysis at once intellectually more satisfying and strategically more relevant. In this effort we took our cue from the words of Amilcar Cabral, who said that "the crisis of the African revolution . . . is not a crisis of growth, but mainly a crisis of knowledge. In too many cases the struggle for liberation and our plans for the future are not only without a

7

theoretical base, but are also more or less cut off from the concrete situation in which we are working." To be sure, some of the essays included here will inevitably seem much too "academic" to many revolutionary purists. But, in aspiration at least, even these are informed by an attempt to identify with the oppressed in their struggle. Above all, particularly at this relatively early stage of our own thinking on such issues, they must be considered mere "openers" for discussion; they will have fully served their purpose if they earn the sort of constructive criticism from concerned radicals, both on the African continent and in the metropolitan centers, that can help all of us to advance the analysis further.

Of course, scholarship which is Marxist and socialist in its aspiration, its method, its spirit, always develops best in a context of collective toil and comradely interchange. And in the course of writing these essays both authors already have profited from work with comrades in Zimbabwe, in Tanzania, and elsewhere, who have debated with us, criticized and encouraged our undertakings, shared in common intellectual and political effort. It would be invidious to single out names from the long list of such associates that might be printed here; they cannot, in any case, share responsibility for the many "failures of analytical nerve" which remain. Our debt to them is very real, nonetheless.

Giovanni Arrighi
John S. Saul

Milan and Dar es Salaam
January 1973

Part I

Overviews

I

Socialism and Economic Development in Tropical Africa

Giovanni Arrighi and John S. Saul

A noted economist (Perroux) has defined socialism as "le développement de tout l'homme et de tous les hommes." The motor for a drive toward socialism is generally to be found in a conviction that man's creative potential can only be fully realized in a society which transcends the cultural centrality of "possessive individualism" and in which a signal measure of economic and social equality, the precondition for genuine political democracy, is guaranteed. In the best of socialist intellectual work, however, socialists have been equally interested in economic development and in the full release of the potential for growth of the productive forces in a society. Within this tradition it was perhaps Marx who most dramatically fused the concern for economic development and the concern for the elimination of class inequalities in his presentation of the socialist case. He argued that the inequalities of the bourgeois society of his day increasingly meant that the potential of the available industrial machine would not be realized: inequality and muffled productive forces thus went hand in hand.[1]

Certain class inequalities have sometimes proved to be historically necessary to foster the full release of the potential for growth of the social productive forces; this is too obvious a fact to require emphasis. But the existence either of some necessary dichotomy between "development" and "equality" or, on the contrary, of some necessary link between the two cannot be postulated a priori. It has to be ascertained empirically through an analysis of the relationship between the class

This article first appeared in *The Journal of Modern African Studies*, no. 2(1968), pp. 141–69. An earlier version was presented to the plenary session of the University of East Africa Social Science Conference in Dar es Salaam in January 1968.

structure of a society and its economic development at each historical juncture. A sophisticated socialist case in contemporary Africa must therefore fuse a concern for an increased rate of economic development with a perception of the role played in the development equation by the existence and emergence of classes and groups with differential interests and access to benefits. Moreover, as will be argued here, one does in fact find the productive potential of African societies, and therefore their development and structural transformation, constrained by the present pattern of world and domestic economy and society; the available surplus is ill utilized—drained away as the repatriated profits of overseas firms, or consumed by self-indulgent domestic elites—and the generation of a larger surplus from, for example, an aroused and mobilized peasantry discouraged. As this suggests, it is the pattern of current inequality, in particular, which tends thus to hamper a rise in productivity.

A viable socialist strategy directed toward these twin concerns will have to face dilemmas of choice in three closely related policy areas. On the level of the international economic and social system, one confronts the specter of international capitalism and a grave inequality of financial power, realities which, as will be shown, can be major constraints on general development. On the domestic scene, one faces the problem of the relationship between "town," the center of administration and of such industrialization as takes place, and "country," an interaction from which real development could spring but which all too often defines the split between unequal and unconnected spheres of a society falling short of genuine transformation. Finally, one has the problem of agricultural development itself in a rural sphere where inequalities can and do begin to emerge, although, at least in the short run, these have a rather more ambiguous impact on the pace of development than the other inequalities already hinted at.

It is the absence of a really hard-headed look at the actual pattern of inequalities within contemporary Africa and in the world at large *and* at the direct relationship of this pattern to the trajectory of growth and development which explains the superficial character of much of the gloss on "African socialism" presented by its practitioners. To this point we shall return. This failure of analytical nerve also explains the generally unsatisfactory character of the bulk of academic commentary on the phenomenon of African socialism. Perhaps the *locus classicus* of this body of work is a much-cited article by Elliot Berg entitled "Socialism and

Economic Development in Tropical Africa." [2] Berg makes much of the failure of the Guinean experience, as well as several points of general interest, culminating in a swinging dismissal of the pretensions of a "socialist case" for tropical Africa. But his analysis is undermined by a seeming disinterest in defining or taking seriously the real dilemma of development common to all African states, or the relationship of a socialist strategy to them. To Berg we shall also return—by way of a brief conclusion.

The purpose of this essay is limited, as, at the present stage of the debate, we can merely hope to raise some neglected questions, juxtaposing them with the theory and *praxis* of African "socialists." The fuller elaboration of a socialist strategy, on the other hand, can only emerge at a more advanced stage of debate and research. In Section 1 we examine the relationship between current class formation in tropical Africa and economic development, focusing on the involvement of international capitalism in the area and on the emergence of what we shall define as the "labor aristocracy" of tropical Africa. In Section 2 we shall look, first, at the ideology of "African socialism" and, second, at the policies of African "socialists," subjecting both theory and praxis to careful critique. From this exercise the reader should gain a broader perspective on the problem of socialism in contemporary Africa. We shall conclude, in Section 3, with some brief remarks on the future course of socialist debate and strategy in Africa, making some reference to the Tanzanian experience.

1. Class Formation and Economic Development

The vast majority of the population of tropical Africa consists of independent producers who do not depend upon wage employment for their subsistence.[3] Any discussion of economic development in tropical Africa must therefore begin with a general description of African pre-capitalist or, as they are more often referred to, traditional economies. This is extremely difficult, in view of their heterogeneity,[4] but some common features of particular relevance to our discussion can be singled out.

Individuals can customarily acquire land for homestead and farms through tribal or kinship rights. Only comparatively rarely is land acquired or disposed of through purchase or sale, though the commercialization of agriculture has often been followed by a marked expansion of private land ownership. The specialization of labor has generally not gone very far in traditional African economies; a relatively small range of commodities is produced and few full-time specialists are to be found. In addition, the technology is rather rudimentary from the point of view of the tools used, storage and transport facilities, the control of plant and animal disease, and the control of water storage. Market exchanges were—and still are in many areas—peripheral, in the sense that most producers do not rely on exchange for the acquisition of the bulk of the means of subsistence. Thus the high dependence on the physical environment, due to the rudimentary technology, is matched by a relative independence from market fluctuations.

Social cohesion is fostered by obligatory gift- and counter-gift-giving between persons who stand in some socially defined relationship to one another, and/or by obligatory payments or labor services to some socially organized center which reallocates portions of what it receives. Security of subsistence is therefore generally guaranteed to the individual in two ways: through socially structured rights to receive factors of production and through emergency allotments of food from the chief and gifts from kin.

It is widely accepted that African peasants have, in general, been highly responsive to the market opportunities that have arisen through contact with European capitalism. This responsiveness has manifested itself in the labor migration system and/or in the rapid expansion of production for the market of both subsistence and cash crops. It seems that this responsiveness was made possible by the existence in traditional African economies of considerable surplus productive capacity in the form of both surplus land and surplus labor-time.[5] This means that the confrontation of a traditional economy producing a limited range of goods with the sophisticated consumption pattern of an advanced industrial system led to a reallocation of labor-time from unproductive traditional activities to the production of a marketable surplus.[6]

It has been pointed out, however, that the increase in peasant production for the market has had the character of a "once and for all" change (though distributed over a number of years), as witnessed by the characteristic growth curve of such production; a curve, that is, rising steeply in the early phase and tapering off gradually.[7] This phenomenon can be accounted for by the fact that the social structure of the traditional economies favors, by maximizing security, the adoption of a short "time horizon" in the allocation of whatever surplus might have been produced as among consumption, unproductive accumulation, and productive accumulation.[8] In other words, peasants still largely involved in a pre-capitalist mode of production are likely to have a strong preference for present consumption and often for unproductive accumulation, which, by maintaining or strengthening social cohesion, preserves the security afforded by the traditional system. This preference is likely to be strengthened by the confrontation of the peasants with the sophisticated consumption pattern of advanced industrial systems mentioned in the previous paragraph.

It would seem, therefore, that we have two problems involved in promoting the growth of productivity of the African peasantry: (1) The problem of creating incentives to exploit whatever surplus productive capacity in the form of surplus land and surplus labor-time may exist; and (2) the problem of raising the productive absorption of the surplus produced in the traditional sector in order to engender the steady growth of the productivity of labor. The first problem concerns the relationship between the modern and the traditional sectors; that is, it concerns the pattern of surplus absorption in the former which is likely to maximize the incentives to increase productivity in the latter. The second problem, on the other hand, relates to the type of organization of production and institutions in the traditional sector which is likely to guarantee the desired responses to the stimuli transmitted by the modern sector. In tropical Africa the first problem seems of primary importance because population pressure on the land, though growing, is generally not yet severe, so that most traditional economies still have some surplus productive capacity. For this reason we shall focus our attention on the development potential of the pattern of surplus absorption in the modern sector.

The "ideal type," in Max Weber's sense, of surplus absorption in the modern sectors of present-day tropical African economies is characterized by three main forms of surplus absorption: the export of profits and investment income in general; discretionary consumption on the part of a small labor aristocracy, as defined below; and productive investment, embodying capital intensive techniques, mainly concentrated in sectors other than those producing capital goods.[9] In order to understand the relationship between these three forms of surplus absorption, it is convenient to begin by examining the causes and implications of the sectoral distribution and factor-intensity of productive investment.

The use of capital intensive techniques of production in tropical Africa is not only the result of technological factors. Two other factors seem equally relevant: the investment policies of the modern international corporations in underdeveloped economies, and the wage and salary policies of the independent African governments, which, in turn, depend upon the character of their power base. With regard to the former, the modern international corporations tend to adopt capital intensive techniques mainly because of managerial constraints and because of their strong financial position.

Techniques of management, organization, and control have evolved in the technological environment of the industrial centers and cannot be easily adapted to the conditions obtaining in underdeveloped countries. In consequence, the spectrum of techniques taken into consideration by the corporations may not include labor intensive techniques. An equally and probably more important factor seems, however, to be the financial strength of these corporations, which they acquire through their pricing and dividend policies in the industrial centers as well as the periphery.[10] The international corporations apply to all their branches technical methods corresponding to their capital;[11] as a result, capital intensive techniques are adopted in tropical Africa irrespective of the situation in the territories where the investment takes place.

But capital intensity of production is also favored by the salary and wage policies of the independent African governments. The salary structure of the independent African states remained as a colonial heritage, and as Africans gradually entered the civil service and the managerial positions in large foreign concerns, they assumed the basic salaries attached to the posts.[12] This unquestioning acceptance of a colonial salary structure brought about a huge gap between the incomes of the elites and sub-elites in bureaucratic employment and the mass of the wage workers. Thus the whole level of labor incomes, from the unskilled labor upward, came into question and, given the political influence of urban workers on African governments, the major employers of labor, a steady rise in wages ensued. This steady rise is also favored by, and tends to strengthen, the capital intensive bias of investment, discussed above. Capital intensity generally means that labor is a lower proportion of costs, so that the individual concern is more willing to concede wage increases (especially foreign oligopolies which can pass on cost increases to the consumer). However, this reinforces the tendency toward capital intensive (or labor saving) growth and a "spiral process" may ensue.[13]

With regard to the sectoral distribution of productive investment, besides obvious technological factors (economies of scale, advantages of operating in an industrial environment, etc.) there seem to be three main reasons for the observed underinvestment in the capital goods industries of tropical Africa. In the first place, the very bias in favor of capital intensive techniques discussed above tends to promote the use of highly specialized machinery and consequently restrains the growth of demand for capital goods that could be produced locally. Other reasons relate more directly to the behavior of the modern international corporations. In nonindustrialized economies the market for capital goods is small; for such goods to be produced there must be good reasons to believe that the whole economy will develop in such a way as to nourish a market for capital goods.[14]

This fact was no serious obstacle in the nineteenth century, when competitive entrepreneurs and financial groups often undertook investment which was "unjustified" by market conditions, thereby fostering the industrialization of less developed economies. Nowadays the great calculating rationality, care, and circumspection in approaching new developments which characterize modern corporations prevent that process from taking place. As Paul M. Sweezy has remarked, it is one of the many contradictions of capitalism that better knowledge may impair its functioning. Finally, the lack of investment in the sector producing capital goods is also determined by the oligopolistic structure of advanced capitalist countries because this implies that producers of capital goods, in deciding whether to establish, or to assist in establishing, a capital goods industry, will generally take into account the effect of the decision not only on their own and their competitors' export interests, but also on those of their customers.

The lack of development of the capital goods sector has important implications for the growth of the modern sector. For such a development, when it does occur, can perform the dual function of expanding both the productive capacity of the economy *and* the internal market. This latter function, too often disregarded, was emphasized by Lenin, who argued that the development of the internal market was possible despite restricted consumption by the masses (or the lack of an external outlet for capitalist production) because "to expand production it is first of all necessary to enlarge that department of social production which manufactures means of production, it is necessary to draw into it workers who create a demand for articles of consumption. Hence 'consumption' develops after 'accumulation.' " [15] Thus underinvestment in the capital goods sector restrains the expansion not only of the productive capacity of tropical Africa but also of its internal market, perpetuating the dependence of the economy on the growth of world demand for its primary products. It is not surprising, therefore, that the economies of tropical Africa have been unable to grow faster than their exports. In the period 1950–1965 real product seems in fact to have grown at an average compound rate of 4.2 percent per annum,[16] which is about 1 percent lower than the rate of export growth.

Given the high rate of population growth, per capita real product has increased at an average rate of 2 percent per annum in the same period. This relatively low rate of growth, combined with the effects of the "wage-mechanization" spiral discussed above, has resulted in a decrease in the proportion of the labor force in wage employment in most countries and has been accompanied by a widening gap between urban and rural incomes.[17] It is far from correct, however, to assume that all classes in the urban areas have benefited from this widening gap. A large proportion of urban workers in Africa notoriously consists of semi-proletarianized peasants, periodically engaged in wage employment. This migrant labor force is not "stabilized" and in general does not acquire that specialization needed in industrial enterprises which use capital intensive techniques. These laborers *as a class,* i.e., as peasants temporarily in wage employment, cannot gain from the "wage-mechanization" spiral we have been discussing, since higher individual incomes are matched by a reduction in their wage employment opportunities.

The higher wages and salaries, however, foster the stabilization of the better paid section of the labor force whose high incomes justify the severance of ties with the traditional economy. Stabilization, in turn, promotes specialization, greater bargaining power, and further increases in the incomes of this small section of the labor force, which represents the proletariat proper of tropical Africa. These workers enjoy incomes three or more times higher than those of unskilled laborers and, together with the elites and sub-elites in bureaucratic employment in the civil service and expatriate concerns, constitute what we call the labor aristocracy of tropical Africa. It is the discretionary consumption of this class which absorbs a significant proportion of the surplus produced in the money economy.

The third significant form of surplus absorption is the profits, interest, dividends, fees, etc., transferred abroad by the international corporations. It seems a well-established fact that foreign private investment in less developed economies (far from being an outlet for a domestically generated surplus) has been, in the recent past, an efficient device for transferring surplus generated abroad to the advanced capitalist countries.[18] It is a highly plausible assumption that, at least with regard to tropical Africa, this transfer of surplus is bound to increase in the future, for two main reasons: the high rate of profit expected by foreign corporations and the relatively slow rate of growth of the economies of tropical Africa. It appears that returns in the order of 15–20 percent on capital, usually on the basis of an investment maturing in about three years, are required in order to attract foreign capital to tropical Africa.[19] The implication is that, in order to offset the outflow of profits, foreign investment in the area must steadily grow at a rate of 11–14 percent, which seems an impossible attainment in economies growing at a rate of 4–5 percent. Thus, while the transfer of surplus has been somewhat contained during the present phase of easy import substitution, the outflow can only become more serious in the years ahead as that phase comes to an end.

We may now discuss the development potential of this pattern of surplus absorption. The focus of attention must be upon the creation of stimuli to exploit the surplus productive capacity existing in the traditional economies. There are two main ways in which African peasants participate in the money economy: through periodic wage employment and through the sale of agricultural produce. It follows that the development potential of a given pattern of surplus absorption in the modern economy is determined by its impact on the demand for peasant labor and produce. From this standpoint the pattern discussed has little, if any, potential. The slow growth of the money economy and the concurrent high rate of mechanization and automation hold back the growth of wage-employment opportunities for the peasantry. More important still, the absorption of a considerable share of the surplus by the discretionary consumption of the labor aristocracy (which creates demand in the industrial countries or in the modern economies of tropical Africa themselves), and by the transfer of investment incomes abroad, restrains the growth of internal demand for peasant produce. As a consequence the creation of stimuli to increase productivity in the rural areas is left to the sluggish expansion of foreign demand for African produce and to those "invocations to effort" which are a prominent feature of much "socialist" practice in Africa and to which we shall return.

The slow growth of peasant incomes and productivity has in turn a negative impact on the growth potential of the modern sector itself, since it further hampers the expansion of the internal market. It would seem, therefore, that an acceleration of economic growth in tropical Africa within the existing political-economic framework is highly unlikely and, as the phase of easy import substitution is superseded, a slowdown may actually be expected. In the light of these considerations, the current economic growth of tropical Africa may be properly characterized as "perverse growth"; that is, growth which undermines, rather than enhances, the potentialities of the economy for long-term growth.[20]

In describing theoretically the current pattern of growth in Africa we have argued in terms of an "ideal type," as we were bound to in an essay of this sort. The full range of historical cases will undoubtedly include exceptions which do not fit our conclusions. Yet it is interesting to note that even the Ivory Coast, model of the international capitalist road to development, is beginning to feel the pinch which accompanies that strategy; several authors have recently commented on the country's pattern of growth "without development," without genuine self-sustaining transformation, which looks increasingly tenuous for the long run as profits begin increasingly to flow back to France and few reinforcing complementarities emerge. Indigenous sources of capital and "entrepreneurial" ability (public or private), which might push in a more fruitful direction, are stifled by the emergent class structure and pattern of international involvement.[21]

The foregoing discussion suggests the advisability of a policy of self-reliance vis-à-vis international capitalism for two main reasons: (1) because of the drain on the surplus which, sooner or later, is engendered by dependence on foreign capital; and (2) because of the impact of foreign investment (with respect to choice of techniques and to its sectoral distribution) upon the structure of the tropical African economies.[22] It does not follow, however, that the disengagement from international capitalism is a *sufficient* condition for development. As we have seen, the emergence of a labor aristocracy, with considerable political power, was brought about not only by the pattern of foreign investment but also by the acceptance of a colonial salary structure on the part of independent African governments. The labor aristocracy will therefore continue to use its power in a state-controlled modern sector in order to appropriate a considerable share of the surplus in the form of increasing discretionary consumption. Under these conditions "perverse growth" would continue notwithstanding state ownership of the means of production.[23] In order to achieve "real" long-term development, disengagement from international capitalism will have to be accompanied by a change in the power base of African governments.

Yet even the re-allocation of surplus from the discretionary consumption of the "labor aristocracy" to productive investment, though a necessary condition, is not sufficient for steady long-term growth. Productive investment in the modern sector must be directed toward the creation of development stimuli in the traditional sector; that is, it must be directed to the expansion of those industries producing the capital and the consumer goods most suited to the requirements of the traditional sector. Failing this, as the history of socialist development in nonindustrial environments has so often demonstrated, the growing demand for labor and produce following upon industrialization would merely lead to unfavorable terms of trade for the traditional sector, restraining the exploitation of its surplus productive capacity.[24]

The problem of creating incentives to exploit surplus productive capacity in the traditional sector is crucial because there still exist, among the peasants of tropical Africa, surplus land and surplus labor-time. The second problem involved in raising the productivity of African peasants (see above) is that of ensuring the *productive absorption of the surplus produced in the traditional sector*. Here the question of rural transformation is more starkly posed, even if difficult to answer at the theoretical level. It will involve some calculations as to whether the transformation of traditional economies is best attained through the formation of an agrarian capitalist class or the gradual absorption of the individual peasant families into larger units (cooperatives, collectives, communes): whether through the utilization or superseding of traditional forms of work cooperation, or through reliance upon central marketing boards or traders for the collection of produce from, and distribution of manufactured goods to, the traditional producers.

Certainly a process of very real differentiation is afoot in many parts of rural Africa. The commercialization of peasant agriculture has often been followed by a marked expansion of private land ownership,[25] and a growing division between the nascent agricultural "entrepreneurs" (the "kulaks," as Professor Dumont recently referred to them in Tanzania), the more marginal cash-croppers, the subsistence farmers, and the agricultural laborers. Increasingly these strata have differential interests with implications for rural strategy. Thus, for example, cooperatives may come to be manipulated by the more economically advanced peasants for their own benefit. If the instruments of "generalized mobilization" become mortgaged to one particular group, the thrust of such a development policy may well be blunted.

On the other hand, it has been ably argued that at this stage in development it may be wise to "let the kulaks run," to allow the logic of the market to *briser la famille* (as Samir Amin has put it), and to break down the attendant traditional economic constraints once and for all.[26] It is not inconceivable, of course, that links of common interest formed between emergent "capitalist" farmers and the labor aristocracy could become a further force to sustain the present pattern of economy and society—one thinks of the symbiosis between planters and bureaucrats in the Ivory Coast. Yet much will depend upon the general framework provided by the trajectory of development in the modern sector as to how short-run compromises with "inequality" in the "traditional" sector are situated and perhaps eventually controlled.

In conclusion, the first part of our analysis raises a number of questions concerning the relationship between current class formation and long-term development in tropical Africa. The growth of a labor aristocracy and the reliance on international capitalism, far from being necessary for such development, seem instead to reduce the growth potential of the economies in question, although the relationship between class formation and development, for the short run at least, is much less clear in the rural areas. It may be argued that the changes in surplus utilization, which we have seen to be necessary for real development, are not possible under present historical conditions, particularly in view of the short-term losses in economic growth and, quite possibly, in political stability that would ensue from any serious attempt at disengagement from international capitalism or reform of the power base of the African governments involved. This question, however, by no means invalidates the historical necessity of the change itself, which should therefore be of central importance in socialist debate.

2. The Theory and Practice of African Socialism

It seems relevant at this point to appraise, using rather broad strokes, the theory and practice of African socialism as evidenced to date. In this way the nature of the limitations, both intellectual and contextual, upon socialist experiment in Africa may be clarified. It would, of course, be artificial to separate too categorically considerations as to "theory" and "practice"; an understanding of the latter must serve to illuminate the real texture and function of the former. Nonetheless, many striking ambiguities are readily identifiable on the ideological plane itself, whether this be seen primarily as a determinant of practice or merely as its reflection and rationalization. The broad outline of the constellation of ideas under discussion, sometimes identified generically as "African socialism," are by now familiar enough,[27] though they remain difficult to capsulize as we must do here. It should be noted that even the overarching label of "African socialism" has been vigorously rejected by some of the continent's more militant practitioners; we must be careful not to schematize away real differences.

Yet there remain certain central themes common to most African writers and speakers on the subject and, more important, some common pattern to the seeming inadequacy of the analysis underlying many of their statements. Professed African socialists are, to be sure, uniformly interested in economic development; they have also sensed that some form of coordinated expansion on the agricultural and industrial fronts is required in order to attain that goal. The precise nature of the problems of "structural transformation" which are involved is less clearly fixed in their minds, though certain echoes of these concerns are sometimes to be found scattered through their speeches and programs.

Even socialists, however, have tended to operate in terms of the conventional model of development based upon the expansion of cash crops for the export market, increased industrial capital formation in consumer goods industries, and the import of foreign—generally private—capital, the requisite amount of infrastructural investment being the responsibility of the state. This is, of course, in essence the ideal type of "perverse growth" in Africa which we discussed in Section 1. Thus the main intellectual limitations, whether they be conscious or unconscious, lie in an inadequate understanding of the process of sustained development and structural transformation, but also, as will become apparent, in an insufficiently subtle and critical picture both of the emerging pattern of African socioeconomic stratification (particularly as regards "town-country" relations) and of the realities of the international economy. Small wonder, then, that ideas about "development" and "equality" are themselves not systematically linked, and, in consequence, that "socialist" strategies emerge which leave much to be desired.

In brief, a thoroughly disabused (and disinterested) look at such patterns has rarely been taken by African leaders. This is reflected by the extent to which the general tone of "socialist" thinking in Africa tends to blur these concerns, despite the occasional admissions and qualifications witnessing to rather greater sophistication. Thus, to take one example, Senghor is sometimes alive in his writings to the dangers of a newly privileged, urban-based group of "intellectuals—liberal professionals, functionaries, employers, even workers"—arising to exploit "the peasants, shepherds, and artisans." But the point is not pushed, nor possible institutional checks hypothesized; rather, he relies largely upon "spiritual values" to avert the danger. Yet excessive self-denial on the part of this "labor aristocracy" (as we have defined it) is certainly not to be expected when so militant a socialist spokesman as Touré himself can note:

> In our denunciation of bourgeois tendencies we must not, as do specialists in confusion, accuse of being bourgeois the peasant, the worker or the civil servant who is a convinced democrat and devoted PDG member and who by his personal efforts has been able to build a modern house, purchase a car or acquire honestly anything which contributes to the material well-being of his family. Since the main objective of our revolution is to make it possible for all to attain through work the highest possible degree of prosperity, we cannot blame these people. On the contrary, a man must utilize his energies and faculties for the constant improvement of his living standard.[28]

Surely this must amount to an overt sanction of the norm of *enrichissez-vous* for the bureaucratic groups (of party and state), "the new elites of tropical Africa," [29] which have emerged to prominence in the post-independence period. There has really been little grasp, within the doctrine of African socialism, of such a form of inequality and the accompanying possibilities for exploitation by this labor aristocracy. The necessity of bridging the urban-rural gap is rarely given sufficient prominence; the sort of assault on privilege which would free a good proportion of the surplus from urban consumptionism for rural incentives and capital formation is deflected away.

Occasionally certain steps are taken and presented with a logic that seems impeccably to combine the twin concerns of development and equality. Thus an argument postulated upon the social necessity of capital accumulation and the imperative of "hard work" is often used when African governments turn to deal with the trade unions. In most "socialist" countries the latter have been brought to heel, absorbed organizationally into the network of the ruling party. It is argued that they represent a privileged cadre of workers and that their gains are being made at the expense of the country as a whole, and of the rural sector in particular. As a step toward general development, they must be disciplined accordingly and redirected from "consumptionist" to "productionist" activities. [30]

Another prime target is the trading community, and again the argument against it is often advanced in terms of the need for both a more egalitarian pattern of distribution and accelerated capital accumulation. The redistribution of excessive profits of local traders and (sometimes) foreign trading houses is demanded, to provide incentive payments for the growers and more financing for productive investment by the state. In addition, it is argued that the marketing cooperatives, which are further encouraged by such steps in the rural areas, represent a collective, and therefore socialist, enterprise which is laudable in its own right. The fact that the trading group to be so displaced is often largely composed of a racial or cultural minority may, of course, ease the acceptance of such policies.

One might be better disposed to accept these latter moves on the terms in which they have been presented by the leaders, were the general line of argument which is used to justify them (that is, the criticism, by presumptive socialists, of inequalities which block development) more consciously and rigorously applied to the society as a whole. Unfortunately this has not been the case: perceived inequalities—what

Touré has termed "contradictions"—get very easily swallowed up and blurred analytically within the framework provided by the continent's distinctive "socialist" ideology. Here we refer to that strand of the argument which has been characterized by Peter Worsley as "populism." [31] In Africa this has involved the claim, by almost all leaders, that African societies are, even now, classless. The foundations for pervasive social solidarity are to be found in traditional society and, mediated by a contemporary "attitude of mind," continue to strike against meaningful stratification.

The most outspoken statement of this "model" is to be found in Nyerere's early paper "Ujamaa," [32] but even so Marxist-tinged a spokesman as Touré has fallen back upon the "communocratic" nature of African society to smooth over, ideologically, certain of the potential class antagonisms he sees in Guinean society. To this Touré adds the argument that such classless uniformity is reinforced by the fact of the whole population's facing, as a body, the neocolonialist exploiter. Not surprisingly, nationalism provides much of the cement for this populist edifice, being useful also for displacing continuing ethnic or tribal consciousness. Countless quotations could be introduced to demonstrate these general emphases in Africa. Nor, within such a "classless" society, is it surprising that any consideration as to the nature of the social relations of production is seen to be of little fundamental concern to socialist aspirations. Thus Kofi Baako, a man as close as anyone to Nkrumah in Ghana:

> In a Nkrumahist-Socialist state, the farmer will not lose his farm; the landlord will not lose his house, but will not be allowed to exploit the tenant; the employer will not be allowed to exploit the worker, nor will the worker be allowed to cheat the employer by idling about; the car owner will still have his car . . . the property or wealth which someone has acquired or earned through hard labor and through honest use of his mental and physical energies [will not] be taken away from him and shared among lazy, unscrupulous, indisciplined but able-bodied citizens.

As Fitch and Oppenheimer observe of such utterances: "Neither landlords nor capitalists will be abolished—they will simply be regulated." [33]

This "populist" strain to African socialism also has important implications for the analysis of the rural sector; moreover, there it is perhaps even more likely to be taken seriously by the ideologues themselves.

Worsley summarizes this theme when he writes: "Africa is its peasantry, subsistence producers and cash-crop producers, but independent peasants. This is the basic fact about the social structures of the new African states." We have already seen this to be suspect, given the character of "town-country" relationships in contemporary Africa, but within the rural area itself solidarity is (once again) felt to arise from these facts. Yet, as we have suggested, even the relatively unrevolutionized rural economies of tropical Africa are no longer as undifferentiated as these African leaders like to profess. What is clear, therefore, is that the issue of nascent rural class formation and its implications for development cannot be squarely faced, or effective "long-run" strategies of socialist control and direction developed, within a populist framework of analysis which masks the process of rural change.

Even in the absence of such a searching examination of rural realities, it nonetheless remains true that the "mobilization" of the peasantry is regarded as a vital necessity much more vocally in states of "socialist" bent than in others. There, a more generalized release of productive energies is looked to; it is in this context that the strand of "African socialism" which Friedland termed "the social obligation to work" becomes most prominent.[34] Socialism is presented as an invocation to effort and, implicitly or explicitly, a certain measure of sacrifice against the promise of some future day is encouraged, in however unspecified a way. Thus *investissement humain* and self-help become a collective exercise in some, often marginal, form of capital accumulation. These projects can be of value in educating people to national consciousness;[35] but, as should be apparent, such emphases may merely encourage the evasion of those more central problems which concern the interaction of traditional and modern sectors and the expansion of surplus productive capacity. All too rarely, for example, is the character of any choice between capitalist and collectivist agricultural accumulation spelled out or related to broader questions of development priorities such as we have posed; policies can therefore quite easily fall between two stools.

Just as the populist strand in African socialism obscures the realities of class formation, so it is important, if somewhat paradoxical, to observe that much of the criticism of "neocolonialism" in socialist Africa has served to obscure the realities of international capitalism's involvement on the continent. Of necessity, therefore, the range of specific policy options is also artificially narrowed. Even the most vocal of socialists assume the necessity of dealing with "the enemy"; as Jean Lacouture observed in discussing the Dakar Colloquium on African Socialism: "The distinction, always somewhat artificial, between 'revolutionary' and 'reformist' Africa now seems altogether obsolete. . . . What is even more striking is that nobody challenged the necessity of calling upon foreign aid and investment." [36]

But neither did anyone feel too compelled, it would seem, to analyze very systematically the arguments concerning the development potential of such investment by an increasingly monopolistic brand of international capitalism in terms of the choice of techniques and the absorption of labor, the reinvestment of profits, and the generation of internal demand. Policy statements thus oscillate rather erratically between the abstract slogans of "neocolonialism"—a useful instrument with which to forge national unity behind the leaders—and a "forced" acceptance of the "necessity" of encouraging foreign investment in order to obtain skills and capital.

Side effects tend to drop out of the equation. The application of a long time horizon might suggest that, despite a time lag, the inflow of unfettered foreign capital must eventually lead to a marked drain of repatriated profits and the like. Therefore an assessment must constantly be made as to its genuine development potential; as suggested, many forms of capital import may be worse than none at all, despite the subsequent existence of plants on the ground and a handful of newly hired indigenous employees. One can, of course, suspect that some of the encouragement given to an increased capital inflow may arise from the elite's concern with short-term balance-of-payments difficulties caused by excessive imports. Nonetheless, for the genuine African socialist, the necessity of *internal capital formation* must be underscored in his arguments and, furthermore, explained clearly to the people.

For, all too often, the promise of a favorable deal to be made by the elite with that most powerful external constellation of technology and economic power which is the Western economic system smacks of an attempt to get something for nothing (an unlikely occurrence, but perhaps a useful political case to make to the mass of the population in the short run). Given a clearer perspective, the definition of firmer conditions for such capital as did come in would also become a more pressing imperative than has been the case, however difficult such conditions are to apply in practice. And a vigorous attack upon "balkanization" and an advocacy of regional groupings, preferably of "like-minded" states, to encourage complementarities and coordinated development would become an even more prominent feature.

The relating of an ideology like African socialism to the complex social structure of changing Africa and the identifying of its functions is not an easy task. We have said enough, however, to suggest that more than mere intellectual confusion is at issue. It is true that in colonial and economically underdeveloped Africa an indigenous dominant class with power grounded in the process of production had, by and large, not emerged;[37] the political and bureaucratic groups which did come forward to prominence were therefore defined by a greater "relative social autonomy and plasticity," as Roger Murray has put it.[38] Nonetheless, after independence, when a combination of past education and/or political record and current bureaucratic position came to be the chief determinants of privilege in the new society, it is clear that, in the absence of more rigorous organization and ideological clarity, a rather narrow vested interest in the system had come to characterize the new elites, "une bourgeoisie plus proche d'un mandarinat," as Dia has called them. Their growing consciousness of a differentiated position vis-à-vis the mass of the population was such that Peter Lloyd, one of the shrewdest observers of this process, could toy with the idea of discarding the "elite" concept and substituting the notion of "class" to describe the position in society of this group.[39]

Thus it is within this sort of context that one must place trends—to an increased centralization of power, the absorption of quasi-autonomous bodies, and ideological myth-making for popular consumption of the sort we have examined—which are then seen to express a clear institutional and, behind that, a class interest.[40] And within this framework much state intervention, insofar as it seems only marginally related to a generalized socialist development strategy, can in part be explained as the conscious proliferation of jobs for incoming recruits to the dominant group. At the very least, given the nature of the bureaucratic elite, any glib identification, by leaders or observers, of socialism in Africa with *étatisme* and policies for centralization of economic control must be viewed with suspicion. In addition, a sustained stand against the blandishments of foreign capitalism, or even a critical scrutiny of its potential contributions, is unlikely from such a group. There is some danger of crude reductionism in such a generalized formulation, but it remains a

hypothesis which illuminates a great deal of the empirical evidence at
our disposal.

A closer examination of the practice of African states conventionally
labeled "socialist" contributes markedly to such a picture. Thus Samir
Amin's valuable study of Ghana, Guinea, and Mali demonstrates, with
telling statistical force, the heavy weight of bureaucratic expense and
conspicuous urban consumption, both public and private, in the budgets
of these states. His conclusion is that: "Austerity, the revolutionary
effort to use new and less costly methods, have not resisted the appetites
of the new bureaucracy." In Guinea, administrative expenditure rose by
80 percent between 1959 and 1962; in Mali, by 60 percent. Salary
structures, inherited from the colonial era, have been only marginally
reformed. The result: "The Guinea and Mali plans implied a great
effort toward domestic, public financing which has not been effected." [41]

Gérard Chaliand's figures for French-speaking West Africa as a
whole reveal an important aspect of this tilting of resources toward an
increasingly consumptionist middle class. Uniformly across these
countries there is a gross discrepancy between the amounts spent abroad
for importation of drink and other luxury items (toiletries, certain kinds
of motor cars) and the amounts of foreign exchange used for capital formation.[42] Similar statistics to document the importance of what we have
termed "discretionary consumption" could be produced for other
countries on the continent. Amin (and others) stress the importance of
this pattern for the traditional sector which in the absence of a genuine
take-off he sees as still the major brake upon development efforts within
the three national experiments he reviews. Certainly it becomes increasingly difficult under these circumstances for a rural population to take at
face value the protestations and demands for sacrifice of such an elite.
And, as should by now be evident, vital resources which could stimulate
the dynamic interaction of the urban and rural sectors are being diverted
from that effort.

In the Ghana of the early 1960s a reasonably sophisticated style of socialist debate which began in certain Ghanaian student circles abroad in
the 1940s was revitalized.[43] This was characterized, for example, by
"the attempt to transcend the 'African socialism' current of thought in
favor of a more universal and scientific theory; and the related effort to
institutionalize and accelerate the formation of an *ideological vanguard* of
cadres who might then strive to make ideology a mass force (Win-

neba)." [44] Similarly the Seven Year Plan took seriously many imperatives concerning the "extension of state economic activity and control
over the private sector" and "accelerated accumulation" in some relationship to a general socialist strategy.[45] Even at the level of analysis
there were inadequacies:

> For if a reading of the Ghanaian plan demonstrates that the leaders are
> aware of the necessity of breaking with this type of development which
> has reached its limits, of revolutionizing traditional agriculture, of radical
> industrialization in the context of closer economic unity in West Africa, it
> is still necessary to say that the specific policies to be undertaken have not
> been sufficiently thought through.[46]

And the results were disappointing.

But the chief constraint remained the quality of the regime's political
and social base. Having over the years cut itself off from mass support,
the CPP became increasingly a "town" organization in the general
sense we have suggested. The political instruments themselves were excessively bureaucratized, with their cadres marked by opportunism.
They could muster little support either for socialism or against those
other "labor aristocrats" of the state bureaucracy (including the military) who were progressively more alienated from the regime by its
overtly socialist drive, however much this was found to be half-hearted
in practice. "The spectacular purges, trials and appeals (Dawn Broad-
cast, etc.) merely revealed the inability to transform the CPP and its
satellite formations by mobilization from the base up." [47] Among other
things, it is not surprising that efforts at rural transformation by means
of novel crops and techniques suffered as a result of this peculiarly Ghanaian variant of the "urban-rural" dichotomy.

Other aspects of so-called socialist "practice" are revealing. We have
spoken of government action vis-à-vis the trade unions, the rationale for
which was often a variant upon the theme "equalization for development." Yet the statistics are again striking—we have already cited
Turner's finding that, while wage and salary employment in Africa has
remained relatively static in the last dozen years, wages have risen markedly.[48] No real line has been held even where organizational control has
been maximized. One may be forgiven the suspicion that jockeying for
political control rather than the logic of a development strategy has dictated much of the interventionism that has taken place. Certainly wage

workers have not been forced, in any marked way, to pay the price of development, despite what often amounts to a government take-over from the incumbent leadership. Organized workers have generally been admitted into the privileged ranks of the "labor aristocracy." Of course, where wage restraint began to be demanded of these junior partners to the "aristocracy," its imposition was made more difficult by the unambiguously privileged position of its other members, the politicians and the salariat: "Essentially the CPP solved the problem of moral versus material incentives by denying both: the workers were ordered to become Stakhanovites to defend a revolution that had never really begun." [49]

Even the character of the take-over of the trading sector, attempted in one form or another in most African "socialist" states, is revealing. It certainly promises a proliferation of jobs; it also provides sources of advantage for a leadership cadre whose highest level of consciousness is often *enrichissez-vous*. Once again, the norm of redistribution is shown to be ambiguous. The Abraham Commission's inquiry into corruption in Ghana's trading corporations makes chilling reading; extended peculation has all too often characterized the substitution of a network of cooperatives and marketing boards elsewhere. Certainly any total take-over of the marketing system is sufficiently difficult to make one hesitate to see it as an early priority for a socialist strategy, especially in the light of our earlier discussion of the ambiguities involved in establishing socialist priorities for the rural areas.

But it is important to note that criticisms such as those by Berg and others concerning Guinea's sweeping "nationalization" of the marketing sector may oversimplify the case; it is not only administrative incapacity that is at stake.[50] Much of the failure had to do with the character of the Guinean elite and the norms of the bureaucratic machine that moved to assert control. A more generalized socialist strategy, establishing, for example, different priorities in training cadres and attempting to raise the socialist consciousness of the people concerned through political education, might possibly transcend some of these problems.

Finally, we should appraise socialist practice in the relations of African states with foreign capital. We have already suggested the extent to which slogans have served to blur the real choices here. Yet the question is a crucial one. As noted, even in a country like the Ivory Coast economic problems are beginning to arise from its "international capitalist" strategy of growth. And most socialist countries have been loath, by and large, to chart very divergent paths. Even in the heyday of Guinean socialism, for example, there was little attempt to question ties with international capitalism in the industrial and extractive sectors, and this tendency has been magnified since 1961.[51]

Nkrumah's regime is again a textbook study of such involvement, one which offers additional explanations of its difficulties. Whereas the "Lewis strategy" to attract foreign capital had been a relative failure in the 1950s, *after* the declaration of a more militant socialism the pace stepped up—especially in the field of supplier credits, as Douglas Rimmer has noted.[52] What was in train was "merely a transformation and redefinition of [foreign private capital's] mode of linkage with the Ghanaian state," a continuance of some form of the "politics of mediation."[53] The Volta River Project seems the apogee of such "peaceful coexistence between sectors": Kaiser obtained a source of cheap power for the transformation of transshipped bauxite into aluminum, with no concomitant necessity of developing local bauxite deposits or of building an integrated aluminum industry.[54] Not that the redefinition of such a neocolonial relationship is easy: investment codes of varying degrees of stringency have in fact been tried in Guinea, Ghana, Senegal, and especially Mali. But if the international economic environment has been a harsh one for such efforts, it is also true that the will to divert international ties in a socialist direction has not been a sustained one.

This is not surprising: any attempt so to face up to international capitalism would suggest a growing awareness of the centrality of the pattern of surplus absorption and utilization to development strategy, and some readiness to correct its "irrationalities." Yet the inevitable corollary of a serious commitment to this goal is a parallel attack on the privileges of those very classes constituting the power base upon which most African governments are likely to rely. We therefore come full circle to that dichotomy observed above between what is historically necessary both for development and socialism, and what may appear at present to be historically possible. Any strategy directed toward socialist construction in Africa must therefore face up to the full complexities involved in creating a state power dedicated to the task, and in generating or tapping social forces capable of underpinning such a state.

It is perhaps possible that such a novel power base could be found by combining elements of a fully mobilized peasantry and a transformed urban and rural proletariat, thereby producing a genuine "workers and peasants" state. Whether the existing political and bureaucratic elites are the men who can realize such a transformation will remain here an open question, though, as noted, the results to date have been anything but reassuring on this score; certainly the quality of the political parties ostensibly working toward such goals has left much to be desired. More strikingly, the character of intra-elite competition in contemporary Africa and, in particular, the rise of the military to a position of special prominence show the strength of forces driving the situation in a counter-revolutionary direction.[55] As noted in the introduction, it has not been our intention to articulate fully a forward strategy for African socialism. Nonetheless, there are themes here which demand the urgent attention of all those concerned.

3. Concluding Remarks

Tanzania is, perhaps, the country in contemporary Africa where socialist aspirations figure most prominently and interestingly in the development equation, and most powerfully affect the kind of policies which are being pursued. To be sure, much remains to be done there; moreover, it is by no means clear that all the relevant dimensions of the problem of socialist development have as yet been considered by the leadership. Another article of this length, in fact, could be written to discuss the implications of the Tanzanian experience to date and its likely trajectory,[56] but perhaps a few brief points can be made here in the light of the preceding discussion.

It remains true that much of the course of recent Tanzanian development has been charted by the evolution of President Nyerere's own thinking, from the rather *simpliste* "African socialist" themes of presumptive solidarity and an automatically socialist "attitude of mind," which are to be found in the paper on *ujamaa* cited above, to a more subtle assessment of African realities; by and large it has not arisen from any concerted group or mass pressure. But the relatively unchallenged acceptance of certain accompanying party policies and, especially, the attainment of widespread ideological conformity to novel socialist aspirations do testify, in some measure, to the "relative social autonomy and plasticity" of the African leadership cadre which was suggested above. Whether the emergent labor aristocracy in Tanzania can really transcend the narrow horizons of its opposite numbers in other African countries remains to be seen. But a genuine attempt is being made to elicit a heightened socialist commitment from them (and, among other things, a consequent curb on the "politics of urban consumptionism"). Of course, the lack of "revolutionary intellectuals" among the leaders is a striking feature, suggesting a possible future drag upon the policy of genuinely transforming the nature of the "elite." [57]

Yet presumably much will also depend upon parallel efforts, using the democratic mechanisms peculiar to Tanzania's one-party system, as well as other institutions, both to rouse the vast mass of the peasant population to express their interests as a social force checking possible abuses of their position by the leaders, and at the same time to raise the level of mass consciousness so that such "intervention" is of a progressive sort. The fact that, given a relatively unmobilized peasantry, this will be a difficult balance to strike should require no elaborate emphasis. It also appears true that the Tanzanian party, TANU, which might otherwise seem the ideal instrument for linking revolutionary intellectuals and the mass of the population, remains a relatively weak reed.[58] It is, unfortunately, too early to assess the likelihood of a dramatic change in this dimension of the Tanzanian situation, but the efforts undertaken to realize such a change may be one of the features making Tanzania an important focus of interest in the next few years.   For the fact remains that President Nyerere has increasingly displayed a sophisticated awareness of many of the patterns of African change which we have discussed: the importance of the "rural-urban" dichotomy, the relative lack of socialist direction provided by a mere "attitude of mind," some of the ambiguities of foreign economic involvement in the domestic economy, and the realities of rural stratification. Regarding the first of these, his actions have been forthright: witness the curbing of student pretensions at the University College, the subsequent civil service salary cuts, the recent disciplining of the extravagant wage demands of NUTA (the national trade union), and, most important of all, the Arusha Declaration of February 1967, which has enacted a self-denying ordinance against certain kinds of economic aggrandizement by the elite (especially as regards the ownership of property) and thus called upon them to exemplify their socialist commitment.[59] A real beginning has thus been made. Similarly, "political education" has become a much more dominant theme, both within the educational system and vis-à-vis the general public, suggesting that there is increasingly an ideology and a commitment to be taught and to be understood, and a higher level of socialist consciousness to be worked toward, rather than merely to be *assumed,* as the basic building block of Tanzanian socialism.

A wide range of firms has been nationalized, including banks, insurance, and some processing and manufacturing concerns, with some eye to relating their investment and other decisions more directly to the interests of national development. In the rural sphere, the peasants have been given an even more exalted rank in the verbal formulations of the national ideology, often, in the president's speeches, at the very explicit expense of the *amour-propre* of the leaders; as noted, the organizational edge to this emphasis has not been fully defined in practice, though local leaders are also being called upon to exemplify their socialism along the lines articulated in the Arusha Declaration.[60] This is an attempt at all levels to introduce certain "vanguard" characteristics into what is otherwise most clearly a "mass" party. More recently the president has also expressed a growing concern with the realities of class formation in the rural areas, particularly with the emergence of what he has himself termed a "rural proletariat," and has suggested, rather tentatively, his solution of the *ujamma* village, with its emphasis upon a communal, though technologically modernized, mode of agricultural production, to meet this challenge to egalitarianism.[61]

However, the full scope of the relationship between agriculture and industry, between the rural and the urban sectors, has not been clearly established, beyond those important actions referred to above which have been designed to rationalize the process of "surplus appropriation" by curbing discretionary consumption in the urban areas. An attendant result is that, hinged upon the constantly reiterated slogan of "self-reliance," mere agricultural expansionism, a rather dangerous strategy when world prices are falling, tends to be substituted for agricultural expansion to meet a planned, industrially induced demand, both direct and indirect. In fact, it is perhaps fair to say that "industrial growth" is still a missing link in the chain of socialist strategy in Tanzania; there is a relative silence on the priority to be given to industrialization, on how capital formation should be divided between the capital goods sector and the consumer goods sector or, again, between the sectors servicing the rural areas and those servicing the urban areas, or how agricultural policy should be expected to fit into this pattern. The related question of external trade and financial links with the socialist countries beyond Africa and with the capitalist world will also demand further consideration. Concern for "surplus utilization" is as important for socialists as concern for "surplus appropriation." Tanzania is making heroic efforts, but it will be easier to assess the direction of its course if and when a presidential paper is issued which concerns itself with policies for industrialization.

One thing is clear: Tanzania is increasingly carrying on the debate about socialism at a high level of sophistication. This is more than can be said for much socialist discourse and ideology-making elsewhere on the continent, as has been shown. It is also more than can be said for Berg, whose article we cited earlier, and many of his academic colleagues. Berg launches an attack on socialist aspirations in Africa in strong terms: "For contemporary Africa it is the wrong ideology, in the wrong place, at the wrong time." [62] He bases this assessment on three main points, all of which are unexceptionable in their place. There is a trained manpower constraint, he argues, and this is seen to make the control of marketing in particular a hazardous exercise. African agriculture he finds uncongenial to mechanization and therefore to large-scale farming; moreover, there is still a need to draw peasants out of traditional subsistence production into the market, and cash stimuli can best accomplish this in the short run.[63] And finally he cites the permeability of frontiers as a major challenge to controlled marketing. From the above he draws his sweeping conclusion:

> [African socialists] believe that maximum growth can only come through socialist solutions, and this is almost certainly not true. . . . This is the saddest part of all—that these most admirable men are also those most firmly gripped by the illusion that socialism provides a quick and true path to economic development. Given power they would lead their countries not forward but backward.[64]

Yet Berg arrives at his conclusion without mentioning most of the aspects of economic development in Africa which we have seen to be central to socialist concern. There is no mention of industrialization except for a brief paean of praise for the "inflow of private capital"; needless to say, the ambiguities as to the nature of the latter's actual contribution to development are nowhere broached. Neither are the patterns of surplus absorption and of productive investment analyzed. And, a related oversight, the nature of class formation (particularly the consolidation of "labor aristrocracies") and the possible role of this process in either blocking or stimulating development are ignored. Yet, at the very least, patterns of industrialization and surplus utilization are relevant to the long-term rise of agricultural output he values so highly, in terms of both increased incentives and future demand—created or forgone—and of potential inputs, produced or not produced.

Berg's arguments do pinpoint some limits of the possible for socialists, particularly in the rural sector. But, because they ignore the most important questions about the relationship between development and the aspiration to eliminate class privileges in Africa, they do not come as close to preempting the socialists' discussion of what is necessary for development as he had perhaps hoped. Berg's contribution is therefore marginal: academics will have to do better than this if they are to be of any assistance to governments who may aspire to turn growth into development and take seriously the possible relevance of socialism to that goal.

Notes

1. On the continued validity of a much refined Marxist critique of contemporary capitalist society along similar lines, see P. Baran and P. M. Sweezy, *Monopoly Capital* (New York, 1966).

2. E. Berg, "Socialism and Economic Development in Tropical Africa," *The Quarterly Journal of Economics*, November 1964. For typical citations see J. S. Coleman, "The Resurrection of Political Economy," *Mawazo* (Kampala), no. 1, (1967); and C. Anderson, F. Van der Mehden, and C. Young, *Issues of Political Development* (Englewood Cliffs, New Jersey, 1967), ch. 10.

3. K. C. Doctor and H. Gallis estimate that the proportion of the labor force of tropical Africa in wage employment is, on average, 11.1 percent. However, migrant labor, characterized by partial dependence upon wage employment for its subsistence, is included in the estimate, so that the proletariat proper accounts for a lower percentage than the above. The estimate is in "Size and Characteristics of Wage Employment in Africa: Statistical Estimates," *International Labour Review* 93 (February 1966).

4. For a bibliography on traditional African systems, see J. Middleton, *The Effect of Economic Development on Traditional Political Systems South of the Sahara* (The Hague, 1966).

5. See H. Myint, *The Economics of Developing Countries* (London, 1964), ch. 3, and also D. Walker, "Problems of Economic Development of East Africa," in E. A. G. Robinson, ed., *Economic Development for Africa South of the Sahara* (London, 1964), pp. 111–14.

6. The adjective "unproductive" has, of course, no negative implication concerning the rationality or the necessity within the traditional society of activities so characterized.

7. Cf. Myint, op. cit. and Walker, op. cit.

8. We define "surplus" as the difference between the aggregate net output produced (net, that is, of the means of production used up in the process) and the means of subsistence consumed by the community, both referred to a given period of time. By "subsistence" we understand goods that are socially recognized as necessities, so that they exclude what may be called "discretionary" consumption. On the concept of the surplus see P. A. Baran, *The Political Economy of Growth* (New York, 1967), ch. 2; and C. Bettelheim, "Le Surplus économique, facteur de base d'une politique de développement," *Planification et croissance accéléré* (Paris, 1965). Our definition is closer to Bettelheim's than to Baran's.

9. This "ideal" type is analyzed in greater detail in Chapter 3 of this volume. The category "capital goods" must be understood in a very broad sense as including all those goods which directly increase the productive capacity of the economy.

10. The concepts of "industrial centers" and "periphery" have been introduced by Raul Prebisch to designate the advanced industrial economies and the relatively underdeveloped countries, respectively.

11. F. Perroux and R. Demonts, "Large Firms—Small Nations," *Présence africaine* 10, no. 38 (1961), p. 46.

12. P. Lloyd, ed., *The New Elites of Tropical Africa* (London, 1966), pp. 10–11.

13. H. A. Turner, *Wage Trends, Wage Policies and Collective Bargaining: The Problems for Underdeveloped Countries* (Cambridge, 1965), p. 21.

14. M. Barratt Brown, *After Imperialism* (London, 1963), p. 419.

15. Quoted in H. Alavi, "Imperialism Old and New," *The Socialist Register 1964* (New York and London, 1964), pp. 106–7.

16. See OECD, *National Accounts of Less Developed Countries* (Paris, 1967), preliminary.

17. See Chapter 3 of this volume, and Turner, op. cit., pp. 12–13.

18. In the case of the United States, for example, figures contained in the *Survey of Current Business* of the U.S. Department of Commerce show that total direct investment abroad, for the period 1950–1963, amounted to $17.382 million, against a total inflow of investment income of $29.416 mil-

lion. Cf. Baran and Sweezy, op. cit., p. 107. Data derived from the same source show that, in the period 1959–1964, U.S. direct investment (excluding oil) in Africa amounted to $386 million and investment income to $610 million.

19. See D. J. Morgan, *British Private Investment in East Africa: Report of a Survey and a Conference* (London, 1965).

20. The concept of "perverse growth" has been introduced by Ignacy Sachs. See his "On Growth Potential, Proportional Growth, and Perverse Growth," *Czechoslavak Economic Papers* (1966), pp. 65–71.

21. See S. Amin, *Le Développement du capitalisme en Côte d'Ivoire* (Paris, 1967); S. Amin, "Côte d'Ivoire: valeur et limites d'une expérience," *Jeune Afrique* (October 1967); Z. Dobrska, "Economic Development of the Ivory Coast from the Winning of Independence," *Africana Bulletin* (Warsaw), no. 5 (1966).

22. It is surprising that apologists of foreign private investment in Africa (who consider the drain on the surplus a payment for technical assistance and finance supplied by the international corporations) have seldom paused to consider whether the managerial, administrative, and technical skills supplied are suited to the requirements of the receiving economies from the standpoint of their growth potential (as opposed to some short-term effects on income and employment).

23. See Sachs, op. cit.

24. For an excellent discussion of problems of socialist development in a nonindustrial environment, see F. Schurmann, *Ideology and Organization in Communist China* (Berkeley and Los Angeles, 1966).

25. See S. Chodak, "Social Classes in Sub-Saharan Africa," *Africana Bulletin*, no. 4 (1966).

26. See S. Amin, *Trois expériences africaines de développement: le Mali, la Guinée, et le Ghana* (Paris, 1965), pp. 10–17 and 230–32; also "The Class Struggle in Africa" (anon.), *Révolution*, no. 1, p. 9.

27. See particularly, J. Mohan, "Varieties of African Socialism," *The Socialist Register 1966* (New York and London, 1966). Also W. H. Friedland and C. G. Rosberg, Jr., *African Socialism* (Stanford, 1964); Charles Andrain, "Democracy and Socialism: Ideologies of African Leaders," in D. Apter, ed., *Ideology and Discontent* (New York, 1964); and Bernard Charles, "Le Socialisme africaine, mythes et réalités," *Revue française de science politique*, no. 15 (1965), p. 856.

28. *Africa Report*, "Special Issue on African Socialism" (May 1963), pp. 26–27.

29. This is the title of a useful book on related themes edited by Peter Lloyd (London, 1966).

30. For this distinction see Isaac Deutscher, "Russia," in W. Galenson, ed.,

Comparative Labor Movements (New York, 1952); and Friedland and Rosberg, op. cit., p. 19.

31. Peter Worsley, *The Third World* (London, 1964), ch. 4. For a detailed critique of "populism" see Chapter 4 of this volume.

32. This essay is reproduced in J. K. Nyerere, *Freedom and Unity / Uhuru na Umoja* (Dar es Salaam and London, 1966 and 1967), pp. 162–71. It was first published in 1962.

33. Both Baako's remark and the subsequent comment are to be found in B. Fitch and M. Oppenheimer, *Ghana: End of an Illusion* (New York, 1966), p. 112.

34. Friedland and Rosberg, op. cit., p. 16.

35. See K. Grundy, "Mali: The Prospects of 'Planned Socialism,'" in ibid., p. 192.

36. *Le Monde*, 11 December 1962, cited in *Africa Report* (May 1963), p. 18.

37. Though the emergence of a small but often outspoken trading class in a country like Ghana, for example, can play an important role in defining the trajectory of socialist experiments.

38. Roger Murray, "Second Thoughts on Ghana," *New Left Review* (March–April 1967), p. 34.

39. Lloyd, op. cit., Introduction.

40. At the extreme, of course, one has the example of Kenya, where the ideology of "socialism" is being used unscrupulously to rationalize the march of the new African elite into all sectors of the economy, public and private. Not all uses of this rationale are so crude, but there is a certain consistency to the African pattern, nonetheless.

41. Amin, *Trois expériences africaines*, p. 277.

42. G. Chaliand, "Indépendance nationale et révolution," *Partisans* (May-June 1966), special issue, "L'Afrique dans l'épreuve."

43. On this subject see Colin Legum, "Socialism in Ghana: A Political Interpretation," in Friedland and Rosberg, op. cit.

44. Murray, op. cit., p. 35.

45. R. Green, "Four African Development Plans: Ghana, Kenya, Nigeria, and Tanzania," *Journal of Modern African Studies* (August 1965); Amin, *Trois expériences africaines*.

46. Amin, ibid., p. 229 (our translation). Perhaps most markedly lacking was a sustained attempt to analyze relations between traditional and modern sectors and to integrate long-term industrial and agricultural strategies along the lines we have suggested in Section 1.

47. Murray, op. cit.

48. Cf. Turner, op. cit., pp. 12–14.

49. Fitch and Oppenheimer, op. cit., p. 105.

50. Berg, op. cit., pp. 556–60.

51. Walter H. Drew, "How Socialist *Are* African Economies?," *Africa Report* (May 1963), p. 12; B. Ameillon, *La Guinée, bilan d'une indépendance* (Paris, 1964). The latter lays particular emphasis not only upon the compromised position (vis-à-vis foreign capital) of the Guinean regime, but also on the consolidation of a "bureaucratic class" in power. See especially part III, ch. 2, "Du Socialisme d'état à l'étatisation de classe."

52. Douglas Rimmer, "The Crisis of the Ghana Economy," *The Journal of Modern African Studies* (January 1966).

53. The former quotation is from Murray, op. cit., the latter from Fitch and Oppenheimer, op. cit. Both echo Fanon's rather more dramatic utterance on the subject: "The national middle class discovers its heroic mission: that of intermediary. Seen through its eyes, its mission is nothing to do with transforming the nation; it consists, prosaically, of being the transmission line between the nation and a capitalism, rampant though camouflaged, which today puts on the mask of neocolonialism." *The Wretched of the Earth* (London, 1967), p. 122.

54. See Tony Killick, "Volta River Project," in W. Birmingham, I. Neustadt, and E. N. Omaboe, *A Study of Contemporary Ghana* (London, 1966).

55. On this subject see Roger Murray, "Militarism in Africa," *New Left Review* (July–August 1966).

56. See Chapter 6 of this volume.

57. For a suggestive discussion of the importance of "revolutionary intellectuals" see John Cammett, *Antonio Gramsci and the Origins of Italian Communism* (Stanford, 1967), ch. 10.

58. On TANU in the pre-Arusha Declaration period, see H. Bienen, *Tanzania: Party Transformation and Economic Development* (Princeton, 1967), a useful work despite the misleading picture which it presents of the ideological dimensions of the Tanzanian experience.

59. See *The Arusha Declaration and TANU's Policy on Socialism and Self-Reliance* (Dar es Salaam, 1967); also *Arusha Declaration: Answers to Questions* (Dar es Salaam, 1967).

60. As one example, such leaders are to be subject to severe restrictions in their hiring of labor, a practice which would involve, in the language of Arusha, "exploitation."

61. Julius K. Nyerere, *Socialism and Rural Development* (Dar es Salaam, 1967). Whether this particular aspiration is premature is, as we have noted, a moot point. The president himself does not fully explore the links between agricultural development and an "egalitarian" mode of production beyond remarking that "if this kind of capitalist development takes place widely over the country, we may get a good statistical increase in the national wealth of

Tanzania, but the masses of the people will not necessarily be better off. On the contrary, as land becomes more scarce we will find ourselves with a farmers' class and a laborers' class, with the latter being unable to work for themselves or to receive a full return for the contribution they are making to the total output."

62. Berg, op. cit., p. 571.
63. For a similar point of view, albeit from a Marxist perspective, see Amin, "The Class Struggle in Africa."
64. Berg, op. cit., p. 573.

2

Nationalism and Revolution in Sub-Saharan Africa

Giovanni Arrighi and John S. Saul

In the previous essay, we stressed the poverty of academic debate on the relevance of socialism to development goals in tropical Africa and advanced the argument that socialism is, in fact, rapidly becoming a historical *necessity* in order to ensure the further development of the area. At the same time it must be noted that the quality of debate among socialists concerning the actual *possibility* of revolutionary, socialist transformation in Africa in the present historical conjuncture also leaves much to be desired.[1] Thus some circles on the Left have fallen back upon a form of "agrarian messianism," as one writer has characterized it; in this model a pure and undefiled peasantry becomes the major vector for progressive change in Africa.[2] Other Western Marxists, in an attempt (legitimate in many respects) to counteract such tendencies, have themselves often taken stands which smack, in turn, of "proletarian messianism."[3] If such extremes are to be avoided, and the intellectual bases for relevant strategies laid, greater attention will have to be paid both to the real nature of pre-capitalist African societies as restructured by capitalist penetration on the one hand, and to the processes of capitalist accumulation in the underdeveloped world under the present conditions of oligopolistic market structures and revolutionized technology on the other.

Another related aspect of such oversimplification has been an absence of sufficient differentiation between the component parts of contemporary Africa. To further minimize the dangers of too undiscriminating a set of analytical categories we must instead attempt to balance an aware-

This article was originally published in Ralph Miliband and John Saville, eds., *The Socialist Register 1969* (New York and London, 1969), pp. 137–88. Copyright © 1969 by Merlin Press. Reprinted by permission.

ness of such similarities as mark the structures of various regions, states, and communities against an adequate understanding of the often more important differences between them. These similarities and differences become more readily apparent within a framework which focuses upon the various kinds of *uneven development* thrown up by capitalist penetration in Africa. For the underdevelopment of Africa as a whole relative to the industrial centers of the West has been accompanied and mediated by uneven development as between regions, states, tribes, and races *within* Africa itself, and this fact adds important dimensions to the class struggle in Africa and to the character of the resistance of progressive African forces to contemporary imperialism.

Not surprisingly, the kinds of oversimplification already mentioned have tended to preclude a correct identification of the major forces underwriting the *stability* of the present continental conjuncture, while at the same time inhibiting an adequate assessment of those *contradictions* relevant to defining the possibilities for progressive action. We feel, therefore, that the general qualifications which we have introduced above urgently require clarification if such revolutionary potential as exists in Africa today is not to be wasted. It is in fact a sense of urgency which has prompted us to attempt a work of synthesis which the lack of relevant research on more limited questions makes difficult and tentative. We hope in this way to contribute to a definition of the problems that demand investigation and clear confrontation, though we are aware that the methods for their solution can only evolve from the revolutionary praxis of the African people.

1

Any attempt to identify the major determinants underlying contemporary African realities and, in particular, to identify those forces which provide the dynamic for uneven development as a continental process, must first assess the structure of Western capitalism's interest in Africa. Such a focus suggests in turn two hypotheses of crucial significance: First, there has been a broadening of Western capitalist interests in the underdeveloped world in general due to the more direct involvement of the multinational corporations in such industrialization as takes place in the peripheries.[4] This relative shift of emphasis away from the pattern of classic "extractive" imperialism (whose drive was postulated primarily upon the guaranteeing of supplies of raw materials and of outlets for the sale of manufacturing goods in the underdeveloped world) has been reinforced by the sharp decline in profitability and attractiveness of the agricultural sector to overseas interests.

Second, the factors determining the drive for export of capital from the advanced capitalist centers have themselves been shifting dramatically in the wake of the postwar technological "revolution." In particular, the exploitation of cheap labor overseas has lost much of its significance;[5] instead, the factor of overwhelming contemporary importance is the existence of a relatively developed and rapidly expanding industrial structure, as the latter ensures the smooth operation of capitalist manufacturing enterprises from the standpoint of outlets for their products and sources of factors of production. Other determinants, such as the aforementioned low relative labor costs, favorable political climate, possibility to export profits, and the like are also important but are highly imperfect substitutes for this dominant factor.[6] The combination of these two novel aspects of capitalist development on a world scale has come to define, in effect, a "second phase" of imperial predominance. Of course, investment in extractive industry retains much of its traditional centrality in relationship to the mining sector,[7] but even here the dominant factors will be the presence and nature of mineral deposits and the degree of freedom accorded to the investing enterprises in pricing output, since this is the main device used by vertically integrated combines to transfer surpluses across political boundaries. One major exception is gold mining, where price is not subject to oligopolistic determination and for which, therefore, cheapness of labor retains much of its significance.

The above considerations suggest a hierarchy of capitalist interests in the various regions of sub-Saharan Africa. Clearly, what we shall call the Southern Africa complex centered around industrial South Africa and Rhodesia and including South-West Africa, Angola, Mozambique, and the quasi-Bantustans of Swaziland, Lesotho, and Botswana—is by far the most important region with respect to the above criteria, since it is characterized by a relatively developed industrial structure and exceptional mineral wealth. Concomitantly, the scope of Western capitalist involvement in the area is vast indeed. This is, of course, a familiar story and will bear only limited repetition here.[8]

Britain, with over £1,000 million invested in the Republic of South

Africa and some £200 million in Rhodesia, remains the major investing capitalist country in the area. Dennis Austin, a veteran British observer of African affairs, has sketched the full scope of British economic interests in South Africa—banks, investments in manufacturing and mining, trade, access to gold—and, characteristically, blanched, as has the British government on all occasions, at any prospect of rocking so profitable a boat.[9] By 1963, South Africa had overtaken the United States and Australia as Britain's biggest earner of investment income abroad.

United States investment in South Africa is still a bad second to Britain's, but its significance lies in its rapid growth. Thus U.S. *direct* investments alone rose from $50 million in 1943 to $140 million in 1950, $286 million in 1960, and $467 million in 1964—when South Africa accounted for almost 30 percent of all U.S. direct investment in Africa.[10] This rapid growth of U.S. direct investments, which are also being rapidly diversified into manufacturing, is not surprising in view of the fact that "in 1964, the last year for which [Dept. of Commerce] figures are available, U.S. direct investments generated earnings of nearly $100 million, equal to 21 percent in net worth, making South Africa the most profitable country for private investment in the world." [11] In 1961, when the panic after the Sharpville massacre caused some investors to pull out, it was perhaps their greater "calculating rationality" which encouraged the eighty American firms then involved in South Africa to stand fast. Indeed:

> When action came in 1961 it was concerted and direct. American firms increased their investments by $23 million (to about $442 million in 1962), and an *ad hoc* financial consortium advanced a $50 million loan to the government, the First National City Bank putting up $5 million, the Chase Manhattan Bank $10 million, the International Monetary Fund $38 million, the World Bank $28 million, and "U.S. lenders not publicly identified" $70 million. The situation was saved. Since that crisis the number of American companies investing in South Africa's future has nearly tripled.[12]

Needless to say, French, German, and other interests have all been involved in the new gold rush.

Not surprisingly, despite verbal protestations, the activities of the American state have not diverged far from the logic of support for the South African status quo already witnessed in such private undertakings. Various observers have catalogued a number of striking instances of such American governmental activity, but similar lists could be compiled for other capitalist powers. Item, the U.S. government contributed $4.9 million or 29.77 percent of the budget of an organization called the Intergovernmental Committee for European Migration which by 1965 had brought 25,000 Europeans to South Africa, mainly in the vital skilled worker category. Item,

> [Despite] widespread African fears and international speculation that uranium-rich South Africa may try to develop both nuclear energy and nuclear weapons, the American Atomic Energy Commission [has] trained South African technicians at the Oak Ridge National Laboratory in Tennessee and loaned the South African Atomic Energy Board a reactor consultant (Thomas Cole of Oak Ridge National Laboratory) to whom the South Africans consider themselves "largely indebted for the successful commission of Safari I," their first nuclear reactor which was dedicated in August 1965 in the presence of Dr. Alvin Weinburg, director of the Oak Ridge National Laboratory.[13]

Item, the many roles of "Citizen Engelhart," American representative to Gabonese and Zambian independence celebrations, the prime mover of powerful Rand Mines, and a director of the Anglo-American Corporation of South Africa, of the Witwatersrand Native Labour Association, and of the Native Recruiting Corporation, confidant of presidents, described by Lyndon Johnson as "a humanitarian of the first order." [14] The list could be extended indefinitely.

Of course, in addition to such a range of involvements in the Republic of South Africa itself, a wide variety of Western capitalist interests are also conspicuously active in the other territories of the Southern African complex, like Rhodesia, South-West Africa, and Angola, although, particularly in the latter two instances, investment is directed mainly to the exploitation of mineral resources.[15]

In sharp contrast to this situation, the rest of sub-Saharan Africa, with its lack of an industrial structure, growing shortage of foreign exchange (which endangers the export of profit), little-developed capitalist relations of production, and low density of population remains a region of relatively small comparative attraction for foreign manufacturing concerns. As a result, that "broadening" of Western capitalist interests which has been observed in other regions of the underdeveloped world,[16] and which was referred to above, remains embryonic in tropical

Africa. As Conor Cruise O'Brien has suggested, the area considered as a whole still occupies something of a "reserve position in the international capitalist strategy." We shall return to this point in Section 3, but it is important to note here that this conclusion does not fully apply to those few countries—like Gabon, the Congo, Nigeria, and Zambia—endowed with known mineral resources of great importance to the world economy and therefore of special concern to international capitalism. It should also be noted that countries like Kenya, Ghana, and the Ivory Coast, which (owing to their relatively more structured economies) play or can play the role of peripheral centers, are important in ways denied to more marginal economies.[17] This is not to deny that such countries, which are those more directly impinged upon by the "second phase" of imperialist economic predominance mentioned above, will also find their genuine transformation constrained in the long run by the logic of their continuing dependent relationship, however novel the terms of that dependency.[18] But the differential patterns of growth involved are, nonetheless, among the most significant aspects of uneven development on the continent and can come to have important implications for differing internal situations as between various African states *and* for the kinds of interstate relationships which are constructed on such foundations.[19] Nor should independent Africa's *relative* unimportance be seen to preclude the possibility of the capitalist world's playing its trump cards when more subtle measures of control, generally successful in the present continental conjuncture, prove inadequate. Thus, French paratroopers intervened in Gabon in 1964 to restore their tottering puppet Mba. America's logistic and military support for Tshombe in his suppression of the threat to his collaborationist government from the eastern Congo in 1964 was equally graphic, though somewhat more nuanced was its support for Mobutu when the game (and American interests) took on a more anti-Belgian character. Certainly, future strategic calculation must never underestimate the implications of such events.

Notwithstanding certain qualifications, however, it can be assumed that the retention within the international capitalist system of so profitable a field of investment and source of strategic raw materials as the Southern African complex occupies the dominant position in the structure of Western capitalist interests in sub-Saharan Africa. In consequence, their main concern vis-à-vis independent Africa is to prevent the growth of strong politico-economic systems independent of Western capitalist hegemony in the countries bordering on the Southern African complex (Congo, Zambia, Malawi, and Tanzania) which could, among other things, seriously threaten (through their support for the increasingly radical liberation movements) white rule in Southern Africa. International capitalism, as noted above, will further have more sectional but nonetheless important interests in controlling political-economic processes of development in those countries which we have singled out as peripheral centers and (in particular) as centers of mineral exploitation. Interests in the other countries can be assumed to be mainly indirect, in the sense that whatever measure of control international capitalism may exercise over them will aim more at their retention as satellites of the peripheral centers or their use as pawns in increasing the strategic security of centers of mineral exploitation, than at securing fields of profitable investment and trade.

The implications of this structure of interests will become obvious as we proceed. We should, however, further clarify these interests by defining them in relation to issues which have traditionally been assigned crucial significance. To begin with, the intensity of conflicts over labor retribution between international capitalism and wage workers in the periphery has been considerably lessened. It is of course true that the immediate effect of a rise in wages and salaries is a reduction in profits. Yet, owing to the low labor intensity of productive processes controlled by the multinational corporations, this effect is likely to be small and, given the oligopolistic character of such corporations, can be largely passed on to those classes and strata (in the industrial centers and especially in the peripheries) that are unable to protect their real incomes.[20] In addition, under African conditions, higher wages can significantly reduce labor turnover, thereby raising productivity, particularly in those enterprises where the stability of the labor force is a requirement for imparting specialized skills. Obviously, this is a fact of the most crucial significance for assessing the likely role of the wage-earning sector in contemporary Africa, a consideration to which we shall return. More generally, the fact of rapidly rising wages and salaries, by introducing a bias in consumption and accumulation patterns in favor of imports, by weakening government finances (the state being the major employer of labor in most independent African countries), and by undermining the competitive position of local capitalist strata (if they exist at all), will be one more powerful force promoting the further political-economic integration of the modern sectors of the periphery with the advanced capitalist centers.[21] That some of the latter results are also such as to sustain a general economic structure inhibiting the full extension of those neocolonial involvements which we have seen to be characteristic of "second-phase imperialism" is merely one of the more dramatic contradictions of international capitalism's presence in contemporary Africa.

International capitalism is inevitably antagonistic to the sorts of comprehensive planning which might definitively rupture such constraints upon the development process. Nonetheless, certain seemingly novel departures do become acceptable to, are even encouraged by, an international capitalism increasingly concerned to free *some* of the continent's potential for industrialization. Thus, a degree of state involvement in the economy, particularly in the nonextractive sectors, has not always seemed a great threat to a flexible contemporary international capitalism. As a matter of fact, partnership agreements or management contracts with African statal and parastatal enterprises are increasingly seen by the international corporations as effective ways of reducing or eliminating altogether entrepreneurial and political risks, while profits are obtained in the form of royalties, fees for "technical services," use of patents and brand names, and through sales of equipment.[22] What is crucial to such a capitalism is the continuation of this stream of payments and therefore the orientation of such industrialization as may take place in Africa toward reliance upon the industrial capitalist centers.

Nor is contemporary international capitalism necessarily antagonistic to the development of larger politico-economic units and common markets. On the contrary, as the phase of import substitution in the light industrial sector draws to a close, the excessive balkanization of Africa becomes a serious constraint upon the extension of its continental role. Paralleling the attitude toward state involvement, it is only unification *aimed at a process of autonomous industrialization* (a historical necessity for the successful modernization of African societies)[23] that would antagonize international capitalism. The latter can, on the other hand, be relied upon to promote African unification provided that it widens the scope for its own involvement on the continent. It is no accident that AID has placed a growing emphasis upon the construction of broader markets and regional groupings, that the Korry Report on Africa stressed that American aid to Africa should be increasingly geared to such units, or that this was also a point of emphasis in the recommendations of the report of a special subcommittee on foreign economic policy of the United States House of Representatives.[24]

The fact that the United States, more than any other capitalist power, is promoting the idea of larger economic units in Africa, is significant in another respect. So far we have not differentiated among national interests within international capitalism. Yet Western capitalism is no simple monolith and its national dimensions must be taken into account in any analysis of its structure. Neocolonial relations continue to be mediated to Africa in diverse ways. By and large, the most prominent remain those channels first established during the period of formal colonial dominance. This is particularly the case for those ex-French colonies which now find themselves entwined with the former metropole through the multiple mechanisms of the franc zone and Common Market agreements, and their economies thereby encouraged in the maintenance of integration with, and effective subordination to, their European counterpart:

> Through participation in formulating and financing African development plans, through the control of money and credit policies, and through tariff and trade agreements, France thus exercises a dominant and detailed influence over the direction of development.[25]

Similarly, but to a lesser degree, privileges for Britain and Belgium have been reproduced in the "decolonization" process of their former colonies.

These national components of center-periphery relations in Africa must, however, be analyzed in historical perspective. It is indisputable, for example, that even in the French case such a component has been significantly weakened,[26] and that the major force behind this tendency has been the consolidation of U.S. hegemony within Western capitalism. For the United States has unquestionably established itself since the war as the world's preeminent economic force, a fact underlying its insistence upon a *liberalisme absolu* in the Third World which gives free play to its economic superiority in what Oglesby has termed the "free-world empire." Critically weighed within such a perspective, the winning of formal independence in Africa must be seen as related to the process of internationalization of center-periphery relations. It is in fact evident that the complex of international capitalism, particularly when seen to be increasingly skewed in an American direction, had little reason to be hostile to the process. Formal decolonization had, in fact, the virtue of liberalizing economic access to the erstwhile colonies. If, as must have seemed a good bet, trustworthy *indigènes* were those likely to seize and hold the reins of power, a neocolonial solution then seemed an acceptable answer to the growth of nationalist pressure in much of the continent. Even in places like Rhodesia and the Portuguese territories, there is little doubt that this could be looked to as a viable solution by many of the interests involved, though, as will be apparent, there were additional complicating factors in these instances. Seen in this light, the mechanisms of French and other ex-colonial powers' control referred to above appear in large measure *defensive* in nature. As Barbe notes:

> Thus, as opposed to the thoroughgoing liberalism advocated by American imperialism, French imperialism tends to interpose a set of controls [*un semidirigisme*], a practice better fitted to its position of secondary importance [*puissance de second ordre*] (in spite of the pretentions articulated by our leaders).[27]

To be sure, Africa has remained less central to American concern than other areas of the globe. In 1964 U.S. capital directly invested in the continent amounted to only $1,629 million, or less than 4 percent of total U.S. capital directly invested abroad. Further, the bulk of it (80 percent) was accounted for by capital invested in South Africa and in a few oil-producing countries.[28] But throughout the continent there is evidence of a growing range of American involvements, as witnessed by the numerous examples of American banks and companies expanding their interests and contacts collated by Vignes.[29] This growing involvement is not always congruent with the interests of, and is therefore resisted by, other Western actors. Thus, according to the former American ambassador to Gabon, "in several African countries de Gaulle's government has been discovered, sometimes in little scheming ways and sometimes in ways not so little, to be working against the United States, to frustrate [U.S.] policies and diminish [U.S.] influence." [30] In Gabon itself, Darlington suggests, the French intervention to restore Mba which was referred to above was as much directed to forestall further American aggrandizement as to realize any other objective. The reasons for this are self-evident to him: in Gabon the French resented U.S. Steel's large participation in manganese and Bethlehem Steel's 50 percent share in the iron ore. They were considerably disgruntled when Foley Brothers of Pleasantville, New York, obtained the contract from the World Bank to make the survey for Gabon's railway. . . .[31]

And the "proxy fight" in the Congo during the past few years over mineral interests has also witnessed an expanding American involvement, presumably related to its expanded military and political role, which has led to overt conflicts between the United States and Belgian businesses.[32]

These conflicts are peripheral manifestations of intracapitalist conflicts in the industrial centers,[33] and speculations on the particular manner (and the timing thereof) in which they will be solved are beyond the scope of our analysis. We shall simply assume that the present phase of relatively intense intracapitalist competition will end with the "survival of the fittest," i.e., the American-based giant corporations and those European- and Japanese-based corporations which will succeed in attaining the size and efficiency of their American counterparts. As current trends already show,[34] nationalities will, in the process, be largely transcended within the corporations themselves, which then tend to acquire a multinational character. The relevance of this phenomenon for Africa is already apparent and can be gauged by following through the complex patterns of interlocking and overlapping corporate structures traced in Nkrumah's book, already cited. Strictly national interests become less clear in such a maze.

Thus, even if it is true that Western "monopoly capitalism" is no simple monolith, there are reasons to expect it to become increasingly so; its political-economic domination of Africa will accordingly be "rationalized." A first implication of this rationalization would be a strengthening of that trend toward capitalist-sponsored economic and political integration in Africa which we discussed earlier, because the obstacles to such an integration traceable to the persistence of links with ex-colonial powers would be relaxed. A second effect would be a weakening of the bargaining position of the African ruling classes in their dealings with Western capitalism, as much of what strength they can presently claim seems to derive from opportunities provided by the competition among capitalist powers. Such a "bargaining position" may have helped the French-speaking African states to gain various concessions in the sale of their primary products to France (and its partners in the EEC), the quid pro quo being privileged access by the metropole for the launching of various forms of investment. This was obviously not part of a development strategy designed to alter drastically the structure of the "colonial" economies, but it did increase the possibilities for the ruling classes to gain a breathing space for themselves and their economies. More controversially, it has been argued that a state like the Congo could hope to obtain more significant leverage over the proceeds from its mining resources because of such competition.[35] And Western aid, though it has in any event tended to serve the primary purpose of reinforcing development strategies reliant upon international capitalism,[36] would be more forthcoming as long as the situation remained an ambiguous one for competing capitalisms. When also placed in the context of an abatement of intense East-West competition characteristic of the present period of peaceful coexistence,[37] one realizes that such general phenomena as the increased difficulties experienced by African states in striking favorable bargains for their agricultural interests[38] and the relative decline in available aid must be interpreted, in the absence of any significant attempts to break out of the overall neocolonialist pattern, as merely reflecting the key trend toward increased subservience vis-à-vis a rationalizing international capitalism which we have been tracing.

2

We have already mentioned the centrality of Southern Africa to international capitalist concern. Among what we might call the various "sub-totalities" of sub-Saharan Africa, characterized by different class and power structures, it is immediately apparent that the Southern African complex is also the most powerful. The development of an organic industrial base in South Africa and Rhodesia, which is a key dimension of the area's strength, must be traced to the presence in these countries of a national bourgeoisie (the settlers) sufficiently strong to uphold a "national" interest vis-à-vis the metropolitan countries. This class, by promoting important structural changes in the economies in question, has in fact restrained that "development of underdevelopment" which is a normal phenomenon in center-periphery relations.[39]

Mainly through the intermediary of the state, and often, especially in South Africa, in opposition to the short-term interests of less nationalistic sections of the capitalist class, the settlers have managed to establish some basic industries and consolidate themselves *qua* capitalists as one important element in the modern sector. Needless to say, these achievements were attained only at the cost of, and indeed through, the relative impoverishment of the African masses, this being a process which has produced an exceptional degree of inequality between European and African incomes. In South Africa the average per capita income of Europeans is more than $1,500, whereas that of Africans is in the order of $100; and in Rhodesia the corresponding figures are approximately £890 and £30.[40]

Such gross income inequalities have important implications for the pattern of development of these settlers' economies. In the first place, they imply high saving rates. In the last ten to fifteen years, gross fixed capital formation as a ratio of Gross Domestic Product has been consistently higher than 20 percent in South Africa and has averaged more than 20 percent in Rhodesia.[41] These rates are obviously exceptional for countries at similar levels of per capita income. But such gross inequalities also restrain the growth of the internal market and it is therefore not surprising that the relative importance of exports in absorbing the productive capacity of the economies in question has remained roughly unaltered for the last three or four decades.

This racial distribution of income is unlikely to change significantly in the near future owing to the determination of the ruling white classes to retain the existing dualistic structure upon which their power and privileges rest. Growth will therefore continue to depend on exports, a fact that raises some problems since the buoyancy of the latter requires a steady change in their composition in favor of manufactured goods in general and capital goods in particular. For these are the sectors which, as in most advanced capitalist countries, are currently providing the South African economy with much of its dynamism.[42] Thus, with further growth, and in order to guarantee the continuance of that growth, internal pressures will be building up in Southern Africa for the expansion of external outlets for its manufacturing industries. However, the competitive position of South Africa's manufactured goods in general and its capital goods in particular on the world market is likely to remain weak relatively to North American, European, and Japanese manufacturers. It is therefore to black Africa—as the London *Economist* observes in closing a recent "optimistic" survey—"that the Republic must hope to sell most of its growing exports of manufactured goods: if black Africa is willing." [43]

To the extent that exports do not expand to absorb the growing productive potential of the South African economy, a related tendency for investable surpluses to be exported can be expected to develop and has in fact already materialized. Its most dramatic expression is the emergence and expansion of the "Oppenheimer Empire," built in the first instance on the extraordinary mineral wealth of Southern and Central Africa, but gradually losing its territorial and sectoral identity. Dominating this complex of over 200 companies are the Anglo-American Corporation of South Africa Ltd., with head offices in Johannesburg, and Charter Consolidated, a new London-based mining-finance company in which members of the Anglo-American group are the largest shareholders. The market value of the former's investments was put in 1965 at £194.2 million and its reported profits after taxes stood at £14.6 million. For the same year, Charter Consolidated reported profits after taxes at £7.8 million and net assets at £171.6 million. As mentioned, the interests of this giant have lately been considerably diversified both geographically and sectorally. Through subsidiaries and often in partnership with European and American corporations (Ferranti, Pennarroya, Highveld Steel and Vanadium Corporation, Imperial Chemical Industries, etc.) the Oppenheimer Empire has entered such diverse sectors as metallurgy, electrical and mechanical engineering, mining machinery, transport equipment, construction materials, industrial explosives, petro-chemicals, paper, textiles, beer, building, transport, banks, etc. Geographical diversification has been equally impressive: the interests of Charter Consolidated in 1965 were 39 percent in the Republic of South Africa, 16 percent in the rest of Africa, 23 percent in North America, and 22 percent elsewhere; while Anglo-American has important interests in Central and East Africa, Australia, the United States, Canada, and Britain.[44] Thus the penetration of the Southern African complex on the part of European and American corporations has been matched by the outward expansion of South African capitalism and a growing interconnection between the two.

Although, as can be gauged from the above, the Oppenheimer Empire has most of the characteristics (in relation to the local economies) of the multinational corporations, its unique dependence on Africa as a basis of surplus accumulation makes its interests in the region much more vital to it than is the case for any other section of international capitalism. For this reason it is possible that the group in question may be prepared, more than other interests, to diversify its investment pattern in independent Africa (particularly in the East and Central sub-regions) with a view toward strengthening its grip on the political economy of the area. Moreover, this diversification would bring other direct benefits to the Oppenheimer Empire. For by moving into the diverse sectors mentioned above, it has come to control, directly or indirectly, much of the South African capital goods industry, and an industrialization, which it would also help to finance and continue to control, of strategically selected countries in independent Africa could help in creating the external demand required for the continued expansion of that industry.[45]

We thus come full circle to the question of trade between white and black Africa and should briefly examine the possibility that the obstacle to such trade which is represented by the settler regimes' racialist ideology may be somewhat relaxed in the near future. Generally, it must be admitted that there have been areas of genuine tension between such regimes and international capitalism, for the racialist ideology of apartheid does impede in certain fields the calculating "rationality" of capitalist interests.[46] Thus, for example, job reservation, which prevents skilled industrial training for black labor, and the Planning Act of Carel de Wet, which restricts the employment of Africans in urban areas, and the like, have led very readily to misallocations of manpower and other resources from a strictly economic point of view. Yet these conflicts are obviously nonantagonistic for one major reason. The white workers and national bourgeoisie derive their social and economic privileges from their control over the state apparatus, a situation which is the direct opposite of that of international capitalism, whose political power is mainly based on control over economic structures. Thus the settlers have everything to lose from an African neocolonial solution and have shown considerable determination in preventing it. Given their entrenchment in the political economy of these countries, such a solution could be brought about only at the expense of the widespread disruption of the Southern African economic system. It is therefore naive utopianism to expect the forces of international capitalism, either directly or as mediated by various Western states, to risk a most profitable outlet for investment and exports for the sake of marginal improvements in the "logic of the market." [47]

But if radical "liberalization" must be ruled out, there are factors at work in Southern Africa that may lead to marginal or formal "liberalization." For one thing, differentials in skills, education, and wealth between the races have been so deepened that market forces can increasingly be relied upon to maintain the existing racial dualism even if some of the political constraints on interracial competition are relaxed or removed. In addition, the structural changes which have increased the importance of manufacturing in the Southern African economies and the spreading to the capitalist sectors of such economies of the postwar technological "revolution" are having a double impact on the contradiction between apartheid and economic growth. On the one hand, it reduces the overall dependence of the capitalist sector on African labor and therefore makes the Bantustan policy pursued in Southern Africa less inconsistent with rapid growth. On the other hand, it requires the stabilization of a small minority of the African population in the modern economy to perform that manual, but skilled, productive work for which white labor is not available. Thus limited "liberalization," by easing the absorption of advanced technology, will, *pace* the *Economist* and other neo-apologists for *baaskap,* make possible a stricter implementation of apartheid vis-à-vis the vast majority of the African population.

Moreover, those forces promoting marginal "liberalization" within Southern Africa will be the more effective the greater the chances that such "liberalization" can succeed in normalizing relations with independent Africa. The economic significance of this normalization has already been discussed. It is also important to emphasize its strategic significance. For the settlers' regimes increasingly realize the opportunities of supplementing the use of force and the threat thereof with the use of political-economic mechanisms in containing pressure from the north. In this connection, there is much evidence of South Africa's growing confidence in "neocolonial solutions" as they have been exemplified in the former High Commission territories and Malawi.[48] Thus Vorster, in a 1966 interview with *U.S. News and World Report*, used words heavy with irony, whether intended or unintended, when he observed:

> We do not at all fear these developments—the establishment of African governments in these states. It is a natural development as far as we are concerned. . . . We want to work with them as independent black states, to their advantage and to our advantage. . . . In many respects we have, with respect to much of Africa south of the Sahara, a responsibility for as-

sisting in development—comparable to the responsibility which the United
States has undertaken on a much larger scale with respect to the underdeveloped areas of the world as a whole. Although we do not publicize it, we
are already doing quite a lot in this field.[49]

It remains possible, of course, that ideological factors in South Africa itself have acquired such a degree of autonomy that they may eventually
prevent *any* type of liberalization and therefore hamper, among other
things, the normalization of relations with black Africa, a possibility
which is also relevant to strategic calculation. Here it is sufficient, however, to conclude that there are undoubtedly particularly strong economic and strategic factors at work within Southern Africa which are
promoting the expansion of its presence in independent Africa at a time
when, as we have seen in Section 1, the relations between the latter and
the advanced capitalist centers are likely to be increasingly internation-
alized. The chances for the continued success of this political-economic
offensive can only be discussed in the next section after analyzing trends
in independent Africa.[50]

To this point we have not differentiated much between the various
political units within Southern Africa; and this emphasis is in part vali-
dated by striking evidence of increased integration under South African
leadership, both in economic terms and as regards defensive alignments
against the thrust from the north.[51] But it would not do to oversimplify
the breadth of South Africa's writ in the area, for there are peculiar elements in the cases both of Rhodesia and the Portuguese territories which
are worth bearing in mind. Thus in Rhodesia, still formally under British control, it seemed probable that some form of neocolonial solution
involving replacement of settler control by a sympathetic black government was deemed an active possibility by representatives of the wider
capitalist world throughout the latter part of the pre-UDI period; moreover, there too the settlers were often a nuisance because antagonistic to
the full rationalization of the economic system in line with corporate interests. It is the political leverage and drive of the settler minority which
have until now undermined that possibility—the activities of the settler
minority and considerable support from South Africa itself, be it noted.
Thus in addition to such considerations as concern for world, and especially African, opinion, it is in part a nostalgia for the latter option which
has given the sanctions program such teeth as it has had. Conversely, it

has been the very lack of interest, suggested above, in standing up to South Africa (along with lack of compliance by various private economic interests, often with tacit state support) which is the major factor in undermining that effort. Whether this can become a division of significance between the various dominant interests in Southern Africa remains to be seen: on the one hand, Britain has seemed willing to offer a number of compromise solutions to assuage settler fears, on the other South Africa, financially burdened by its assistance to Rhodesia and nervous at the growth of linked ANC and ZAPU guerrilla activities there, has given some signs of pressing Smith and his colleagues to themselves make further concessions to minimal African aspirations.[52] Here South Africa's growing confidence in the "neocolonial solution" might even bring its calculations into line with those Western powers for whom this has become a time-tested recipe. But this is merely speculative; much will depend, inevitably, both on the emerging character of the African forces which seem most likely to take power in Rhodesia and upon the actions of the prickly band of Rhodesian settlers themselves.

The Portuguese territories present some further complications. Here links with Portugal itself have been rather more direct, intense, and economically central to the "mother country" than elsewhere, facts which prompted Perry Anderson to coin the phrase "ultracolonialism" ("the most primitive, the most defective, and the most savagely exploitative colonial regime in Africa") to describe the situation there.[53] The contributions of agricultural and mineral earnings from Angola and Mozambique have long been central to the health, such as it is, of the creaking Portuguese economy and with bright prospects in oil and iron ore figure to be even more central in the future. Domestic manufacturing is also on the upswing, all these facts prompting William Hance to observe that "Angola's potential for development is undoubtedly one of the best in Africa. Mozambique, while less impressive, is nonetheless comparatively favorable and its potential is also large." [54]

Predictably, Western economic involvement in these colonies has been great and on the upswing; this is seen most dramatically in the prominent role of the Gulf Oil Corporation in the sphere of Angolan oil, especially as regards the recently opened rich Cabinda fields. But Portugal itself remains very much an active and interested element in the equation, reportedly having vetoed direct investment by South Africa in the new Portuguese-dominated Portuguese Exploration Company, for example. From such a perspective, it is certain that its strategic bargaining position would be weakened relative to other interests if it was to sacrifice direct political controls. Despite the cost of resistance to growing African pressures—Salazar himself gave the figure of £86 million a year and a force of 120,000 troops—there thus seems little likelihood that Portugal can afford to gamble on an alternative mode of guarding what are quite vital interests. Nor is there any real evidence that its Western allies have, for the moment, any alternative approach in mind: investments continued to rise as noted, U.N. resolutions are resisted and ignored, and, most important, Western arms flow to Portugal, ostensibly under NATO agreements,[55] but with the result of freeing Portugal's hands for more aggressive colonial wars. South Africa too lends a helping hand, economically and strategically. The time for a "neocolonial solution" has certainly not arrived, though some future turn of the wheel might increase the likelihood of such an attempt. But Portugal, on the other hand, is not strong and the costs of the struggle are high—Portuguese Africa may yet prove to be an Achilles' heel.

It is in fact in the Portuguese territories that the armed struggle is furthest advanced, furthest of all in that Portuguese territory which lies quite outside Southern Africa itself—Portuguese Guinea or Guinea Bissau. There an exemplary guerrilla struggle, radical in its ideological premises and characterized both by considerable military success over two-thirds of the country and a markedly socialist transformation of the economic and social structure in the extensive liberated areas, has at the very least stalemated any Portuguese attempt to recoup lost ground.[56] The area is rather marginal to Portuguese interests and therefore might at some point be easily dispensed with were this not to seem, as it inevitably would, a bad precedent. Moreover, the possible Marxist orientation of the emergent state, the cadres for such an attempt being quite literally forged in the current struggle, is likely to be viewed, prospectively, as an even worse precedent.

Things have not come to quite so dangerous a pass in the other two territories. In Angola, after the initial dramatic successes of 1961, the struggle has leveled off into a long, hard, and bitter grind. But the Africans have more than held their own to date and may well be winning the current war of attrition. Equally important, MPLA, currently the most successful movement operating in the area, is also articulating a more systematic political line, as well as beginning to duplicate some of Guinea Bissau's social restructuring in its own liberated areas.[57] FRELIMO, in Mozambique, later into the struggle and with a leadership less ideologically coherent, has also made military advances of some significance, particularly in the northern parts. In Angola and to a lesser extent in Mozambique there is evidence that guerrilla activities are linking up with a great many vectors of internal discontent, urban and rural, throughout the country, though no easy road can yet be prophesied. Even in Portuguese Africa, "revolutionary time" for Africa must certainly still be measured in terms of numbers of long years, rather than numbers of months.

Most important, the struggle itself is having an educative effect. The true dimensions of the Southern African situation are the more graphically apparent when the enemies' arms are standard NATO issue and the only sources of active military support for the liberation movements are to be found in the East. Anticapitalist and anti-imperialist sentiments of a very different order and depth from those which characterized conventional African nationalist movements are likely to be the result; already there is talk of the "dangers" of a "neocolonial solution" among some activists in both Mozambique and Angola. Similarly, as one American observer had occasion to note with reference to the struggle in Portuguese Africa,

> nationalist sentiments reflect a deepening reaction against the United States. The African revolutionaries denounce what they consider the hypocrisy of American lip service to self-determination as well as American racism at home and "overkill" in Vietnam, and declare these to be the antitheses of the values they are fighting for.[58]

Clearly, if socialist consciousness rises and organizational forms are increasingly forged to express it and demand a more meaningful victory, the chances of a neocolonial solution appearing a trustworthy one to international capitalism are by that very fact diminished. Indeed, the reverse situation is the more likely, and the possible development of more subtle and intense forms of coordinated resistance by imperialist interests must therefore be expected.[59]

The establishment of revolutionary governments in Angola or in northern Mozambique would create an entirely new situation in the whole of Southern Africa.[60] For this reason the struggle for their establishment and future consolidation is structurally linked with the struggle in the centers of the Southern African complex: Rhodesia and South Africa. This latter struggle is, however, qualitatively different from those which have been waged or are likely to be waged in the rest of sub-Saharan Africa. We are not here referring to the fact, so obvious by now, that the pattern of "decolonization" characteristic of the situation north of the Zambezi is not going to repeat itself in South Africa, but to other crucial considerations. One such consideration of more long-term significance concerns the possible results of a successful liberation struggle in the centers in question. Given the central position they occupy in the structure of international capitalist interests in Africa, their advanced stage of industrialization, and their abundant resources, their seizure by revolutionary forces could have far-reaching implications for the whole of Africa. Particularly within the possible framework of a progressive pan-Africanism to be characterized both by greater economic integration *and* more meaningful planning (some such form of unity being one prerequisite for genuine continental advancement, as we shall see) they could provide the cornerstone for a really effective development strategy. Indeed "only with the full liberation of the entire Southern and Central states of Africa can optimum division of interstate production be achieved." [61] The likely character of the participation of such liberated territories in future continental economic organizations (as well as the actual degree of their control over their own economic decisions) is of course of essential importance to these speculations. Here too the Southern African situation provides some promise; a second consideration of more immediate relevance therefore relates to the unique problems and potentialities (relative to the rest of Africa) of revolutionary action itself in South Africa and Rhodesia, a uniqueness which also largely derives from the advanced stage of economic development attained by these countries.

For unlike the situation elsewhere on the continent, the African peasantry here has been effectively proletarianized in the sense that the balance between means of production outside the capitalist sector (mainly land) and the subsistence requirements of the African population has been severely and irreversibly upset: the latter can only to a very limited extent be satisfied within the framework of a peasant economy. This fact has some important implications. In the first place, the *minimal* aspirations of the African people cannot be fulfilled by a peasant revolution aiming mainly at land redistribution, reduction in the burden of taxation, and other "populist" objectives. These aspirations can only be fulfilled by seizing control over the industrial apparatus itself and its reorientation toward the economic and social uplifting of the African masses. Moreover, contrary to what has sometimes been supposed, this reorientation of the industrial apparatus clearly cannot be initiated by an African bourgeois "revolution" aiming in the first instance at removing the racialist component of South African capitalism. For one thing, such a component is integral to South African capitalism and we have already identified as utopianism the expectation that international capitalism will provide its essential support for such a political transformation.[62] More important still, the structural weakness of the African bourgeoisie and middle class in these societies, resulting from a pattern of development that has, in defense of the settlers' interests, systematically restrained the upward mobility of the African peasants and workers, prevents them from assuming a hegemonic role in the struggle. In conclusion, the revolution in South Africa and Rhodesia, if it is to come, can only be a proletarian and a socialist revolution and the liberation struggle will not succeed unless it is restructured in accordance with this premise.

Much revolutionary energy has been wasted in the past in pursuance of reformist objectives and this has probably increased the sense of hopelessness felt by the masses in the face of a growing repressive apparatus. As in the Portuguese territories, the struggle itself has begun to have an educative effect and the liberation movements have by now realized the nonantagonistic nature of the conflict between the liberalism of international capitalism and the racialism of the settlers' regimes. However, further energies and revolutionary potential may now be misdirected in pursuance of a peasant revolution. As we have already emphasized, the African peasantry in these countries has been effectively proletarianized, notwithstanding the persistence (encouraged by the settlers' regimes as part of their tacit or open Bantustan policy) of remnants of precapitalist relations of production in the African areas. The composition of the population in these latter areas is notoriously unbalanced, the majority of the able-bodied males spending most of their time in wage employment in the European areas. Remittances from the latter are an essential component of the subsistence income of the children, women, and the aged who make up the bulk of the population in the African areas. In consequence, unlike the peasantry of the Portuguese territories (southern Mozambique excluded), still largely self-sufficient for most of their basic subsistence requirements, the radically restructured peasantry of South Africa and Rhodesia can hardly be expected to start struggles which "build up to a crescendo over a [long] time, are capable of pinning down large government forces, and are maintained at comparatively lower cost," as Govan Mbeki suggests.[63] This conclusion is further warranted by the fact that there are no reasons for expecting that large government forces will get themselves pinned down in the Bantustans, both because of the negligible economic importance of these areas as sources of public revenue or private profit, and of the ease with which they can be "sealed off" militarily, for relatively long periods, from the centers of industrial and mineral exploitation on which the wealth and power of the white ruling classes are based. This is not to deny the necessity of establishing guerrilla foci in the rural areas as a means of building up morale and revolutionary consciousness among the masses and of "spreading the enemy thin"; rural struggles can be important, particularly if they are also seen to include guerrilla and terrorist activity in the areas of European farming. The point is simply that the decisive battles in Rhodesia and South Africa will have to be fought in the "cities" and that a failure to prepare politically and organizationally the urban masses for such battles will ultimately lead to the suppression of the guerrilla foci. Put somewhat differently, it could be argued that, if the relevant model for the struggle in the Portuguese territories is perhaps some blending of the Chinese and Cuban experiences, the relevant model for Rhodesia and South Africa may be a blend of the Cuban experience and that of the Afro-Americans in the United States!

In the future in the cities themselves the steady absorption of advanced technology and growing importance of manufacturing may lead, as we have noted, to the full integration of a small section of the African working class into the wage economy. Yet at the same time it will tend to reduce the ability of the mass of the African workers to earn a subsistence from the sale of their labor (while their ability to do so outside the wage economy has long been negligible). The materialization of this tendency, which in South Africa has been counteracted by the rapid economic growth of the 1960s, would therefore increase the already great revolutionary potential of these industrial centers. It is important to bear in mind, however, that, besides the subjective factors discussed above, any revolutionary action faces here a formidable repressive apparatus. As a matter of fact, the high stage of economic development attained in these countries, while leading to the effective proletarianization of the peasantry, has also (owing to the exceptional inequalities in income distribution) enhanced the repressive potential of the white ruling classes by making available large surpluses for the steady expansion of a complex police and military apparatus. Indeed, given the industrialized structure of the South African economy, the armament program of the South African government, which has raised military expenditures to £150 million in 1966 (six times the 1960 expenditure and 20 percent of the budget) has had a stimulating effect on the economy.[64] In Nelson Mandela's words, there can indeed be "no easy road to freedom."

An elaboration of two important and related points will serve to conclude this section, the first concerning the interdependence of revolutionary action within the Southern African complex. As noted, the "periphery" of the Southern African complex (i.e., the Portuguese territories) is undoubtedly the "weakest link." If the struggle in these territories gains momentum, the financial and above all the white manpower resources of the "centers" (South Africa and Rhodesia) can be considerably strained, thereby easing the more complex task of seizing power in the latter; if it succeeds, they will provide the Rhodesian and South African liberation movements with more reliable bases than are at present available. A revolution in the "centers" of Southern Africa, on the other hand, is probably necessary to guarantee the survival of revolutionary governments in the "periphery" or to prevent their bureaucratic involution. Fortunately, some of these lessons too are being learned in the course of the struggle and growing contacts between ANC, ZAPU, FRELIMO, and MPLA, for example, give promise for the future. Thus perhaps the most noteworthy aspect of the growing seriousness of the effort to light from outside the spark in the "centers" may be the military alliance forged in 1967 by ANC and ZAPU, and the assistance rendered by the ANC of South Africa during the course of the actual fighting of 1968 within Zimbabwe.[65]

Equally important is a second point which emphasizes the relevance to the liberation struggle in Southern Africa as a whole of the emerging character of relations between independent Africa and Southern Africa, discussed briefly above. If established Southern African interests are at all successful in obtaining further rapprochement, the already shaky sup-

port of independent Africa for the liberation movements would fade
completely at a crucial stage of the struggle—this being one of the main
objectives of the settlers' regimes in seeking "northern" contacts. In addition, as such "normalization" of relations would give new momentum
to the growth of the industrial centers in Southern Africa (and might induce some marginal internal liberalization) it would at one and the same
time restrain the deepening of internal contradictions and, possibly, re-
vive the myths of the African "middle-class revolution" and of peaceful
transition from under the yoke of apartheid. Inevitably, in the light of
such emphases, the necessarily *continental* character of revolutionary
strategy in contemporary Africa becomes all the more apparent.

3

The decisive fact about contemporary independent Africa is the continuance of its subservient economic position vis-à-vis the industrial centers of the West. This subordination originated, as is well known, in the
pattern of trade and investment of colonial times, whereby Africa came
to play, within the international division of labor, a role of supplier of
raw materials and outlet for the manufactures of the centers of accumulation in Europe. It is important to reemphasize that, as compared with
other areas of the underdeveloped world, this "classic" pattern of extractive imperialism has remained relatively untransformed in Africa. Thus
the exports of twenty leading primary commodities accounted for 65.7
percent in 1960, and 70.1 percent in 1965, of all exports from Africa
(South Africa excluded); at the same time, the imports of industrial
manufactured goods accounted for 70.6 percent of all imports in 1960
and 71.8 percent in 1965.[66]

Nonetheless, such shifts in the pattern of capitalist involvement on the
continent as have emerged in the last decade have merely increased the
structural dependence of the economies of independent Africa upon the
advanced capitalist centers. As we have shown elsewhere, such a pattern
is characterized by the use of capital intensive techniques of production
and low rates of reinvestment of surpluses, especially in the capital goods
sector, and results in a growing integration of the modern sectors of the
African economies within the international capitalist system, and in a
deepening of internal dualism.[67] Under these conditions, attempts to
step up economic growth soon result in shortages of foreign exchange
which leave these countries wide open to a predictable variety of politi-

cal pressures and to the lure of economic deals with foreign governments and private investors which, while possibly "buying time" in the short run, ultimately strengthen their structural dependence on international capitalism and consolidate a pattern of "perverse growth." [68]

The internal sociopolitical structure of the independent African states is directly related to these trends and comes in fact to sustain them. The fundamental characteristic of such a structure, in contrast to the situation which we have observed in South Africa and Rhodesia, is the absence of a proletariat in the classical sense of the term and, at best, the likelihood that one will emerge only very slowly indeed. Owing to an overall absence of population pressure on the land in most African countries and to the capital intensive character of production, the wage-working class is polarized into two strata. Wage workers in the lower stratum are only marginally or partially proletarianized as, over their life cycle, they derive the bulk of the means of subsistence for their families from outside the wage economy. Wage workers in the upper stratum, generally a very small minority, receive incomes sufficiently high (say three to five times those received by wage workers in the lower stratum) to justify a total break of their links with the peasantry. This is a type of "optional proletarianization" which has little in common with processes of proletarianization resulting from the steady impoverishment of the peasantry. We therefore feel justified in considering wage workers in the lower stratum as part of the peasantry (which participates in the wage economy through labor migration) and in including the upper stratum with the much more important "elites" and "sub-elites" in bureaucratic employment in what we have called the "labor aristocracy," notwithstanding the confusion that the use of this term may generate.[69]

The present pattern of growth is rapidly improving the lot of this labor aristocracy (stabilized in the wage economy and increasingly detached from the peasantry) which appears as the hegemonic class and the guarantor of the "neocolonial solution." By emphasizing the centrality to the formation of such a labor aristocracy of the process of Africanization of the bureaucratic structures characteristic of colonial rule, we may further suggest that to this dominant group applies Régis Debray's characterization of what he calls the "progressive petit bourgeoisie" of Latin America:

[It] does not possess an infrastructure of economic power before it wins political power. Hence it transforms the state not only into an instru-

ment of political domination, but also into a source of economic power.
*The state, culmination of social relations of exploitation in capitalist Europe,
becomes in a certain sense the instrument of their installation in these countries.*[70]

There is some danger of oversimplification here. As Samir Amin has
had occasion to note in a recent and most suggestive article, the phenomenon of a "national bourgeoisie" is by no means absent in contemporary Africa, though it has been inordinately weak in relation to international capitalism and thus unable to bring about structural changes
which would restrain black Africa's underdevelopment relative to both
the metropolis and to peripheral centers where an immigrant bourgeoisie was present. In those parts of the continent where such a "national
bourgeoisie" is most prominent, it is to be found in the agricultural
economy and in commercial roles, though seldom in the industrial sector. Thus Amin instances in the Congo "une nouvelle bourgeoisie com-
merçante et riche" which has developed and which has "attained in a
few years an exceptional degree of maturity." For "organized into a
powerful professional association—APRODECO—the Congolese traders today represent perhaps 20 percent of the total turnover of whole-
saling and import-export trade—something which is unequaled elsewhere in Africa." [71] Considerable evidence also exists, for example,
which suggests that, particularly in the case of pre-colonial systems
characterized by class differentiation, there was a greater response to the
stimuli to expand production for the market created by colonial penetration. The reasons for this tendency were the assumption by privileged
classes of entrepreneurial roles and their utilization of opportunities for
extorting labor services from the underprivileged groups: here, then, a
rural bourgeoisie emerges at a faster pace.

The present pattern of growth may very well have the result of further fostering the formation and consolidation of a "kulak" class, for, as
we shall see, it steadily increases the supply of cheap labor for wage employment in agriculture. Amin easily (no doubt with his own investigations of the Ivory Coast prominently in mind) assimilates these and
other trends toward rural differentiation to the major thread which we
have ourselves emphasized: "However, as a rule, the bureaucratic bourgeoisie [*la bourgeoisie d'état*] has never eliminated the private bourgeoisie
[*la bourgeoisie privée*], but contents itself with co-opting it or fusing with
it." [72] There are certainly no reasons for assuming any major conflict of

interest between the labor aristocracy and international capitalism on the one side, and the African national bourgeoisie on the other. Their relationship in production is more complementary than competitive (the latter being concentrated in agriculture and petty trade) and, as mentioned, the present pattern of growth tends to increase the availability of wage labor in the rural areas. It should also be borne in mind that the concentration of government agricultural expenditure on the so-called progressive (i.e., wealthy) farmers compensates the rural bourgeoisie for worsening "town-country" terms of trade and urban biases of government expenditure. More important still, the tendency observable in most independent African countries for the labor aristocracies to be drawn from the "kulak" class and/or to invest in capitalist agricultural enterprises can be expected to smooth over even the marginal conflicts which still separate these classes.

In part, of course, differences of opinion over the proper emphasis to be given in analyzing these developments and the pace of the emergence of various groups and classes may result from the lack of differentiation, in much of the relevant debate, between the component parts of independent Africa. Thus a heightened emphasis upon the role of the African bourgeoisie (and of traditional authorities who have significant private economic involvements, both urban and rural) is probably not misplaced when West African countries are analyzed. However, it is very much less significant an emphasis when the vast sub-region of East and Central Africa (including the Congo) is being analyzed. In any event, regardless of the variations, the broad and converging trends which underpin both the dominance of international capitalism and the key position of mediation of the indigenous labor artistocracy (supplemented in some generally nonantagonistic manner by a national bourgeoisie) remains the core. Indeed, the military coups which have pockmarked the continent in recent years signal the meshing of these external and internal trends and their ultimate apotheosis in a most dramatic manner: through them the labor aristocracy moves to take over power directly, no longer content to have it exercised by a cadre of residual "heroes" from the independence struggle.

That this is true may be suggested by the haste with which military leaders have moved to assure themselves of Western, and particularly American, backing in the aftermath of their various coups: ". . . the U.S. is now the major economic factor to be reckoned with, given the urgent and crude financial needs of the new regimes in pursuit of popularity." [73] The almost mandatory expulsion of Eastern embassies becomes merely the prolegomenon to a round of visits to Western capitals for chats with government ministers and "officials from various companies who may be interested in investing"; ever more attractive investment incentives are unveiled and the words of the IMF assume the status of Holy Writ. This pattern is most striking in those states where some effort to articulate more radical development strategies had been made prior to the takeovers, viz., Ghana and Mali, but it evidences itself at each turn of the wheel in even the most pliant of client states.

For in all areas such a pattern doubtless reflects the fact that the old guard of nationalist politicians has often seemed at best an inconvenient and irrational element to international capitalism. Military rule, usually stabilized with the full cooperation of the civil service, seems to offer the promise of "technocratic" transformation to eliminate the grosser forms of corruption and to rationalize the environment of economic penetration; what this amounts to in practice is, in fact, a "pattern of rule . . . military-bureaucratic in type, politically repressive, espousing conservative finance and free enterprise, culturally null." [74] In addition, though an expression of the labor aristocracy, such regimes are by no means hostile to the national bourgeoisie, and in many instances, as is again most apparent in Ghana, predicate themselves upon the removal of the latter's fetters. Writing about the reversal of Nkrumah's plans for a growing state sector, I. G. Markowitz notes that "what is striking as a group about the industries denationalized is their suitability for development by Ghanaian entrepreneurs, involving as they do ready markets and relatively small capital outlay." In general, "the apparent overall effect of Ghana's new domestic policies is to foster the development of the fast-rising Ghanaian commercial bourgeoisie as well as that of the civil servants, technocrats, and careerists." [75] But even if these systems were to be so streamlined by such interventions, it remains clear that the military regimes, though more varied than can be suggested here, in general offer little other than an intensification of the pattern of structural subordination to international capitalism.

Under the circumstances, ideological styles which exemplify an "aspiration for solidarity" within the boundaries of the new nation-states come to be manipulated by the ruling classes to paper over the social and economic distance emerging between themselves and the masses.[76] "Nation-building," a concept transferred from the pages of American textbooks on political development, takes pride of place over "socialist construction"—just as American financiers are increasingly the world's bankers, so American social scientists are the ideologues of the epoch. To be sure, such reiterated "nationalism" is also in part articulated as a response to the fragility of political structures and identifications which results from the legacy of ethnic and cultural diversity in the states of sub-Saharan Africa. But the alternative socialist option, by debouching upon actual strategies for meaningful development and by raising the level of consciousness in ways closer to the felt experience and exploitation of the masses, might be expected to more readily assault parochialism in any event. It would, however, involve striking in significant ways at the internal dualism which sustains the labor aristocracies' privileges and for this reason continues to be shunned.

Such nationalism can, of course, be a springboard for certain kinds of pressure at the international level. Here, in the world produce markets and the like, the African ruling classes would like to see market forces subordinated to political decisions in such a way as to sustain prices and make available more assistance of a useful variety. Similarly, in individual countries, under propitious circumstances, an effort may be made to shift the terms of the bargain struck with international capitalism in a more favorable direction: the dominant groups are certainly not averse to increasing the revenues available to them within the established structure. It has been argued, for example, that Mobutu's activities vis-à-vis Union Minière in 1966–1967 represented a particularly aggressive and admirable exemplification of such a strategy. In this regard Paul Semonin notes that

> greater efforts should now be made to distinguish him from other African rulers brought to power through military coups. . . . Under Mobutu the state functions as a differential gear within the context of limitations imposed by the country's continued economic dependence. His regime has attempted to expand the Congolese national "space" within the interstices of competing corporate interests.[77]

In the event, of course, despite a somewhat expanded role for such a firm as American Newmont Mining Co., "the Congo government was forced to accept an agreement that returns essentially to the *status quo ante*," [78] and the conditions for any confrontation, if such indeed this was, have since further deteriorated in the context of monetary problems. Zambia, too, has more recently moved to redefine certain of its "terms" by imposing restrictions upon the export of profits and by the nationalization of marginal enterprises, but under existing conditions of total dependence on international capitalism for the operation of its productive apparatus the limitations of such tactics in contributing to the structural changes necessary for development have been obvious. More generally, government involvement in the economies of independent Africa has been ambiguous in the sense already discussed in Section 1. Thus state enterprises are generally managed by the international corporations, with little if any attention being paid to broader problems of structural change and long-term development.

The lack of an industrialization strategy which is at the root of this phenomenon must to some extent be traced to the difficulty of envisaging full-fledged economic transformation taking place within the African political and economic units in their present balkanized form. The major strength of Nkrumah's efforts in the cause of African unity always lay in the vision of meaningful continental planning for development which accompanied them. This is a case which has been spelled out cogently in a recent book by Green and Seidman:

> The gravest barrier to African economic development becomes apparent at this point. No African state is economically large enough to construct a modern economy alone. Africa as a whole has the resources for industrialization, but it is split among more than forty African territories. Africa as a whole could provide markets able to support large-scale, efficient industrial complexes; no single African state nor existing subregional economic union can do so. African states cannot establish large-scale productive complexes stimulating demand throughout the economy as poles of rapid economic growth because their markets are far too small. Instead the separate tiny economies willy-nilly plan on lines leading to the dead-end of excessive dependence on raw materials exports and small-scale inefficient "national factories" at high costs per unit of output. Inevitably, therefore, they fail to reduce substantially their basic dependence on foreign markets, complex manufactures and capital.
>
> The only way to achieve the economic reconstruction and development essential to fulfil the aspirations, needs and demands of the peoples of Africa is through a sustained shift to continental planning so as to unite increasingly the resources, markets and capital of Africa in a single substantial economic unit.[79]

In brief, existing dualism can only be eliminated by the subordination of market forces to political direction which could (through a planned re-orientation of capital accumulation, technical progress, and international and intersectoral trade) steadily reduce geographical and functional im-balances. Most dramatically, of course, land-locked interior African states "can participate effectively in a continental economic system—ei-ther as producers or consumers—only if special attention is given to their problems as underdeveloped areas in an underdeveloped conti-nent." The industrial location policy made available through planning "is certainly critical to the adequate provision of growth points for the poorest and least developed areas." [80] But in the long run, the continent as a whole will be the loser when circumstances dictate that potential "poles of growth" are not rationally distributed to encourage their maxi-mum mutual reinforcement. Once again, the sting is in the planning: if, in fact, market forces are not subordinated to a strategy of long-term political-economic development and the formation of larger units is aimed at easing the further penetration of the African economies by the multinational corporations whose profit-oriented calculations are thereby allowed to determine the pattern of accumulation and technical progress, then unification can only encourage further the process of growth without development which is already afoot. This brings us back to the essential question raised in Section 1 as to the likely purposes to be served by the realization of "unity" under differing conditions, and it is surprising to find such a question blurred over even by some of the more radical spokesmen of the pan-Africanist ideology.

Thus Kofi Baako, Nkrumah's spokesman in the hey-day of Ghanaian concern for pan-Africanism, states that "to wait until a common ideol-ogy is reached will delay both union and solution to our problems. When Africa is united, problems will themselves call forth the best methods of solution";[81] and similarly, Green and Seidman, in an almost propagandist attempt to make their powerful intellectual case as palat-able as possible to all concerned, argue with calculated blandness that "minimal thresholds" dictate only that

there must be African state—not foreign—control over internal economic decisions that affect the attainment of production targets in multi-state in-dustries. The exact institutional pattern of ownership and management may vary from state to state, or from industry to industry within a state, so long as African state control is sufficient to implement continentally agreed policies and output goals.[82]

But in contemporary Africa this is a *maximalist* demand, of course, and Green and Seidman's failure to emphasize this fact is of a piece with their general lack of concern to articulate political strategies capable of assuring efficacious coordination in practice. Benot is clearly closer to the point in discussing Amin's own emphasis upon the need for economic integration, when he notes:

> Indeed, unity such as that conceived by Samir Amin can only be the unity of countries which accept and apply the principles and methods of a particular development strategy, that of rapid accumulation [*accumulation accélérée*] with all that that implies, that is to say, a profound sociocultural revolution. And even then problems of doctrine would remain and doubtless continue to provide an obstacle.[83]

No meaningful continental or regional African integration such as that envisaged by Amin and Benot seems therefore possible in the present historical conjuncture. For the whole complex of forces—economic, cultural-ideological, sociopolitical—which we have identified as defining this conjuncture undermines any thrust in that direction. As noted above, the narrow, self-interested, and defensive nationalism of the labor aristocracies, coupled with the hostility to meaningful planning of both that group and their neocolonial tutors, are likely instead to promote an integration aimed merely at giving new momentum to international capitalist penetration which is increasingly fettered by excessive balkanization. It is in this perspective that one must in fact view the proliferation of so many regional groupings on the continent in recent years, groupings which reflect the growing interest of actual or potential "peripheral centers" like Kenya, the Congo, Gabon, Ivory Coast, etc., to stabilize their access to an economic hinterland (although in the East African case there have been attempts, as yet of marginal efficacy, to balance benefits, present and future).

The quality of pan-African cooperation on other fronts is of a piece with this experience in the economic sphere, and reflects the same underlying realities. Immanuel Wallerstein, in his book *Africa: The Politics of Unity*, has traced in some detail the development of pan-African organizations, culminating in the establishment of the Organization of African Unity. In doing so he identifies two active elements or viewpoints relating to the scope and character of pan-Africanism active on the continent. There has been a radical element conceptualizing pan-Africanism as a "movement" transcending "artificial" national boundaries and placing considerable emphasis both upon the threat of "neocolonialism" (with its corollary, the centrality of the anti-imperialist struggle) and upon aggressive activities to assure the success of Southern African liberation and, at least on the rhetorical plane, upon real sacrifices of existent sovereignty to assure meaningful economic unity. In this effort a core of "radical" states—Ghana, Algeria, Mali, UAR, Tanzania, Guinea—have played a leading part in conjunction with the more radical of the liberation movements and a number of parties of militant opposition in independent African states. Increasingly opposed to such trends, a conservative reaction, springing in the first instance from French-speaking Africa, has conceptualized unity merely as an "alliance" of existing states. In so doing it has sought to drain off any and all radical dimensions from the thrust of pan-African sentiment. Wallerstein sees in the construction of the OAU in 1963 a major victory for the latter forces, a victory which has evidenced itself in even more striking form subsequently. Thus the radical bloc in the compromises of 1963 obtained verbal guarantees of staunch support from all concerned for the liberation struggle, chips which, despite (or because of) the subsequent establishment of a Liberation Committee of the OAU, have proven to be most difficult to cash. For their part, the more conservative members saw to it that the OAU, in the words of the charter, guaranteed the principle of "noninterference in the internal affairs of states," thereby meeting their desire to underwrite strongly their own internal security. Furthermore, it provided for certain minimal organs of socioeconomic cooperation of a confederal nature, cemented by assurances as to the acceptability of the "maintenance of economic assistance from the Western world," as Wallerstein phrases it. As he further notes, this new structure "was in itself reassuring to Western powers, promising greater economic rationality without the threat of a political structure strong enough to attempt to transform world economic relationships." [84] It is significant that it was two of the radical opposition groups in French-speaking Africa who most clearly sensed the drift of events. Thus the UPC of the Cameroon in 1962, in its pamphlet "African Unity or Neocolonialism," argued:

> There is an Africa of the peoples and one of the servants. . . . The road
> of true African unity is not that of the fusion of the groups of Brazzaville,

Monrovia, Lagos, and Casablanca. That would be a confusion which would profit only neocolonialism and imperialism and which would induce African leaders to relegate to the background the fundamental problem of the struggle against neocolonialism in order to amuse themselves with economic and social hocus-pocus.

And in 1963 Djibo Bakary, leader of the opposition Sawaba group in Niger, warned crisply: ". . . in no way must African unity become a sort of trade union of men in power who will seek to support one another to resist popular currents." [85] It is safe to say that the worst fears of such men have been borne out amply in subsequent pan-African practice. The institutionalization of pan-Africanism, in particular through the OAU, has become the guarantor of defensive, conservative "nationalism" and a force for smothering significant challenges to the status quo.[86]

Noteworthy in this context has been the constant preoccupation of the vast majority of states to assault any and all potential sources of *radical* challenge to their positions. Even in the case of Tsombe's regime in the Congo, complete with the most aggressive sort of American support and at a time where there was much sentiment on the continent in support of the 1964 rebels, no states withdrew recognition and any proposed intervention by the OAU was rendered nugatory. French-speaking states in particular "seemed to place the threat to their immediate security so high, either directly or through further revolution in the Congo, that the alliance of African states against the external world seemed a secondary consideration." [87] Nkrumah, major publicist of an ideological stance which tended to discuss "subversion" in rather broader terms than his fellow heads of state and to see its clearest exemplification in the category of "client-states" of Western economic power, not unnaturally became a major target of contumely in the period. It is as yet unclear how far he himself actually posed and underwrote an active threat of more direct and potentially "progressive" subversion against such states, but it is significant that by 1965 so strong was the pressure against any activity of the sort that he made "the extreme concession of agreeing to deport from Ghana all political refugees and their families opposed to the Ivory Coast, Upper Volta, and Niger, such deportation being final." [88] It seems probable that Nkrumah had in fact never fully worked out in his own mind the place of various possible forms of "intervention" into the affairs of other African states within an effective and radical pan-Africanist strategy. It is, however, doubtful whether, under the circumstances, Nyerere, often a courageous spokesman for a more meaningful pan-Africanism, comes closer to articulating a meaningful strategy when he notes:

> Like-mindedness even on major social and economic issues is not likely to be achieved even after unity; it will never be achieved before. To imagine a merger of sovereignties will automatically solve inter-African conflicts is to invite disaster. Unity will simply change the context in which these problems can be tackled. *The socialist policies of our own countries must be safeguarded, the African-oriented policies of nonsocialist/African states will also have to be safeguarded.*[89]

Moreover, the conservative turn taken by pan-Africanism and the "Congress of Vienna" atmosphere which has come to pervade the OAU can be expected to become increasingly evident in the attitude of independent Africa to the liberation struggle in Southern Africa, especially as regards the activities of the organization as they are focused in the Liberation Committee. Already much dragging of feet over financing characterizes the policy of many African states in this sphere. And the continued paralysis of independent Africa in relation to the Rhodesian situation must be viewed as being particularly symptomatic of the general malaise.

The changing attitudes toward the regimes of Southern Africa will increasingly find a further rationale in some of the trends already discussed. As mentioned at the beginning of this section, the present pattern of growth without development leaves independent Africa wide open to political and economic deals with international capitalism which can sometimes help to shore up stability in the *short run,* and this will become all the more important a factor as the limits of growth are reached. In particular, it may create favorable conditions for that northward expansion of South African capitalism which we discussed in the previous section. Whether such expansion will actually materialize is an open question, though, as Bowman has noted,

> there is evidence that South Africa is having some success in breaking out of its isolated position. . . . In Parliament on January 31, 1967, Dr. Muller [South Africa's Foreign Minister] said that "those countries willing to cooperate with South Africa are increasing. Contact on different levels has increased day by day." The statement is at least partially

substantiated by South Africa's trade figures with the rest of Africa. Although for political reasons South Africa does not break down its African trade on a country-by-country basis, there have been sharp increases in recent years.[90]

In part, the degree of success depends on the extent to which marginal internal "liberalization" in Southern Africa and/or the establishment of military dictatorships in independent Africa will relax ideological barriers. But the crucial determinant will be the strength of those social forces which can be expected, in the near future, to oppose neocolonialism in independent Africa and capitalism in Southern Africa. The latter we have already discussed; to the former we must now turn.

We have already noted the polarization of wage workers in Africa into two strata and we should now further clarify the differential roles of these strata within the current pattern of development. Those wage workers who have been fully integrated into the wage economy and have cut their links with the peasantry partake of some of the privileges enjoyed by the "elites" and "sub-elites": not only do they have incomes (especially when they are employed by the state and by multinational corporations) which compare satisfactorily with those of the latter but, in addition, they benefit from the developed overhead capital of the urban areas (educational and health facilities, transport, water, electricity, etc.). They thus tend to become partners, albeit junior partners, of the dominant power bloc in the post-independent context. The short- and medium-run costs which the stratum in question would have to bear in the event of a radical restructuring of relations with international capitalism are too high relative to the likely benefits for one to expect much revolutionary initiative to come from this source. To be sure, worker demands have occasionally triggered movements with real menace for the dominant circles: one thinks of the Sekondi-Takoradi strike in Ghana, and the near general strike in Nigeria in 1964. Yet only in Congo-Brazzaville has such worker agitation seemed an unequivocally progressive force, becoming, as it did, a major instigator and prop of the progressive regime which emerged there for a time.[91]

Our assumption may seem to conflict with the fact that certain African labor leaders have in the past been among those articulating the most aggressively radical philosophies on the continent, a force finding its broadest expression in trends within certain pan-African trade union organizations, notably the AATUF. This may in part merely evidence the relative ideological autonomy of the labor leadership from the interests of the upper stratum of the working class, but it may also reflect the presence within such organizations of elements belonging to the lower stratum of the wage workers. This lower stratum, consisting of workers and unemployed who retain strong links with the peasantry, has in fact interests which are antagonistic to the present order. For the very pattern of capital intensive accumulation which is promoting the rapid growth of the incomes of the labor aristocracies is restraining the absorption in the wage sector of the migrant workers who seek employment to supplement the meager rural incomes of their families. This phenomenon is an important aspect of the impact of the current pattern of "perverse growth" in the peasant societies of independent Africa, a pattern strengthening external linkages at the expense of internal linkages and thereby limiting the peasantry's opportunities to improve their lot through participation in the labor and produce markets. In consequence, while growing income and wealth differentials between and within "town" and "country" steadily raise the desire of the peasantry to participate in the money economy, its ability to do so is being restrained and, as population pressure on the land builds up, it increasingly loses its economic independence and tends to be transformed into a rural proletariat or an urban lumpenproletariat.

Given such realities, it is evident that considerable attention must continue to be paid to the emphasis of Frantz Fanon, who placed his hopes for significant transformation in post-colonial Africa upon the peasantry's outrage at widening economic and social differentials, especially as between the mass of the population and the new "middle-class" (between, in effect, the rural and urban worlds), and upon their consequent dramatic insertion into the political equation.[92] However, the depth and likely impact of this contradiction must not be misconstrued. For on a continental basis the general absence of population pressure on the land and the relatively unrevolutionized nature of traditional rural economic systems—family centered with many communal constraints upon the full play of individualism—mean that the range of pressures characteristic of either full-fledged feudal or capitalistic exploitation are much less in evidence. As Benot points out:

> Because of the importance of the subsistence economy and of self-sufficiency, because of the importance of social structures marked by resid-

ual communalism and parochialism, because, too, of the fact that [in Africa] the same complex of gerontocratic and familiar traditions and customs encompass the exploited and the exploiters alike (who are, so to speak, often relatives), because of all these things the class struggle of which Sekou Touré speaks does not manifest itself within present-day African society as an internal conflict *(affrontement interne)* but as a conflict with the state, which remains a far-off abstraction, unconnected with felt experience—a conflict with which *everyone* can eventually identify himself in some vague way.[93]

Thus in the absence of immediate and widespread exploitation at the level of the mode of production (which has, however, begun to emerge in some areas, as mentioned earlier) politically relevant consciousness of the gap separating the peasantry from the labor aristocracy tends to be truncated and may merely lead to apathy and parochialism.

Not that this is the sole response conceivable; certain moments in Africa have suggested more progressive possibilities. Thus much of the turbulence in the Congo around 1964 seemed to take on the characteristics of a peasant resistance to the sorts of exploitation characteristic of a situation of dominance by a "new class" such as we have been describing; in particular, Mulele's rising in the Kwilu may be accurately characterized as being, primarily though not exclusively,

> a revolt of impoverished and exploited peasants for whom the enemy was not only the foreign colonialist but above all those Congolese who had monopolized all the fruits of independence, and also those policemen, administrators and even teachers who served the new class and sought to imitate its style of life.[94]

Other areas of the Congo, deprived of leadership of the quality of that provided by Mulele and his associates, were able to articulate their grievances rather less coherently, but some such elements of "class struggle" were apparent in many areas of the country and may simmer still, despite military defeat.

Less satisfactorily, the resentment thus directed toward the "elites" can be utilized to underwrite further mystification in a national context,[95] and, of course, similar strands of resistance could, in the absence of sustained political work, even frustrate future radical development efforts. For it must be underscored that the spreading of progressive political consciousness among the peasantry of independent African countries meets formidable obstacles. Though the politically relevant boundaries and major arena of self-aggrandizement for the elite have increasingly become those of the states of contemporary Africa, for the peasant rather narrower tribal and sub-tribal affiliations may still be the most prominent social horizon. To be sure, the latter is not solely a superstructural phenomenon but rather reflects, in part, the uneven development which capitalist penetration in colonial times has as a rule promoted not only among African territories but also among tribes. It can therefore become a reality to be manipulated by the elite itself to fragment growing mass consciousness or to provide the basis of pawns to be played in intra-elite competition: Richard Sklar, for example, in drawing upon his intensive Nigerian investigations, suggests that under such circumstances it is far from unusual for "tribalism [to] become a mask for class privilege." [96] Moreover, as Fanon himself recognized, even in times of heightened general tension, which evidence some potential for radical change, "what can be dangerous is when [the African people] reach the stage of social consciousness before the stage of nationalism. If this happens, we find in underdeveloped countries fierce demands for social justice which paradoxically are allied with often primitive tribalism." [97] In other words, protest itself, instead of giving rise to a critique characterized by socialist content, may be so mediated and thereby inflected into narrower and usually self-defeating channels. In such a situation some sort of achieved nationalism may become a precious commodity. For, in its absence, "mass discontent against the new class [in the Congo] was in many ways diverted into tribal wars often initiated by traditional chiefs intent on restoring ancient kingdoms";[98] even in Kwilu there are clear signs that the Mulelist movement itself contained backward-looking dimensions which tended to become more prominent as the level of tensions inherent in the Congo situation rose.

These ethnic dimensions must figure prominently in any African balance sheet as they give hostages to unwelcome international pressures. The blend of tribalism, oil, and opportunistic intervention by various rival capitalist and great power concerns which has characterized the Nigeria-Biafra war is a case in point. Nor should the possible ways in which the availability of such leverage can link up with other dimensions of the continental struggle be ignored. The tribalism fostered in Zambia by intra-elite competition has, for example, become the main entering wedge in the Southern African regimes' attempts to tame Kaunda's support for the liberation movements;[99] and one of the accomplishments of Portuguese aid to Biafra was the defection of a prominent (now) Biafran, seconded to the headquarters of the Liberation Committee in Dar es Salaam, who surfaced eventually in Lisbon bearing information of strategic relevance to the liberation struggle in Southern Africa.

Uneven development has also created contradictions among various African states, especially between the peripheral centers and those countries which form their periphery. These contradictions are still embryonic but can be expected to deepen, especially if the wave of capitalist-sponsored economic liberalization discussed earlier becomes an even stronger one: in this context, for example, the recent decision of a country like Chad to impose customs duties on goods entering the country from its former partners of the Central African Customs Union assumes more general significance. But in such instances (as with the more serious clashes which may emerge in the future) any progressive potential inherent in such an implicit critique of continental imbalances will, for the reasons which we have discussed, be vitiated in the absence of alternative strategies designed to complete a break with international capitalism at home.[100] Under existing circumstances it is probable, in fact, that these conflicts, and the "nationalist" sentiments they may arouse, will merely be manipulated by the ruling classes in the countries concerned to further fragment and mystify mass consciousness on the continent (while at the same time making available another possible instrument for use as leverage by outside—including South African—interests).

In conclusion, class contradictions in independent Africa are less dramatic than in Southern Africa and many areas of the underdeveloped world. Moreover, they are blurred by racial, ethnic, and nationalist dimensions which hamper the development of subjective conditions favorable to radical change. The development of a rural proletariat and of an urban lumpenproletariat will steadily restructure this situation, but for some time to come class antagonisms are unlikely to contribute in a determinant way to the internal dynamics of independent Africa. This very underdevelopment of revolutionary social forces further underscores the potentially important contribution both of intellectuals, who might play the role of generalizing protest and raising it to a level of significant revolutionary praxis, and of disciplined political movements which can over time turn discontent into a drive for radical change. Though some African students, especially when in the metropoles, have been among the most *articulate* radicals (a radicalism exemplified in the militancy of a number of their organizations, most prominently the Paris-centered FEANF) it is nonetheless true that with education classically so prominent a factor in recruitment into the labor aristocracy, the intelligentsia has tended to be a central prop to the unbalanced African power structure. Here too, however, there are reasons for expecting change. When the eclipse of the easy opportunities inherent in replacing the European colonial establishment has been coupled both with the expansion of educational opportunities *and* much slower expansion of positions concomitant upon a bankrupt development strategy, we may expect a growing frustration of that segment of the intelligentsia (understood in very broad terms) which the increasingly exclusive top levels of the labor aristocracy are unable to absorb. Such frustration may simply lead to an intensification of the manipulation of the masses in the service of intra-elite struggles. It might, however, lead to a genuinely revolutionary vanguard if, in line with other changes, the instrumentalization of the masses is subject to increasingly diminishing returns.

The potentially important contribution of a radical leadership is in some respects corroborated by the Tanzanian experience, where a transformation of the consciousness of the very ruling strata which inherited power at independence has been attempted under the creative leadership of Julius Nyerere. Here "self-reliance" vis-à-vis foreign capital has become rather more aggressively than elsewhere the order of the day, and state ownership has been extended to a sizable segment of the modern economy. To be sure, the ambiguities of state ownership without a radical development strategy,[101] mentioned earlier, are far from being resolved in Tanzania and it is by no means clear that the mass base that must underwrite the attempt can be generated. Yet the nationalizations have fulfilled a basic precondition for such a strategy to emerge, and the power of the labor aristocracy and international capitalism to inflect social transformations in a neocolonial direction has been contained. But even if this remains a situation of some continuing promise, it has arisen from a peculiar concatenation of circumstances—involving, among other things, a low degree of direct involvement, historically, on the part of international capitalism, a slower crystallization, in a setting of extreme "backwardness," of the interests and the consciousness of the nascent Tanzanian labor aristocracy relative to many other African situations, *and* the presence of a leader of great tactical skill and genuine commitment who could take considerable advantage of the breathing space thus allotted him[102]—the moment for which, if it ever existed, has probably passed unused in most other African states. In much of independent Africa root and branch challenge to the incumbent regimes is the relevant historical necessity, however difficult the task.

4

The picture which emerges from our discussion is not bright. International capitalism, under the hegemony of the United States, seems about to rationalize its domination of black Africa, a trend which may be supplemented by an economic and diplomatic offensive from South Africa. The bankruptcy of independent Africa's development policies in the last decade has, at the same time, prepared a favorable environment for the success of both such moves. Thus the victorious "nationalisms" of the fifties and early sixties, which seemed the crystallization of an effective challenge to imperialism, must now be generally reinterpreted, in the light of independent Africa's "false decolonization" (in Fanon's suggestive phrase), as no real defense but rather as so many myths designed to legitimate the dominant position of the new ruling classes. Similarly pan-Africanism, originally drawing upon a living tradition of racial and cultural themes and a sense of shared grievance, is itself being transformed from a radical force seemingly capable of offering real resistance to the further subordination of Africa to Western capitalism, into a conservative alliance guaranteeing the stability of existing neocolonialist structures. Moreover, though some among the African countries (especially the peripheral centers) find themselves bound into the imperialist system in ways which provide (in the short run) more of the illusion of development, ultimately all are effectively constrained by such a continental pattern. In sum, the "Latin Americanization" of independent Africa is well underway.

The social forces which might be expected to underpin any drive to reverse these trends are, generally speaking, either absent (as in the case of the proletariat proper) or ideologically and politically fragmented (viz., the peasantry). Moreover, given the present pattern of capital intensive development, the proletarianization of the peasantry will be too slow and long drawn out a process on which to base hopes of revolutionary change in most of the area. In time the fruits of bankrupt development strategies—impressed upon lumpen elements in the urban areas, sections of the peasantry, and some members of the intelligentsia, for example—will come to define real contradictions, but in the short run greater authoritarianism, occasionally complemented by "mass" incursions into politics whose regressive and parochial character reflects the fragmented and mediated consciousness which we have mentioned, is a more likely outgrowth of tension than any concerted revolutionary activity.

Hopes must instead be focused upon the liberation struggle in Southern Africa, the implications of which are bound to have truly continental dimensions. In the "centers" of Southern Africa the peasantry has been effectively proletarianized and the social structure produced by a pattern of development in which the white settlers play the hegemonic role leaves little, if any, room for a neocolonial solution. Moreover, in the periphery of this region (the Portuguese territories) the neocolonial solution has been blocked by the "ultra-colonialism" of Portugal and the peasant revolution which has ensued is creating subjective conditions for socialist transformation which are generally absent elsewhere in independent black Africa. The intensification of the struggle in Southern Africa, drawing South Africa out of its own fortress (and perhaps eventually drawing the United States and others ever more overtly into the fray), can in turn have an educative effect upon receptive circles in independent Africa. Much more important, a successful socialist revolution in Southern Africa would radically restructure neocolonialist relationships on the whole continent since, after a necessary (and admittedly difficult) period of reconstruction, it would act as a powerful pole of politico-economic attraction for the less developed and less wealthy nations of tropical Africa. Our discussions should have dispelled any illusions concerning the nature and short-term prospects of the struggle in Southern Africa. Yet, at the present historical moment, this provides the main, if not the only, leverage for revolutionary change in sub-Saharan Africa.

It follows that the countries bordering upon the Southern African complex deserve special attention as their support is crucial to the liberation struggles, especially those in Rhodesia and South Africa where, as we have seen, the peasantry cannot provide a sure and sustained base for revolutionary action. In this regard the Congo, and particularly Malawi, have already been effectively neutralized by the neocolonial control of

the United States and South Africa respectively; this has in turn enhanced the strategic significance of Zambia and Tanzania. In assessing
the present and likely future contributions of these countries to the liberation struggle in Southern Africa, it must be stressed from the outset
that the constraints upon the development of revolutionary consciousness within their own borders are formidable; the combination of forces
which we have seen to be promoting the entrenchment of neocolonialism are present also in these countries. In addition, Zambia, like Malawi,
finds itself in the unique position of having an economy closely integrated with that of South Africa, its links with Rhodesia having been reduced since UDI largely through greater dependence upon South Africa
and the Portuguese territories. This situation obviously narrows further
the options open to the Zambian nationalist leadership, which, in addition, has been rather less coherent and radical than that of Tanzania in
conceptualizing the problems of its country's development.

   Yet, given this situation, the consolidation in power of the present
leadership there and in Tanzania, and the retention by such leaderships
of their present attitudes toward the liberation movements, is the most
favorable trend that the liberation movements can expect—though the
confrontation with Southern Africa in its various dimensions (involving
the backing by the white regimes of internal opposition groups, as in
Zambia, the tacit encouragement by those same regimes of the expansionist ambitions displayed by Banda, and, of course, the direct military
intervention exemplified most graphically to date by Portuguese border
raids into Tanzania and Zambia) may have a further radicalizing effect
on both countries. For this trend to have any chance to materialize it is
necessary, however, that the Zambians succeed in reducing the integration of their economy with Southern Africa to a much greater extent
and at a faster pace than they have to date. In this connection the further
rapid expansion of various links with Tanzania, particularly in the field
of communications and trade, would represent an important development, and one is therefore tempted to look upon the success or failure to
execute the projected Tanzam railway project, to be financed and built
by China, as a major indicator of future trends in sub-Saharan Africa.[103]

   In any event, developments in Zambia will be closely related to those
in Tanzania. Of course, the long-run success of the latter country's bid
to escape the neocolonial pattern of development could in and of itself
begin to have some educative effect upon the rest of the continent. More

immediately relevant to our purposes here, however, is the fact that its failure would almost inevitably lead Zambia to join Malawi and the Congo in surrendering completely to internal and external neocolonialist pressures. We have already mentioned some of the positive features, as well as some of the continuing ambiguities, of the Tanzanian experience; we will here add only some brief mention of the important implications of Tanzania's integration into the regional East African economy. For Tanzania has traditionally played the role of an economic satellite vis-à-vis Kenya, which, owing to the pressures of a European and Asian national bourgeoisie, had acquired many of the features characteristic of the settler economies of Southern Africa. Prominent among such features was a relatively developed productive structure which, together with Kenya's total subservience to the West, has made that country the "natural" base for international capitalism's operations in the whole of East Africa in the post-independence era. It is not surprising, therefore, that Kenya is one of the countries where United States presence has become most marked.[104] Under these conditions, and irrespective of short-term advantages, the participation with Kenya in what seems to be primarily a neocolonialist-sponsored common market could severely constrain meaningful planning in Tanzania at the very moment when it begins to sense the need for a coherent domestic industrial strategy.[105] On the basis of our earlier general argument, it should be clear that Tanzania's efforts would benefit greatly from participation in larger economic units characterized by rational and equitable planning. But it is equally evident that some forms of unity, whether continental or regional, can be more damaging than none at all for many of the participants.

Such a consideration provides one reason why radical change in Kenya would significantly ease the way for the ultimate success of the Tanzanian policy of "self-reliance." It is therefore relevant to recognize that the prospects for such change are marginally brighter in Kenya than elsewhere in black Africa. For another feature which Kenya has inherited from the colonial period is a class structure similar to that of Rhodesia and South Africa, which is to say that the Kenyan peasantry has been more deeply proletarianized than the peasantry in most other African countries. For this reason class conflicts are likely to emerge as a dynamic factor as soon as the limits are reached in the current Africanization of the settler economy, this latter process having created considerable consensus for the present regime but having also assured the consolidation of Kenya's black labor aristocracy in a position of gross privilege even more graphic and exposed than is the case in other parts of the continent.[106] Admittedly, fragmentation of consciousness along tribal lines is a deep-seated problem, but there is also a living tradition, in Mau Mau, of peasant violence to redress socioeconomic grievances which can be drawn upon.[107]

Here, too, such realities may merely lead to greater authoritarianism and are in fact doing so. But if adequate subjective conditions are being created, grievances generalized, and the basic tasks of organization begun, Kenya could at some future date underwrite a qualitatively different situation in East Africa and, through the repercussions on Zambia and the liberation movements, in Southern Africa. Finally, certain parallel points might be made about potential developments in the strategically important state of Zaïre, for the character of its integration into the Southern African mining complex and the degree to which its rural structures were shaken up by the Belgians' own version of "ultra-colonialism" [108] also give its sociopolitical system a certain unique volatility. This has been best exemplified by those post-independence peasant outbursts mentioned in an earlier section which are without ready parallel elsewhere on the continent—though here again, as noted, subjective factors undermined much of the creative potential inherent in the situation.

We are here moving toward the realm of the merely speculative, for in fact the possible permutations and combinations of events and their likely timing are vast in number. It is enough in conclusion to take note of two main elements that are readily apparent in the preceding argument. On the one hand, a concluding focus upon the important interconnections between the various states and liberation movements in the "battle area" serves to reemphasize the necessarily *continental sweep* of strategic calculation in contemporary Africa. On the other hand, the importance of the development of *subjective conditions* which has been noted reinforces the concern expressed in our introduction for increased clarity of analysis and a deeper understanding of the forces involved on the part of all concerned.

The former point raises a number of difficulties, of course, for the sets of priorities which should be adopted by states, groups, and individuals in Africa in defining their revolutionary praxis are by no means self-evident. Benot has raised some relevant points in his discussion of Nkrumah's pan-African strategy, arguing that much of the latter's emphasis on this issue led to an unfortunate dispersion of vital energies. He concludes that

> a state embarked upon the difficult struggle for development and economic independence is of necessity forced to consider the demonstration through its own achievements and its own progress of the real possibilities of independence as the crucial contribution which it can make to the liberation of the continent.[109]

Nationalism, so potentially mystifying an element on the African scene, can in certain contexts be revitalized, used (and controlled) as a progressive instrument providing the rationale for struggle and/or the framework within which social reconstruction proceeds.[110] But nonetheless, for reasons which we have indicated, it must certainly be balanced by a continental concern, though not one cast in the conventional mold of the present day. Indeed, what must be a most pressing necessity is to recapture in new terms the vital spirit of continental *division* which characterized the hey-day of the Casablanca and Monrovia blocs. This will involve calculations of particular relevance to the socialist states which may emerge from the liberation struggle (though it should probably be of increased immediate concern to a state like Tanzania, for example). For links among the like-minded will become particularly important as such states move to sustain each other and to spread their influence. Clearly the groundwork should now be laid by African revolutionaries for consideration of the full range of possible activities in the next stages of continental evolution.

Needless to say, answers to the questions raised in the course of such calculations are dependent upon the clarity of vision whose necessity was introduced as the second major element of our summary above. Only when concepts of "nationalism" and of "pan-Africanism" are fully demystified and liberated from the cultural grip of the ruling classes and their ideologues can they be put to progressive use as political instruments.[111] It is then too that a patently two-edged sword like *racial consciousness* can realize its full progressive potential—when, in other words, it is related to (though not submerged by) a growing realization on the part of African radicals that their revolution is part and parcel of a worldwide *anti-imperialist struggle*. Of course, as Roger Murray has cogently observed, the demands for both intellectual probity and intellectual honesty to be made upon "metropolitan socialists" can be no less severe, and must lead them to transcend such "misinterpreted application of revolutionary responsibility and commitment" as has led to "the general default of meaningful and critical solidarity" with the Third World in the past; his injunctions in this regard should be required reading and need not therefore be paraphrased here.[112]

Many parallel points might also be made with reference to the role of the socialist countries for whom collaborationism with "national democracies" is a temptation and opportunism, as exemplified in the Nigerian case, an ever present danger. Partly this may spring from an atmosphere of "peaceful coexistence" which all too often means merely a retirement before the sort of aggressive global "rationalization" by international capitalism whose African version we have elaborated upon above. And even where more fruitful involvement is the rule as in the struggle in Southern Africa the division between the Soviet and Chinese wings of the socialist camp can, in its crudest expressions, have a most deleterious effect. Yet the contribution from the East can and must be great, not only during the stage of the liberation struggle itself, but also as socialist states struggle to emerge on more secure bases than was the case for the first wave of radical states in sub-Saharan Africa. Often isolated (as would be the case for an independent Cabralist Guinea, for example) and inevitably in need of meaningful short-run assistance (as in contemporary Tanzania), these should be the foci of concentrated effort. In the current continental conjuncture, characterized by a graphically uneven development of revolutionary possibilities, there is little to be gained from spreading one's efforts thinly and uncritically.

In sum, for all concerned outsiders of radical persuasion anxious to maximize their contribution, more sophisticated theory and analysis and clearer insight into African realities are almost as important as for the new African revolutionaries themselves. Too little advance has been made beyond the situation described in 1960 by Amilcar Cabral, among the most admirable of African militants, when he identified what he chose to call "a crisis in the African revolution":

> It is not a crisis of growth, but mainly a crisis of knowledge. In too many cases the struggle for liberation and our plans for the future are not only without a theoretical base, but also more or less cut off from the concrete situation in which we are working.[113]

Notes

1. We have limited our inquiry to sub-Saharan Africa despite the fact that, for many important purposes, this artificially excludes North Africa from the continental balance sheet which we attempt to sketch. A more adequate account would have to pay particular attention to the often radical role played by North African states (the UAR and Algeria in particular), both within various continental organizations and vis-à-vis the liberation struggle in Southern Africa.

2. The phrase is Braundi's, in E. R. Braundi, "Neo-Colonialism and Class Struggle," *International Socialist Journal*, no. 1 (1964). Romano Ledda ("Social Classes and Political Struggle," *International Socialist Journal*, no. 22 [August 1967], p. 560) in adopting a somewhat similar line is particularly critical of the writings of Frantz Fanon, in particular *The Wretched of the Earth*. For an extreme version of one form of "agrarian messianism" with reference to Africa see Peter Worsley, *The Third World* (London, 1964), especially ch. 4, "Populism"; for a critique see Chapter 4 of this volume.

3. Thus Ledda (op. cit., p. 580) emphasizes the central importance of "the emergence of a working class, made up essentially of wage earners—industrial, agricultural, and tertiary proletariat—in the cities and rural areas; and it is this class that will form the backbone of a revolutionary movement" in Africa.

4. Hamza Alavi, "Imperialism Old and New," in *The Socialist Register 1964* (New York and London, 1964); H. Magdoff, *The Age of Imperialism*, (New York, 1969).

5. Alavi, op. cit.

6. This hypothesis is of course consistent with the fact that there is a net outflow of private capital from the periphery to the industrial capitalist centers. See Alavi, op. cit.; Magdoff, op. cit.; and J. P. Vigier and G. Waysand, "Revolucion Cientifica e Imperialismo," *Pensamiento Critico*, no. 13 (1968).

7. For the importance of the mining industry to advanced capitalism see Pierre Jalée, *The Pillage of the Third World* (New York, 1968) and *Third World in the World Economy* (New York, 1970).

8. On foreign investment in South Africa see "A Special Report on American Involvement in the South African Economy," *Africa Today* (January 1966); Dennis Austin, *Britain and South Africa* (London, 1966), especially ch. 6; "Foreign Investment in South Africa, Part I: Britain," *Sechaba* (Dar es Salaam), no. 11 (1968); "Foreign Investment in South Africa, Part II: U.S.A., West Germany," *Sechaba*, no. 12 (1968). On foreign investment in Rhodesia, South-West Africa, and Portuguese territories see United Nations, A/6868/Add. 1 (October 1967).

9. Austin, op. cit.

10. U.S. Department of Commerce, *U.S. Business Investment in Foreign Countries* (1960); and *Survey of Current Business* (August 1964).

11. "South Africa," *New Republic*, 13 August 1966, p. 8.

12. Carl Oglesby and Richard Schaull, *Containment and Change* (New York, 1968), p. 98. Oglesby draws heavily upon the data in the *Africa Today* special report mentioned above.

13. These two instances, among others, are cited in John Marcum, "Southern Africa and United States Policy: A Consideration of Alternatives," *Africa Today* (October 1967).

14. See the *Africa Today* special report chapter, "Citizen Englehard."

15. United Nations, op. cit.

16. See Alavi, op. cit. For a valuable case study see M. Kidron, *Foreign Investment in India* (London, 1965).

17. In this article we shall distinguish between "peripheral centers" and their "satellites." The development of capitalism on a world scale has not only produced the relative underdevelopment and subordination of the "periphery" as a whole (the present underdeveloped world); it has also led to uneven development within the periphery itself, where some countries, regions, and communities play the role of "peripheral centers" and others those of their "satellites." See Gunder Frank, *Capitalism and Underdevelopment in Latin America* (New York, 1967).

18. See Samir Amin, *Le Développement du capitalisme en Côte d'Ivoire* (Paris, 1967), especially the conclusion. Difficulties similar to those described by Amin for the Ivory Coast are also becoming apparent in Kenya.

19. It is along some such lines that one might hope to pursue Roger Murray's goal of "a much finer discrimination of the variant forms of a 'neocolonialism' which embraces much of the world; and which therefore has to be liquidated as an autonomous category." See Roger Murray, "Second Thoughts on Ghana," *New Left Review* (March–April 1967), p. 39. On this subject, most definitely, further work is needed.

20. As noted earlier, this assumption does not apply to concerns engaged in gold mining.

21. See Chapter 3 of this volume.

22. Alavi, op. cit.; K. Nkrumah, *Neo-Colonialism: The Last Stage of Imperialism* (London, 1965); R. H. Green and A. W. Seidman, *Unity or Poverty?* (London, 1968); A. W. Seidman, "Reshaping Foreign Economic Relations" (unpublished manuscript).

23. See Chapter 1 of this volume.

24. A. Astrachan, "AID Reslices the Pie," *Africa Report* (June 1967); Farbstein, et al., *The Involvement of U.S. Private Enterprise in Developing Countries* (Washington, 1968).

25. Green and Seidman, op. cit., p. 138.

26. M. Saint-Marc,"Diversification des courants d'échange des anciennes colonies françaises," *Le Mois en Afrique* (December 1967).

27. R. Barbe, "Le Rapport Jeanneney et le néo-colonialisme," *Economie et politique* (October 1964), p. 66 (our translation).

28. U.S. Department of Commerce, op. cit.

29. J. Vignes, *L'Afrique contemporaine* (Paris, 1968). An extract from the chapter "Dépendance et exploitation économique de l'Afrique" appears in *Tricontinental* no. 3 (1967), p. 168. See also Nkrumah, op. cit.

30. Charles and Alice Darlington, *African Betrayal* (New York, 1968), p. 169.

31. Ibid.

32. Paul Semonin, "Proxy Fight in the Congo," *The Nation*, 6 March 1967, p. 303.

33. The main manifestation of these conflicts is probably the series of international monetary crises which Western capitalism has been undergoing lately. See M. Kidron, *Western Capitalism Since the War* (London, 1968).

34. See E. Mandel, "International Capitalism and 'Supra-Nationality,' " in *The Socialist Register 1967* (New York and London, 1967); S. Hymer, "Transatlantic Reactions to Foreign Investment," Yale University, Economic Growth Center, Discussion Paper no. 53 (1968).

35. See Paul Semonin, "Mobutu and the Congolese," *The World Today* (January 1968). We will return to this theme in Section 3, below.

36. For a revealing case study see H. Alavi and A. Khusro, "Pakistan: The Burden of U.S. Aid," *New University Thought* (August 1962). Also Farbstein, et al., op. cit.; Green and Seidman, op. cit., part II, ch. 3.

37. On the importance for the weakening of Africa's "bargaining position" of the decline of an aggressive Soviet presence in independent Africa see Immanuel Wallerstein, "African Unity Reassessed," *Africa Report* (April 1966).

38. For example, B. J. Oudes in his article "OCAM Comes of Age," *Africa Report* (February 1968) strongly emphasizes the weakened bargaining position of the African leaders vis-à-vis the EEC.

39. See Frank, op. cit. The phrase "development of underdevelopment" is used to emphasize that the underdevelopment of the peripheries must not be viewed as an "original state" but as the "joint product" of the historical process which has brought about the development of the advanced capitalist centers.

40. United Nations, E/CN/14/370, p. 179 for South Africa; and Central Statistical Office, *National Accounts and Balance of Payments of Rhodesia, 1965* (Salisbury, 1966), for Rhodesia.

41. Ibid.

42. United Nations, E/CN/14/370, and *Sechaba*, no. 7 (1967).

43. "The Green Bay Tree," *The Economist,* 29 June–5 July 1968, p. xlv. The subtitle of this fifty-page special report by the *Economist*'s deputy editor is, significantly, "A survey by the *Economist* of why South Africa is getting richer so quickly, and of why it is almost certainly to everybody's advantage that it should continue to do so."

44. United Nations, A/6868/Add. 1.

45. It should be noted that as regards these trends the "Oppenheimer Empire" is only the most far-sighted and aggressive of a number of actors in the Southern African economy with similar interests.

46. See R. Horwitz, *The Political Economy of South Africa* (London, 1967); and Chapter 7 of this volume.

47. The classic instance in this regard is Colin and Margaret Legum, *South Africa: Crisis for the West* (London, 1964); for an alternative prognosis see Chapter 7 of this volume.

48. The Malawi case is a particularly striking one; for a succinct analysis see "Introduction to Malawi," *New Left Review,* no. 45 (1967).

49. Cited in Z. Nkosi, "South African Imperialism," *The African Communist,* no. 30 (Third Quarter, 1967), p. 35, which presents a number of revealing statements by important actors in the South African political economy on this subject; see also *The Economist,* op. cit., p. xlvi; "Vorster's Political Deception," *The Nationalist* (Dar es Salaam), 4 November 1968; D. Austin, "White Power?," *The Journal of Commonwealth Studies* (July 1968). Nkosi also mentions, for example, that "Dr. Robert Gardiner [a Ghanian], executive secretary of the U.N. Economic Commission for Africa, on his return to his headquarters in Addis Ababa from a visit to the Republic last March called for 'an agonizing reappraisal' of how black Africa should approach the problem of South Africa" (p. 37).

50. Nor should one ignore, in the last instance, the threat of direct South African military action against the North: "Three months ago Mr. Botha [South Africa's Minister of Defense] declared that South Africa regarded assistance given to the guerrillas as an act of provocation—'provocation can lead to hard retaliation in the interests of self-respect and peace.' Significantly he drew the analogy of Israel's raids against al-Fatah bases across the Jordan." ("In the Steps of Dayan," *The Economist,* 3–9 August 1968).

51. Dennis Austin is very much to the point when he argues that "particularly interesting are the joint development undertakings in Lesotho, Mozambique, and Angola, including the very large hydroelectric projects on the Orange, Zambezi, and Cunene rivers. One can also list a growing number of mining ventures and industries directly financed by South Africa in Botswana, Swaziland, both the Portuguese territories, Rhodesia and Malawi" (in "White Power?," op. cit.). Clear evidence of the military and logistic

presence of South Africa in the Southern African struggle beyond its borders is best situated by Botha's remark: "True friends do not need signed treaties. South Africa has an interest in what is happening in Angola, Rhodesia, and Mozambique" (quoted in "In the Steps of Dayan," op. cit.).

52. "Vorster Says Settle," *The Economist*, October 1968.

53. P. Anderson, "Portugal and the End of Ultra-Colonialism," *New Left Review*, nos. 16, 17, 18 (1962).

54. W. A. Hance, "Three Economies," *Africa Report* (November 1967), p. 30. This is a special issue devoted to the situation in Portuguese Africa.

55. For evidence of more direct American involvement see David Welsh, "Flyboys for the CIA," *Ramparts* (December 1966).

56. See Gérard Chaliand, *Armed Struggle in Africa* (New York, 1972).

57. Donald Barnett, "In the Liberated Areas of Angola" (interview with Spartacus Monimambu), *Guardian* (New York), 27 April, 4 May, and 11 May 1968; Roy Harvey, "Angolan Liberation Group Confers," *Guardian* (New York), 19 October 1968.

58. J. Marcum, "Three Revolutions," *Africa Report* (November 1967), p. 22. Similarly, this "educative effect" helps to facilitate the transcending of tribal consciousness and other forms of parochialism; for a closely related and more detailed analysis of the revolutionary situation in Mozambique as it has developed *since* the writing of the present essay (1968), see Chapter 8 of this volume. Some of the possible ambiguities inherent in peasant political involvement in sub-Saharan Africa are discussed at greater length in Section 3, below.

59. Nonetheless, Marcum is no doubt grossly premature with his argument (presented in the most "respectable" American journal of African affairs) that "the possibility of U.S. intervention to preserve the status quo hangs over the three revolutions in Portuguese Africa like summer smog over Washington." Ibid.

60. Parts of southern Mozambique are, of course, particularly tightly integrated into the South African economy and a variety of further complexities may arise from this important fact.

61. Green and Seidman, op. cit., p. 149n. For example, in their catalogue of possible sectoral growth plans for a rejuvenated economic unity in Africa, Green and Seidman cite (p. 245n.), among other instances, the fact that "continental policy in iron and steel would particularly benefit from the liberation of Southern Africa. South Africa and Rhodesia have the first and third largest iron and steel industries respectively in Africa and virtually all the coking coal. Along with Swaziland—whose deposits are now being opened up for the Japanese market—they possess a very large share of the high-grade iron ore reserves. Finally, production of pig iron and basic steel

products in this area to serve the steel (and iron ore) deficit of Asian countries appears to be one of the logical entry points for Africa into intermediate and manufactured products for export to world markets."

62. See Frank, op. cit., on the relationship between capitalist development and feudal relations of production in Latin America. In our opinion, however, Frank oversimplifies the problem of the coexistence of different social relations of production under what he correctly identifies as capitalist systems.

63. Govan Mbeki, *South Africa: The Peasants' Revolt* (London, 1964), p. 131.

64. It has, however, been argued that this has recently given rise to dangerous inflationary pressures. See Martin Legassick, "The Consequences of African Guerrilla Activity for South Africa's Relations with Its Neighbors" (unpublished paper).

65. See "Forward from Wankie," *Sechaba*, no. 11 (1968).

66. United Nations, E/CN 14/UNCTAD II/1.

67. See Chapters 1 and 3 of this volume.

68. See I. Sachs, "On Growth Potential, Proportional Growth, and Perverse Growth," *Czechoslovack Economic Papers* (1966), pp. 65–71.

69. We would welcome a term other than "labor aristocracy" for the group which we have in mind should any be forthcoming; the genesis of a much clearer conceptualization of the African class structure must, in any event, be an immediate priority. For a discussion of the "elites" and "sub-elites" of tropical Africa see P. Lloyd, ed., *The New Elites of Tropical Africa* (London, 1966), especially the Introduction by the editor.

70. R. Debray, "Problems of Revolutionary Strategy in Latin America," *New Left Review* (September–October 1967), p.35 (emphasis in the original).

71. S. Amin, "Le Développement du capitalisme en Afrique noire," *L'Homme et la société* (October–December 1967), pp. 107–19; see also Y. Benot, "Développement accéléré et révolution sociale en Afrique Occidentale," *La Pensée* (April 1966) (our translation).

72. Amin, ibid., p. 117; see also S. Amin, *Le Développement du capitalisme en Côte d'Ivoire*, op. cit. (our translation).

73. Roger Murray, "Militarism in Africa," *New Left Review* (July–August 1966), p. 56. This is much the most valuable analysis of the wave of military coups which has yet appeared.

74. Ibid.

75. I. G. Markowitz, "Ghana Ten Years After Independence: The Development of Technocracy-Capitalism," *Africa Today* (January 1967), p. 11.

76. See Chapter 4 of this volume.

77. Semonin, "Mobutu and the Congolese," pp. 27, 29. Compare this emphasis, however, with that of Murray ("Mitarism in Africa," p. 56): "American penetration into the Congo (Rockefeller, etc.) is such that one can assume

that Mobutu, in his dealings with Belgium, is playing the American card."
This latter seems in many ways to be the stronger hypothesis.

78. Alvin W. Wolfe, "Economies in Bondage: The Mining Industry," *Africa Today* (January 1967), p. 19.

79. Green and Seidman, op. cit., p. 22. While we broadly agree with the views expressed in this quotation we feel uneasy, to say the least, at the lack of concern shown by the authors for the problem—which we consider central to a strategy of economic development in Africa—of evolving a technology better suited to the task of mobilizing productive forces in Africa than that imported from the advanced capitalist centers. See Chapter 3 of this volume.

80. Ibid., pp. 255–56. Wolfe (op. cit., p. 19) has also stressed the extent to which division undermines a strong continental bargaining position, arguing, for example, that the Congo's failure to effectively renegotiate its copper position foundered on this reef: "The African states, weak as they are individually, have not methodically utilized what resources they have for enhancing collective influence vis-à-vis the developed centers."

81. Quoted in Green and Seidman, op. cit., p. 229.

82. Ibid., p. 230.

83. Benot, op. cit., pp. 54–55 (our translation).

84. I. Wallerstein, *Africa: The Politics of Unity* (New York, 1967), pp. 66–67.

85. Both these quotations appear in Wallerstein, ibid., p. 63. The latter thought was echoed some three years later by President Boumedienne of Algeria when he observed that "there has been since [Addis Ababa] a certain decline of African solidarity. . . . We must avoid at any price the danger of this trade union [of heads of states] which would hold back the necessary evolution of our people" (quoted in Wallerstein, p. 106).

86. In fact, the French-speaking states have in the past not always trusted the OAU to play this role and have relied as much or more on their own defensive alliances (viz., OCAM).

87. Wallerstein, *Africa: The Politics of Unity*, p. 93.

88. Ibid., p. 101.

89. Quoted in Green and Seidman, op. cit., p. 350 (emphasis added). It is from a speech delivered to the UAR National Assembly, 9 April 1967.

90. Larry W. Bowman, "The Subordinate State System of Southern Africa," *International Studies Quarterly* (September 1968), p. 254. He also paraphrases a report from the *Times* (London) of 25 June 1967, to the effect that "Dr. Muller . . . attended the Independence Day celebrations in both Lesotho and Botswana where he met African leaders from all over the continent. He subsequently reported that in 1966, fifty African ministers passed through Jan Smuts Airport in Johannesburg and that South Africa

sent eight official or semi-official delegations to African states in 1966." In recent years the South African government has also proven willing to "liberalize" certain marginal elements of superstructural apartheid (e.g., restrictions concerning accommodations for diplomats) in order to avoid offending the sensibilities of prospective new black allies. See also Nkosi, op. cit.

91. Murray (op. cit., p. 46) has in fact generalized the *potential* significance of the Brazzaville pattern in the following terms: "The 'egoistic' oppositional action of urban wage workers (and peripheral semi-employed) can debouch into a genuine critique of the power system of postcolonial clientage—if the confrontation is sufficiently *sharp* and *sustained* and if it is relayed by groups with a wider social vision and program (revolutionary intellectuals)." Yet he himself reckoned the possibilities of such a development to be "admittedly dim" with reference to several other situations which he discusses. Further work on this important subject should also avoid eliding consideration of the likely involvements of the two strata of wage workers as Murray has done here. Even in the Brazzaville case, insufficient data is presently available to assess retrospectively the exact roles of such strata, for example.

92. Frantz Fanon, op. cit.

93. Benot, op. cit., pp. 52–53 (our translation).

94. J. Gérard-Libois, "The New Class and Rebellion in the Congo," *The Socialist Register 1966* (New York and London, 1966), p. 278.

95. Thus Andrew Ross cogently argues that in Malawi Banda has moved skillfully to manipulate the crudest sort of "populist" resentment in order to consolidate his popularity and his position in power, while inflecting it away from any broader critique which might challenge his own ultra-collaborationist policy. See his "White Africa's Black Ally," *New Left Review* (September–October 1967), p. 85.

96. In his article "Political Science and National Integration," *The Journal of Modern African Studies*, no. 1 (1967), p. 1, Sklar takes the view that "tribalism should be viewed as a dependent variable rather than a primordial force in the new nation."His *Nigerian Political Parties* (Princeton, 1963) provides much concrete evidence to support this notion.

97. Fanon, op. cit., p. 164.

98. Gérard-Libois, op. cit., p. 272. See also R. C. Fox, W. de Craemer, and J. M. Ribeaucourt, "The Second Independence: A Case Study of the Kwilu Rebellion in the Congo," *Comparative Studies in Society and History* (October 1965).

99. The recent Zambian election (December 1968) saw the opposition ANC making gains in key areas of the country, particularly in the strategically important south and west. This was done in part by encouraging and playing upon growing tribal tensions, but it is significant that Nkumbula,

the ANC leader, spoke openly of seeking extended economic ties with South Africa. See "UNIP Emerges Only Truly National Party," *The Nationalist* (Dar es Salaam), 31 December 1968; "New Threats of Secession," *The Nationalist,* 7 January 1969.

100. The Chad decision was reported in the *Tanzania Standard,* 20 January 1969; as will be noted below, Tanzania's own involvement in the East African community, and the tensions which have arisen upon occasion in that forum, are rather less easy to characterize because of the latter country's attempts to articulate a more radical *domestic* strategy.

101. To date the few investment projects carried out, or in the process of being carried out, with Chinese assistance—with their emphasis on labor-intensive and agriculture-oriented industrialization—seem to be the main signs of a radical development strategy that nonetheless still awaits sustained and sophisticated elaboration.

102. For a more detailed analysis of these and other aspects of the Tanzanian experience, see Chapter 6 of this volume.

103. Interestingly, in a recent *Newsweek* article ("Profits from Africa," January 20, 1969) devoted to the African investment offensive of the ubiquitous Lonrho Corporation (a company which works, in the words of one of its directors, "through personal contacts with ministers and heads of state") attention is drawn to that corporation's intention to construct a railway link to Zambia through the Congo which "would thus pose a massive threat to the Communist Chinese-backed plan for a 1,000-mile railroad running the other way."

104. "Already some 61 U.S. firms are operating in Kenya with an investment reported to be about $85–100 million and employing over 5,000 persons," according to Ann Seidman in an unpublished manuscript on foreign capital in East Africa. See also the revealing report by the National Christian Council of Kenya entitled *Who Controls Industry in Kenya* (Nairobi, 1968).

105. See Seidman, ibid. On some of the limitations of the mechanisms designed to readjust the imbalances created and sustained within the community by the free play of market forces see D. Rothchild, "Experiment in Functional Integration," *Africa Report* (April 1968).

106. See the speech in the Kenya National Assembly (3 September 1968) delivered by M. Muliro, a KANU M.P., veteran of the nationalist movement and by no stretch of the imagination a radical: "Today, sir, politically we have a wind of change in Africa. . . . The respect the people have for [President Kenyatta] is the only thing which is keeping us together. . . . The danger in concentration of population in Nairobi lies in the threat of revolution. It will explode one day. . . ."

107. See D. Barnett and K. Njama, *Mau-Mau from Within* (New York, 1966); L. Cliffe has, however, stressed the continuing importance of the process of Registration and Consolidation, originally launched by the colonial government to undermine Mau Mau, in stabilizing the rural situation in some vital areas of potential discontent, at least in the immediate future (oral communication).

108. M. Merlier, *Le Congo de la colonisation belge à l'indépendance* (Paris, 1962).

109. Y. Benot, "Kwame Nkrumah et l'unification africaine," *La Pensée*, (August 1964), p. 74 (our translation).

110. See R. Debray (op. cit., p. 20), ". . . the existence of separate American nations, even mutually hostile ones, is an irreversible fact, and revolutionary struggle today can only be a struggle for *national* liberation. To require of national revolutionary processes in South America the previous condition of continental unity is to postpone them to the Greek Calends." There are clear differences between the South American situation and that of Africa, of course, but Debray's powerful insistence that "South America is not yet a continent" is an equally important emphasis there.

111. See J. Mohan, "A Whig Interpretation of African Nationalism," *The Journal of Modern African Studies* (October 1968). In reviewing the recent writings of Ali Mazrui, Kenyan Professor of Political Science at Uganda's Makerere University College, Mohan suggests (p. 408) that the latter "is a representative of the intelligentsia, a spokesman of elite nationalism, and an ideologist of the ruling class in Africa."

112. Murray, "Second Thoughts on Ghana," especially pp. 25–28.

113. Quoted in Ledda, op. cit., p. 561, n. 3.

Part II

Perspectives

3

International Corporations, Labor Aristocracies, and Economic Development in Tropical Africa

Giovanni Arrighi

The emergence of the large-scale corporation as the typical unit of production in advanced capitalist economies has had momentous implications for the process of development in the still underdeveloped lands. Implicitly or explicitly, this is generally acknowledged by all but those who continue to base their theories on the competitive model, thus assuming away the problem. It is also agreed that such implications are, on balance, negative. There is no agreement, however, concerning the nature of the relationship between the growth of oligopoly in the advanced capitalist countries and the permanence of underdevelopment.

All theories that emphasize the size of the market and its growth and/or technological discontinuities as important factors in hampering development are, to some extent, implying the relevance of the increased scale of capitalist production and of oligopolistic behavior.[1] However, this relationship between oligopoly and underdevelopment is often seen in purely technological terms, that is, as having little to do with the political-economic systems obtaining in the advanced and underdeveloped economies. Perroux has made the point explicitly:

> The organization of nations on a one-by-one and separate basis goes against technical and economic requirements which do not depend on democracy or dictatorship, communism or capitalism, but which are the direct and unavoidable consequence of techniques used in industry in the twentieth century.
>
> The conflict between the exigencies of the political and territorial or-

This essay was written in 1967. It was first published in Robert I. Rhodes, ed., *Imperialism and Underdevelopment: A Reader* (New York and London, 1970), pp. 220–67. Copyright © 1970 by Monthly Review Press. Reprinted by permission.

ganization of the social life of peoples and the exigencies of the multinational administration of the large-scale industries is a continuing reality.

It may be doubted whether Marxism has yet accurately and sufficiently grasped this fact.[2]

An emphasis on oligopolistic behavior, rather than on technological factors, can be traced in Prebisch's[3] argument that the terms of trade between the "industrial centers" and the "periphery"[4] of the world economic system have behaved in the opposite way than one would expect from the competitive model. In that model the faster technical progress in the industrial centers, relative to the periphery, ought to result in falling prices of industrial products relative to primary products. However, the market power of workers, in pressing for higher wages, and of oligopolists, in resisting a squeeze on profit, in the industrial centers is considerably greater than the market power of capitalists, workers, and peasants in the periphery. As a consequence, in the centers the incomes of entrepreneurs and of productive factors increase relatively more than productivity, whereas in the periphery the increase in income is less than that in productivity.

Marxist theorists have, of course, been far more explicit in tracing the inability of contemporary capitalism to promote development in the nonindustrialized lands to the oligopolistic structure of advance capitalist countries. The argument has been succinctly expressed by Oskar Lange:

> With the development of large capitalist monopolies in the leading capitalist countries, the capitalists of those countries lost interest in developmental investment in the less developed countries because such investment threatened their established monopolistic positions. Consequently, investment in underdeveloped countries of capital from the highly developed countries acquired a specific character. It went chiefly into the exploitation of natural resources to be utilized as raw materials by the industries of the developed countries; and into developing food production in the underdeveloped countries to feed the population of the developed capitalist countries. It also went into developing the economic infrastructures . . . needed to maintain economic relations with the underdeveloped countries.
>
> . . . the profits which were made by foreign capital . . . were exported back to the countries where the capital came from. Or if used for investment . . . they were not used for industrial investment on any major scale, which, as we know from experience, is the real dynamic factor of modern economic development. . . .

Furthermore . . . the great capitalist powers supported the feudal elements in the underdeveloped countries as an instrument for maintaining their economic and political influence. This provided another obstacle to the economic development of these countries. . . .[5]

With regard to Africa, Nkrumah has emphasized another aspect of the problem by pointing out that the balkanization of Africa has created a superstructure that makes it impossible for individual nations to cope with the bargaining power of the international corporations which, by means of interlocking directorships, cross-shareholding, and other devices, effectively act on a pan-African scale.[6]

The purpose of this essay is to analyze the relationship between capitalist centers and periphery in order to assess the validity of these assumptions. The analysis will be limited in two ways. In the first place, it will be concerned with tropical Africa and, within that region, with East and Central Africa in particular. The main reason is that, while it may be legitimate to deal with an "ideal" or "average" type of underdeveloped country when the interest of the analysis is centered on the advanced capitalist countries, the procedure may be misleading when the interest is focused on the periphery.

The discussion is limited in another direction. The pattern of relationships between centers and periphery is changing and considerable confusion concerning such relationships stems from the fact that different conclusions are drawn according to whether the "old" or the "new" pattern is emphasized. The relative importance of the two is difficult to assess, though the former is still predominant. Notwithstanding this, we shall focus our attention on the new pattern, i.e., that emerging from the relative decline in importance, not only of foreign portfolio investment in colonial government and railway stock, but also of foreign capital attracted to tropical Africa by the combination of rich natural resources and cheap labor, on the one hand, and the growing relative importance of direct investment by large-scale oligopolies on the other.[7] By limiting the study in these two ways we shall be in a position to gain an insight into the developmental potential of the emerging pattern of center-periphery relations under conditions of embryonic class formation in the periphery itself.

The advantage of an analysis of center-periphery relations under conditions of embryonic class formation is that it enables us to examine the position of the "intelligentsia" and the proletariat in the political economy of the periphery in the absence of "conservative" classes. The alliance of foreign interests with conservative elements in the periphery (feudal elements, landowning classes, some sections—or the whole—of the national bourgeoisie, upper ranks of the armed forces, corrupted bureaucrats, etc.), is usually thought to be the most powerful factor determining the stability of center-periphery relations.[8] The working class and the "intelligentsia" are left in a rather equivocal position. While it is sometimes acknowledged that the exploitation of cheap labor no longer represents an important determinant of foreign investment in the periphery,[9] suggestions that the interests of the proletariat proper and of the intelligentsia may conflict with those of the peasantry (often semi-proletarianized) have called forth some strongly worded criticism:

> [The working class is] the object of systematic defamation, to which some European idealists, infatuated with agrarian messianism, have unconsciously lent themselves. It is true that the wages of the workers are incomparably higher than the income of the African peasants; it is true that their standard of living is higher . . . it is normal that the bourgeoisie in power should use this state of affairs to set the peasants against the workers by presenting them as the privileged. It is, on the other hand, aberrant to find the same arguments coming from the pens of socialist theoreticians. The Russian workers in 1917 also formed a privileged minority with regard to the mass of mouzhiks, but what does that prove? [10]

In East and Central Africa in particular, the classes or groups usually singled out as likely to form alliances with foreign interests are economically and/or politically too weak to compete successfully for power with the intelligentsia (normally in bureaucratic employment), the wage workers, and the peasantry. We shall, therefore, have to look for some other factor contributing to the stability of the present center-periphery relations.

We shall proceed as follows. In Section 1 we shall analyze the emerging pattern of foreign investment in tropical Africa with particular reference to the choice of techniques and of sectors implicit in that pattern and to its developmental potential. In Section 2 we shall analyze the changes in the class structure of tropical African societies associated with that pattern. In Section 3 we shall examine the implications for growth and development of the conclusions reached in the previous two sec-

tions. And finally, in Section 4 we shall discuss the limitations of state
action in the light of the political economy of tropical Africa.

1

The growth of oligopoly as the dominant structure in the advanced
capitalist countries has been accompanied by a relative decline in importance of rentier capital as an independent center of economic and political power, and of competitive capitalism as a dynamic factor of growth.
Small competitive firms still exist but in a subordinate position with respect to the large manufacturing or distributive corporations.[11] The latter, on the other hand, are increasingly able to take care of their investment needs from internal financing (especially depreciation
allowances),[12] thus freeing themselves from outside financial control.
The reciprocal recognition of strength and retaliatory power on the part
of competitors, suppliers, and customers, characteristic of oligopolistic
structures, enables the corporations to protect their profit positions
through adjustments in prices, techniques, and employment. The long
time horizon in investment decisions that the financial independence of
the corporations makes possible, and the greater calculating rationality
of corporate managers enable the oligopolies to approach new developments with care and circumspection and to calculate more accurately
the risks involved.[13] These changes in the competitive structure of the
industrial centers have, since World War II, been reflected in the pattern of investment in the periphery.

The declining relative importance of rentier capital has been matched
by a decline in portfolio investment in the periphery relative to direct
investment on the part of the corporations.[14] At the same time, the vast
financial resources available to the corporations favored further vertical
integration, while oligopolistic behavior encouraged the formation of
consortia in mineral extraction and processing.[15] These tendencies were
strengthened by the process of "decolonization." The "colonial preserves of European imperialism" were opened up to American capitalism,[16] where the oligopolistic corporation plays a more central role than
in French or British capitalism. More important still was the outflow of
small-scale, competitive capital that accompanied independence. In fact,
decolonization was, among other things, the result of a conflict between
the dynamic elements (big companies) and the backward elements

(marginal enterprises, small planters, small trading houses, small semi-artisanal workshops) of colonial capitalism.[17] Independence favored the outflow of the latter. For example, the accession to independence of French-speaking Africa was accompanied by capital outflow in the sector of small colonial enterprises and trading houses and a capital inflow in mining, manufacturing, and industrial agriculture.[18] Similar tendencies were at work in English-speaking countries: the flight of small-scale colonial enterprise was undoubtedly an important factor in the drastic fall of British private investment in Sterling Africa, from £30 million in 1960 and £33.4 million in 1961 to £8.8 million in 1962, £2.5 million in 1963, and *minus* £9 million in 1964.[19] The upshot of these changes has been the emergence of a new pattern of foreign investment in which financial and merchanting interests and small-scale capital (mainly in agriculture but also in secondary and tertiary industries) have declined in importance relative to large-scale manufacturing and vertically integrated mining concerns. The typical expatriate firm operating in tropical Africa is more and more what has been called the "multinational corporation" [20] or the "great interterritorial unit," [21] i.e., an organized ensemble of means of production subject to a single policy-making center which controls establishments situated in several different national territories.

An analysis of the factors determining the investment policies in the periphery of such multinational corporations is therefore necessary in order to assess the impact that foreign investment is likely to have on the process of development of tropical Africa. It is useful to break down the analysis into two problems: (1) The sectoral distribution of investment; and (2) the type of techniques adopted in each sector. As we shall see, the two problems are interrelated but, as a first approximation, their separate treatment is analytically convenient.

There is a lack of basic quantitative evidence on the *sectoral distribution of foreign investment* in tropical African countries. Most of what exists is aggregated in such a way as to be of little use for our purposes. There is, however, considerable agreement on a few broad generalizations:

1. The colonial pattern of capital investment in production for export has basically remained unaltered: investment in mining and petroleum absorbed the preponderant amount of private funds in the last decade.[22]

What has changed in this respect is that complementary investment in the infrastructure, which used to be undertaken by private interests, is now the responsibility of the public sector. Private capital is now invested in more directly productive enterprises.[23]

2. Industrial investment other than in mining has been almost entirely concentrated either in primary products processing for the export market[24] or in import substitution in the light branches of manufacturing such as food, beverages, textiles, clothing, footwear, furniture, soap, and other consumer goods. More recently, the development of import substitution has begun to move gradually into branches of manufacturing industries producing intermediate goods (cement, nonmetallic mineral products, and, less often, fertilizers and chemical products).[25]

3. Notwithstanding these developments, heavy industry in tropical Africa is either nonexistent or, being export-oriented, is totally unrelated to the structure of the national and supranational African economies in the sense that it can hardly constitute a basis for the production of the capital goods required for the industrialization of the areas in which it is located. Rhodesia is possibly the only exception to the generalization. This situation is in sharp contrast with that of South Africa, where metallurgy, chemicals, and rubber are relatively advanced, and, to a lesser extent, with that of some North African countries, where chemicals and some basic metal and metal products industries have been developed.[26]

This sectoral pattern of foreign investment is likely to change slowly or not at all for reasons that are partly technological and partly political-economic. The sectors in question (mainly heavy engineering and chemical industries) are those in which economies of scale and the advantages of operating in an industrial environment (low costs of buying, erecting, maintaining, and operating machinery) are greatest. Hence the very underdevelopment and the balkanization of tropical Africa hinder the development of an organic capital goods industry.[27]

However, as Michael Barratt-Brown[28] has pointed out, there are more fundamental reasons than these:

> The main reason for the failure of capitalism to invest more in the industrialisation of the less-developed lands has arisen from a real doubt about the possibilities of success, and, therefore, of a profitable return. Investment in heavy industry is a big business, on which a return may only be seen in the

very long term. There must be good reasons to believe that the whole overseas economy will develop in such a way as to nourish a market for capital goods. . . . It is not surprising that capitalist firms and financiers . . . should prefer to wait and see how the establishment of light industries and the development of power supplies and a marketable surplus of food goes, before wishing to sink their capital in heavy industry.

Bearing this in mind, it would seem that the greater calculating rationality and the greater care and circumspection in approaching new developments of the modern international corporations, relative to competitive capital and to chartered companies and finance capital of old, are an important obstacle to the development of capital goods industries in the periphery. The oligopolistic structure of advanced capitalist countries, however, plays a more direct role in favoring the bias of investment in the periphery against the capital goods industry. As we have seen, oligopoly favors the reciprocal recognition of strength and retaliatory power. This means that when a large-scale manufacturer is deciding whether to invest in a new area, he will take into consideration, among other things, the effect of the decision on: (1) his own export interests, (2) his competitors' export interests, and (3) his customers' export interests, if any.[29] A textile manufacturing concern, for example, will take into consideration only (1) and (2). A manufacturer of capital goods, on the other hand, will also consider possible effects on his customers' interests which may be impinged upon by the growth, in the periphery, of a competing industry induced by the local production of capital goods. In consequence, quite apart from its effects on the level of investment to be discussed later on, the oligopolistic structure of the industrial centers strengthens the other factors mentioned above in producing in tropical Africa a sectoral pattern of foreign investment biased against the capital goods industry.

With regard to *choice of techniques,* it seems fairly well established that foreign investment in tropical Africa has a capital intensive bias.[30] This bias is sometimes due to technological constraints. In mining, for example, the nature of the deposits may be responsible for differences in capital intensity. The scattering of Rhodesian gold deposits favored labor intensive techniques, while the concentration of high-grade copper deposits in Zambia favored capital intensive techniques.[31] In the latter case, even if highly labor intensive techniques exist, such as those used by Africans prior to European penetration, the technological gap is too great for such techniques to develop the industry on a significant scale.[32] However, even in extreme cases like the one in question, alternative techniques are always available,[33] though within a relatively limited range. Thus technological constraints are only one factor in determining the capital intensity of investment, and, in the case of many industries (e.g., light industries) in which foreign investment shows an equally strong bias toward capital intensity,[34] they are rather unimportant. Other determinants have to be sought. Somewhat related to technological factors, management constraints have to be mentioned. Techniques of management, organization, and control have evolved in the technological environment of the industrial centers and cannot be easily adapted to the conditions in the periphery.[35] Often, therefore, either the conditions in the periphery can be modified, at least partially, to make capital and skill intensive investment possible or no investment at all will be undertaken by the multinational corporations.[36] In other words, the spectrum of techniques taken into consideration by the multinational corporations may not include labor intensive techniques.

There is another reason, probably more important than management constraints, why labor intensive techniques may be disregarded.

As Perroux and Demonts have pointed out,[37] the multinational firm applies to all its branches technical methods corresponding to its capital, whatever the importance of the factors at work in the territories where it settles. There is a tendency in discussions of underdevelopment to overlook the fact that a shortage of finance is an important impediment to the growth of the small enterprise and of the public sectors of African economies, but it is no problem for the multinational firms. The latter not only have access to the capital markets in the industrial centers,[38] but, as we have mentioned, they are in a position through their pricing and dividend policies (in the industrial centers as well as in the periphery) to build up large accumulated reserves of capital for their investment programs. Financial strength makes the large firm adopt capital intensive techniques, not only in the industrial centers but also in the periphery.[39]

In a way, capital intensity is favored also by the qualitative characteristics of the labor force in tropical Africa. The problem is too often overlooked because of insufficiently clear definitions of the various categories of labor.[40] Let us classify labor as follows:

1. *Unskilled labor,* characterized by versatility (in the sense that it can

be readily put to varied unskilled activities), and by lack of adaptation to the discipline of wage employment.

2. *Semi-skilled labor,* characterized by specialization, regularity, and identification with the job.

3. *Skilled labor,* characterized by relative versatility (in the sense of having complex skills), e.g., carpenters, mechanics, supervisors, etc.

4. *High-level manpower,* characterized by specialization and by educational qualifications other than, or besides, training on the job, e.g., maintenance and production engineers, purchase and sales experts, designers, cost and accounting personnel, etc.

Capital intensive techniques will not only require less labor for each level of output, but they will also require a different composition of the labor force than labor intensive techniques, as they make possible the division of complex operations, which would need skilled labor, into simple operations that can be performed by semi-skilled labor. In other words, labor intensive techniques are associated with a pattern of employment in which labor of types (1) and (3) predominate, whereas capital intensive techniques are associated with a pattern of employment in which labor of types (2) and (4) predominate. As we shall see in the next section, provided that employers take a sufficiently long time horizon in their wage and employment policies, it is easier, under African conditions, to provide the remedy for a shortage of the latter types of labor than it is to do so for a shortage of skilled labor. Thus, from this point of view as well, the longer time horizon of the multinational corporations favors the adoption of capital intensive techniques.

These two biases of the pattern of investment emerging in tropical Africa (i.e., in favor of capital intensive techniques and against the capital goods sector) reinforce each other. The choice of capital intensive techniques within each industry favors the use of specialized machinery and consequently restrains the growth of demand for capital goods that could be produced in the periphery. The lack of investment in the capital goods sector, in turn, prevents the development of capital goods embodying a *modern* labor intensive technology which may reduce the bias in favor of capital intensity. This double bias has many implications for growth, development, and class formation in tropical Africa that will be examined in the following sections. What must be considered here is *the relationship between the pattern of investment* just discussed and *the size of the internal market* that is a key determinant of foreign investment in the region.

The development of the capital goods sector performs the double function of expanding both the productive capacity of the economy and the internal market. The latter function was emphasized by Lenin in a controversy with the Narodniks on the subject of the possibility of the "*internal* expansion of capitalism." The development of the internal market, Lenin argued, was possible despite the restricted consumption by the masses (or the lack of an external outlet) because to expand production it is first of all necessary to enlarge that department of social production which manufactures means of production, and it is necessary to draw into it workers who create a demand for articles of consumption. Hence, "consumption" develops after "accumulation".[41] The crucial assumption in the argument is that the demand for capital goods is largely autonomous, i.e., that it is not induced by the preexisting size of the market and its growth. However, this autonomous development of the capital goods sector presupposes a type of behavior which may characterize competitive capitalism, but which cannot be expected from the modern corporations.[42] These corporations tend to expand productive capacity in response to market demand and in consequence restrain the endogenous generation of growth stimuli.

In the case of tropical Africa and the periphery in general, the position is made worse by the fact that the multinational corporations (whenever the nature of the productive process permits it) usually prefer to expand productive capacity in the industrial centers where they are more secure and where they can take advantage of operating in an industrial environment.[43] Expansion in the periphery is usually undertaken by a foreign concern in response to protectionist policies on the part of national government in order either to protect its own export interests, or to establish itself anew in the area.[44] In other words, the existence of a local market for the production of the foreign concern, though a necessary condition, is not sufficient for the actual establishment of a plant. This presupposes the ability of individual governments either to set up production in competition with foreign interests or to play one oligopoly off against the other. The fact that this ability on the part of the governments of tropical Africa is most limited in the case of capital goods industries is an additional factor strengthening the bias of the emerging pattern of investment against such industries.

It follows that the emerging pattern of investment is unlikely to reduce the basic lack of structure of the tropical African economies. Growth in these economies continues to depend on the growth of outside markets. In fact, the dependence is even greater than it used to be in view of the fact that industrialization tends to take a capital intensive path which presupposes the importation of specialized machinery. For this reason the integration of the modern sectors of tropical Africa (due to the need of the multinational concerns to operate on a supranational scale) is accompanied by their greater integration with the industrial centers. We shall return to these conclusions in Section 3, where their implications for growth and development are discussed. We must now analyze the impact of the emerging pattern of foreign investment on the class structure of tropical African societies.

2

The analysis in this section will be focused on wage and salary workers and their direct and indirect relationships with other classes and interests. *Wage employment in tropical Africa* is at a low stage of development. Table 1 [45] gives no more than an idea of the order of magnitudes involved. As will be pointed out below, this small participation in wage employment is matched by qualitative characteristics of the wage-labor force which reduce even further the relative importance of the proletariat proper in tropical Africa. Equally important is the fact that wage employment has been relatively static over the last ten to fifteen years,[46] though in almost every country there have been periods, coinciding with heavy investments in infrastructure and with installation investments, during which the proportion of the labor force in wage employment temporarily rose. This relatively static wage employment has been accompanied by rising wages; the average annual rate of increase in African wages during the 1950s, for example, appears to have been on the order of 7 to 8 percent.[47] In general, wages are not merely chasing prices but are running ahead of them, the rise often implying an increase in real wages considerably faster than that in real national product.[48] In consequence, the employees' share of national income rose sharply in many countries.[49] As Turner remarks, "It seems rather hard to find a case where the general level of real wages has in recent years behaved as it theoretically ought in an underdeveloped economy—i.e., has lagged

Table 1

Estimated Population Labor Force and Total Nonagricultural Wage Employment in Africa

(by region, around 1960)

Region	Population	Labor force		Total wage employment		Non-agricultural wage employment	
		in millions	as per-cent of pop.	in millions	as per-cent of labor force	in millions	as per-cent of labor force
East Africa	67.6	24.7	36.5	3.8	15.4	2.5	10.1
Central Africa	32.8	13.8	42.1	2.1	15.2	1.6	11.6
West Africa	71.8	32.9	45.8	2.0	6.1	1.7	5.2
Tropical Africa	173.2	71.4	41.2	7.9	11.1	5.8	8.1
North Africa	65.4	22.6	34.6	7.5	32.2	4.6	20.4
Southern Africa	16.9	6.0	35.5	3.8	63.3	3.0	50.0
All Africa	254.5	100.0	39.3	19.2	19.2	13.4	13.4

behind other incomes, and particularly profits." [50] Thus the main characteristics of the wage working class are relatively static numbers and rising incomes. With regard to the structural characteristics of wage employment, the table below illustrates them for selected tropical African countries.[51]

It can be observed from the table that the public sector, as a rule, employs a substantial proportion of wage workers and that nonagricultural employment is heavily concentrated in the service sector. The underdevelopment of industry is an obvious determinant of that structure. Another important factor is that the colonial powers superimposed a complex administrative structure on near-subsistence economies which tended to control not only the public services but also many economic and social agencies, such as marketing boards. After independence, African governments have taken over these functions and expanded them in their attempts to step up economic growth and to enlarge social services

Table 2

Structures of Wage Employment in Selected Tropical African Countries

Country	Year	Nonagricultural wage employment		
		Percent of total wage empl.	*Percent employed in public sector*	*Percent employed in services sector*
Kenya	1965	65	30	77
Uganda	1965	82	39	77
Tanzania (Tanganyika)	1965	62	32	75
Malawi	1961	65	—	61
Malagasy Rep.	1961	77	—	77
Nigeria	1962	98	34	46
Ivory Coast	1961	55	—	68
Ghana	1960	73	35	55
Sierra Leone	1963	95	—	53

(agricultural extension work, development corporations, education, etc.).

Unfortunately, there are no data on the relative importance of wage employment in concerns to which the analysis of the previous section may apply (viz., in enterprises with international affiliations including the vertically integrated combines and mixed or state enterprises managed by international corporations). This lack of quantitative data, however, is only a partial obstacle to our analysis as our main concern is with the qualitative changes in the wage-labor force that can be associated with the pattern of investment discussed in the previous section. In this connection, the first point that has to be emphasized is the heterogeneity of the African salary and wage-working class. We have already classified the labor force according to skills, singling out four categories: unskilled, semi-skilled, and skilled labor, and high-level manpower. This classification only to some extent overlaps with two other classifications that are relevant in the present context. The first, to be discussed presently, concerns the degree of commitment to, or dependence upon, wage employment and gives rise to the two main categories of "proletariat" and "semi-proletarianized peasantry" (or, less frequently in tropical Africa, semi-proletarianized artisans). The other classification focuses on status and prestige and distinguishes an elite, a sub-elite, and the mass of the wage workers.[52]

At a seminar of the International African Institute on the New Elites of Tropical Africa (Ibadan, July 1964) it was suggested that the term "elite" could be appropriately used to denote those who were Western educated with an annual income of at least £250.[53] The sub-elite, on the other hand, is made up of the less well educated, i.e., those with post-primary education or some secondary education (executive-clerical grades, primary school teachers, and skilled artisans).[54] The rapid growth of the African elite and sub-elite in the last decade can be traced to the expansion of educational facilities and of job opportunities for Africans in highly paid employment that accompanied and followed the accession to independence. This expansion has been phenomenal but it is still a fortunate few who manage to reach secondary school. In no African state does the proportion exceed 2 percent, though in some constituent regions this figure is exceeded.[55] The fast rate of expansion of highly paid job opportunities for Africans has been due mainly to the Africanization of the complex administrative structure inherited from colonial rule, the scope of which, as I have mentioned, was extended by the African governments. Another factor favoring this expansion, the Africanization policy of expatriate firms, is of lesser but growing importance as the top posts in government service are uniformly held by young men with decades of service ahead of them. Expatriate firms have become increasingly conscious of their "public image" and have quickly Africanized their office staffs, middle commercial posts, and some managerial posts, especially in personnel management and public relations. Production, engineering, and other technical and higher executive posts are still mainly in expatriate hands, though in a few instances Africans have been recruited to nominal directorships.[56] In the colonial period the private professions held great attraction for Africans who were subject to discriminatory practices in the civil service. These professions are still popular, but, though in general lawyers remain in private practice, most doctors are now employed in the public service.[57] Thus the overwhelming majority of the elite and the sub-elite in tropical Africa is in bureaucratic employment, and, though employment in the public sector is predominant, the international corporations are becoming an increasingly important outlet for the newly educated African.

When we come to analyze what in the classification just discussed is lumped together as the "masses of wage workers," the distinction focusing on the commitment to, or dependence upon, wage employment becomes relevant. The mass of English migrants in the early nineteenth century were landless agricultural laborers. In tropical Africa the mass of migrants are peasants with rights to the use of land. While the former were proletarians, the latter are peasants at different stages of proletarianization and therefore present a much greater heterogeneity. Labor migration in Africa is compounded of various elements of "push" and "pull," the former relating to the maintenance of subsistence or essential consumption and the latter relating to the improvement of the preexisting standard of living.[58] "Push" factors are usually associated with a deteriorating relation of the population to the traditional means of subsistence (e.g., land shortage), or changes in the nature of essential consumption due to the penetration of the money economy. The improvement of the existing standard of living, on the other hand, can be achieved either directly or indirectly—directly when the aim of labor migration is a net addition to the consumption of the extended family; indirectly when the aim is the purchase of equipment to improve production in the traditional sector or the accumulation of sufficient financial means to enter some petty capitalistic activity (e.g., commercial farming, trade, contracting, etc.). The two main characteristics of the labor force under the system of labor migration are low wages and high turnover. The wage rate is customarily based on subsistence for bachelor workers. Such a wage may or may not allow some saving according to whether "pull" or "push" factors predominate in the economy. Low wages strengthen the tendency for the participation in the labor market to be of a temporary nature, which in turn accounts for the persistently unskilled character of the labor force. These factors interact, favoring the development of a poorly paid and unskilled labor force.[59] In addition, the lack of division of labor between agricultural and nonagricultural activities and between wage employment limits the internal market, especially for agricultural produce. Thus, by hampering the development of capitalist agriculture, it further entrenches the labor migration system.

Under these conditions the complete *proletarianization of the wage workers,* i.e., the severance of the ties with the traditional sector, is largely optional. It occurs when the incomes derived from wage employment are high enough to make the worker uninterested in the maintenance of reciprocal obligations with the extended family in the traditional sector. More specifically, his income must be sufficiently high and reliable to allow him to support his family in the town and to save enough to insure himself against distress in periods of unemployment, sickness, and in his old age. The difference between this income and the low migrant-labor wage rate will normally be considerable. This differential is reflected in the high cost of semi-skilled and skilled labor relative to unskilled labor. The time horizon of the migrant worker is typically short and therefore as soon as his acquired skill commands remuneration in excess of that which he presently receives, he leaves the employer.[60] In consequence, either the employer is willing and able to pay the much higher wages that can induce greater stability of the labor force or he must adapt his techniques to the existing qualitative characteristics of the labor force rather than train the workers for more skilled activities. The nature of the typical enterprise in colonial times militated against a breakthrough in the vicious circle "high turnover–low productivity–low wages–high turnover" and therefore against the development of a semi-skilled, relatively highly paid, stabilized labor force. Small planters, small trading houses, small workshops could hardly be expected to take a long time horizon in their investment decisions. Similarly, the large enterprises engaged in primary production were either indifferent toward the use of mechanized techniques or positively against it in view of the instability of markets or, whenever technological constraints imposed capital intensity and the use of skilled and semi-skilled labor, found it more convenient to resort to the importation of expatriate workers than to embark upon the expensive exercise of stabilizing the African labor force.[61] Thus traditional colonial employers relied on African migrant labor for their requirements of unskilled labor and on racial minorities (Europeans, Asians, Levantines) for their requirements of skilled labor. The demand for semi-skilled labor remained, on the whole, very limited. In the 1950s important changes took place. As we have seen, the pattern of foreign investment altered, especially in the immediate pre-independence period when the importance of small-scale colonial enterprises declined and that of the multinational concerns increased. This change was accompanied by the slackening of the influence of the former interests and of the racial minorities on government policies, and by the correspondingly greater influence of the international corporations and of the African elite, sub-elite, and working class. These two changes can be assumed to have been instrumental in bringing about the breakthrough in the vicious circle "low wages–high turnover–low productivity–low wages." Various factors were at work in producing the breakthrough and their relative importance is not only difficult to assess (given their interaction), but varies considerably from country to country. Let us first analyze some of the most important factors and later suggest what their relative contribution to the change might have been.

The salary structure of the independent African states remains a colonial heritage. As Africans gradually entered the civil service and the managerial positions in large foreign concerns, they assumed the basic salaries attached to the posts since, so far, the principle of equal pay between African and expatriate for equal posts has generally been maintained.[62] In consequence, Africanization brings about a huge gap between the incomes of high-level manpower (the African elite and sub-elite), and the incomes not only of unskilled labor but also of semi-skilled and skilled labor. Thus the whole level of wages, from the unskilled laborer upward, comes into question.[63] The workers' capacity for industrial conflict may be negligible but their political influence is often considerable, while increases in wages and salaries seem an easy route to prove the value of the recently acquired independence.[64] For these reasons governments in tropical Africa are easily induced to steadily raise wages either through increases in legal minimum wages or, being major employers of labor, by acting as wage leaders. Thus the Africanization of high-level manpower and greater influence of the working class on government policies favored a gradual rise in wages at the lower levels.

Another important factor was the *emerging pattern of foreign investment* discussed in the previous section. As we saw, the greater capital intensity of production associated with that pattern requires a labor force in which semi-skilled labor predominates. For the multinational concerns, therefore, stabilization of a section of the indigenous labor force is essential and actively sought after as the importation of skilled labor becomes impracticable and indeed unnecessary as complex operations are broken down into simpler operations that can be performed by semi-skilled labor. Capital intensity of production (which makes wages a small proportion of total costs and requires labor stability), the ability to pass on to the consumer increased labor costs (in the periphery in the case of manufacturing concerns, in the industrial centers in the case of the vertically integrated companies operating in primary production), and the ability to take a long time horizon in employment and investment decisions, make the multinational companies willing and able to pay sufficiently high wages to stabilize a section of the labor force. In other words, for the companies in question the exploitation of natural resources or of market opportunities in the periphery with capital intensive techniques is far more important than the exploitation of cheap labor. These factors are undoubtedly responsible for the observed tendency to pay relatively high wages and to experiment with modern training and management methods on the part of large expatriate firms.[65]

Governments' and international corporations' wage and salary policies interact and the ensuing steady rise in wage rates induces further labor saving, not only on the part of expatriate firms, but also on the part of those locally based enterprises which can afford it.[66] Capital intensity, in turn, generally means that labor is a lower proportion of costs to the enterprise than it would otherwise be, so that the individual concern's willingness to concede wage increases is higher; but this reinforces the tendency to capital intensive (or labor saving) development *and a "spiral" process* may ensue.[67] Some disagreement is bound to arise concerning the extent to which growing capital intensity in tropical Africa is induced by the investment and employment policies of the international corporations. The question is largely academic as such policies, either as a casual or as a permissive factor, are undoubtedly a crucial element in the "spiral" process. The importance as a "prime mover," on the other hand, will vary from country to country. In Uganda, for example, it would seem that government policies have played a predominant role in bringing about the steady rise in wages and, in consequence, most mechanization has been "induced." [68] In Rhodesia, on the other hand, African workers have hardly any power to influence government policies and the steady rise in wages in the 1950s and in the early 1960s seems to have been induced by the stable labor requirements of the large-scale expatriate firms. Thus, while African money wages rose between 1949 and 1962 at an average annual rate of 9 percent, the increase was largely concentrated in those sectors where labor stabilization mattered most (viz., manufacturing and services). In the sectors where stabilization mattered least (viz., agriculture), money wages rose at a rate not much higher than that of price increases.[69]

An assumption that seems unacceptable is that the rise in wages has been due, to any important extent, to *monopolistic action* on the part of

African workers, as distinct from their power to influence government policies. This is Baldwin's assumption concerning the rise of wages on the Zambian copperbelt:

> Since the war . . . African and European wages have been raised by monopolistic actions to levels considerably above the rates necessary to attract the numbers actually employed. The consequences of this wage policy have been the creation of unemployment conditions in the Copperbelt towns, especially among Africans, and the widespread substitution of machines for men in the industry.[70]

That European workers, in the colonial situation, were in a strong bargaining position is a generally acknowledged fact. But it is equally acknowledged that the prevalence of the migrant-labor system and related lack of skills and specialization among Africans militates against the workers' capacity for industrial conflict.[71] Moderately effective trade union organization normally follows and does not precede labor stabilization and mechanization,[72] as witnessed by the fact that, apart from the public services, the most important instances where anything like normal collective bargaining has been established appear to be in large-scale enterprises under foreign ownership and management.[73] It is possible therefore that, though trade union organizations have in the past mainly played a dependent role in the spiral process of rising wages and mechanization, they may, with the growing stabilization of the labor force, become a partly autonomous factor. However, the effect, if any, will be felt primarily on the differential between the remuneration of stabilized skilled and semi-skilled labor and that of the semi-proletarianized unskilled labor whose market power is bound to remain negligible.

This consideration brings us to the question of the stratification of the working class. The conclusion that emerges from the foregoing analysis is that the changes in the pattern of capital investment and in government policies in tropical Africa that have occurred in the last decade have resulted in a breakthrough in the vicious circle "low wages–high turnover–low productivity–low wages"; such a breakthrough, however, concerns only the small section of the working class that is being rapidly proletarianized by enabling it to earn a subsistence in the wage economy. The breakthrough is therefore achieved at the cost of a relative reduction of the overall degree of participation of the labor force in wage employment. Whether this relative reduction can be assumed to be a short-term phenomenon which leads in the longer run to faster economic growth and greater participation in wage employment is a problem to be discussed in the next section. Here we are concerned with structural problems. From this standpoint it is correct to assume that the spiral process of rising wages and mechanization tends to produce a situation of rising productivity and living standards in a limited and shrinking modern sector, while the wage-employment opportunities in that sector for the unskilled, semi-proletarianized peasantry (which increasingly becomes a noncompeting group vis-à-vis the semi-skilled proletariat) are reduced.[74] To find out to what extent this tendency is a special aspect of a more general trend toward a growing cleavage between the modern capital intensive sector and the rest of the economy we must analyze the impact of the emerging pattern of foreign investment on the other classes of tropical African society.[75]

Let us begin by examining the implications of the emerging pattern of foreign investment for the rural sector. The first point that has to be made is that the sectoral distribution of such investment enhances the dependence of agriculture on world markets for its expansion. The bias against the capital goods sector not only restrains, as we have seen, the growth of the internal market, but also increases the dependence on foreign sources for the supply of the capital goods necessary for the transformation of traditional agriculture. This transformation comes, therefore, to be subject to balance-of-payments constraints which, as it will be argued in the next section, are likely to become increasingly severe. The bias in favor of capital intensive techniques has equally important implications. There are two ways in which the African peasantry can participate in the money economy: through periodic wage employment and through the sale of produce. We have seen that the emerging pattern of foreign investment restrains the growth of wage-employment opportunities in the modern sector for the unskilled, semi-proletarianized peasantry. But, in addition to this, the low income-elasticity of the demand for agricultural produce in general and local produce in particular implicit in the capital intensive growth of the modern sector also restrains the growth of demand for peasant produce.

It would seem, therefore, that the emerging pattern of foreign investment tends to reduce both the complementary links between urban and rural sectors (i.e., to increase further the lack of structure of the econo-

mies of tropical Africa), and the spreading of development stimuli from
the modern to the traditional sector. These conclusions hold for whatever assumptions one may want to make concerning the type of development of the agricultural sector, i.e., whether the expansion of agriculture takes place through the formation of a "kulak" class employing
wage labor, or through the formation of cooperatives, collectives, and
communes, or through the expansion of production by self-employed
producers.

It may, however, be argued that the *relative* impoverishment of the
peasantry associated with the emerging pattern of investment will speed
up the spreading of capitalist relations in African agriculture,[76] i.e., the
simultaneous formation of a kulak class and a rural proletariat, that
would enhance the growth of agricultural productivity. This argument,
however, misses the point that the relative impoverishment of the peasantry is accompanied by the negative impact of the emerging pattern of
investment on the growth of demand for local agricultural produce.
Such a pattern, therefore, restrains the incentive for, and financial ability
of, the emerging kulaks to expand wage employment so that, other
things being equal, it tends to produce an impoverished peasantry without fostering its absorption in capitalist agriculture.

The last point we have to discuss in this section is the implication of
the emerging pattern of investment for the national bourgeoisie in nonagricultural sectors. In the colonial period most commerce (not directly
in the hands of expatriate companies), and small-scale industrial enterprise[77] was in alien hands—the Levantines of West Africa, the Indians
of East Africa, the Europeans, and, to a lesser extent, the Indians of
Central Africa. African traders were almost totally absent in Central
and East Africa while part-time trading activities were widespread
among West Africans, especially in Ghana and Nigeria. This pattern
started to change with the approach of independence. In East and Central Africa the Africans, with official support, began to challenge Asian
dominance in the commercial sphere. In West Africa the large expatriate firms, while Africanizing their staff, began to let slip into African
hands the less sophisticated types of trade, particularly the produce
buying and the retailing of simple goods—many of the licensed buyers
are in fact men trained by these companies.[78] In industry, on the other
hand, locally based capitalist enterprises are still largely in the hands of
racial minorities and, though there are exceptions,[79] they are generally

small and managed by people whose background is commerce rather than industry.[80] Africanization in this sphere is proceeding more slowly than in petty trade, but in Ghana and Nigeria Africans own businesses and workshops in a wide range of light and service industries.

There are various factors hampering the growth of a locally based capitalist class. Lack of specialization generally characterizes African petty capitalism: wage employment, trade, farming, and artisanal activities are often combined, though the combination of more than two occupations is rare.[81] This lack of specialization favors the dispersal of capital, labor, and managerial resources, and in consequence it hampers the growth of productivity and credit-worthiness in each line. The emerging pattern of investment in tropical Africa creates additional and more powerful obstacles. The rise of an African elite, sub-elite, and proletariat proper, all enjoying a relatively high standard of living, both imposes consumption patterns which discourage accumulation,[82] and makes business unattractive relative to salary employment or even wage employment in the capital intensive expatriate or mixed enterprises.[83]

The new pattern of foreign investment, however, has more direct repercussions on the supply and demand conditions facing existing or potential local capitalism. On the supply side, we must consider the effects of foreign investment on the labor force. We saw that large-scale foreign corporations contribute to the rising trend in wages. While those local enterprises which can afford it adapt themselves to the new market situation by stepping up labor saving, the rise in labor costs tends to discourage the expansion of the smaller scale, financially weaker enterprises which cannot afford mechanization.[84] However, to the extent that a dual wage structure obtains, *de jure* or *de facto,* the possibility of survival or expansion of small-scale local capitalism depends on how effectively labor intensive enterprise can compete, in quality and price, with capital intensive large-scale enterprises. The experience of advanced countries shows that, given a sufficiently large market in relation to the minimum scale which makes capital intensive production economical,[85] it is difficult to think of industries, besides construction, some servicing industries, and the exceptions mentioned below, where small-scale labor intensive enterprise has a competitive advantage.

The pattern of consumption associated with the capital intensive production of the wage sectors of tropical Africa aggravates the position. The income elasticity of demand not only for agricultural produce but also for simple consumer and capital goods in the production of which small-scale industry may have a competitive advantage, is much smaller than it would be in the case of a labor intensive type of growth of the money economy. This pattern of demand, therefore, makes it easier for modern manufacturing based on the latest technology to undersell, or to preempt, the market opportunities for local small-scale enterprises.[86] This possibility threatens the latter even when no competition from large scale enterprises is expected in the short run; the greater risks involved in undertaking production may thus discourage the exploitation of profitable opportunities by small entrepreneurs.

In each industrial process, however, there are *operations* which can be profitably subcontracted to smaller labor intensive enterprises by the large-scale expatriate firms. It is not inconceivable, therefore, that investment by multinational corporations in tropical Africa will encourage the growth of a satellite, small-scale national bourgeoisie. Such a subordinate role is all that this national bourgeoisie will, at best, play in the area. In other words, the polarization of the business world, so aptly described in the following passage by C. Wright Mills with regard to the industrial centers, can be expected to grow in the periphery as well:

> Roughly speaking the business world is polarized into two types: large industrial corporations and a "lumpenbourgeoisie." The latter is composed of a multitude of firms with a high death rate, which do a fraction of the total business done in their lines and engage a considerably larger proportion of people than their quota of business. . . .
>
> Their remarkable persistence as a stratum . . . should not be confused with the well-being of each individual enterprise and its owner-manager . . . [as there] is a great flow of entrepreneurs and would-be entrepreneurs in and out of the small business stratum. . . .

The small businessmen are increasingly concentrated in the retail and service industries, and, to a lesser extent, in finance and construction. Their most important characteristic from the standpoint of our analysis is the subordinate role they come to play:

> The power of the large business is such that, even though many small businesses remain independent, they become in reality agents of larger businesses. . . .
>
> Dependency on trade credit tends to reduce the small businessman to an agent of the creditor. . . .

[By means of] "exclusive dealing contracts" and "full line forcing" . . .
manufacturers, who set retail prices and advertise nationally [interna-
tionally, in our context], turn small retailers into what amounts to salesmen
on commission who take entrepreneurial risks. In manufacturing, subcon-
tracting often turns the small subcontractor into what amounts to a risk-
taking manager of a branch plant.[87]

The main implication is that the national bourgeoisie will be increasingly incapable of creating growth stimuli independently of international capitalism in the sense that its expansion comes to be almost entirely induced by the complementary growth of the multinational
concerns. In consequence, the integration of tropical Africa with the international capitalist system can be assumed to exclude the possibility of
a national capitalist pattern of development.

3

In this section we will analyze the implications for growth and development in tropical Africa of the main assumptions that have emerged in
the previous discussion. A brief summary of the main conclusions so far
reached is in order. In Section 1 we argued that the financial strength
and managerial characteristics of the multinational concerns are
reflected in the choice of capital intensive techniques within individual
sectors or industries. In addition, the oligopolistic behavior and greater
calculating rationality of the multinational concerns are reflected in a
sectoral pattern of investment which is biased against the capital goods
sector. Both biases (in favor of capital intensity and against the capital
goods sector) contribute to the low demand-generating potential of investment which is already implicit in oligopolistic behavior. We concluded that this pattern of investment tends to promote the integration
of the modern sector in the periphery and of these with the industrial
centers but does not contribute to the reduction of the lack of structure
of the national and supranational economies of tropical Africa. In Section 2, where attention was focused on the changes in the class structure
of tropical Africa that can be associated with the emerging pattern of investment, we saw that the multinational corporation contributes to the
reproduction of an environment in the modern sector of the periphery
that suits its operations: a semi-skilled proletariat, a white-collar elite and
sub-elite, a dependent "lumpenbourgeoisie." This tendency deepens the

cleavages between modern and traditional sectors for two main reasons:

1. Because of the growing qualitative differences between proletarianized and semi-proletarianized labor. The former, through relatively high income and consequent greater stability, acquires specialized skills, while the latter's dependence on the traditional sector is increased by the labor-saving development of the modern sector.

2. Because of the lessening of the links between the traditional sector and the modern sector as the capital intensity and bureaucratization of the latter minimizes the income elasticity of its demand for the output of the former.

Growing internal cleavages and greater external integration tend, of course, to reinforce each other in a process of circular causation. The various "demonstration effects" which influence the pattern of consumption, investment, technology, and administration in the modern sector, are strengthened by greater external integration and, in turn, deepen the internal cleavages.

It may be argued that whatever the outcome in the short run, the long-term development potential of the tropical African economies is increased rather than reduced by this pattern of growth. The argument may seem to be implicit in those theories of development which uphold the advisability—in definite conditions, to be discussed presently, and from the standpoint of long-term consumption and employment maximization—of a choice of capital intensive techniques in underdeveloped economies.[88] The argument is based on the consideration that each technique of production has a double impact on employment and consumption. There is a direct effect on output and employment in the short run, and there is an indirect effect in the long run as the technique of production, through its influence on income distribution and the size of the investable surplus, affects the rate of growth of output and employment. Labor intensive techniques are associated with high levels of employment in the short run and with a large share of wages in output. Capital intensive techniques, on the other hand, imply a smaller share of wages in output, and may therefore yield a larger investable surplus and a faster rate of growth of employment.

The argument, implicitly or explicitly, is based on a number of restrictive assumptions. We shall limit our discussion to the following crucial ones:

1. The real wage rate is fixed whatever technique of production is adopted and it is constant through time.

2. The reinvestment of the larger surplus associated with capital intensive techniques is feasible in the sense that either the productive capacity of the capital goods sector is sufficiently large to supply the capital goods required by such reinvestment, or foreign exchange is available to make up the deficiency of capital goods through purchases abroad.

3. The reinvestment of the larger surplus is not only feasible but desired by whoever controls its utilization.

Let us discuss the validity of these assumptions in the context analyzed in Sections 1 and 2.

1. The real wage rate is constant whatever the technique of production and through time.

Both assumptions are generally untrue in the context of tropical Africa. Capital intensive techniques require a semi-skilled and therefore stabilized labor force committed to wage employment. As we saw, the "price" of stabilization, and therefore the differential in real wage rates according to whether capital or labor intensive techniques are used, is considerable. In consequence, even though the share of output accruing to wages is smaller in the case of capital intensive techniques, the size of the investable surplus (and therefore the rate of growth of output and employment) may be greater in the case of labor intensive techniques. The case for capital intensive techniques is further weakened by the fact that, either as a permissive or as a causal factor, they encourage a steady rise in wages. In consequence, capital intensive techniques may foster the rapid growth of consumption on the part of employed workers rather than the rapid growth of employment.

2. The reinvestment of the larger surplus associated with capital intensive techniques is feasible.

In a closed economy, if the capital goods sector cannot supply the means of production necessary for the investment of the larger surplus associated with capital intensive techniques, the ceiling to the rate of growth of output and employment will be determined by the capacity of that sector. We saw that the emerging pattern of investment in tropical Africa has a double bias, in favor of capital intensive techniques and against the capital goods sector. The implication of this double bias for growth is that the positive impact of the former bias is counteracted by the latter. In other words, the bias against the capital goods sector of the emerging pattern of investment reduces the problem of the feasibility of a faster rate of growth through capital intensive development to one of foreign exchange availability to purchase capital goods abroad.

The lack of structure of tropical African economies makes them dependent for their foreign exchange earnings on the export of primary products. With the exception of the oil-producing countries and certain metal producers, underdeveloped economies relying on sales of primary products have, since the end of the Korean War boom, experienced a slowing down in the rate of growth of output and an actual fall in prices which has led to a decline in total earnings.[89] In the case of tropical Africa, while the value of exports rose about 55 percent between 1950 and 1955, it rose only 15 percent between 1955 and 1960,[90] and lately the position has probably worsened. In addition, it must be borne in mind that, in the case of many agricultural exports such as coffee, tobacco, short-staple cotton, oilseeds, sisal, etc., the position would have been seriously worsened in the absence of restrictive actions and/or lack of expansion in competing areas.[91] As tropical Africa is principally an agricultural producer, though its world position is strongest in minerals, it is safe to assume that a steady and rapid expansion of exports in the future is highly unlikely. A few individual countries with important mineral deposits will, of course, represent the exception to the general rule.

Imports, on the other hand, have been growing faster than exports with the result that, in recent years, there seems to be no surplus in the trade account for tropical Africa as a whole.[92] When investment income paid abroad and "services" are taken into account, tropical Africa has a considerable deficit on current account.[93] Given this situation, the ability of tropical Africa to sustain a high rate of capital intensive investment will depend on the inflow of private and public capital from abroad.[94]

Let us first discuss foreign private investment. Such flow of capital has positive and negative effects on the balance of payments. The most obvious negative effect is the outflow of profits which, after a lag, the investment will bring about. It seems that returns of some 15 to 20 percent on capital, usually on the basis of an investment maturing in about three years, are required in order to attract foreign investment in tropical Africa.[95] Table 3 gives the rates of growth of foreign investment, for different maturation lags and rates of profit, which must be maintained if

Table 3

**Rates of Growth of Gross Foreign Investment Necessary to Offset
the Outflow on Investment Income**
(percent values)

	Rates of profit (percent)			
	10	15	20	25
Maturation period:				
3 years	8	11	14	16
4 years	7	10	12	14
5 years	7	9	11	13

the outflow of investment income is not to exceed gross foreign investment. The combinations denoted with a circle can be conservatively assumed to be the most relevant to our context. Rates of growth of foreign
private investment in the order of 10 to 12 percent are very high from
the standpoint, not only of past performance,[96] but, as we shall see later
on, of future prospects. It seems, therefore, highly unlikely that a net
inflow of private capital can, with occasional exceptions, be expected to
ease the shortage of foreign exchange in tropical Africa.

Let us now see whether we can expect a positive effect of foreign investment on the trade account. In the case of investment in mining, foreign investment can, in many cases, be expected to bring about a steady
increase in the value of exports. These gains, however, may be offset by
related effects of such investment on imports. As we have seen, the
emerging pattern of foreign investment in tropical Africa, in mining as
well as manufacturing, favors (either as a permissive or as a causal factor), the development of a pattern of consumption and of production in
the modern sector that weakens the links between the modern sector itself and the rest of the economy in the periphery. The pattern of demand for productive inputs and of consumption, associated with a capital
intensive and bureaucratized modern sector, tends to promote a pattern
of derivative demand that will be mainly satisfied either by imports from
the industrial centers or by production within the modern sectors of the
periphery. In the former case the negative impact on the balance of payments is direct and immediate. In the latter case, on the other hand, it is
indirect. In order to understand this more roundabout effect we must

consider the impact on the trade account of the balance of payments of foreign investment in manufacturing. The biases of investment in tropical Africa in favor of capital intensity and against the capital goods sector are relevant in this connection.

They are in fact largely responsible both for the fact that import substitution has largely been self-defeating[97] and for the poor prospects for tropical African economies to become competitive on the world markets for manufactures.[98] As a result, manufacturing tends to be undertaken to supply almost exclusively the national or supranational markets of tropical Africa.[99] While a positive net impact on the trade account may obtain in the early stages of import substitution, the negative effects that we have earlier traced in the pattern of derivative demand associated with the emerging pattern of investment become overwhelming in the longer run. If we take into account the fact that it is also in the early stages of import substitution, if ever, that foreign private investment is likely to attain the "critical" rate of growth of 10 to 12 percent discussed above, the general conclusion emerges that after that stage foreign private investment, far from easing the shortage of foreign exchange of tropical African economies, increasingly worsens the situation.[100]

Let us now consider the possibility that the foreign exchange necessary for the capital intensive development of tropical Africa will be made available by the advanced capitalist countries through bilateral long-term financial loans, multilateral loans, and "aid." The inflow of finance from these sources is essentially a postwar phenomenon and has replaced private portfolio investment in financing expenditure in infrastructure. The net flow to tropical Africa rose steadily in the 1950s[101] and, as the interest payments on loans credited to African countries has begun to rise rapidly,[102] it seems to have reached a ceiling of \$0.9–1.0 billion in the 1960s.[103] There is a strong possibility that these financial flows, other than for military purposes (which have no positive effect on the availability of foreign exchange), are, for the most part, a dependent factor, i.e., it is likely that they are determined by the flows of direct private investment. In the first place, this financial assistance is more and more made available on the basis of the "economic viability" of the projects which it is supposed to support. This, in general, means that private capital must be forthcoming to make use of the overhead capital financed by public capital. In the second place, as mentioned above, a large proportion of bilateral assistance aims at easing the balance-of-payments position of tropical African economies in order to make possible either the importation of capital goods or the repatriation of profits and capital. For these reasons official flows of financial resources cannot but marginally be considered an independent variable in determining the availability of foreign exchange necessary for the capital intensive development of tropical Africa.

Such availability will ultimately depend on the level and growth of foreign private investment in the sense that public capital will in general reinforce whatever tendencies are favored by the inflow of private capital—in the case of a high propensity to invest in the area, it will provide the financial resources necessary for the materialization of that propensity; in the case of a low investment propensity, it will ease the shortage of foreign exchange to make possible the outflow of capital, thus worsening the situation in the long run. In conclusion, the problem of the feasibility of the higher rate of growth made possible by the capital intensive development of tropical Africa is largely related to that of the propensity to invest in the area of private foreign capital. We must now discuss this propensity.

3. The reinvestment of the larger surplus associated with capital intensive techniques is not only feasible, but desired by whoever controls its utilization.

In the present context the utilization of the surplus is controlled by the international corporations.[104] Thus in order to assess the likelihood that the surplus will be reinvested in tropical Africa, we must briefly discuss the determinants of their propensity to invest in the periphery. Three main considerations seem to be relevant in this context.[105]

1. The extent to which tropical Africa is a "growth area," as it is in fast-growing economies that the profitable opportunities necessary to attract foreign investment will present themselves.

2. The extent to which tropical Africa is affected by a shortage of foreign exchange which would restrain the freedom of foreign corporations to repatriate profits and capital.

3. The extent to which investment in tropical Africa is subject to the risks of expropriation of assets and for nationalization without "full" compensation.

The last question is not particularly relevant in the present discussion as we assume that, in this respect, conditions favorable to foreign capital obtain. We shall return to it in the next section.

The fact that the propensity to invest in tropical Africa is affected by its balance-of-payments position, on the other hand, gives rise to a problem of circular causation. Recalling what we said earlier in this section, if foreign private investment grows at a rate higher than the critical value of some 10 to 12 percent, then such investment eases the shortage of foreign exchange, and if other favorable conditions obtain, additional foreign investment will be attracted to the area, improving further the balance-of-payments position. But if the rate of growth of foreign capital invested in the area falls short of that critical value, the opposite cumulative process of falling propensity to invest and growing shortage of foreign exchange will take place. As we have seen, the flows of official capital will, in general, strengthen these tendencies. This cumulative process is more likely to operate in a downward than in an upward direction, since in the latter case other conditions connected with the extent to which tropical Africa is a "growth area" must obtain to make the process self-sustaining. Let us take the lower limit of 10 to 12 percent as the mimimum rate of growth of foreign investment that would create the conditions for the reinvestment in tropical Africa of the surplus accruing to foreign corporations. This rate seems of impossible attainment for two main reasons:

1. With the exception of a few countries with particularly rich mineral deposits, the prospects for a rapid rise of tropical African primary exports, i.e., at a rate exceeding the present 3 to 5 percent per annum, are very poor.[106]

2. Given the bias of the emerging pattern of investment in the area against the capital goods sector, the autonomous growth of the internal market is severely restrained.

The combination of these two factors makes it safe to assume that, given the behavioral and institutional framework we have been analyzing, tropical Africa will not, in the foreseeable future, become a "growth area." In consequence, whatever the situation might be during the so-called phase of easy import substitution, foreign investment will increasingly become a mere device for transferring surplus generated in tropical Africa to the investing country.[107] Under these conditions the higher surplus associated with capital intensive techniques does not lead to faster growth of employment but to higher exports of profits.

We see, therefore, that none of the three crucial assumptions on which the argument for capital intensive techniques is based apply to our context. In consequence, the bias of the emerging pattern of investment in favor of capital intensity and against the capital goods industry cannot be expected to lead, in the long run, to a faster growth of wage and salary employment; it will simply allow a larger outflow of surplus from the area and growing incomes for a small, and, in relative terms, constant or contracting section of the working population. This type of growth, which, as we have seen, already characterizes tropical Africa,[108] we shall call growth without development. In the last section of this essay we must turn to discuss the reasons for the stability of this pattern of growth.

4

The analysis in the previous sections has been carried out in some detail in order to show the complexity of the relationship between the integration of tropical Africa with the international capitalist system and the obstacles to African development. The assumption of a connection between the persistence of underdevelopment and the evolution of oligopolistic structures in the advanced capitalist countries seems to be valid; we need, however, to qualify it in many ways to take into account various technological and behavioral factors that act independently of the form of ownership of the means of production in the periphery and in the industrial centers with which the former is integrated.

It should be clear that the mere participation of the state in stimulating or undertaking major industrial and marketing functions (a phenomenon that can be observed in many countries of tropical Africa), or even the nationalization of foreign enterprises, does not necessarily alter the nature of the relations between periphery and industrial centers and among sectors and classes within the periphery itself. For example, it is normal in tropical Africa for managerial control of enterprises wholly owned by the state (or in which the state holds a majority participation) to remain in the hands of international corporations.[109] Minority participation and management agreements ensure the foreign corporations a regular flow of payments in the form of royalties, patents, licensing agreements, and technical assistance fees, etc., which to some extent replace the export of profits in affecting the balance of payments negatively.[110] But even if state ownership increases the share of the surplus retained in the periphery, the bias of investment in favor of capital intensive techniques may remain unaffected not only because of the persistence of managerial constraints, but also because the managing corporations profit from the supply of equipment, components, materials, and technical services which embody capital intensive techniques. Similar considerations apply to the bias against the capital goods sector. In fact, though the state may have greater confidence in the future industrialization of the economy, which would justify the expansion of the capital goods sector ahead of demand, the other obstacles discussed in Section 1 are not removed by the mere public ownership of the means of production. Indeed, if capital intensity is retained, the balance-of-payments problems, discussed in Section 3, may be intensified.

Our analysis also implies that a disengagement from the international capitalist system and greater integration with the socialist economies of Eastern Europe and China may not in itself alter the pattern of growth without development. It is true that such reorientation of external economic relations, if it were possible,[111] might remove the various obstacles to development we have seen to be related to the existence of oligopolistic structures in advanced capitalist countries. It is also true that the integration of tropical African countries with planned economies would make planning in the former less of a gamble. Yet the problems connected with the balkanization of Africa which make the individual national economies inefficient planning units would persist. More important still is the fact that many technological and managerial constraints are independent of the mode of production obtaining in the industrial centers.[112]

In other words, there is no panacea for African economic development, and African unity is no such panacea either. The fact that international capitalism acts on a pan-African—indeed on a world—scale undoubtedly reduces the bargaining strength and ability to plan of the small African nations. However, we have seen that the lack of development in tropical Africa originates in a pattern of growth that is only partly due to the balkanization of the area. Whatever the relative importance of these factors (i.e., ownership of the means of production in the tropical African economies and in the industrial centers with which they are integrated, and the balkanization of Africa) may be in determining the pattern of growth without development, none can be singled out as the crucial variable. Institutional changes alone cannot be expected to change that pattern.

African governments will have to face up to the problem of primary accumulation, a process that has not gone very far in tropical Africa. Broadly speaking, this process has two related aspects: the mobilization of the saving potential implicit in the underutilized productive resources of the pre-capitalist economies; and the reallocation of the surplus from export of investment income and from conspicuous or nonessential consumption to serve the requirements of that mobilization. In this connection two patterns of growth of the modern sector seem to confront each other. The existing pattern is characterized by a high capital intensity of production within each sector and by a sectoral distribution of investment implying a low "implicit capital intensity." [113] We have seen that this pattern has a very low development potential because it restrains the growth of the internal market and (being associated with a high income elasticity of imports), it creates balance-of-payments problems which frustrate the further expansion of productive capacity. An alternative pattern of growth would be one characterized by a lower capital intensity within each sector but a higher "implicit capital intensity." [114] This pattern would have greater developmental potential because it would foster the autonomous growth (i.e., independent of external stimulants) of the internal market and would reduce the dependence of steady increases in productivity upon the availability of foreign exchange.

The importance of this last point warrants some detailed discussion. Increases in productivity involve a "learning process" that enhances the rationality of productive combinations. The existing pattern of growth not only restrains the spreading of the learning process over large sections of the population; in addition, even in the state-owned enterprises, it limits considerably the range of experiences that can be undergone in the periphery as crucial economic and technological decisions are made in the industrial centers. Furthermore, the bureaucratization and narrow specialization that capital intensive large-scale enterprises entail limit the number of different arrangements and situations in which learning can take place.[115] The use of labor intensive techniques would not only spread the learning process to larger sections of the African population but also make it more complete and varied. The use of labor intensive techniques is also more likely to make possible the mobilization of the underemployed labor of the African pre-capitalist system. Disguised unemployment in Africa is typically seasonal and periodic since no general population pressure on the land exists. The labor migration system (an adaptation to African conditions of the "putting-out" system that has characterized primary accumulation in the now advanced economies), however inefficient, performed the function of mobilizing this type of disguised unemployment for productive purposes. As we have seen, the emerging pattern of investment is displacing the system but no alternative way of mobilizing underemployed labor has emerged. The main failure of the labor migration system in colonial times was that it did not create the conditions that would have made it obsolete. In other words, migrant labor was employed in primary production for export which, with some marginal exceptions, did not lead to industrialization and to the transformation of traditional agriculture that would have enabled the African economies to supersede the system. This consideration leads us to a fundamental question. As Nurkse[116] has pointed out, the state of disguised unemployment implies a disguised saving potential as well. The emerging pattern of growth with its bias in favor of capital intensity and against the development of a sector producing the capital goods most suitable for the modernization of the African economies makes the mobilization of that potential unlikely if not impossible.[117] In consequence, it leads to reliance on outside finance which, as we have seen, frustrates development in the long run. Labor intensive techniques and the development of a capital goods industry would, on the other hand, make possible the mobilization of the disguised saving potential of tropical Africa and therefore the internal generation of the surplus necessary for long-term growth and development.

It is, however, important to bear in mind that the question of a shift toward more labor intensive techniques within sectors and toward a different allocation of the investable surplus among sectors cannot be divorced from the second question mentioned above, namely, that of the distribution of the surplus among classes. We shall presently turn to this question; at the moment it is sufficient to point out the obvious incompatibility between the absorption of the surplus by the export of profits and by the conspicuous or nonessential consumption of a small section of the population, on the one hand, and its utilization to step up capital accumulation and to provide incentives for the transformation of traditional agriculture, on the other.

Thus, changes in techniques of production and in the sectoral distribution of investment, like the institutional changes discussed above, are only necessary and not sufficient conditions for the development of tropical Africa. In other words, development must be seen as a total process in which technical, behavioral, and institutional factors are interrelated. This does not mean, of course, that institutional, technical, and behavioral obstacles to development all have to be tackled at the same time; it certainly means, however, that changes in each of the various factors can only make sense *as tactical moves in a strategy which aims at some special transformation in the total situation.* In concluding this essay we must attempt to find out why such strategy has failed to emerge in tropical Africa.[118]

The emphasis is usually put on external obstacles. By not dealing with such obstacles it is not our intention to belittle them. We disregard them because, whatever the retaliatory power of foreign capital, it is more important to understand the causes of the failure to evolve a valid strategy of development, which are rooted in the political economy of tropical Africa itself, namely in the power base of the African governments. As pointed out in the introductory section, in most countries of tropical Africa feudal elements, landowning classes, and national bourgeoisies are either nonexistent or not sufficiently significant, politically and/or economically, to constitute the power base of the state. The implication is that the stability of the existing system of internal and external relationships must be sought in a consistency between the interests of international capitalism and some classes other than the abovementioned. Our analysis has suggested that such classes are, in all likelihood, the African elite, sub-elite, and *proletariat proper* (i.e., excluding migrant labor), which we shall collectively refer to as the "labor aristocracy" of tropical Africa.

The labor aristocracy, as we have seen in Section 2, owes its very emergence and consolidation to a pattern of investment in which the international corporations play a leading role. The displacement costs involved in the disengagement from international capitalism therefore have to be borne mainly by the labor aristocracy itself. The most important consideration, however, concerns the reallocation of the surplus that is necessary for the mobilization of the disguised saving potential of tropical Africa. Such a reallocation directly hits the labor aristocracy, which has most benefited from the present pattern of growth without development,[119] and whose consumption therefore has to be significantly curtailed. State ownership and management of the means of production is not sufficient to prevent the present unequal distribution of incentives.

As we saw in Section 2, the steady rise in wages and salaries of the last ten to fifteen years is only partly due to the investment and employment policies of the large-scale foreign corporations. Governments' wage and salary policies have also played a leading role. It follows that even though the labor aristocracy may not be opposed to state ownership and management of the means of production, it can be expected to resist that reallocation of the surplus on the part of the state which must be an essential component of the strategy for the transformation in the total situation of the societies of tropical Africa.

It may be argued that there is no real conflict of interests between the semi-proletarianized peasantry and the labor aristocracies, as growth without development is, in the long run, self-defeating. The argument is ambiguous because the definition of class interests without a time dimension does not make much sense. Of course, we can always take a point in time distant enough to be able to show that the labor aristocracy can only gain from the organic development of the economies of tropical Africa. However, in defining class interests one must make assumptions not only about the benefits derived by a class from a certain pattern of growth and development at a point in time, but also on whether that point in time lies within the time horizon that can be realistically expected from that class. Disregard of the time dimension may lead both to a kind of "proletarian messianism" and to unrealistic assumptions concerning the class interests that can be attributed to international capitalism. The view that international corporations have an interest in the development of the periphery is held by most non-Marxist economists and, to some extent, seems to have influenced some Marxist scholars. Barratt-Brown,[120] for example, in answering the question, "What chance is there of the great corporations embarking upon the policies of worldwide industrial expansion?" argues that since wider markets, rather than cheap labor, represent the most important interest of international capitalism:

> This gives rise to the hope that capitalist firms and governments will see . . . that economic development in the as yet underdeveloped lands is very much in their interest. . . . It seems hardly to be in the nature of capitalism to undertake such development, but British capitalism did it once for the lands of European settlement and we must consider the possibility of continuing the job in the less developed lands of Asia and in Africa.[121]

That international capitalism is made up of heterogeneous sectional interests and that some of its sections have an interest in the industrialization and development of the periphery is widely accepted. The point, however, is that the "freedom of action" of what we may call the "progressive" section of international capitalism and of the governments of capitalist countries are severely limited, in the case of the former, by the oligopolistic structure of the international capitalist system and, in the case of the latter, by their power base in which the "progressive" capitalist element is normally of little consequence. These two factors considerably curtail the time horizon of international capitalism so that its long-term interests in the industrialization of the periphery are irrelevant to the determination of its behavior.

Proletarian and bourgeois "messianism" seem therefore to be closely related, both being rooted in the competitive models of capitalism of, respectively, Marx and Smith. A shift in the focus of attention from competition to oligopoly is most needed to understand both contemporary capitalist systems and the problems of development and socialism in their periphery.

Notes

1. Individual, small-scale, competitive producers assume that, at the ruling price, the market demand for their output is unlimited. Furthermore, under competitive conditions the flexibility of the rate of profit ensures the expansion of demand to match supply. See below.
2. F. Perroux, "La Nation en voie de se faire et les pouvoirs industriels," *Les Cahiers de la République* (July–August 1959), p. 51.
3. R. Prebisch, "The Role of Commercial Policies in Underdeveloped Countries," *American Economic Review Papers and Proceedings* (May 1959).
4. The terms "periphery" and "industrial centers" will be retained throughout to designate the underdeveloped and the industrial countries with which the former are economically integrated.
5. O. Lange, *Economic Development, Planning, and International Cooperation* (New York, 1963), pp. 10–11.
6. Kwame Nkrumah, *Neo-Colonialism: The Last Stage of Imperialism* (New York, 1965).
7. See below.

8. Cf., for example, Lange's passage quoted above and also P. A. Baran and P. M. Sweezy, *Monopoly Capital* (New York, 1966), p. 205; and Hamza Alavi, "Imperialism Old and New," *The Socialist Register 1964* (New York and London, 1964), p. 124.

9. Cf., for example, Alavi, ibid., p. 116.

10. E. R. Braundi, "Neocolonialism and Class Struggle," *International Socialist Journal*, no. 1 (1964), p. 66.

11. Cf. C. Wright Mills, *White Collar* (New York, 1956), pp. 23–38.

12. Baran and Sweezy, op. cit., pp. 102–105; S. Tsuru, ed., *Has Capitalism Changed?* (Tokyo, 1961), pp. 51–53.

13. Baran and Sweezy, op. cit., p. 50.

14. R. Vernon, "The American Corporation in Underdeveloped Areas," in E. S. Mason, ed., *The Corporation in Modern Society* (Cambridge, Mass., 1959), pp. 238–39; W. A. Chudson, "Trends in African Exports and Capital Inflows," in M. J. Herskovits and M. Harwitz, eds., *Economic Transition in Africa* (London, 1964), pp. 349–50; M. Barratt-Brown, *After Imperialism* (London, 1963), ch. 8; Baran and Sweezy, op. cit., pp. 196–97.

15. Cf. Nkrumah, op. cit.

16. Ibid., pp. 58–60.

17. Braundi, op. cit., pp. 55–56.

18. Ibid., p. 60. See also the staff paper by G. Benveniste and W. E. Moran, Jr. (Stanford Research Institute, International Industrial Development Center), quoted in S. F. Frankel, "Capital and Capital Supply in Relation to the Development of Africa," in E. A. G. Robinson, ed., *Economic Development for Africa South of the Sahara* (London, 1964), pp. 431–32.

19. D. J. Morgan, *British Private Investment in East Africa: Report of a Survey and a Conference* (London: The Overseas Development Institute, 1965), p. 6.

20. "Multinational Companies, a Special Report," *Business Week*, 20 April 1963.

21. Cf. M. Byé, "La Grande unité interterritoriale," *Cahiers de l'I.S.E.A.*, quoted by F. Perroux and R. Demonts, "Large Firms—Small Nations," *Présence Africaine*, no. 38 (1961), p. 37.

22. Chudson, op. cit.

23. Loc. cit.

24. UNESCO, *Policy Aspects of Industrial Development in Africa: Problems and Prospects*, E/CN. 14/AS/II/2/K/1 (1965), pp. 22–27, mimeographed. In some cases increases in manufacturing activities merely represent classification changes. Cf. R. E. Baldwin, *Economic Development and Export Growth: A Study of Northern Rhodesia, 1920–1960* (Berkeley and Los Angeles, 1966), p. 181.

25. UNESCO, *Policy Aspects of Industrial Development in Africa.* See also G. Hunter, *The New Societies of Tropical Africa* (London, 1962), pp. 161–62.

26. UNESCO, op. cit.

27. Intermediary and capital goods industries generally require, especially in nonindustrialized countries, supranational markets. The possibility of using protectionist policies or setting up competing units in neighboring countries increases the risks of, and therefore discourages, investment in each country. This consideration points to the possibility of conflicts of interest within international capitalism concerning the balkanization of tropical Africa.

28. Barratt-Brown, op. cit., p. 419.

29. We are assuming that the new plants will not compete in the national market from which the investment originates. The argument holds *a fortiori* if this assumption is not made.

30. Cf. Hunter, op. cit., pp. 60–61. See also H. A. Turner, *Wage Trends, Wage Policies, and Collective Bargaining: The Problems of Underdeveloped Countries* (Cambridge, 1965), p. 21; and below.

31. Baldwin, op. cit., pp. 79–80.

32. Loc. cit.

33. Ibid. This is also shown by the fact that the copper mines of Uganda have a lower degree of mechanization than the Katangese mines. Cf. A. Baryaruha, *Factors Affecting Industrial Employment: A Study of Ugandan Experience, 1954–1964* (Nairobi, 1967), p. 58.

34. Cf., for instance, Baryaruha, op. cit., and Hunter, op. cit., pp. 60–61.

35. Cf. Vernon, op. cit., pp. 253–54.

36. See below.

37. Perroux and Demonts, op. cit., p. 46.

38. Cf. D. J. Viljoen, "Problems of Large-Scale Industry in Africa," in Robinson, op. cit., pp. 253–54.

39. Capitalist enterprises always tend to adopt those techniques which "maximize" the surplus. Such techniques are relatively capital intensive (see Section 3). However, financial stringency prevents the smaller firms from taking a long time horizon in their investment decisions and therefore from adopting capital intensive techniques. The large corporation, on the other hand, is to a large extent free from financial constraints upon its investment decisions.

40. One notable exception is W. Elkan, *Migrants and Proletarians: Urban Labor in the Economic Development of Uganda* (London, 1960).

41. Quoted in Alavi, op. cit., pp. 106–107.

42. Degree of competition is not the only variable in this context. As already

mentioned, the calculating rationality of the capitalist concerns is equally relevant, giving rise to the discrepancy in the behavior of the chartered companies and concessionaries of old and that of the modern corporations.

43. Cf. Alavi, op. cit., p. 121. This point is discussed more fully in Section 3, where the determinants of corporate investment in the periphery are dealt with.

44. Cf. Vernon, op. cit., pp. 248–49; Barratt-Brown, op. cit., pp. 273–76; Morgan, op. cit., p. 47.

45. Derived from K. C. Doctor and H. Gallis, "Size and Characteristics of Wage Employment in Africa: Some Statistical Estimates," *International Labor Review,* no. 2 (1966), p. 166. The estimates are very rough.

46. Cf. Turner, op. cit., p. 14; D. Walker, "Problems of Economic Development in East Africa," in Robinson, op. cit., p. 123; T. L. V. Blair, "African Economic Development," *Présence Africaine* (English edition), no. 56 (1965), p. 34. That the rate of growth of employment has been considerably less than the rate of growth of the population is clearly shown in the following table which gives data for selected countries of East and Central Africa:

| | *Annual rates of growth (compound)* | | | |
Country	*Employment*	*Population*	*Real product*	*Period*
Uganda	1.2 (a b)	2.5 (c)	3.5 (c)	1952–65
Kenya	.9 (d b)	3.0 (c)	4.8 (c)	1954–64
Tanzania				
(Tanganyika)	−2.1 (e)	1.8 (c)	3.5 (c)	1953–65
Rhodesia	1.3 (e)	3.3 (c)	5.4 (c)	1954–64
Malawi	.3 (e)	2.4 (c)	2.5 (c)	1954–64
Zambia	.4 (e)	2.8 (c)	2.5 (c)	1954–65

The data were calculated from: (a) Uganda Government, *1963 Statistical Abstract* (Entebbe, 1963), p. 89; (b) East African Statistical Department, *Economic and Statistical Review,* no. 20 (1966), p. 51; (c) OECD, *National Accounts of Less-Developed Countries* (Paris, 1967), pp. 5–9; (d) Kenya Government, *Economic Survey, 1964* (Nairobi, 1964), p. 39; (e) International Labor Institute (ILO), *Year Book of Labor Statistics* (1961), p. 100; *Yearbook of Labor Statistics* (1966), p. 288.

47. Cf. Turner, op. cit., pp. 12–13.

48. Loc. cit.

49. Ibid., p. 14.

50. Ibid.

51. Sources: For Kenya, Uganda, and Tanganyika, see East African Statistical Department, *Economic and Statistical Review*, p. 51; data for the other countries have been derived from Doctor and Gallis, op. cit.

52. The terms "elite" and "sub-elite" have ideological connotations. They are used in this essay for want of a better terminology and not because of any implicit agreement with the view that no conflict of interest exists between the "elite," on the one hand, and the "masses," on the other, or that there is a lack of class structure within the "non-elite." This view seems to justify the use of the terms by some writers. Cf. P. Lloyd, ed., *The New Elites of Tropical Africa* (London, 1966), p. 60.

53. Ibid., p. 2.

54. Ibid., pp. 12–13.

55. Ibid., p. 22.

56. Ibid., p. 8; and Hunter, op. cit., p. 8.

57. Lloyd, op. cit., pp. 7–8.

58. What follows is based on my own unpublished research on the proletarianization of the Rhodesian peasantry (see Chapter 5 of this volume) and, unless otherwise specified, on standard works on the subject such as J. C. Mitchell, "Labour Migration in Africa South of the Sahara: The Cause of Labour Migration," *Bulletin of the Inter-African Labour Institute*, no. 1 (1959); W. Watson, *Tribal Cohesion in a Money Economy* (Manchester, 1958); and, especially, Elkan, op. cit.

59. Cf. W. E. Moore, "The Adaptation of African Labor Systems to Social Change," in Herskovits and Harwitz, op. cit., pp. 293–94 and 297.

60. Cf. Elkan, op. cit., pp. 52–54.

61. A distinction has to be made between stabilization in the sense of "long service in one type of employment" and stabilization in the sense of proletarianization or urbanization implying "a severance from rural ties combined with a tendency to settle down forever as a town dweller." Obviously employers in Africa have always been keen on the former type of stabilization. However, as they were not prepared to bear the costs (and the risks) involved in the latter type of stabilization, their interest remained purely hypothetical. Cf. Baldwin, op. cit., p. 138.

62. Lloyd, op. cit., pp. 10–11.

63. Hunter, op. cit., pp. 230–31.

64. Turner, op. cit., pp. 20–21.

65. Cf. Hunter, op. cit., p. 207; Elkan, op. cit., p. 85; Turner, op. cit., pp. 17–18, 48.

66. Baryaruha, for example, shows that locally based enterprises also stepped up mechanization in response to the steady rise in wages.

67. Cf. Turner, op. cit., p. 21.

68. Cf. Elkan, op. cit.

69. See Chapter 3 of this volume.

70. Baldwin, op. cit., p. 105.

71. Cf. Moore, op. cit., p. 290; Elkan, op. cit., pp. 61–62.

72. Moore, op. cit., p. 290.

73. Turner, op. cit., p. 48.

74. Cf. ibid., p. 21.

75. The following analysis is rather cursory as the focus of our attention is on the wage-working class and foreign capital. Its only purpose is to bridge the gap that would otherwise arise between the foregoing discussion and the analysis of the next two sections.

76. Some rural economies of tropical Africa are already some way along the road to class formation. Those of southern Ghana, parts of eastern and western Nigeria, the Ivory Coast, and Buganda are examples. They still are, however, rather exceptional, particularly in East and Central Africa.

77. Enterprises are here defined as small scale if they have no international affiliations and employ a relatively small number of workers.

78. Hunter, op. cit., pp. 129–31, 156. New opportunities have also arisen in the field of gasoline service stations as the oil marketing companies have become some of the largest investors in sub-Saharan Africa.

79. The Madhvani Group of East Africa is certainly the most conspicuous exception. In Uganda, Kenya, and Tanzania it controls twenty-three enterprises, excluding subsidiaries and associates, in a wide range of industries: sugar, vegetable oil, beer, steel, textiles, glass, confectionery, matches, and others. Obviously groups such as this, though locally based, must be included in international capitalism.

80. Cf., Elkan, op. cit., pp. 111–12.

81. Cf. M. Katzin, "The Role of the Small Entrepreneur," in Herskovits and Harwitz, op. cit., pp. 179–80; Hunter, op. cit., pp. 100–101, 137–40.

82. Hunter, op. cit., pp. 137–40; S. Chodak, "Social Classes in Sub-Saharan Africa," *Africana Bulletin,* no. 4 (1966), p. 35. In Buganda, it is the consumption pattern imposed by a prosperous farming community which frustrated the accumulation of savings on the part of would-be petty capitalists. See Elkan, op. cit., p. 47.

83. Cf. Katzin, op. cit., p. 195; Lloyd, op. cit., p. 8.

84. In addition to this, the advantage that small enterprises may derive from the imparting of skills among the population on the part of large-scale enterprises is considerably reduced by the use of highly capital intensive techniques. The less capital intensive small enterprises will generally need either unskilled labor or labor fully skilled in one of the traditional crafts. As we have seen, however, the large-scale corporations will tend to create a semi-skilled, specialized force largely unsuitable for the local employers.

85. The obstacles of the small national market can be overcome by the large-scale corporation by means of multinational operations.

86. This is another reason for assuming that international corporations may benefit from rising wages and salaries. As we have seen, large numbers are employed by the public sector (see Table 2 above); in consequence, the increase in demand for the products of the corporations brought about by the rise in labor incomes makes it easier to pass the increased labor costs on to the consumer.

87. Mills, op. cit., pp. 23–28.

88. See, for example, Maurice Dobb, *An Essay on Economic Growth and Planning*, orig. pub. 1960 (New York, 1969); W. Galenson and H. Leibenstein, "Investment Criteria, Productivity and Economic Development," *The Quarterly Journal of Economics* (August 1955); A. K. Sen, *Choice of Techniques. An Aspect of the Theory of Planned Economic Development* (Oxford, 1962). Since implicitly or explicitly these authors assume a socialist economy, what follows does not represent a critique of their theories.

89. Barratt-Brown, op. cit., p. 354.

90. Chudson, op. cit., p. 337.

91. Ibid., p. 340.

92. A. M. Kamarck, "The Development of the Economic Infrastructure," in Herskovits and Harwitz, op. cit., p. 75.

93. Loc. cit. The "guesstimates" of the deficit on current account given by Kamarck are $1.0 billion for 1963 and $0.9 billion for 1964. These deficits amount to 24.4 and 19.2 percent, respectively, of the exports from tropical Africa in the two years.

94. We are excluding for the time being reductions in imports of nonessential consumer goods. This possibility is discussed in Section 4.

95. Cf. Morgan, op. cit., pp. 15–16.

96. For the trend of the private investment from advanced capitalist countries to the underdeveloped economies see "The Slow-Down on Aid," *Economist*, 26 August 1967, pp. 736–37. With regard to tropical Africa, gross private foreign investment seems to have reached a peak of about $800 million per year sometime between 1950 and 1957 and to have since then fallen. See Frankel, op. cit., p. 428. The table on the following page gives U.K. and American foreign direct investment (excluding oil) in Sterling Africa and Africa, respectively, for the period 1959–1964. It was derived from Morgan, op. cit., p. 6 (for the U.K.), and Kamarck, op. cit., pp. 266–67 (for the U.S.).

97. In the sense that import substitution leads to a faster growth of imports of semi-finished goods, capital goods, and raw materials.

98. Kamarck, op. cit., p. 155.

99. Chudson, op. cit., p. 352.

		Private direct investment, excluding oil *(millions of \$U.S.)*				
	1959	1960	1961	1962	1963	1964
U.K. (Sterling Africa)	81	83	83	25	7	−25
U.S. (Africa)	92	13	8	93	105	75
Total	173	96	111	118	112	50

100. This conclusion refers to tropical Africa as a whole and to the majority of countries. There will probably be exceptions of two kinds: countries with particularly rich mineral deposits, such as Gabon, and countries in which foreign investment in manufacturing will tend to concentrate to take advantage of a relatively industrialized environment.

101. Cf. Chudson, op. cit., p. 349.

102. Cf. Blair, op. cit., pp. 29–30; Nkrumah, op. cit., pp. 241–42.

103. Kamarck, op. cit., p. 202. As Braundi has pointed out (op. cit., pp. 241–42), these flows of public funds have been instrumental in making possible the export of profits from tropical Africa which would otherwise have been paralyzed by disequilibria in the balance of payments.

104. Problems connected with the investment of the surplus on the part of the state are discussed in Section 4.

105. Cf. Morgan, op. cit.

106. See p. 246 above.

107. Baran and Sweezy have shown, on the basis of official data, that in the case of the U.S. (the industrial center par excellence), foreign investment is in fact a most efficient device for transferring surplus generated abroad to the investing country. In the period 1950–1963, while the net direct investment capital outflow from the U.S. amounted to \$17,382 million, the inflow of direct investment income amounted to \$29,416 million. See *Monopoly Capital*, pp. 106–108.

108. Cf. n. 46 above.

109. Cf. Hunter, op. cit., pp. 183–84.

110. Cf. Alavi, op. cit., p. 119; Nkrumah, op. cit., p. 178.

111. For the feasibility of a strategy of development that includes the institutional changes under discussion, see below.

112. The experience of China is instructive in this respect. In the early and mid-1950s the rapid industrialization of China was made possible by Soviet assistance. However, the nature of this assistance tended to produce a pattern of growth without development which contributed to the

difficulties of the late 1950s. Cf. Franz Schurmann, *Ideology and Organization in Communist China* (Berkeley and Los Angeles, 1966).

113. By "implicit capital intensity" is here understood the proportion of the labor force employed in the sector producing means of production.

114. It would be futile and quite beyond the purpose of this essay to give a detailed and concrete description of this alternative pattern of growth. While its broad characteristics can be perceived at the theoretical level, its concrete characterization can only emerge from the *praxis* of African development.

115. On this last point cf. H. W. Singer, "Small-Scale Industry in African Economic Development," in Robinson, op. cit., pp. 640–41. The spread of an organic "learning process" is particularly important in connection with the development of a *modern* labor intensive technology which might very well be necessary for the development of Africa.

116. R. Nurkse, *Problems of Capital Formation in Underdeveloped Countries* (Oxford, 1953), p. 37.

117. Cf. Singer, op. cit., pp. 641 and 653. The capital goods sector must be understood in a broad sense to include, for instance, capital construction and land improvements in the rural sector.

118. Tanzania may turn out to be an exception to the general rule.

119. Turner (op. cit., pp. 12–14) estimates that the whole benefit of economic development in Africa during the 1950s accrued to the wage and salary earners. In fact, however, we have seen that the unskilled semi-proletarianized peasantry (as a class) can have benefited but marginally from this rise in labor incomes because of the loss of employment opportunities ensuing from increased mechanization. Hence, not wage earners as such, but the labor aristocracy has gained from the present pattern of growth.

120. Barratt-Brown, op. cit., pp. 324–27.

121. From the conclusions of this study it would seem that Barratt-Brown deems possible a coalition between the British government and "progressive" giant corporations to promote the industrialization of the underdeveloped world.

4
On African Populism

John S. Saul

We enter here upon treacherous and uncharted waters. Those few authors who do make use of the notion of "populism" in their analyses of things African rarely bother to define it; furthermore they seldom deign to grace the use of the "concept" in the body of their text with so much as a citation in the index! We shall look at some of this literature in an attempt to gain initial purchase on our subject, but our critical function must transcend its limitations. Even then we can only hope, at this stage, to lay down certain distinctions and guidelines of use for further discussion; as we shall see, any definitive evaluation of the meaning of "populism" in an African context must await the genesis of more nuanced observation and theorizing as to the nature of the overall process of change in Africa, a program of work only now beginning to yield its first fruits.

Two initial distinctions must be made, for a failure to make them has, in the past, led to a measure of confusion. Firstly, in the literature and in our thinking about populism there are two different "definitions" of the phenomenon rattling around. These will be seen to be related in certain important ways; nonetheless, the choice of one definition rather than the other, whether made explicitly or implicitly, carries discussion in divergent directions and they must therefore be spelled out. Thus, on the one hand, we find Lloyd Fallers considering "populism" to be an ideology which postulates that "legitimacy resides in the people's will"—popu-

This article was originally published in G. Ionescu and E. Gellner, eds., *Populism: Its Meaning and National Characteristics* (London, 1969), pp. 122–50. Copyright © 1969 by Weidenfeld & Nicholson. Reprinted by permission.

I would like to thank a number of friends and colleagues in Dar es Salaam for assistance, both conscious and unconscious, in the writing of this paper, but particularly Roger Murray, John Iliffe, and Giovanni Arrighi. Needless to say, all errors of fact or judgment are my own.

lism as radical democracy, as it were.[1] On the other, Peter Worsley sees it as a response generated "wherever capitalism has penetrated into traditionalistic peasant society," an "ideology of small rural people threatened by encroaching industrial and financial capital." Giovanni Arrighi has made a similar point rather more sharply: "Populist ideologies are unorthodox precisely because they uphold the resistance against the spreading of capitalist relations."[2]

In contrasting these two notions, the stress of our examples has been on matters of ideology, but this is premature; a second important distinction must be introduced. For "populism," in both the above senses, has been used in each of two different ways (though these two overlap). It may be used as an analytical category, thought to be descriptive of aspects of reality. To take an example, a movement may be described as populist because it is felt by the observer to be an actual movement of "the people" in some important sense, a movement distinctive because it is "popular" as regards participation in a way that other movements are not. It may also be used as a term which characterizes a body of ideas or an ideology. To return to the example of the so-called populist movement: here one might wish merely to characterize the ideology of such a movement as "populist" (in either or both of the senses suggested in the preceding paragraph). The actual "truth" of that ideology in relationship to the composition or interests of the movement or the society as a whole could well be another matter. We shall see that the uses to which men and women, particularly leaders, can put those ideas thought to be best described as "populist" are most varied. These sets of rather abstract distinctions by way of introduction, then; they will be fleshed out as the paper proceeds.

1. Populism as the Will of the People

We may begin by working out from Fallers' definition. A closely related note is echoed by a number of observers of Third World developments: that this is an era characterized by the real or potential involvement of the "masses" in politics in a way unknown before this century. "Populism" for David Apter is a word which sums up this novel surge forward:

> Today, however, most governments operate in a climate of populism and mass participation. How much populism is controlled and shaped, as well

as the degree of responsiveness by government to the demands of the public, constitutes the characteristic problem of government, especially in
modernizing societies.[3]

Manfred Halpern uses the word in order to characterize the ideologies
summoned forth by this fact; the distinction in emphasis is not unimportant. "Every politician everywhere in the modern age prefers to speak in
the name of the 'people' . . . populism can be a mask for almost any
program, or else a nostalgic emotionalism for no program but immediate
satisfaction." [4] Furthermore, in the Third World, and especially Africa,
the term "mass" tends immediately to take on a predominantly rural
referent; it is in the countryside that the "people" are to be found in
their hundreds and thousands.

The reality of growing popular participation and awakened popular
consciousness in recent African history has been most explicitly identified in the literature as the quintessential "populism" by Apter himself
and by D. A. Low in their respective works on Buganda. In particular,
an important article by Low may serve, all too briefly here, as a *locus
classicus* for documenting certain strengths and weaknesses of "populism," so used, as an analytical category.[5] Low summarizes with admirable precision the process by which, around the turn of the century, the
then current generation of administrative chiefs, with British assistance
(especially within the terms of the 1900 agreement), consolidated a position of power both politically and economically as a landed oligarchy.
In so doing they aggrandized themselves at the expense of the hitherto
extremely powerful Kabaka (or king) and also of the people (in Buganda, the *bakopi*), the mass of the peasantry, whose significant measure
of bargaining capability vis-à-vis the chiefs was now seriously undermined. Low then traces the manner in which "the people" gradually asserted themselves over the next sixty years after the agreement, occasionally with the important assistance of the colonial government; this is
the phenomenon which he terms "populism."

In particular he notes the recurring importance of the network of
clans (the "Bataka" pattern) within the society, closer to the people than
the chiefly administrative hierarchy and more egalitarian, as a rallying
point for resistance to overweening chiefs. He also mentions the impact
of the gradual transformation of the landed-estate system of the agreement into a primarily small-scale, peasant, cash-cropping system, thus
making possible a new bargaining position for an "independent yeo-

manry." Importantly, as Apter also stressed, this populism has tended to take on a "neo-traditional" cast, defensive about many traditional ideas and practices and fiercely "nationalistic," but its general thrust against an elite of chiefs within Buganda tended to remain undampened. He concludes that it was this thrusting populism, suspicious of the chiefs and whetted by complementary economic grievances against Protectorate and Asian control of marketing, that led to riots in Buganda in 1945 and 1949 and, after the incident of the Kabaka's deportation, to a real curtailment of the chiefs' position in the name of "the people."

Low thus builds his model of social and political change quite squarely on the triad of "Kabaka, chiefs and people" and the interaction of the three, concluding that there "have been changes not of the structure itself but of the distribution of political power within it" and between, that is to say, its three monolithic components.[6] Yet one suspects that Buganda society was, quite simply, rather more complex than this; so used, "populism" can become a dangerous metaphor. Compare C. C. Wrigley:

> The rise of an active, broad-based economic middle class is acting as a ferment which is steadily dissolving the fabric of traditional society. . . . The uniform mass of rustic commoners has begun to split up into groups which are notably well-to-do and others which are notably poor; and the economic structure has been further complicated and diversified by the rise of a professional class, by the influx of migrant labourers and by the growth of commerce and urban wage-employment of every kind. As a result society has become fluid and amorphous; there is great economic differentiation but hardly any clear-cut stratification.[7]

As early as 1952, Wrigley noted the following division of farmers in one village: 19 percent well-to-do; 27 percent middling peasants; 33 percent poor peasants; 20 percent landless laborers.[8] To be sure, most of those at the very bottom were immigrants, but Bugandans were to be found at every level. One must suspect that such divisions among the people found some expression, if only in variable degrees of consciousness and involvement.

And such was, of course, the case. Apter mentions from time to time a number of sub-groups of importance as, for example, chiefs who had been removed:

> With inherited land, a sense of their own worth, and considerable education, such farmers attempted to engage in economic enterprise to restore

their social status. . . . In most cases they could not compete successfully with Asians and European business groups, or else they came up against government restrictions.[9]

These men, clan leaders, businessmen, mission employees, are mentioned as activists; Low himself cites the important role of African rural shopkeepers and African taxi-drivers, in competition against Asians. What of the possibly differential role of the varying strata of cultivators themselves? Unfortunately no one has thought to check. In any event, Low is forced to conclude his apotheosis of "populism" with the observation that changes, such as the important redressing of the balance of chiefs' power in the late fifties

> have been effected, not by determined mass movements (either of the chiefs on the first occasion, or of the people on the second) but of aroused minorities—the Christian chiefs in the 1880s and 1890s, the "political malcontents" (as Professor Pratt has called them) in the 1950s. In many respects these minorities may not have been typical of their order: but in a Burkean sense they were representative of it.[10]

One is justified in feeling uneasy with this last formulation. Like the term "populism" as used so broadly and inclusively throughout the article, it explains, or rather explains away, too much. The term itself threatens to stand in the way of more comprehensive data collection and theory building by prematurely closing questions that should remain open. Throughout our discussion we must face the distinct possibility that such a concept only seems useful because of the relative superficiality of our analysis of the modernization process and the relative poverty of our present vocabulary of dealing with "mass" phenomena. In the present instance, three important areas of inquiry are threatened with being blurred. First, the term encourages an overestimation of the *spread of popular involvement.* In social analysis it is all too easy to exaggerate the degree to which a population can be or has been aroused to action; our metaphors tend to impose hyperbole upon us. A warning against this seems particularly apt in an African setting where the pull upon individuals of the most localized of social units and of subsistence agriculture is strong.

Secondly, and closely related, it is tempting to overestimate the *level of consciousness* of the mass of the population; this encourages a failure to perceive differences in social situations (as, for example, class) among the people which can fundamentally determine variable degrees of involvement and complementary retardations of consciousness. Thus despite Low's final bow to a more complex reality, the centrality for his analysis of a monolithic, primarily peasant, block has hampered his systematic pursuit of this line of inquiry. Finally, one fears that even when dealing with those peasants who are more conscious and aroused to action, the concept "populism" encourages the assumption of a *unity of view* which may pass over the wide range of local variation of causes often characteristic of activity in a period of upheaval and tend to lump all such activity under an inadequate covering rubric. In this context it becomes particularly tempting to take the claims of leaders for a clear reflection of realities at the base, though evidence suggests that the interaction of such men with "grassroots" protest may be most ambiguous.

These points must be underscored, for in fact the term, in the sense currently under review, is a tempting one, catching as it does the mood of a novel and valuable emphasis articulated by some recent students of African affairs. Complementing the tendency of a first generation of Africanists to place almost exclusive emphasis upon the emergence of town-based, Western-educated elites as the progenitors of nationalism,[11] there has been a tendency to bring the "masses" back into the picture as a vital force. John Lonsdale writes:

> In short, there would seem to be some justification, in Western Kenya at least, for regarding the development of national consciousness as being stimulated to a large extent by local rural grievances and aspirations, directed and coordinated by men with local roots.[12]

Lionel Cliffe has made a similar point for Tanzania, stressing that the proto-nationalist associations which " 'provided the cells around which a nationwide political organization could be constructed' were essentially rurally based," expressing "the resentment of country people against outside interference in the things closest to them, their land and its use, their cattle and their way of life." [13] Popular grievances, then, played a vital role in the articulation of a successful nationalist movement. Was this "populism"?

There are familiar ambiguities and complexities. Certainly in Tanganyika rural protest was important but its character varied greatly from area to area. In some it was a force with a rather clear and sophisticated perception of economic matters and beyond them of political implications; in other areas it was much more conservative, instinctive, back-ward-looking, narrow in focus—responding, for example, to immediate threats from programs of agricultural change, with no broader view on questions of authority and legitimacy that might seem logical corollaries. Only a leadership cadre could generalize this protest for political ends and control at the center, yet that leadership's ties to the actual eruption of individual cases of rural protest were often largely peripheral and op-portunistic. In addition, in areas where protest was more sophisticated, as in Sukumaland with the rise of the cooperative movement which soon became a bulwark of TANU activity in the Lake Province in the 1950s, differentiation among the mass was important. Even today this coopera-tive cannot claim membership of over 50 percent of the growers in some areas and members tend to be the most economically advanced growers there. More information on the realities of "involvement" would clearly be most helpful. Similarly, Lonsdale's work reveals a rather more com-plex model of a popular movement, suggesting the interaction of, among others, local clan leaders, African traders, and Nairobi politicians and the "mass"; there was thus, in his words, merely a "coincidence of rural fears and national aims."

Perhaps Martin Kilson, among recent writers, has reflected in the most rewarding manner on these and other aspects of Africa's nationalist phase. Interestingly enough, in so doing he has articulated a usage of the concept "populism" which avoids at least some of the limitations we have mentioned above. Implicitly he attempts to situate "populism" as merely one element of broader movements and processes of change, not as a global characterization of relatively more complex phenomena.

> In describing local political pressures as "populist," I do not suggest that they were part of a systematic egalitarian ideology. I simply mean that they represent the lower reaches of provincial society, they came nearest to reflecting the political feelings of what we call the masses—the little people.[14]

For Sierra Leone he compiles an impressive catalogue of examples of rural outbursts which, generally, have taken a violent, riotous form. These outbursts have tended to be directed against the chiefs who have aggrandized themselves as the agents of colonialism, but they are often confused and visceral.

> Populist demands for local political change were not precise about the institutional form the desired change should take. This, of course, was not

surprising insofar as the rural masses lacked both the knowledge and the experience necessary to formulate details of institutional change. Nor was it always clear that populist political pressures were directed against the traditional authority structure as such, seeking its destruction as a legitimate political institution. Given the ambivalence of most rural Africans toward the chiefly groups, they were unable to push their grievances to the point of outright revolution. . . . The groups who spearheaded popular protest not infrequently asserted their demands within a traditional framework.[15]

While admitting the seemingly chaotic, aimless, and undefined nature of much of this protest, he nonetheless insists that

on closer observation, the violent populist responses may *themselves* reveal something about the goals of their perpetrators. More specifically, by considering the objects of populist violence one may gain insight into both the goals of the populist groups and the causes of their violent behavior.[16]

He is thus at pains to note that implicit in the attack on the chiefs, especially in their role in local tax administration and novel exploitation of customary rights, is some demand for reform of the structure of authority, if only at the local level.

In some sense, then, "populism" becomes more than just an expression of mass feelings of any sort; even for Kilson the implication is that these protests are "populist" because in one way or another they do challenge authority from a democratic perspective. As he points out, it was "only when colonial government rectified these features of local administration, mainly through the extension of democratic reforms to the rural masses, that a more orderly mode of local political change was possible." [17] Despite his earlier definition it therefore remains unclear whether he considers that *any* rural outburst can be considered populist in a useful sense or whether its use must be restricted to outbursts which contain elements of this latter dimension. It is, of course, true that any rural protest will tend to have implications for the existent structure of authority. But "protest" in Africa has taken many forms, from anti-witchcraft movements, independent churches, and riots through participation in articulate political movements. We are back to the same conundrum: how conscious does a movement have to be of the "legitimacy" question and of related implications for action in order to be usefully described as "populist." Certainly there are some aspects of this conscious sort to the politics of colonial Kenya, Tanganyika, and Sierra Leone, whether or not "populism" can be sufficiently differentiated as a term to serve in filtering them out.

Kilson's empirical work is useful in another respect, for he enriches our perspective on the ambiguous relationship between "elite" and "mass" within contemporary African society in suggestive directions; we again take up the fact of his having situated "populism," as he defines it, as merely one aspect of the broader decolonization process. In this case study, he counterpoints mass frustration and the violent "populist" forms of its release against the politics of the new, educated elite of the capital; differences of interest emerge most starkly. In fact, the elite are shown to have rather more in common with the colonial government than with their rioting fellow-countrymen.

> These [governmental and social systems] are after all the system the new elite aspires to control once colonial authorities transfer power to them. Populist behavior, in their reckoning, could hardly be permitted to threaten the transfer of this power.[18]

The advanced elements of the society use the contrast between their reasonableness and the "lawlessness" of "revolutionists" (to quote Sir Milton Margai) as a cat's paw to force the colonial power's hand; the latter willingly strikes a bargain.

In other areas circumstances dictate a more positive elite identification with such protests than seems to have been the case in Sierra Leone, though even there the language of democracy was imposed by the colonial electoral system. In fact, as we have seen, it has often been a leadership cadre itself which has generalized protest and given it any coherent demand for popular control of authority which it may have, particularly, though not exclusively, at the national level. Once again more dilemmas are raised than answers given. Is such elite consciousness of questions of legitimacy within a movement enough to earn for that movement the "populist" sobriquet; if not, how much "mass" awareness is necessary and of what kind?[19] And even where such consciousness apparently has moved the leadership cadres one must continue to ask questions concerning the sincerity of their protestations and the real degree of solidarity with the masses which is involved.[20] Evidence from the post-independence period, as for example that suggesting the growing gap between the leaders and the led, may be brought to bear in order to cast retrospective light on such questions concerning the late colonial period. It also leads to some related considerations about the place of "populism" in contemporary Africa.

It is a closely related theme that Frantz Fanon has seized upon in his important writings and any student of populism in Africa must consider the relevance of the term to his work. For he sees the whole of the movement of anticolonial nationalism through radically disabused eyes. The elite, presumptive leaders of the mass, have compromised with the values and institutional structures, economic and governmental, of the metropole, ignoring, in any real way, the potential of the countryside. Even in the case of rural risings,

> we see that even when such an occasion offers, the nationalist parties make no use at all of the opportunity which is offered to them to integrate the people of the countryside, to educate them politically and to raise the level of their struggle. The old attitude of mistrust toward the countryside is criminally evident.

This despite the fact that "in their spontaneous movements the country people as a whole remain disciplined and altruistic. The individual stands aside in favor of the community." Fanon is equally certain about the pattern that this can be said to have imposed upon present-day Africa:

> National consciousness, instead of being the all-embracing crystallization of the innermost hopes of the whole people, instead of being the immediate and most obvious result of the mobilization of the people, will be in any case only an empty shell, a crude and fragile travesty of what it might have been.[21]

Elsewhere, more prosaically and explicitly, he argues that the elite will govern the ex-colonial machine for its own ends as a "new class," and the mass will remain as it began.

In this crisis period he calls for a new kind of political party that can in fact identify with the peasantry in ways that the nationalist movements have failed to find and rouse them to an active participation in the building of the new nation. The other corollary, of course, is that, failing such changes and given the continuance of this state of "false decolonization," rural radicalism, of one kind or another, must again assert itself. There is much truth in this characterization, however much Fanon may overestimate the unity of the populace or fudge certain ambiguities as to the quality of their consciousness. It is also true that for many revolutionary students and others, both in and outside Africa, this has been read as a call to arms for a new generation in the name of "the people" —whatever its merits as description, it is providing the basis for an archetypal populist ideology.

Experience in post-colonial Africa bears out many of Fanon's observations, though rivalries among the "new class" (especially the marked assertion of claims to power by the military) have hitherto been more important than any spontaneous assertion of mass desires. However, there are already examples of the eruption of rural radicalism and if this should prove a continuing pattern the descriptive vocabulary of "populism" will again be temptingly near at hand. We might conclude this section by looking very briefly at Mulelism and the Kwilu rebellion of 1964 in the Congo; it is an example which suggests both the importance of the focus a continued preoccupation with "populism" might bring as well as the familiar ambiguities. Crawford Young and Herbert Weiss have noted the role of rural radicalism in earlier periods of Congolese development; Young, J. Gerard-Libois and others have traced the emergence of the "new class" to power there, the extent of "false decolonization." [22] What is striking to note is the degree of explicit reaction to this latter phenomenon in Kwilu. As three recent writers have noted:

> Our understanding of the Kwilu rebellion takes its clue from the way in which it was described and heralded by many persons of this province. "La Deuxième Indépendance," "the Second Independence"—they called it. This suggests, as do the materials we have examined, that the Kwilu rebellion was a revolutionary attempt to correct some of the abuses and injustices by which large segments of the population felt oppressed four years after official independence, and an effort to try once again to express and concretely realize the goals and dreams promised by the "First Independence" of 1960.

In this pursuit of "the Second Independence" there are clearly actual and important elements of popular assertion as well as an ideology, articulated by a most active and vocal leadership cadre, calling "to the oppressed class engaged in such [agricultural, manual] work to unite in brotherhood and in the revolutionary intention to overthrow the existing regime." On the other hand, like most other "mass movements" its character is not easily capsulized in a phrase:

> In sum the social distribution and the motivation of the followers and adherents of Mulelism in the Kwilu suggest far more than a banding together

of "oppressed classes" versus "exploitative classes of privilege." Tribal, political, economic, religious and magical influences of various kinds have attracted persons of many different social groups in the Kwilu to the movement (and detracted still others). In later stages of the Kwilu rebellion, when the partisans began to make wholesale use of methods of terror and violence, many other people supported the rebels primarily because they were afraid.[23]

2. Populism and the Defense Against Capitalism

We must complement the preceding analysis by turning to the other strand of "populist" debate identified in our introductory paragraphs, thus taking up the hints offered by Worsley and Arrighi. Worsley has made "populism" the crux of his analysis of the Third World (but particularly of Africa), and has in fact found it useful as a category both to describe African realities and to codify the ideological themes currently being articulated there. Within this framework the highlighting of preoccupations with authority as the defining characteristic of populism yields pride of place to a focus upon the substantive or policy considerations that stimulate political action. And, as mentioned above, this is seen to involve a critique of the capitalist mode of production and way of life felt to be encroaching upon more traditional methods of ordering society. In Worsley's view this was also the distinguishing feature of Russian Narodnikism and North American rural radicalism, both of which have been assigned the label "populist"; to this roster he would add the *total experiences* of existent African states.

We will want to investigate further Worsley's theses for they provide one of the few relatively systematic formulations of an explicitly "populist" analytical framework being brought to bear upon African realities. But initially it is useful to expand upon the whole question of the incursion of capitalism into Africa and some of the more obvious results of that process. Once again Kilson has advanced a suggestive point of view:

> The term "modernization" refers to those social relationships and economic and technological activities that move a social system away from the traditional state of affairs in which there is little or no "social mobilization" among its members. More specifically, the term "modernization" refers essentially to those peculiar socioeconomic institutions and political processes necessary to establish a cash nexus, in the place of a feudal or socially obli-

gatory system, as the primary link relating people to each other, and to the social system, in the production of goods and services and in their exchange.[24]

One may quarrel over shades of emphasis here but it remains difficult to overestimate the disruption caused by such an insertion, as the solidarities of clan, kinship, and tribe falter.

It is perhaps this added dimension of change in Africa that helps explain the seeming "irrationalities" of much rural radicalism and its apparent lack of consistent focus, as, for example, upon centers of authority. With tradition no longer a wholly stable guide, a variety of reactions and frameworks for protest (again ranging from witchcraft eradication movements to more overtly political groups) become possible. This is one of the reasons for the "unreliability" of populist or radical response under such conditions when one attempts to conceptualize them in terms of the dichotomy of Left and Right.

> Unlike the emergent African bourgeoisie, the masses are generally not themselves modernized and thus their relationship to colonial modernizers is different. But they do desire to be modernized, or at least to rationalize and clarify the complicated and disturbing situation of partial or peripheral modernization in the midst of traditional life and ways.[25]

A partial vacuum is created for leadership, armed with even perfunctory organizational techniques and an ideology, to play a politically creative role as regards this protest (if such leadership should become available). The often random impact of the cash economy also provides some key to the uneven development of consciousness which has been noted earlier. In a great many instances and in different areas of a given country traditional forms and attachments linger on in important ways, cutting across, in a far from uniform manner, the logic of modernization which Kilson has defined.

"Capitalist relations," the "cash nexus"—unfortunately many necessary subtleties of vocabulary for dealing fully with such important aspects of modernization are not available; this becomes particularly obvious when one's focus is upon the responses elicited by such developments. It is clear, however, that if we are to use the term "populism" to cover these responses we must see them as varying in conjunction with various epochs or phases in capitalist development. Thus it may seem useful to lump together Russian Narodnikism and North

American populism under the analytical rubric of "populism" because both represent largely rural responses to the onward march of "capitalism" or "modernization" or "industrialization," but it is just as important to distinguish them. The first may be schematized as a *communalistic* response, defending the traditional unit of solidarity, at the first impact of capitalism, against breakdown and the emergence of new and unwelcome forms of interpersonal relationships; the second is *individualistic* and essentially market-oriented, defending itself against the further "rationalizations" of an expansive capitalism (embodied, for example, in the threat of large-scale agriculture) and the power of centralized urban financial and marketing institutions (both national and international) that have tended to emerge over time. Worsley, as seen in our initial two linked quotations and in the rest of his book, and others tend to lump these together for too many purposes, but the mere existence of what Worsley calls "communitarian" aspects in the "individualistic" phase (involving, say, the tendency to form cooperatives) is not sufficient justification for this.

This is especially true for the African setting where some traditional, unrevolutionized communities are just now being markedly subjected to the pressures of the cash nexus at the same time that elements within individual countries, especially leadership cadres and certain economically advanced geographical areas, are facing the full implications of involvement in a complex national and international economy. Responses are scarcely likely to be uniform, even if in some sense "populist," and once again the label may merely work to obscure these differences and the full implications of uneven development.[26] Indeed, four potential elements of the rural sector might be very roughly factored out at this stage: traditional, more communal modes of agriculture; small-scale peasant farming; growing differentiation with some farmers breaking through to rather large, more capitalistic modes of production; attempts to transcend individualistic agriculture by creating novel communal modes of production, possibly on the basis of the original traditional units. The exact mix of these elements in any given instance will be a factor of some importance.

The sense of phasing may be suggestive in another way as well, for it further illumines the substance and character of much rural protest. It reminds us that, historically, such protests have arisen as much out of the rearguard actions of declining groups at major turning points of development as from the positive thrust of progressive elements. As Barrington Moore has put it, brilliantly and with a characteristically elegaic note,

> the chief social basis of radicalism has been the peasants and the smaller ar-
> tisans of the towns. From these facts one may conclude that the well-
> springs of human freedom lie not only where Marx saw them, in the aspi-
> rations of classes about to take power, but perhaps even more in the dying
> wail of a class over whom the wave of progress is about to roll. Indus-
> trialism, as it continues to spread, may in some distant future still those
> voices forever and make revolutionary radicalism as anachronistic as cunei-
> form writing.[27]

Be that as it may, our attention is at least directed once again to the probability of a most variegated membership in any so-called populist movement, and the possibility of its having rather Janus-like characteristics.

We must now grapple, more directly, with one of the main premises of this whole approach: this concerns the position to be assigned in analysis to "the impact of capitalism." To some extent "capitalism" becomes coterminous here with "modernization"—we have seen that for Kilson the latter term is virtually indistinguishable from the process of establishing the cash nexus as the central human relationship. In an African setting it has been suggested that the overriding logic of the colonial system is just this as well; though missions, for example, may educate with rather different reasons in mind, their main impact, like that of other colonial institutions, will be to hasten the replacement of traditional ties with "capitalist" ones. We have mentioned already the great importance of this force in breaking down the preexisting rural systems of Africa; if this point is pushed to the extreme, of course, most radicalism of the colonial period becomes populist almost by definition. Thus even when peasants attack the chiefs for abuses of power it is because they are part of the colonial system. And the colonial system is in turn a part of the world market system into which the colonialists are, without doubt, plunging African cultivators. Opinions will differ over this breadth of definition and its actual utility for analysis; however, this does indicate some of the broader questions which must be asked as to the range of possible supporting premises underwriting a particular usage of the term "populism" in the literature. Thus the data which is relevant will vary with such decisions as to how wide to cast one's net; to this end more thinking is obviously necessary on the real meaning and import of colonialism and neocolonialism. But there is in any case much evidence of direct and immediate reaction of a seemingly populist sort to capitalist economic forces.

Any studies of the colonial period will reveal some examples. Kilson's work on Sierra Leone is rich with data concerning resistance to hut taxes and other devices designed to pitchfork the African into a monetary relationship with the wider environment, whether as cash-cropper or migrant laborer.[28] A rather different "phase" of response is evidenced by the manner in which economic grievance against price manipulation and the like by the protectorate government (in the form of money held back for stabilization funds—and British exchange reserves) and Asian buyers supplemented Buganda protest against the chiefs. Crawford Young, writing on the Congo, has linked the genesis of widespread rural radicalism there directly to this process:

> The totality of policies pursued in the rural areas—land alienation, national parks, creation of *paysannats,* obligatory cultivation, other forced labor, relocation of villages along the roadways—imposed modernity upon the countryside. If we follow Martin Kilson in suggesting that integration into a cash nexus is the key factor in distinguishing the political transition from traditional to modern, then we may conclude that there is no parallel in tropical Africa for the degree of penetration of a modern economic-social system throughout the entire territory. If we add to this the impact, first of evangelization, then education, we find the simultaneous infusion of new norms, of new cosmologies. . . . The colonial system had in part succeeded in eliminating the subsistence economy, in methodically reconstructing an entire society by its own blueprint. . . . But at the same time, the colonial system had engendered a profound frustration at the level of the mass. This is perhaps the key to understanding the astounding politicization of a large part of the countryside in so brief a period of time.[29]

And in Tanganyika the sort of rural resistance that underwrote TANU's success in the 1950s was largely in response to the attempts by the colonial government to rationalize peasant agriculture and make it a more successful financial enterprise.

The range of responses found in the Tanganyikan case (which we discussed in Section 1) is illuminating in this context as well. For in some areas the essential thrust of resistance was against a disruption of traditional ways even if it would mean a real benefit in market terms; in others the desire was for extended control of the market by peasant growers and one result was the genesis of cooperatives. "Narodniks" and "populists" perhaps, but certainly not exactly the same. As might be expected, a similarly mixed pattern is widespread throughout Africa. Here too we might mention an additional analytical problem: that of sorting out and classifying the content of various rural outbursts. Were attacks on the chiefs in Sierra Leone launched because of abuses of authority and consequent sentiments as to legitimacy or because of the content of chiefly policies and consequent fears of "proletarianization"? Or if, as is likely, both were in some vague way involved, what sort of blend of the two defines their "populism"; logic-chopping again, yet unless the question is asked the term remains a most open-ended one.

Uneven development, such as that suggested by the Tanganyikan example above, will be present after independence, though individualistic patterns of economy will obviously continue to increase in importance; it seems likely, too, that the most articulate political actors will tend to rise from the ranks of the "individualists." Of necessity they will be more conscious of broader horizons, less traditional in their bias. Insofar as they are moved to protest and not absorbed into the existing system, their focus is more on the national level; their outbursts will once again involve some mixture of distaste for abuses of authority per se and mistrust of certain policy implications. For example, Fanon stresses both these aspects in his "populist" polemic, finding the policy dimension of his critique to lie in an anti-capitalist stance. However, this component of his "populism" is a direct response to a capitalism of a very advanced type indeed, a response to international capitalism in its neocolonial phase and to the continuing role of the ex-colonial states themselves. His characterization of African leadership is crisp:

> The national middle class discovers its historic mission: that of intermediary . . . it consists, prosaically, of being the transmission line between the nation and a capitalism, rampant though camouflaged, which today puts on the mask of neocolonialism.[30]

And this can indeed become a dimension of popular revolt against the "new class." To return to Kwilu:

> Since January 1964, the ideology of Mulelism preached in the Kwilu seems to have changed in at least one significant respect. Greater emphasis has been placed on the extent to which the Congo and its workers and

peasants have been exploited by the foreigners (who, to be sure, the doctrine continues to assert, have been aided and abetted by the present Congolese government). . . . Belgians, Americans, Portuguese, Dutch, and Germans are accused of stealing "the wealth of the Congo," "our peanuts, the fruits of our palms, our corn and our cotton . . . and the earth on which these are planted," and of sending this wealth back to their own countries.[31]

Even when such a leadership cadre assumes power and genuinely seeks to guide the country along lines considered to be "populist" in the present sense, the ambiguities already mentioned make it difficult to assess their activities. For such a leadership could be defending an image of a traditionally communal society and attempting to build an indigenous socialism on that basis; some African leaders have made this claim. Or it could be rallying growers against the threats and controls of the international economic system. But the latter preoccupation does not necessarily involve concern about decaying traditional modes of social order or even about the degree of internal class formation possibly attendant upon the articulation of an individualistic pattern of development. Thus a leader in pursuit of development might find himself the gravedigger of the traditional system, subject to attacks by what we might call "phase one populism," even while articulating an ideology which would earn him the title of a "phase two populist" and the support, presumably, of people further removed, psychologically and socially, from traditional ways. The spectre of varying levels of consciousness again haunts any ready application of the term "populism."

Similarly, the efficacy of the elite-mass distinction central to Fanon's populist perspective becomes subject to further reevaluation from a related vantage point. It may well be useful to see the present leadership elite in many African countries as the intermediaries for neocolonial economic pressures and to seek for some of the roots of popular revolt in the reaction to that fact. But one must not lose sight of the realization, already suggested by our Buganda data, that the social transformation from traditional communalists to peasant individualists does not stop there. For individualism has in turn tended to lead to rural differentiation, especially in the more advanced areas of African countries. A third level of popular consciousness is thus a likelihood as "well-to-do" farmers so motivated may increasingly find themselves in alliance with a "new class" of administrators and politicians, interpenetrating with them as beneficiaries of the existing system. The character of the "populace" must therefore be viewed dynamically. With time many of the more articulate potential protestors against various stages of capitalist development may be absorbed through their own success (with others, needless to say, being totally displaced); the nature and intensity of rural protest will be subject to great flux, dependent upon lags and spurts in the development process.

This invocation of a "third phase" of development is a further useful warning against any underestimation of the complexity of contemporary African societies, merely because they seem at least marginally less complex than many societies elsewhere. Even in pre-colonial Africa the decay of a village community remotely resembling "primitive communism" was far advanced throughout much of the continent. For example, "the formation of castes and the reinforcement of the power of the 'old men' which derived from this evolution . . . constitute the genesis of antagonistic social classes." [32] And where state systems and sophisticated pre-colonial markets had emerged this was even more the case. Similarly, the impact of capitalism in conjunction with the colonial period has been rather more sweeping in this connection than many observers care to admit.

> Modern exploitation occurs behind and through "traditional" tenurial and legal forms . . . the village is situated at the end (or beginning) of a long line of increasingly commercialized relationships. Accumulation of productive resources (land, cattle, exploitation of hired and family labor, usury, manipulation of credit, exercise of political power to economic ends, the deepening network of internal trade and transportation) all bear witness to the growing pressures of the market on the "primitive community." [33]

The various elements of the rural landscape referred to earlier can in this way be further concretized, though, as P. J. Harding cogently observes, a fully adequate "rural sociology" for Africa remains an urgent priority.

One final ambiguity must be introduced relating to the nature of the demands of participants in particular instances of protest: it becomes important to ask how conscious they are of the implications of their expressed discontent. It is legitimate to argue, as we have seen, that much protest has been stimulated by the impact of the cash economy at the heart of the colonial experience. It was observed that Young traces "frustration at the level of the mass" in the Congo to this process, for example. But he also notes the quality of initial reactions:

Symptoms of the frustration broke in the widespread outcropping of syn-
cretistic religious movements. These . . . in their millennial, apocalyptic
vision of change reflect the conviction that the colonial system was im-
pregnable, a permanent source of humiliation.[34]

We alluded to this at the start of this section; here it serves to under-
score a familiar problem. There is often little overt awareness of the reasons underlying disruption or much sophistication in the reaction to
them; the "cash nexus" or the "international economy" looming behind
the immediate grievances impinging upon farmers may well be lost to
their view. Are such examples therefore populist, and if not, at what
point would they become such? And at what level should this minimal
awareness express itself—that of the leadership, the mass, or both?

With this and other queries in mind we may finally turn to Worsley's work, but we shall find that he himself is rather loath to confront
them. As mentioned earlier, he not only identifies a "populist" ideology
as a key dimension in contemporary Africa, but he takes that ideology to
be an accurate rendering of the character of African social reality. Thus
he cites at length the various statements of African leaders as to the
"classlessness" and peculiar solidarity of African society. Of these leaders Julius Nyerere has been perhaps the most eloquent and may be
quoted as an example:

We, in Africa, have no more need of being "converted" to socialism than
we have of being "taught" democracy. Both are rooted in our own past—
in the traditional society which produced us. Modern African Socialism
can draw from its traditional heritage the recognition of a "society" as an
extension of the basic family unit.[35]

But the echoing of similar sentiments, of greater and lesser degrees of
sophistication, relating to a broad range of "socialist" issues is an easy
phenomenon to document. Worsley himself concludes: "Africa is its
peasantry, subsistence producers or cash-crop producers, but independent peasants. This is the basic fact about the social structure of the new
African states . . ." [36]

This latter fact is felt to militate against relevant differentiation; those
few slight differences are "nonantagonistic," as Sekou Touré and others
have argued. For Worsley the logic is that, in addition to the fortunate
fact that "classes are only slightly developed,"

the major antagonisms arise between the indigenous population and foreign capitalist and trading classes. . . . And even where there are class di-

visions amongst the *indigènes,* these are, in reality and not just as a matter of illusion, overriden by common solidarity vis-à-vis the alien exploiter.[37]

"Populism" in Africa, a "rural idiom in a modern world," is thus an ideology which springs from these facts and reflects the desire of such a populace for both continued classlessness and opposition to international capitalism.

Many difficulties with such a formulation will be readily apparent on the basis of our earlier discussion; the first premise as to lack of internal differentiation is especially suspect. By adopting it Worsley misses two important phenomena. Firstly, he underestimates the drama, which is in fact often the tragedy and pain, of the transformation from "subsistence producers" with a wealth of traditional involvements to "cash-crop producers" of increasingly individualist bent. This is a process still going on, and very much a dimension of certain sorts of "populist" outburst. And he misses much of the potential conflict among the interests of those already "transformed"; more accurately, this is a conflict between the transformed individuals, the nascent agricultural "entrepreneurs," and the semi-transformed, or marginal cash-croppers. In other words, the representatives of three different levels of development in the agrarian community find expression in both local and national arenas. His apotheosis of the cooperative as the ideal expression of the "natural *Gemeinschaft*" of "the indigenous society" is, in such a setting, somewhat suspect.[38] My own research on cooperatives in Tanzania, a relatively unrevolutionized society in economic terms, hints at the extent to which the more economically liberated farmers can turn these institutions to their advantage at the expense of their less "awakened" associates.[39] In addition, as regards many sorts of growing differentiation, the cooperative form of marketing and credit distribution is obviously at best a neutral agency. The danger for socialist aspirations of certain of these aspects of the "populist" perspective is therefore that it diverts attention from the question of "the mode of production" best suited to realizing socialist goals, in favor of pursuing a will-o'-the-wisp of presumptive solidarity which, even in Africa, has all too likely fled.

Similarly, Worsley's invocation of the specter of "international capitalism" is excessively schematic. Certainly he vastly overestimates the degree of awareness and the uniformity of response of the mass of the African populace, even among those most plugged into the international economy. And he provides no conceptual tools with which to differentiate the activities of leadership cadres throughout Africa in their responses, though the range of possible "bargains" that can be struck between such leaders and the external economic and political forces impinging upon them has in fact been vast. There is no need to extend the discussion, for such failures are of a piece with the general inadequacy of an approach pitched on too high a level of generality and thus seemingly incapable of fully spanning the realities of uneven development in Africa and the many ambiguities in the relationships between leaders and led which we have cited. The difficulties experienced by so interesting a scholar as Worsley in working with the concept of "populism" should again serve to sensitize the reader to the amount of pre-theorizing necessary if so potentially woolly a frame of reference as the "populist" one is to prove of any utility.

3. Populism and the Aspiration for Solidarity

This paper in its attempt to provide basic data, a survey of the literature, and some critical apparatus is already overlong. A final dimension growing out of the preceding discussion must therefore be mentioned rather more briefly. Yet it is important to note that whatever the weaknesses of the populist framework as a description of reality, ideas that may be called "populist" serve wide-ranging purposes as political rallying cries, both for those in power and for those in pursuit of power. The major aspect of such "populisms," whatever amalgam of emphases upon the "will of the people" and the "defense against capitalism" any given example may represent, is the stress upon solidarity and the unity of vast sections of the populace that it provides: a "populism" is thus a creed most attractive to leaders. In very many cases the stress upon solidarity will represent neither the real situation of the mass of the people, nor their views of that situation, as we have seen. Rather it will represent an aspiration to make a particular view as to the characteristics that unite people prevail over any continuing awareness of the elements that divide. Instead of assuming solidarity to be the actual norm, therefore, it is wiser to look to the tensions between various elements and various perspectives as defining the dynamic of any so-called populist movement.

Insofar as a populist ideology may thus represent the aspirations of people leading a particular African movement or state, it can be put to a number of uses. Here we move into the difficult region of "intent" and as mentioned previously one of the most tortured questions will be to assess the sincerity of key actors when they advance such ideas. In the African case we can perceive, in the first instance, a real measure of *self-deception* among the leadership in their use of these notions. This was, to some extent, a legacy of the anti-colonial struggle. It was then as easy for the leaders, as for subsequent scholars, to overlook the diversity of elements constituting their movements and to subsume them within the analytical frame of misleading rhetoric. Nyerere himself has pointed this out succinctly: *Uhuru* provided a lowest common denominator for people with a wide variety of views as to what the future independent state should look like.[40] It seems probable too that much of the rhetoric of "African socialism"—with its emphasis upon the automatic carry-over of traditional communalities to a modern Africa and the undifferentiated front to be presented to a rather hostile international economic environment—came rather easily to the lips of a leadership fresh to power and hot in pursuit of neutralism and a distinctive ideology.

It was only subsequently that the rather grimmer realities of induced internal differentiation and continued economic pressure from the outside began to demonstrate that choices would be rather more complex. Nyerere, for example, has moved from a reliance upon socialism as an "attitude of mind" to be underwritten automatically by the continuing impact of the traditional environment, to a clearer statement in the recent Arusha Declaration on socialism and self-reliance that it is also an "ideology" to be learned and sustained.[41] And this has led in Tanzania to a growing emphasis upon the role of the educational system as an instrument for socialist education and to certain structural reforms. This sort of populist mode of thought exemplified by the creed of "African socialism" in a good many of its specific embodiments does have a continuing legacy for those in power, however, and tends to bring with it the same limitations that we saw in our discussion of Worsley: choices concerning the internal economic structure, as for example those relating to the modes of production to be fostered and encouraged, are blurred and subtle questions as to the costs and benefits for future social structure and national self-determination of various forms of possible compromise with the international market system are set aside. Solidarity is socialism, and real social trends which may be working against meaningful solidarity are lost to view.

Other leaders are rather more conscious of the loss of focus encouraged by the high level of generalization of the populist framework.

However, as Halpern's earlier statement suggested, it can then be transformed into an aspiration for solidarity useful to the interests of post-colonial elites—this is *interested, manipulative* populism. For it has been mentioned that a populist vision can divert attention from internal contradictions; used consciously, it may thus become a most conservative force, even a cynical cover for continuing privilege. Growing differentiation either between the elite and mass or within the rural community itself, as well as subtle compromises with international capital, can be masked behind a rhetoric of homogeneity and national interest. This has in fact become the underpinning for a number of self-indulgent one-party regimes; the manner in which emergent military elites, now so prominent a force in many African states, have found this appeal to the solidarities of the countryside attractive is also striking, in spite of their absence of interest in socialist aspirations, their most compromised position vis-à-vis external capitalism,[42] and their seeming reluctance to indulge in democratic experiments. Colonel Afrifa, prominent in the Ghanaian military leadership, captures something of this note in his recent book in commenting upon pre-coup days:

> Perhaps people who lived in Accra or visited Accra would not have felt the suffering of the people who lived in the rural areas. Accra is organized in such a way as to give an impression of happiness and affluence; there were new streets and new lights, while vast areas of this country were planted with misery and suffering. I spent all my leaves at home on our farm, seeing and thinking about the helpless condition to which our people had been reduced. I became convinced that Nkrumah had failed the nation.[43]

And the extrapolation of similar themes and rationalizations for "post-liberation" society has followed apace. Where "populism" becomes the official ideology of states, more nuanced tests than ever are necessary to assess the degree of correspondence between its pretensions and the actual state of the rural masses.

There is one final possible use of "populism" which must be mentioned all too briefly here. For "populist" arguments and vocabulary that stress solidarity can be manipulated for ends beyond mere maintenance of power by ensconced elites. They can also be used as part of *a development strategy* designed to maximize the chances of economic breakthrough in a poor country and, therefore, even be intended to work for the well-being of the masses themselves. There is much skepticism about the capacities of a capitalist route to development, a decision in favor of "betting on the strong," to ensure sweeping economic success in the rural sector of backward societies. Where so many need awakening to the potentialities inherent in a new way of life, premature differentiation may merely confront the vast mass with a local political environment manipulated by "kulaks" and thus sap their interest and initiative. This is already a factor to be reckoned with in Africa. On the other hand, forced march methods seem equally unattractive. The alternative, as W. F. Wertheim suggests, may lie in "betting on the many," rallying the people "through organization and intensive education toward efficiency and self-reliance." [44] This is not an approach that assumes solidarity, but one that aspires to it and works to attain it. There are, in fact, increasingly fewer African regimes that seem willing to choose to implement such an option, for it must involve some attempt to exemplify equality and independence in a convincing manner; in addition, like most "populisms," such an aspiration carries its share of familiar ambiguities when brought up against complexities of the African context which we have seen. If implemented aggressively by a committed elite (Amilcar Cabral's "revolutionary petty bourgeoisie") it is just possible, however, that it carries a promise of progressive results beyond that of more romanticized versions postulated upon preexistent harmony and presumed egalitarianism.

Notes

1. Lloyd Fallers, "Populism and Nationalism," *Comparative Studies in Society and History*, no. 4 (July 1964).

2. Peter Worsley, *The Third World* (London, 1964); Giovanni Arrighi, "Black and White Populism in Rhodesia," unpublished seminar paper presented to the Political Science Seminar, Dar es Salaam (March 1967).

3. David Apter, *The Politics of Modernization* (Chicago, 1966), pp. 223–24.

4. Manfred Halpern, *The Politics of Social Change in the Middle East and North Africa* (Princeton, 1963), pp. 290–91.

5. D. A. Low, "The Advent of Populism in Buganda," *Comparative Studies in Society and History*, no. 4 (July 1964). See also David Apter, *The Political Kingdom in Uganda* (Princeton, 1961).

6. In a similar vein Apter speaks of populism, that is, "the people" in action, in the following terms: "Thus thwarted, populism which had led to conflict and bitterness in the past was simply provided with fresh fuel and a new

quota of grievances." The criticism of Low which follows in the text must apply equally to such a regrettable example, as it seems to me, of reification.

7. C. C. Wrigley, "The Changing Economic Structure of Buganda," in L. Fallers, ed., *The King's Men* (London, 1964), pp. 59–60.

8. C. C. Wrigley, "African Farmers in Buganda," East African Institute of Social Research, *Conference Papers* (1953).

9. Apter, *The Politics of Modernization*, p. 193.

10. Low, op. cit., p. 443.

11. The classic text here is, of course, Thomas Hodgkin's *Nationalism in Colonial Africa*; whatever revisions of emphasis may prove useful, however, this will certainly stand the test of time as an exceptionally fine contribution.

12. John Lonsdale, "Rural Resistance and Mass Political Mobilization Amongst the Luo of Western Kenya," paper delivered at the Conference of the East African Academy, September 1965; see also his *A Political History of Western Kenya* (forthcoming).

13. Lionel Cliffe, "Nationalism and the Reaction to Enforced Agricultural Improvement in Tanganyika During the Colonial Period," paper delivered at the East African Institute of Social Research Conference, Makerere, December 1964.

14. Martin Kilson, *Political Change in a West African State* (Cambridge, Mass., 1966), p. 179.

15. Ibid., p. 183.

16. Ibid., p. 186.

17. Ibid., p. 189.

18. Ibid., p. 192.

19. There is, of course, reason to be uneasy with this dichotomy between "elite" and "mass" itself. Though suggestive, it is probably not nuanced enough, particularly as regards the category of "mass," to catch gradations among the populace which can be important for many purposes. The distinction is central to the term "populism" as used by Kilson. Yet one might have liked from him some rather more detailed evidence about involvement and participation, especially in the local instances he cites, before being altogether satisfied with his use of it.

20. Richard Sklar, in his book *Nigerian Political Parties* (Princeton, 1963), is another scholar who has specifically used the term "populism," though without definition. Thus he describes the Northern Elements Progressive Union in Northern Nigeria, a party of marginal economic groups (mainly small traders and craftsmen), as populist on the basis of its ideology, which presents a radical demand for extended democracy and social reform. Its opponents, the ruling Northern People's Congress, is an "elitist" party, dominated by chiefs and wealthy bourgeois interests. Unfortunately, the former group presents the paradox of being a relatively unpopular "populist move-

ment." The NPC, by manipulating both traditional and "populist" values, has retained a considerable grip on the rural masses' loyalties, even eliciting their quite active support. Added to this there is the attendant difficulty of measuring the sincerity of protestations of NEPU leaders so long as they, unlike their rivals, remain out of power. Despite the valuable nature of his account, one wishes Sklar had confronted some of these possible ambiguities in his discussion (and his definitions) more explicitly.

21. Frantz Fanon, *The Wretched of the Earth* (New York, 1963), pp. 94, 90, 121.

22. Crawford Young, *Politics in the Congo* (Princeton, 1965); Herbert Weiss, as reported in *African Studies Bulletin* (December 1961), pp. 8–9; J. Gerard-Libois, "The New Class and Rebellion in the Congo," *Socialist Register 1966* (New York and London, 1966).

23. Renée C. Fox, Willy de Craemer, and Jean-Marie Ribeaucourt, "The Second Independence: A Case Study of the Kwilu Rebellion in the Congo," *Comparative Studies in Society and History* (October 1965), pp. 78, 96, 103. It is also true, as these same authors observe, that the ideology and organization present in the Kwilu was rather more explicit and refined than elsewhere in the Congo. The dominant characteristic of much rural radicalism is often ambiguous indeed. Crawford Young, also speaking of the Congo (op. cit., p. 231), captures an important note: "But the oppressive, omnipresent system had to go. No more taxes, no more cotton, no more census-takers, no more vaccinations, no more identity cards, no more army recruit-ers. Whether such a happy world could exist was, of course, beside the point." Another important example of something very like an outcropping of post-independence "populism" may well be, paradoxically, Dr. Banda's Malawi. According to Rev. Andrew Ross in an unpublished paper ("Tribalism or Counter-Revolution in Malawi"), Banda has been able to rally the masses (though particularly the often ill-educated local political leadership groups and the once-displaced traditional chiefs and headmen) against the more educated and well-to-do "new class" represented by his ex-ministers now in exile, and has consolidated his position on that basis.

24. Martin Kilson, "African Political Change and the Modernization Process," *Journal of Modern African Studies,* no. 4, p. 426.

25. Ibid., p. 435.

26. Arrighi (op. cit.) cites one excellent example with a ring familiar to students of North American populism but certainly to be differentiated from many other forms of rural radicalism in Africa. From the Rhodesia Front's news bulletin *Newsfront,* 20 March 1964, "The Smell of Treachery": "The world we live in is in a pretty mess. And at the root of it all are pressure groups in high finance—big dealings in big money. It is no secret that when Southern Rhodesia was first opened up, the big financiers were there, al-

ways on the alert for a good investment. Today the names of the individual financiers have changed. The smell of money has not. The financiers are all there in the ring . . . and it seems unlikely to worry the contestants if the referee, in the person of the common man, gets hit on the head in the course of the struggle. . . . The traitor is the man who safeguards investment at the expense of his country's economy."

27. Barrington Moore, Jr., *Social Origins of Dictatorship and Democracy: Lord and Peasant in the Making of the Modern World* (Boston, 1966), p. 505.

28. Kilson, *Political Change in a West African State*, lists a number of interesting examples of rural outbreaks across Africa taking place at various periods (pp. 60–61, 110–11); in general this remains a relatively uncharted area of research.

29. Young, op. cit., p. 230.

30. Fanon, op. cit., p. 124.

31. Fox et al, op. cit., p. 108.

32. "The Class Struggle in Africa," *Revolution*, no. 9, p. 30. See also Claude Meillassoux, "Essai d'interpretation du phénomène économique dans les sociétés traditionelles d'autosubsistance," *Cahiers d'etudes africaines* (December 1960). For an excellent bibliographic introduction to the problems of class in Africa, B. Verhaegen, *Bibliographie sur les classes sociales en Afrique* (Brussels, 1965).

33. P. J. Harding, review of Worsley's *The Third World*, in *Views* (Summer 1965).

34. Young, op. cit., p. 230.

35. Julius K. Nyerere, "Ujamaa: The Social Basis of African Socialism," in W. H. Friedland and C. G. Rosberg, eds., *African Socialism* (Stanford, 1964), p. 246.

36. Worsley, op. cit., pp. 162–63.

37. Ibid., p. 165.

38. Ibid.

39. John S. Saul, "Marketing Cooperatives in a Developing Country," in P. Worsley, ed., *Two Blades of Grass* (Manchester, 1971), and reprinted as "Marketing Cooperatives in Tanzania," in Lionel Cliffe and John S. Saul, eds., *Socialism in Tanzania: Politics and Policies* (Nairobi, 1972), vol. II.

40. See Julius K. Nyerere, *Freedom and Unity* (Dar es Salaam, 1966).

41. *The Arusha Declaration and TANU's Policy on Socialism and Self-Reliance* (Dar es Salaam, 1967).

42. For a useful perspective on this phenomenon, see Roger Murray, "Militarism in Africa," *New Left Review* (July–August 1966).

43. A. A. Afrifa, *The Ghana Coup* (London, 1966), p. 95.

44. W. F. Wertheim, "Betting on the Strong," in his collection of essays *East–West Parallels* (The Hague, 1964), pp. 276–77.

5

Labor Supplies in Historical Perspective:
A Study of the Proletarianization
of the African Peasantry in Rhodesia

Giovanni Arrighi

In an article that was to become a classic of modern development theory,[1] W. A. Lewis proposed a two-sector model of labor reallocation from a low productivity "subsistence sector" to a high productivity "capitalist sector." In the former all individuals have a right to receive means of subsistence in quantities determined by custom and, in the last instance, by average productivity in the sector in question. In addition, Lewis postulates that in this sector there is a surplus of labor ("disguised unemployment") in the sense that part of the labor force could be withdrawn without causing a reduction in total output, or at least without causing a reduction greater than the amount of means of subsistence customarily allocated to them. Under these conditions, individuals are assumed to be prepared to leave the subsistence sector and seek employment in the capitalist sector when the wage rate in the latter is some 30 to 50 percent higher than the conventional subsistence income in the former.[2] Since productivity in the capitalist sector is postulated to be sufficiently high to make the payment of the above wage rate consistent with the rate of profit that employers expect in order to undertake production, the capitalist sector is said to enjoy "unlimited" supplies of labor in the sense that, at that level of wages, practically everybody in the subsistence sector is prepared to enter wage employment.

Provided that average productivity in the subsistence sector does not increase, pushing up the conventional subsistence income, the capitalist sector can therefore expand indefinitely without an increase in wages

This article was originally published as Chapter 2 of *Sviluppo economico e sovrastrutture in Africa* (Milan, 1969). It was first published in English in *The Journal of Development Studies*, no. 3 (April 1970). Reprinted by permission.

becoming necessary to attract growing amounts of labor. In this way, the per capita income of workers and peasants remains constant and the investable surplus increases absolutely and as a proportion of aggregate output. Since Lewis further postulates that the entire surplus is always reinvested in a way that increases the demand for labor, the process continues until the "surplus of labor" in the subsistence sector disappears.

Lewis points out, however, that wages may rise before the process is completed, thus slowing down capitalist accumulation, if average productivity in the subsistence sector increases, something that may happen for any of the following reasons: (1) Because the expansion of the capitalist sector is rapid enough to reduce the *absolute* population in the subsistence sector; (2) because of technological progress in the subsistence sector; and (3) because the terms of trade turn against the capitalist sector (assuming that the subsistence sector supplies foodstuff and raw material to the capitalist sector). As we shall see, the last-named possibility is of special interest to our analysis.

The above theory has inspired a good many studies of concrete development experiences. One such study is W. J. Barber's interpretation of the development of the African wage labor force in Rhodesia. Barber distinguishes four stages of such development:

1. To begin with, the indigenous African economy is organized so as to be self-sufficient: real incomes and output are low and tastes are modest.[3]

2. The second stage is inaugurated by the introduction of the money economy from outside. Because of the narrow horizons of the traditional society, the response of the indigenous peoples to "unfamiliar" opportunities for increasing their real incomes may be "delayed." Historically, "a prodding from the tax collector has been required."[4]

3. "After a period of adjustment," however, the indigenous peoples have attempted to acquire cash either through the sale of agricultural surpluses or through the sale of their labor. The latter is attractive only when it increases the total real income—in other words, it must supplement more than it subtracts from the income achieved through agricultural production.[5] This opportunity cost of labor is determined by the social organization of production in the indigenous economies. According to Barber, the customary division of labor was such that the male's role was essentially one of providing at periodical intervals the development works of the community, besides hunting and the care of cattle,

while most of the routine tasks in peasant agriculture were the lot of women.[6] Development works were undertaken periodically, so that rather than "general disguised unemployment," as postulated by Lewis in his model, there was "periodic disguised unemployment" of male labor in the sense that individual members of the family productive unit could be withdrawn for at least a full annual cycle without any sacrifice in indigenous agricultural production. Barber assumes that the proportion of the total adult male population required to maintain the integrity of the indigenous economy is, and has always been, 50 percent. The capitalist sector could therefore expand without inducing an increase in real wages until its African labor requirements rose above this proportion. Up to the mid-1940s the employment of extraterritorial African workers prevented the proportion of able-bodied indigenous males in wage employment from rising above 45 percent.[7] Consequently, in the period 1929–1945, while real wages showed a tendency to decline, the volume of African employment continued to expand.[8]

4. The fourth stage is attained when the demand for African labor of the capitalist sector rises above 50 percent of the total adult male population. An expansion of the supply to meet this level of demand implies a fall in the agricultural output of the indigenous family and therefore the supply of labor ceases to be perfectly elastic:

> To attract additional indigenous workers, . . . the employer in the money economy [is] obliged to offer a real wage which [offsets] the loss in the real income of the family in indigenous agriculture, and to provide a further increment to the real wage sufficient to induce the African worker to make this break with his accustomed way of life.[9]

This stage, which Barber calls "quasi-full employment," was, according to him, attained in the late 1940s when the proportion of able-bodied males claimed by wage employment reached the 50 percent mark. He then finds confirmation of this in the fact that, after 1950, African real wages began to rise.[10]

As we shall presently see, this interpretation of the development of the African wage labor force is questionable on a number of grounds. Before we proceed, however, it is interesting to point out some general assumptions which underlie Lewis's and Barber's analyses. These authors conceive of the underdevelopment of the African peoples as an original state which the development of a capitalist sector gradually eliminates. The development of capitalism thus emerges as an ultimately *beneficial and rationalizing influence* notwithstanding the fact (acknowledged by Barber) that, over long periods, African workers and peasants derived little, if any, advantage from it. Moreover, the development of capitalism is conceived of not only as an ultimately beneficial process but also as a *spontaneous process* in the sense that it is induced exclusively, or almost exclusively, by "market forces" (i.e., the free choice of individuals on the market place) with no or little role assigned to open or concealed forms of compulsion.[11]

The purpose of this essay is to show that neither Barber's interpretation of the development of an African wage labor force in Rhodesia nor his and Lewis's general presumptions concerning the relationship between underdevelopment and the development of capitalism find much supporting evidence in the Rhodesian experience. At the same time an attempt will be made to organize the above critique into an alternative theoretical explanation of the development of the African wage labor force in Rhodesia.

1

The first of Barber's assumptions that is inconsistent with the facts is that up to the late 1940s a situation of excess supply obtained in the labor market. Before 1920, owing to the combination of a relatively sluggish response of indigenous Africans to wage employment opportunities and unreliability of extraterritorial sources of labor, acute shortages of African labor were normal in periods of rising demand, i.e., 1896–1903, 1905–1911, and 1916–1919.[12] Thus, the situation in the African labor market of the late 1940s and early 1950s was no more one of "quasi-full employment" than that obtaining during the abovementioned periods. Moreover, Barber's assumption that the situation of "quasi-full employment" lasted through the late 1950s, when African real wages continued to rise, is equally unfounded.[13] In conclusion, far from starting off from a situation of normal labor abundance and ending up with one of normal labor shortage, the Rhodesian capitalist sector seems to have moved in the opposite direction.

Nor did real wages rise for the first time in the late 1940s. In the period 1896–1903 they rose markedly,[14] and if thereafter they became sticky upward and flexible downward—so that in 1922, after fifteen years of predominant labor shortage, they were lower than in 1904—the reason cannot be sought in the operation of market forces. The different behavior of African wages before and after 1903 must instead be traced to the structural changes that occurred in the Rhodesian capitalist sector during the 1903–1904 crisis, a discussion of which is beyond the scope of this study.[15] Suffice it to say that, prior to that crisis, production was predominantly undertaken with a view to the speculative gains which a small group of promoters and financiers could reap by floating companies on the London financial markets. What mattered was the working of gold deposits *irrespective of the costs involved.* Profitability considerations did not therefore hamper the competitive upward pressure on wages resulting from the shortage of labor. The realization of the low profitability of Rhodesian enterprises, under existing cost conditions, led in 1903 to the collapse of the Rhodesian speculative boom in London and precipitated the abovementioned crisis. The subordination of production to speculation ceased, and efforts were directed at reducing costs in order to enhance the profitability of those enterprises which had survived the crisis. One of the main aspects of this economy drive was to undertake the monopsonistic organization of the African labor market.[16]

This situation was at the root of what Bettison has aptly called "the tradition of a subsistence wage":[17] market mechanisms were largely discarded in the determination of wages, and the real wage rate came to be customarily fixed at a level that would provide for a subsistence of a *single* worker while working in the capitalist sector and a small margin to meet the more urgent of the *cash* income requirements of his family (which continued to reside in the peasant sector). The problem then became one of expanding the supply of labor to match demand at this customary level of wages. Like British capitalists in earlier times, Rhodesian employers, "when they spoke of plenty in connection with supply, [they] had in mind not only quantity but also price." [18] Thus, as changes in wages were no longer to be the equilibrating factor in the labor market, political mechanisms became of crucial importance in closing gaps between supply and demand, and they must therefore figure prominently in any interpretation of the development of the African wage labor force.

Since Barber ignores political mechanisms, the shortcomings of his analysis are immediately apparent. It might be argued, however, that the labor shortages of the first three decades of white rule in Rhodesia were due to a "delay" in African response to market opportunities for increasing their incomes and that extra-economic factors played the role of leading the African peoples on to the "path of a rational behavior." Once this had been attained, an excess of supply over demand appeared in the labor market and Barber's model became applicable. No evidence is, however, to be found to substantiate the assumption of so long a "delay" in African response to market opportunities. It is possible that in the 1890s the African peoples showed some "unfamiliarity" with such opportunities, but by the turn of the century this was no longer the case. Prior to 1904 European farming in Rhodesia was insignificant and the African peasantry supplied the bulk of the foodstuffs required by the mines. In 1903, for example, it was estimated that the annual amount received by Africans for sale of grain, other produce, and stock was in the order of £350,000,[19] and there is much evidence that trade with the African population was at the time the most, if not the only, profitable activity carried out by the Europeans.[20] Further, when the development of European mixed farming and ranching created a demand for African-owned cattle, Africans were ready to sell them in large numbers.[21] Though mainly limited to the sale of what may be called "traditional" produce (grain, cattle, and beer), African participation in the produce market also took other forms: the production for the market of green vegetables, potatoes, wheat, groundnuts, and tobacco, for example, was either introduced or expanded, and the practice developed in the mining areas of deriving a regular income from hiring out bullocks to the mines for purposes of transport.[22] And as we shall see, Africans were equally prompt in investing and innovating in response to market opportunities.

As regards African response to opportunities for increasing their incomes through the sale of labor-time, the first point that has to be made is that there is no evidence to support the view that 50 percent of the male labor force was in "disguised unemployment." Among the Shona peoples (who, at the end of the last century, represented over two-thirds of the African population in Rhodesia) and among lower-caste Ndebele,[23] men were not only in charge of development works, hunting, and the care of cattle. They also helped the women in cultivating the land, especially at planting and harvesting time, and were in charge of a number of nonagricultural productive activities (weaving, net-making, iron-working, etc.) which must have absorbed a non-negligible amount of labor-time until they were supplanted by the importation of capitalist manufactures.[24] In addition, we should not ignore the fact that the labor-time of African males was not only absorbed by material production but also by activities which, though unproductive, were socially necessary. The point has been emphasized (perhaps overemphasized) by J. van Velsen:

> There are several fallacies [in the notion of "leisure"]. Those who hold this notion seem to think that unless people are working manually they are not using their time gainfully. . . . If a similar view were adopted for an industrialized European society all judges listening to cases in court, all bankers or business managers concluding important contracts, . . . and all those who are not actually using muscle power or even pushing a pen would be considered to be enjoying "leisure" instead of working for their livelihood. This would, of course, be wholly unrealistic. It is equally unrealistic to think that people in tribal societies are indulging in unprofitable leisure unless they are handling a hoe or an axe or are doing otherwise physical labor. When men and women are sitting together the chances are that they are not just wasting their time in idle talk but are in fact settling a dispute over, say, garden boundaries or are discussing the desirability of moving the village to a better site, or, again, are arguing about the merits of some new farming techniques. . . . These are *activities* which vitally affect the welfare of individuals or the community as a whole.
>
> In literate societies the knowledge of new laws, of new farming methods, of market trends, of new possibilities for earning money, and so forth, is very largely spread through the written word. . . . But in societies where many people cannot read such information is spread through the spoken word.[25]

In view of the above, we cannot assume that much "disguised unemployment" existed in traditional African societies, though it can be safely assumed that a certain amount of *seasonal underemployment* existed among both Shona and Ndebele.

As this study will attempt to demonstrate, "disguised unemployment" in Barber's or Lewis's sense was itself the result of the process of capitalist development which steadily restructured and eventually disrupted "traditional" African societies. The very imposition of white rule on the Shona and Ndebele peoples, which opened up the territory to capitalist penetration, was a first cause of the appearance of some "disguised unemployment." For the Pax Britannica and the pillage of the African people that followed the establishment of white rule threw Ndebele men belonging to the upper castes into what may be called a state of "structural underemployment." While the imposition of the Pax Britannica prevented them from engaging in martial pursuits, the expropriation from cattle and land prevented them from fully reallocating their labor-time to productive activities *within* the peasant sector (care of cattle and cultivation of the land).[26] The type of underemployment that the imposition of white rule induced among the vast majority of the African people (lower-caste Ndebele and all the Shona) was, on the other hand, of a very different nature. The imposition of the Pax Britannica released the labor-time (and means of production) previously allocated by the Shona to production of the surplus appropriated by the Ndebele (tribute and raids) and to a variety of defense preparations. It also released the labor-time of lower-caste Ndebele which used to be absorbed by the labor services exacted by upper-caste Ndebele. At the same time, expropriation of land did not *immediately* restrict the quantity of land available to this section of the population because, as we shall see, they were generally allowed to remain on their ancestral lands. Moreover, they were also less affected by the expropriation of cattle because of the smaller quantities involved in the expropriation and because of the less central role played by cattle in their economies.[27]

It follows that, in the short run and in as far as the vast majority of the African population (i.e., excluding upper-caste Ndebele) was concerned, the imposition of white rule did not lead to a structural disequilibrium between means of production and (given techniques, size of population, tastes, and wants) subsistence requirements of the peasant producers and their families. As a consequence, if some labor-time remained unutilized *within the peasant sector* ("disguised unemployment"), this was not due to a shortage of means of production relative to the total labor-time available, but rather to seasonal variations in agricultural production or to a *lack of incentives* to apply such labor-time to agricultural production;[28] and if "little" labor-time was sold on the labor market, this was more likely to be due to the fact that the effort-price of cash income earnable through the sale of produce was lower than that earnable through wage employment, rather than to an alleged lack of African response to market opportunities for increasing their incomes.[29]

Most contemporary observers did in fact agree that the effort-price of participation in the produce market was far lower than that in the labor market. For example, in 1903 it was estimated that the latter was generally three times as large as the former.[30] The conclusion that the behavior of the African peoples during these early days was consistent with an allocation of labor-time aimed at increasing their incomes is further warranted by the existence of marked seasonal variations in the supply of African labor and by discrepancies in the Ndebele and Shona rates of participation in the labor market.[31] While the seasonal variations in labor supplies show that, to the extent that there existed underemployment in the peasant economies, Africans were ready to enter wage employment to supplement their incomes, the greater participation of Ndebele men in the labor market shows that the more "structural" in character the disguised unemployment (and therefore the lesser the possibilities of absorbing all labor-time within the peasant sector) the greater the amount of labor-time allocated to wage employment.

Besides misinterpreting the situation in the labor market at the initial and terminal points of the process of formation of the African wage labor force, Barber misses some significant tendencies in African response to wage employment opportunities. These tendencies can be perceived by comparing the relationship between changes in real wages and changes in the rate of African participation in the labor market at different points in time. A first set of relevant data has been collected in Figure 1, which shows trends of three crucial variables during the period 1904–1945. These variables are:

1. The rate of African participation in the labor market (Li/Ni), i.e., the ratio of the average number of indigenous African males in wage employment at any given time (Li) to the total number of indigenous African males over fourteen years of age (Ni).

2. The wage employment/population ratio (L/Ni), i.e., the ratio of the total number of African males (indigenous and extraterritorial) in wage employment (L) to the total number of indigenous African males over fourteen.

3. The proportion of extraterritorial Africans in the total African labor force (Lf/L).

Variations in the first ratio may be taken to reflect changes in the responsiveness of the indigenous population to wage employment opportunities, *provided that their participation in the labor market was not unduly restrained by difficulties of obtaining employment.* This condition can be assumed to have been fulfilled when the Li/Ni ratio was rising or when there was a labor shortage. For this reason we shall limit our inter-temporal comparisons to five periods: 1904–1911, 1915–1922,[32] 1922–1926, 1932–1938, and 1939–1943.

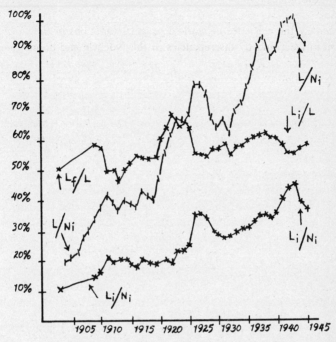

Figure 1: Trends in the African Labor Market, 1904–1945

Source: Derived from *Annual Report of the Chief Native Commissioners* and *Annual Report of the Chamber of Mines of Rhodesia.*

The scanty evidence on money wages and costs of living during these five periods has been collected in Table 1.[33] Though the data, especially those in brackets, are not sufficiently reliable to form the basis of accurate estimates of the magnitude of the changes in African real wages, they are satisfactory for our purposes, namely for identifying the *direction of change* of real wages and, secondarily, for a rough assessment of their comparative magnitude. Taking into account the fact that the European cost of living index shown in the table grossly underestimates the rise in African cost of living between 1914 and 1922 and between 1939

Table 1

African Money Wages and Cost of Living Indexes for Selected Years

Year	Average wages			Cost of living indexes	
	Mining		Agriculture	European cost of living (food, fuel, and light) 1914 = 100	African imports price index 1914 = 100
	including rations s.	excluding rations s.	including rations s.		
1904	46/9 (a)	39/–(a)			148 (g)
1911		(32/–) (b)			94 (g)
1914		(28/–) (b)		100 (f)	100 (g)
1922	45/– (c)	(28/–) (b)	20/– (c)	114 (f)	195 (g)
1926			21/8 (d)	109 (f)	(168) (g)
1932		25/10 (e)		94 (f)	
1938	32/6 (e)	23/6 (e)		93 (f)	
1939	34/– (e)	24/11 (e)		94 (f)	
1943	42/– (e)	27/5 (e)		112 (f)	

Notes and sources: (a) *Annual Report of the Chamber of Mines of Rhodesia.* (b) Estimated by the author on the basis of information on changes in African wages given in the following: *Annual Report of the Chief Native Commissioners; Annual Report of the Chamber of Mines of Rhodesia;* B.S.A. Co., *Directors' Report and Account* (various years); Southern Rhodesia, *Report of the Native Affairs Committee of Enquiry, 1911;* Southern Rhodesia, *Report of the Cost of Living Committee, 1921.* (c) "Natural Resources" (summary of lecture delivered by Mr. L. Cripps before the Rhodesian Scientific Association) in *Official Yearbook of the Colony of Southern Rhodesia,* no. 1 (1924). (d) Southern Rhodesia, *Report on Industrial Relations in Southern Rhodesia by Professor Henry Clay,* 1930. (e) *Economic and Statistical Bulletin of Southern Rhodesia,* II, 13; VI, 8; VI, 10; XIV, 4; and XIV, 5. (f) *Official Yearbook of the Colony of Southern Rhodesia,* no. 3 (1932); *Official Yearbook of Southern Rhodesia,* no. 3 (1952). (g) Calculated by the author on the basis of data taken from the *Annual Report of the Controller of Customs.* The commodities included in the index are those which according to the controller of customs were purchased by Africans and for which physical quantities were available, i.e., biscuits, coffee, preserved fish, rice, sugar, candles, matches, soap, boots and shoes, hats and caps, hoes and picks. The weights used in the calculation of the index are not based on the amounts spent on them by the African population, about which we have no information, but on the value of imports (which includes consumption on the part of Europeans).

and 1943,[34] the figures of Table 1 show that African real wages decreased rapidly in the two periods 1904–1922 and 1939–1943, that they increased moderately fast in the two periods 1904–1911 and 1922–1926, and that they probably decreased (or at best remained constant) in the period 1932–1938. In Table 2 (on the next page), these data on real wages are juxtaposed to the rate of African participation in the labor market for the corresponding periods.

The most striking fact emerging from this table is the changing relationship between the two variables. A few inter-temporal comparisons will illustrate the point. A roughly similar increase in real wages was associated with a moderate increase in the Li/Ni ratio in 1904–1911 but with an exceptionally large increase in 1922–1926; a roughly similar decrease in real wages was associated with a constant Li/Ni ratio in 1914–1922 but with a large increase thereof in 1939–1943. Conversely, a moderate increase in the Li/Ni ratio was associated with rising real wages in 1904–1911, but with falling (or at best constant) real wages in 1932–1939; a large increase in the Li/Ni ratio was associated with rising wages in 1922–1926 but with a fall in real wages in 1939–1943.

These comparisons suggest that the conditions affecting the supply of African labor did not change once and for all after an initial "prodding from the tax collector," as Barber puts it, but that they altered *continuously* and in the direction of greater responsiveness to wage employment opportunities. Moreover, while before 1922 African participation in the labor market did not increase in periods of falling real wages, after that year it always increased irrespective of whether real wages were falling, rising, or remaining constant. It is hardly necessary to emphasize that these phenomena have to be taken into full account in our analysis of the development of the African wage-labor force.

2

We have seen that available evidence does not support the view that the low rate of African participation in the labor market during the early days of white rule was due to an alleged lack of response on their part "to unfamiliar opportunities for increasing their real incomes" as Barber and others have presumed.[35] The reasons for this low rate must be sought elsewhere, namely in the "discretionary" character of African

Table 2

Changes in the Rate of African Participation in the Labor Market
(Li/Ni) and Changes in Real Wages, Selected Periods

Period	Change in Li/Ni (yearly average)	Change in Real Wages (increase: +; decrease: −; no change: =.)
1904–1911	+1	+
1915–1922	0	−
1922–1926	+4	+
1932–1938	+1	− (or =)
1939–1943	+3	−

Notes and sources: The data of the first column have been derived from Fig. 1 and represent the average yearly increase in the percent values of the ratio. The increase in the Li/Ni ratio for the period 1904–1911 has been adjusted downward (from 1.5 to 1) for two reasons: (1) because in 1911 "abnormal" extra-economic pressure was exercised on the African people to induce them to seek wage employment; and (2) because in this period there was a reduction in the rate of participation of Rhodesian Africans in the South African labor market so that the increase in Li/Ni recorded in Rhodesia partly reflected a "territorial shift," rather than an overall increase, in African participation in the labor market. Available data do not permit an accurate assessment of this "territorial shift," but estimates given in the *Annual Report of the Chief Native Commissioners* indicate that the proportion of Rhodesian African males working in South Africa declined from 3.9 percent in 1905 to 2.7 percent in 1910.

participation in the money economy and in the low comparative effort-price of income earnable through the sale of produce.

Let us distinguish between "necessary" and "discretionary" material requirements of a society—the distinction being based on custom and habits as well as physiological criteria. We may then assume that in these early days, and with the exception of some sections of the Ndebele people, there existed a rough balance between means of production and means of subsistence (i.e., the "necessary" requirements of the population) within the peasant sector of the Rhodesian economy. Participation in the money economy, *whatever its form,* was therefore "discretionary" in the sense that it was not essential to the satisfaction of the subsistence requirements of the African population. In such a situation the stimulus to participate in the money economy is obviously weaker than in a situation in which the sale of labor-time and/or of produce fulfills subsistence requirements. This is a factor, however, that affects the *intensity* rather than the *form* of participation in the money economy. That is to say, whether such participation is "discretionary" or "necessary" is something that affects more the *total* amount of labor-time allocated to it than the *distribution* of this total amount between wage employment and production for exchange. This distribution, on the other hand, will be mainly determined, as previously noted, by the comparative effort-price of cash income obtainable from the two forms of participation.

We have already seen that the comparatively small effort-price of cash income earnable through the sale of produce was in fact the main factor restraining African participation in the labor market. We may now add that this factor was in turn traceable to the lack of population pressure on the land and the high prices paid for African produce. The latter is of particular significance because it highlights one aspect of the relationship between the development of capitalist agriculture and the development of the African wage-labor force. Lewis mentions this relationship by way of qualification of his theory outlined at the beginning of this article:

> The increase in the size of the capitalist sector relatively to the subsistence sector may turn the terms of trade against the capitalist sector (if they are producing different things) and so force the capitalist to pay workers a higher percentage of their product, in order to keep their real incomes constant. . . .
>
> If the capitalists are investing in plantation agriculture side by side with their investment in industry we can think of the capitalist sector as self-contained. The expansion of this sector does not then generate any demand for anything produced in the subsistence sector, and there are therefore no terms of trade to upset [our theory].[36]

Thus in Rhodesia, the expansion of the mining industry and of tertiary activities without a comparable development of capitalist agriculture generated a demand for, and tended to raise the price of, African produce, and this discouraged African participation in the labor market at the wage rate fixed by "the tradition of the subsistence wage."

Against this background, and bearing in mind that political rather than market mechanisms were to be the equilibrating factor in the African labor market, let us see what measures were taken by the government to eliminate the labor shortage.

Forced wage labor was an obvious device for closing gaps between supply and demand in the labor market and it was widely resorted to in the early days of settlement:

> Native Commissioners or Inspectors of Police called on the various chiefs and headmen, informing the villagers that a certain percentage must work for the white man in return for a minimum wage of 10s. per month as well as board and lodging; these orders were enforced by African policemen who often exceeded their authority.[37]

This practice was one of the causes of the African rebellions of 1896–1897 and was subsequently abandoned, at least in its crudest forms, in order to avoid a costly repressive apparatus. But even as late as the early 1920s "a hint from the Native Commissioner to some of the headmen [would] usually bring out the desired number of young ones to work."[38] In 1908–1909 a "hint" of this sort increased the supply of labor in two districts by 50 percent, and the abnormally high rate of African participation in the labor market recorded in 1911 was largely due to pressures of this sort.[39]

Measures of a different order—less risky and costly and more permanent in their impact—were necessary if capitalist development in Rhodesia was not to be seriously restrained. Taxation seemed at first to provide the solution as it would reduce the "discretionary" nature of African participation in the money economy. A hut tax of 10s. for every adult male and 10s. extra for each wife exceeding one was imposed as early as 1894, and ten years later it was replaced by a poll tax of £1 on each male over sixteen and 10s. upon each wife exceeding one. When the hut tax was first introduced, payment in kind was accepted, but it was soon discouraged in order to induce Africans to earn their tax by wage labor.[40]

Taxation had, however, some shortcomings. For taxation, by not discriminating between incomes obtained from sale of produce and incomes obtained from the sale of labor-time, did not alter the discrepancy between the effort-prices of the two types of income. It could therefore, as it did in many instances, simply lead to the extension of the acreage under cultivation and/or to more intensive cultivation of the land. This was not, of course, the case in those areas which were located far from the centers of capitalist development (mines, towns, and lines of communication) and were not reached by traders. For Africans living in these areas the only way to earn money to pay taxes was to sell their labor-time.[41]

Our previous discussion of the causes of low African participation in the labor market suggests that those measures which would significantly increase the effort-price of participation in the produce market would also be the most effective ones in solving the labor problem. Land expropriation was undoubtedly the major such measure though, as we shall see, its effects materialized in a more complex way than is commonly assumed. By 1902 the African people had been expropriated from more than three-quarters of all the land in the country.[42] This expropriation did not, however, mean an immediate restriction upon the land resources available to the African peasantry, for they were generally allowed to remain on their ancestral lands upon payment of rent or commitment to supply labor services. Roder has remarked the "feudal" nature of these relations:

> The moment a man had pegged his farm, he regarded the African villagers on it as his serfs, who would have to work for him. The chief means of mobilizing this pool of labor in the first years was the *sjambok* or hippo-hide whip, and after 1908 labor agreements which committed tenants to work several months, usually three, for the privilege of remaining on their ancestral land.[43]

In 1909 the British South Africa Company (B.S.A. Co.) imposed a rent charge on the so-called unalienated land (i.e., land which had been appropriated, but not yet sold or granted to individuals or companies, by the B.S.A. Co.) so that all Africans residing outside the Native Reserves came to pay a rent.[44] In addition to rents and labor services, European landowners exacted various fees (grazing fees, dipping fees, etc.) which were so exorbitant that "within a few years [they went] far toward paying the purchase price of the farm." [45]

The reasons why Africans were not removed from their ancestral lands at this stage are not far to seek. As the Native Affairs Committee of Enquiry (1911) pointed out, "It would be very shortsighted policy to remove these natives to reserves, as their services may be of great value to future European occupants." Land was abundant and labor scarce, so that land with no labor on it had little value. That is to say, the establishment of semi-feudal relations was the most effective short-term solution to the labor problem. Also valuable to the capitalist economy were the rents and other payments exacted from African tenants. Quite apart from the financial contribution that they made to the nascent European agriculture, companies and individuals who had acquired vast tracts of land for speculative purposes and who were still influential with the government welcomed this source of revenue which did not depend on development efforts on their part. Another reason why the administration allowed Africans to reside on expropriated land was in fact that the capitalist sector continued to rely heavily upon African supplies of produce, and any reduction thereof would have seriously hit the dominant mining interests. The development of capitalist agriculture had therefore a double significance for the expansion of African labor supplies, for it would at one and the same time eliminate the terms-of-trade effect of capitalist development and free the hand of the administration in expelling Africans from expropriated land, thus further raising the *effort-price* of their participation in the produce market.[46]

Market forces were, however, hampering the establishment of capitalist agriculture on a sound economic footing: the low opportunity cost to the African peasantry of supplying surpluses of "subsistence produce," the scarcity of cheap wage labor,[47] and the smallness of the financial resources at the command of would-be European farmers, were all factors that made the latter's economic position precarious. Moreover, capitalist agriculture was a highly risky enterprise. For the market was relatively small and prices, being mainly determined by African production of marketable surpluses, fluctuated widely from season to season.[48] It is not surprising, therefore, that the white settlers chose the more profitable opportunities offered by trading, transport work, and various occupations connected with mining, construction, commerce, and speculation rather than farming. Prior to the 1903–1904 crisis, those Europeans who were interested in agriculture were either part-time farmers devoting themselves to more profitable activities or, as was the case with many Afrikaaners who had trekked to Rhodesia, they were subsistence cultivators indistinguishable (by style of life, techniques of production, and crops cultivated) from the African peasantry.[49] Even during the season 1903–1904, when European agriculture had begun to develop, there were only 948 holdings in occupation by Europeans who accounted for approximately 5 percent of the total acreage under cultivation and for less than 10 percent of the total marketed output.[50]

Under these circumstances, the "take-off" of European agriculture after the 1903–1904 crisis could only be brought about by other than market mechanisms. The establishment of semi-feudal relations, discussed above, was one such mechanism, probably the main one; while the exaction of labor services remedied the labor shortage, rents and fees were an important source of finance for capital accumulation. It also became customary for European landowners to market their tenants' produce, and often that of neighboring peasants as well, a practice that must have effectively prevented Africans, or traders on their behalf, from underselling European producers.

State power was brought to bear in other ways upon the strengthening of the white farmers' competitive position. In 1904 there occurred a major shift of the burden of taxation, i.e., from the settlers and foreign capital on to the African population (see Table 3), and while government expenditure on African agriculture remained negligible for at least another decade, expenditure on European agriculture soon became one of the major items in the government budget.

Table 3
Distribution of Public Revenue by Sources

	Period April 4, 1901 to March 31, 1904 (yearly average)		Year ended March 31, 1905	
	thousand £	% of total	thousand £	% of total
Paid by Africans	122.1	26.8	187.6	41.4
Paid by non-African residents	150.1	33.0	122.8	27.1
Paid by foreign capital	87.3	19.1	67.1	14.8
Services rendered (posts and telegraph, land sales, etc.)	96.4	21.1	75.7	16.7
Total	455.9	100.0	453.2	100.0

Source: Annual Report of the Administrator of Southern Rhodesia.

A Department of Agriculture was set up in 1903 to assist European agriculture, and four years later the B.S.A. Co. established central farms, where settlers could acquire a knowledge of local farming before taking up their own holdings. Subsequently the technical work carried out by the Department of Agriculture greatly expanded: it distributed various kinds of improved seeds and plants; it advised on the cultivation of new crops; it carried out various experiments in collaboration with individual growers; it opened an experimental farm at Gwebi; it assisted in water boring works by providing equipment and expert advice at cost price.[51] White farmers also received significant financial assistance at subsidized interest rates.[52]

In the next section we shall analyze the process whereby the development of capitalist agriculture contributed to the solution of the labor problem and we shall see that that process took roughly two decades. In the meantime, however, such development, by increasing the demand for labor, intensified the shortage. The role played by the recruitment of extraterritorial African workers in making possible rapid capitalist development during a transitional period can therefore hardly be exaggerated. Since capitalist development in the southern African subcontinent generated demand only for the labor and not for the produce of the African peasantries of the northern territories, the extension of taxation to such territories, the recruiting activities of various government and private agencies, and, subsequently, the spreading of new tastes and wants, soon turned Northern Rhodesia (Zambia) and later Nyasaland (Malawi) and Mozambique into reservoirs of cheap labor which enabled Rhodesian employers to overcome the labor shortage of the first two decades of this century: as shown in Figure 1, the proportion of extra-territorial Africans in the total African wage labor force rose from less than 50 percent in 1904 to 68 percent in 1922.

3

In analyzing the process whereby the sale of labor-time became a necessity for the African population of Rhodesia, attention must be focused upon two tendencies: (1) the transformation of "discretionary" cash requirements into "necessary" requirements; and (2) an upward tendency in the effort-price of African participation in the produce market resulting from a growing disequilibrium between means of production (mainly land) and population in the peasant sector and a weakening of the peasantry's competitive position on the produce market.[53]

1. The introduction of the compulsory payments discussed in the previous section was the main factor making necessary African participation in the money economy. In addition, there were forces which worked in the same direction in a more gradual way. As mentioned, the terms "necessities" or "subsistence" are not to be understood in an exclusively physiological sense: people get used to what they consume and "discretionary" consumption items can, with the mere passage of time, become necessities whose consumption is indispensable.[54]

In *periods of rising incomes* the subsistence requirements of consumers tend to increase, for *new* goods are added to their budgets and, though in the short run their consumption remains discretionary, in time some of them become necessities. Thus, in the short span of ten years of intense participation in the produce market, the subsistence requirements of the African peasantry changed significantly, as the following observations referring to successive points in time seem to suggest:

> There is a steady increase in the demand for trade goods, of which the articles most in request are hoes, picks, cutlery, blankets, clothing, salt, beads, etc., with occasionally such luxuries as coffee, sugar, golden syrup, and corned beef.[55]

> The natives' progress is becoming more marked each year. This does not apply to any great extent to requirements of articles of civilized manufacture, but of correspondence by post, railway travelling, cleanliness in dress and person.[56]

> The large number of town and country stores catering for the native customer is a striking illustration of the increasing wants of the native. The stock-in-trade comprises agricultural implements . . . boots and shoes, ready-made clothing of all descriptions, hats, shirts, drapery, coffee, tea, jams, sugar, salt, flour, candles, paraffin, and such luxuries as golden syrup, cigarettes, confectionery and perfumery.[57]

> Natives are noticeably dressing better, and on enquiry it is found that many of them demand better quality in suits, shirts, and boots than formerly.[58]

> There is amongst natives, an increasing demand for European medicines.[59]

> That the natives are depending more and more on European goods to supply their wants is manifest by the increasing number of applications for general dealers' licences, in town and country. The class of goods stocked by Europeans for native trade formerly consisted of beads, blankets, limbo,

and brass wire; this has now given place to ready-made clothing, woman's apparel, boots, bicycles, paraffin lamps, candles, cigarettes, sugar, coffee, tea, fish, tinned meat and other groceries, and there is besides a ready demand for farming implements and carpentering tools.[60]

In *periods of falling incomes,* on the other hand, while discretionary consumption tends to be cut, consumers resort to dissaving, to increasing their supply of labor, and, in the case of self-employed producers, to a more intense use of the means of production in order to preserve their consumption of necessities. The protracted period of sustained demand for African produce and the participation in the money economy that it induced can thus be said to have performed the function of making such participation increasingly indispensable for the African population: should the sale of produce become uneconomic or impracticable, the African people would be compelled to sell their labor-time in order to satisfy their *subsistence* requirements.

Many of the articles mentioned in the above passages were substitutes for the products of the traditional economies. And in fact the nonagricultural productive activities of traditional African society soon succumbed to external competition.[61] The main reasons for this were the superior quality and lower prices of capitalist manufactures and the fact that it was difficult for African craftsmen to obtain their *cash* requirements through the sale of nonagricultural goods within the peasant economy: trade had traditionally been a matter of barter, and the peasants were reluctant to pay cash for something that they could, if necessary, make themselves.[62] Despite the fact that during the two world wars, when capitalist manufactures were in short supply or altogether unavailable, there was a revival of the African handicraft industry,[63] the African peasantry underwent an "unlearning process" whereby they gradually lost their ability to produce nonagricultural goods,[64] a tendency that also contributed to increasing their dependence upon the sale of agricultural produce or labor.

The process of growing African dependence on exchange with the capitalist sector tended to be cumulative. As cash payments became an essential part of African society, traditional transactions, such as marriage payments, began to assume a cash value,[65] further increasing the necessary character of participation in the money economy. And gradually, the spreading of missionary education became one of the most powerful factors in altering the nature of such participation. Not only did education (even of a merely religious kind, as it often was) change tastes and wants;[66] in addition, as wage employment became more and more a source of means of subsistence, expenditure on education also lost its discretionary nature, and was later to become one of the major expenditure items in African families' budgets.

2. The tendency toward greater African dependence on exchange with the capitalist sector was matched by an upward tendency in the effort-price of African participation in the produce market. Available official estimates of acreage under cultivation, yields, and population point to two broad trends in African peasant agriculture during the first half of this century: a constant grain output per capita of the rural African population and a steady increase in the acreage under cultivation, also per capita of the rural African population.[67] These two trends taken together imply a steady increase in the effort-price of a given quantity of produce and therefore an upward tendency in the effort-price of African participation in the produce market.

A first point that has to be made in tracing the causes of the above tendency is that, at least prior to the late 1930s, it was not due to an abnormally high rate of population growth. Taking the Chief Native Commissioners' figures of the number of indigenous African males over fourteen as a basis for the calculation of the rate of growth of the African population, we find that that rate remained roughly constant at 1.6 percent per year between 1906 and 1936, it rose to 2.7 percent in the period 1936–1946 and to 3.4 percent in the subsequent decade. Given the low density of population existing in the country as a whole at the turn of the century, we can assume that, before the late 1930s, falling yields per acre were not due to an abnormally high rate of population growth that forced the African peasantry to bring under cultivation increasingly inferior land.

The main causes of the trends in question must rather be traced to the long-term effects of the institutional framework that had been established at the beginning of the century. For one thing, the high rentals, dipping fees and stringent labor clauses on European land occasioned a widespread movement of Africans into the less fertile lands of the Reserves. Moreover, with the development of capitalist agriculture, land values steadily appreciated and the labor situation improved. In consequence, the advantages of retaining African tenants were reduced in many instances since labor was more easily obtainable on the market and competition for grazing between African-owned and European-owned cattle on European farms intensified. European farmers became anxious to have their former tenants removed and, as farms were alienated, the African occupants were given notice and told to leave.[68] As a result, the proportion of the African population residing on Reserves rose from 54 percent in 1909 to 59 percent in 1914 and 64 percent in 1922.[69]

This shift of the African population into the Reserves was, owing to the inferior quality of land therein, a major cause of falling average yields in African agriculture. But other, less apparent, forces were also contributing to the tendency in question, an understanding of which presupposes an analysis of the pattern of surplus absorption in the peasant economy. Disregarding for the time being the problem of the terms of trade with the capitalist sector, the surplus is here defined as the difference between the aggregate net output (net, that is, of the means of production used up in the process in the peasant sector) and the means of subsistence consumed by the peasantry, both referred to a given period of time. For our purposes it is sufficient to distinguish three main forms of surplus absorption: discretionary consumption, socially necessary unproductive absorption, and productive investment. The significance of the *pattern* of surplus absorption lies in the fact that it determines the size of the surplus itself in subsequent periods. Thus, for example, the greater discretionary consumption, the faster the growth of future subsistence requirements and, other things being equal, the smaller the surplus in subsequent periods; the greater and the more "efficient" [70] the productive absorption of the surplus, the greater, other things being equal, the size of future surpluses.

Bearing in mind previous observations, we may say that the imposition of white rule in Rhodesia had a contradictory effect on the surplus-generating capacity of the African peasantry. By generating a demand for their labor-time and produce, it tended to bring about an increase in peasant per capita output, though the limitations imposed on land use soon counteracted this tendency. At the same time, however, the development of capitalism tended to restrain the productive absorption of the surplus *within* the peasant sector. For one thing, much of the surplus was appropriated by the Europeans in the form of labor-services, taxes, rents, etc. In the second place, the confrontation of a pre-industrial society, producing a limited range of goods, with the sophisticated consumption pattern of an industrial society (while it led to the abovementioned increase in the productive exertion of the African peasantry) also tended, as we have seen, to foster discretionary consumption and therefore a rapid increase in African subsistence requirements. Lastly, the development of capitalism did not, to any great extent, reduce the insecurity of existence of the African peoples since it substituted market uncertainty for ecological uncertainty (which, of course, was only partially eliminated). As a consequence, the necessity of certain unproductive forms of surplus absorption which enhanced social cohesion was only marginally lessened.[71]

A substantial amount of productive investment was nonetheless carried out by the African peasantry during the first two decades of the present century. Africans bought wagons and carts for the transport of produce to the towns and mining centers, some invested in corn crushers and in water boreholes, though the latter were rather exceptional and to be found only among those engaged in market gardening near the towns and mining centers or under conditions of acute water scarcity.[72] But by far the most prominent forms of productive investment were cattle and ploughs. In the period 1905–1921 the number of African-owned cattle increased from 114,560 to 854,000 head, or at an average compound rate of 12.5 percent per year; subsequently this rate fell drastically to 6 percent in the period 1921–1931 and to 1 percent in the period 1931–1945.[73] This rapid accumulation was partly traceable to the existence of traditional mechanisms of transformation of current surpluses into cattle[74] and to the role played by cattle in enhancing social cohesion. Equally important, however, was the conscious response of the African peasantry to the opportunities afforded by this form of accumulation for increasing their future incomes. For, with the introduction of the ox-drawn plough and the increased importance of transport, cattle had come to play a more significant productive role in African agriculture, and the development of capitalist agriculture was, as we shall see, steadily raising the market value of African-owned cattle. The Africans readily responded to these new opportunities by supplementing the abovementioned traditional mechanisms of accumulation with improved methods of stock management, investment in dipping tanks, and purchase of imported cattle, breeding stock in particular.[75]

The other major form of productive investment was the plough, the number of ploughs in use by Africans increasing from 440 in 1905 to 16,900 in 1921, to 53,500 in 1931, and to 133,000 in 1945.[76] The common characteristic of these two main forms of productive surplus absorption was their "land-consuming bias." [77] Given the general absence of population pressure on the land before the 1920s, this bias was fully justified by the factor-endowment of the peasant sector. In the long run, however, it tended to eliminate the relative abundance of land, a tendency that was already being promoted by the population movements into the Reserves discussed above. As we shall see, this tendency was soon to materialize in an actual shortage of land which radically altered the position of the African peasantry vis-à-vis the capitalist sector.

In previous sections we have discussed the relationship between the supply of African labor and the development of capitalist agriculture, as well as the role played by political mechanisms in the "take-off" of the latter. The policy of vigorous encouragement of European agriculture pursued by the government brought immediate and impressive results (see Table 4). Taking into account the fact that a considerable proportion (between four-fifths and nine-tenths, according to the season) of African grain production was not marketed, it can be stated that, in as far as grain supplies were concerned, the capitalist sector had become largely self-sufficient by 1915.

The immediate effect of the expansion of European maize production was a downward pressure on grain prices. The scanty available evidence suggests a decline in the price of maize on the order of 30 to 50 percent between 1903–1904 and 1911–1912, [78] which by itself must have significantly raised the effort-price of African participation in the produce market. But the fall in prices received by the African peasantry was even more drastic than the above decline would indicate. For only 30 percent of the land assigned to Africans—as against 75 percent of that alienated to Europeans—was within twenty-five miles of a railway line (and therefore also of towns and mining centers),[79] while it was generally recognized that grain crops could not bear the cost of more than fifteen miles of ox-wagon transport when railway costs were to be added.[80] In consequence, as the development of capitalist agriculture occasioned the migration of the African peasantry into the Reserves, not only were the land resources available to Africans reduced, but their ability to compete on the grain market was progressively curtailed.

Table 4

Comparative Growth of European and African Agriculture, 1904–1921
(in thousands)

	1904	1911	1915	1918	1921
European maize production:					
Total bags	46	393	743	807	1,001
Retained for farm use	n.a.	n.a.	142	149	194
African grain production:					
Total bags	2,151	2,190	2,161	2,495	2,630
External trade:					
Imports of maize (bags)	50	17	44	37	162
Export of maize (bags)	—	41	225	300	386
Cattle population:					
European owned (head)	30	164	395	600	905
African owned (head)	105	330	446	610	845
External trade:					
Cattle imports (head)	n.a.	3	7	1	1
Meat imports (lb.)	1,715	669	151	28	22
Cattle exports (head)	—	—	—	23	9

Notes: Crops are shown under the year in which they were harvested. Production figures for 1915, 1918, and 1921 are averages for three seasons. Figures of African-owned cattle and meat imports for 1904 are annual averages for the two years ended March 31, 1905.

Sources: Censuses of the European Population, 1904 and 1911. *Official Yearbooks,* op. cit., 1924 and 1932; *Annual Report of the Chief Native Commissioners; Annual Report of the Controller of Customs.*

The development of capitalist agriculture did, however, have some positive effects on African agriculture which, for a while, counteracted the above tendency toward a rising effort-price of African participation in the produce market. Since the stock of European-owned cattle was largely built upon cattle purchased from Africans and upgraded by the use of imported bulls,[81] the growth of European mixed farming and cattle ranching generated a demand for African-owned cattle whose price steadily advanced from £1–£2 per head around 1905–1906 to £4–£7 in 1909, and to £9 in 1918.[82] However, this counteracting tendency was necessarily of a temporary nature: after a time the natural increase in

European-owned cattle would become large enough to supply the whole of market demand and the relationship between European and African agriculture would become an exclusively competitive one.

It is probable that this situation would have been reached some time in the mid-1910s had it not been for the boom in external demand for Rhodesian cattle and maize brought about by World War I and lasting through 1920. During this period the downward trend in maize prices was reversed, and African-owned cattle came in great demand to supply the export market. The war and postwar boom thus delayed the full materialization of the effects of the development of capitalist agriculture upon the effort-price of African participation in the produce market. As we shall presently see, however, it also made such materialization all the more sudden and drastic in its impact when it came to an end in 1921.

4

The various tendencies analyzed in the foregoing section were precipitated by the slump in cattle and maize prices of 1921–1923 which radically altered the position of the African peasantry in the structure of the Rhodesian economy. The extent to which the slump affected cash earnings from sale of produce can be gauged from the following data: in 1920 African sales of grain to European traders were estimated at 198,000 bags at 10s. per bag; in 1921, the average price fell to approximately 5s. per bag, at which price trade became uneconomic in many districts, with the result that, notwithstanding a plentiful harvest, only 43,600 bags were purchased from Africans.[83] A similar reduction occurred in receipts from cattle sales: though no figures are available for 1920, it was estimated that at least 20,000 head of cattle were sold by Africans in 1919 at prices in the order of £7–£8; in 1921, the demand for African stock "diminished" and in 1922 "practically ceased," a head of cattle being "worth little more than a sheep." [84] In 1924 there was a recovery followed by a short-lived boom that lasted until 1929, when prices collapsed again.

The immediate effect of the drastic increase in the effort-price of African participation in the produce market brought about by these slumps was a sharp increase in African participation in the labor market (see Figure 1). As a result, the relative importance of wage employment and sale of produce as sources of African cash earnings was reversed: while the sale of produce had accounted for some 70 percent of the total cash earnings of the indigenous African population at the beginning of the present century (see n. 30) it accounted for less than 20 percent of such earnings in 1932.[85] It is important to note that *this change cannot be considered as merely a cyclical phenomenon. It rather was an "irreversible" change in the sense that subsequent recoveries could not restore the previous position of the African peasantry vis-à-vis the capitalist economy.* In order to understand this it is necessary to analyze the short- and long-term impact of the slumps in question on the economy of the peasant sector.

Both slumps were followed by an acceleration in the movement of Africans into the Reserves.[86] One reason for this acceleration was that the financial stringency in which the slumps had thrown the African peasantry had greatly diminished their ability to meet the various charges to which they were subject outside the Reserves.[87] Moreover, since the fall in produce prices had made participation in the labor market the more economic way for many Africans to meet their cash requirements, the payment of such charges in order to reside close to the markets and lines of communication had become less justified than previously.

Once the migration had taken place, the future ability of the Africans who had migrated to obtain their cash requirements through the sale of produce was, of course, jeopardized. More important still, these migrations into the Reserves precipitated the appearance of land shortages therein: in 1926 it was observed that "several Reserves" were becoming "overcrowded";[88] in 1928 "general overstocking" was reported, especially from Matabeleland;[89] and in 1932 the first symptoms of "a vicious and expanding circle of destruction" were detected. Already the first signs of the possible deterioration of the land in native areas from cumulative evils in the shape of soil erosion, the drying up of springs, the extirpation of valuable pasture grasses through overstocking, and the exhaustion of fertility were "discernible in some of our more congested native Reserves, and it is plain that we must take more positive control, if we are to see an increase, and not a reduction, in the life-supporting capacity of our native areas." [90] The cumulative evils of population pressure on the land soon materialized: in an attempt to maintain output, land began to be brought back into cultivation before the soil had a chance to regenerate fully and grazing areas were destroyed as the number of stock increased.[91] As a result of this "expanding circle of destruction," supplemented after the late 1930s by the acceleration in population growth, a general shortage of land developed in the African areas: by 1943 the Department of Native Agriculture estimated that out of 98 Reserves, 62 were overpopulated (19 more than 100 percent overpopulated) and 50 were overstocked. Several of the remaining areas were either in, or dangerously close to, the tsetse fly zones and could not safely carry cattle.[92]

As the African peasantry began to be affected by a shortage of land, the production of a marketable surplus on their part tended to become "impossible," not just "uneconomic," and a return to the status quo ante in relative produce prices would not restore their previous ability to participate in the money economy through the sale of produce. It is mainly for this reason that the enhanced importance of wage employment as a source of African cash earnings after the 1920s must be considered as largely "irreversible" rather than "cyclical." It may be argued, however, that a land shortage is nothing more than a structural disequilibrium between labor, capital, and land, and that a "land-saving bias" in accumulation can in due course eliminate such disequilibrium. This is certainly true and we must therefore analyze the qualitative and quantitative characteristics of peasant surplus absorption in the 1920s and 1930s in order to trace the causes of the persistence, indeed aggravation, of the land shortage.

The pattern of peasant productive investment did alter with the appearance of population pressure on the land. In the 1920s the rate of growth of African-owned cattle fell to half what it had been in the previous fifteen years, while greater attention began to be paid to the quality of herds as witnessed by the increase in the number of grade bulls owned by Africans.[93] There were also attempts to counteract the emerging land shortage by substituting wheeled vehicles for the traditional sleighs which caused soil erosion besides making marketing from distant areas uneconomic.[94] In the 1930s there occurred a further shift in a land-saving direction: the rate of growth of African-owned cattle fell drastically (it averaged only 1 percent per year in the period 1931–1945) and land began to be manured, a practice that became "common" by 1940.[95]

However, these changes were not significant enough to affect the trend toward a general land shortage. Particularly striking was the absence of any major shift from production of marketable surpluses of footstuffs (mainly cattle and grain) to the production of purely commercial crops such as tobacco (which was particularly well suited to the soil and climatic conditions of Rhodesia). Given the more favorable market conditions faced by, and the lesser land requirements of, tobacco production relative to maize and cattle, a shift of this kind could have gone a long way in counteracting the tendency toward a sharply increasing effort-price of African participation in the produce market.

This partial failure of the African peasantry to adjust production patterns to the market conditions and factor endowment must be traced in the first place to the worsening of their terms of trade with the capitalist sector during the 1921–1923 slump and the Great Depression.[96] This worsening, on the one hand, reduced the means available to the peasantry to carry out the investment which must normally accompany innovation. On the other hand, when little surplus is produced, production is almost entirely directed to satisfying short-term subsistence requirements. Innovation in crops and techniques may therefore be highly hazardous as it diverts labor and/or land from the production of means of subsistence, leaving no margin to meet a possible risk of starvation should something go wrong with commercial crops or should a bad harvest occur before the full effects of land-saving innovations have materialized.[97] In other words, while before the 1920s the absence of a land shortage and the good prices of grain and cattle discouraged, respectively, a shift toward land-saving patterns of investment and the cultivation of commercial crops,[98] after the slump of the early 1920s (and especially in the 1930s) these changes were impeded by the smallness of the surplus.

There was, however, another factor at work. Low wages and lack of security in the capitalist sector maintained the African worker's interest in the security afforded by membership of a rural-based kinship group; at the same time, fading opportunities for African participation in the produce market made the peasantry at large more reliant on wage worker's remittances for their cash requirements. There was therefore little incentive for all involved to break up traditional structures which in some ways tended to hamper innovation in techniques and patterns of production. For example, in the 1930s "centralization" of arable land came to be considered as a measure necessary to prevent haphazard interspersing of arable and grazing land which was one of the main causes of soil erosion. This innovation, however, made it increasingly difficult to provide land for a growing family in the vicinity of the parents' kraal, with the result that either the family land holdings, or the family itself, had to be fragmented.[99] As the latter alternative would undermine social cohesion, centralization was resisted or, if implemented, it led to excessive fragmentation of holdings and further deterioration in land fertility.[100]

These factors were preventing a radical reorientation of peasant production patterns in the face of a growing land shortage, which in the late 1930s began to be made more acute by an acceleration in population growth. Moreover, the process tended to become cumulative. For one thing, as the surplus-generating capacity of the African peasantry began to fade, a tendency developed among them to sell more of their crops than they could spare in an attempt to maintain their consumption of purchased necessities. They then had to buy food at enhanced prices from capitalist producers before the next crop was ready[101]—presumably by parting with their accumulated wealth (mainly livestock) or by working for wages—thus further reducing their future surplus-generating capacity. The urge to maintain subsistence consumption also led to the degeneration of agricultural practices noted above and to the persistence of types of productive investment and innovations whose efficiency had been diminished by the changed conditions facing production. For example, the substitution of maize for traditional crops (millets, groundnuts, sweet potatoes), which were less land-consuming but which had become more difficult to dispose of on the market, gained momentum in the 1930s, probably relieving the shortage of cash income in the short run but leading to faster soil erosion in the long run.[102] Similarly, as participation in the money economy through the sale of produce became increasingly uneconomic or altogether impossible, the plough acquired new importance as a labor-saving device necessary to release male labor for wage employment. It thus remained one of the main forms of investment notwithstanding its land-consuming bias which could only worsen the land shortage.[103] Equally important was the fact that, since male labor was traditionally in charge of management and capital formation, the steady increase after 1920 in the proportion of indigenous males in wage employment (see Figure 1) became a factor hampering the adjustment of techniques of production and composition of output in peasant agriculture to the changing factor endowment and market conditions.[104]

In the late 1930s a major reorientation in the pattern of surplus absorption in the peasant sector did occur. A considerable amount of labor-time and expenditure began to be allocated to education. The interest of the rural African people (with exceptions among the youth) in education had previously been lukewarm, but with the deterioration in the income-generating capacity of the peasant sector, education (owing to the advantages it conferred in the wage economy) must have become more and more a "necessary" rather than a "discretionary" expenditure item. The first sign of a changed attitude was a dramatic increase in school attendance, soon followed by an equally dramatic increase in enrolment: average attendance in mission primary schools, after stagnating at around 45,000 for over a decade, shot up from 46,000 in 1936 to over 86,000 in 1943, and to 140,000 in 1947, while enrolment rose from 87,000 in 1936 to 117,000 in 1943, and to almost 180,000 in 1947.[105] Whatever its long-term political and economic implications, this "rush" for education, by diverting a significant proportion of the labor-time and financial resources of the African people away from investment in agriculture, added new and probably decisive momentum to the process of their proletarianization.

Throughout the period under consideration the government continued to play an important role in undermining the African peasantry's ability to participate in the produce market. To be sure, government policy toward African agriculture was modified in the late 1920s. In 1926 the government appointed an Agriculturalist for the Instruction of Natives, and three years later it began to pursue the policy of centralization of arable land mentioned above. In conjunction with this policy the government subsequently introduced other measures meant to check the degeneration of agricultural practices; these included extension services, irrigation schemes, culling of cattle and destocking, voluntary at first but compulsory after the war. Yet even official reports often admitted that these schemes failed to have any significant impact on the trends that we have been analyzing. This failure can be partly traced to the already discussed difficulties of changing techniques and patterns of production in the peasant sector, but the main reason was the smallness of the financial resources allocated by the government to African agriculture: approximately one-fortieth, in the period 1939–1945, of what was being spent on European agriculture.[106] Moreover, Africans, quite justifiably, feared that "any success [in raising land productivity] will be a reason for depriving them of a portion of the Reserves set aside for them or a ground for refusing their demands, which are insistent, for the extension of the Reserves." [107] For this reason they opposed government action in the peasant sector, thus contributing to its failure.

That African suspicions were fully justified is shown by the fact that the land resources available to the African people were further restricted in this period. Though in 1931 they were formally increased through the allocation of previously unassigned land, this *de jure* increase was not matched by a *de facto* increase since Africans were already residing on the land newly assigned to them. In addition, the *de jure* increase was accompanied by the introduction of the Land Apportionment Act (1931), which came to bar Africans from purchasing land outside designated areas at a time when the shortage of land in the Reserves was likely to induce them to enter the land market in greater numbers. More important still, population movements from the European to African areas, due to the factors discussed earlier on and increasingly also to government-organized expulsions, continued to reduce the *de facto* availability of land to Africans: 50,000 Africans moved to the Reserves between 1931 and 1941, and at least as many between 1941 and 1945.[108]

Government action in other spheres was equally *graphic*. With the decline in the importance of the African peasantry as suppliers of foodstuffs to the capitalist sector, and with the rise of the European farmers to a position of hegemony among the ruling classes, the earlier reluctance of the government to discriminate against African marketed produce largely disappeared. Thus in the early 1930s the government monopolized the marketing of locally produced maize and instituted a two-price system which protected the small European producer and discriminated against the African;[109] similar discriminatory practices were introduced in the marketing of cattle.[110] These formal checks on African competition in the produce market simply supplemented what had been and still was the main discriminatory device: the distance of African lands from the consumption centers and the lines of communication. The development of motor transport did not significantly change the situation in this respect, for unless an African area happened to be in the track of a main road between European areas there was no provision for the construction of a road to its boundaries. As a consequence, most African areas had to rely on tracks which were unsuitable at any time for motor transport.[111]

All this having been said, it is probable that political mechanisms were progressively losing their *dominant* role in undermining the peasantry's ability to participate in the produce market and in strengthening the competitive position of European agriculture. For, once capitalist agriculture has overcome the initial difficulties related to its competitive weakness in the produce market and to its low productivity relative to the market wage rate, market forces themselves tend to widen the gap between productivities in peasant and capitalist agriculture. The main reason for this is that capitalist producers in reinvesting surpluses tend to choose those techniques which increase the surplus itself at some future date rather than current output as the peasantry can be expected to do.[112] In time this leads to a higher rate of accumulation[113] and faster growth of land and/or labor productivity in the capitalist sector. In the second place, capitalist agriculture is not subject to the constraints which we have seen to hamper certain types of innovation in peasant agriculture. It is therefore free—and indeed compelled under the pressure of competition—to innovate as trends in market conditions and factor endowment change. For these reasons we can assume that the contraction of the surplus-generating capacity of the African peasantry was matched by a steady increase in the surplus-generating capacity of capitalist agriculture, something that progressively reduced the importance of political mechanisms in deepening the dualism of the Rhodesian economy.

5

We are now in a position to explain why, after the early 1920s, African responsiveness to wage-employment opportunities increased continuously, irrespective of whether real wages were rising, falling, or remaining constant. Our analysis has shown that this tendency must be traced to the increasingly "necessary" character of African participation in the money economy and to the steady increase in the relative effort-price of participation in the produce market which was in turn the result of the development of capitalist agriculture and of the pattern of surplus absorption in the peasant sector. The significance of the 1920s is that the slumps of 1921 and 1929 precipitated a qualitative change in the economic position of the African peasantry: thereafter African participation in the labor market ceased to be largely "discretionary," i.e., a way of transforming *surplus* labor-time which could not be absorbed economically in agricultural production into a surplus of commodities (discretionary consumption, productive and unproductive accumulation), and became the normal and only way in which a growing section of the peasantry could obtain a significant proportion of their means of subsistence.[114] To put it differently, the disguised unemployment of the peasant sector was no longer due to a lack of incentives to apply unutilized labor-time to agricultural production *within* the peasant sector but to a structural disequilibrium between means of production and subsistence requirements of the peasantry.

An analysis of the supply of African labor in historical perspective has thus invalidated Barber's interpretation of the development of the African wage-labor force in Rhodesia. For one thing, dualism in Rhodesia (i.e., the technological, economic, and political distance between the two races) was less an "original state," progressively *reduced* by market forces, than it was the outcome of the development of capitalism itself.[115] Related to this oversight is Barber's failure to see that market forces did not *ab initio* favor capitalist development. Real wages remained at a level which promoted capitalist accumulation not because of the forces of supply and demand, but because of politico-economic mechanisms that ensured *the "desired" supply at the "desired" wage rate*. Before the determination of wage rates and rates of accumulation could be "safely" left to market forces, the Rhodesian capitalist system had to undergo the process of "primary accumulation," a concept that has no place in Barber's analysis and to which Lewis refers in an off-hand way.[116]

Broadly speaking, "primary accumulation" can be defined as a process in which nonmarket mechanisms predominate and through which the gap between productivity in the capitalist sector and productivity in the noncapitalist sector is widened. The process is completed when the gap is so wide that producers in the latter sector are prepared to sell their labor-time "spontaneously" at whatever wage rate is consistent with steady accumulation in the capitalist sector. Once this situation has been attained, the Lewis postulate of the predominance of market mechanisms in the reallocation of labor from the noncapitalist to the capitalist sector of the economy becomes realistic, though political mechanisms may continue to play a subsidiary role. The Lewis model, like any other theoretical model, must therefore be situated historically. In the case of Rhodesia, our analysis suggests that it begins to be relevant in the 1920s when the capitalist sector had become "self-contained" and the peasants' independence of wage employment was being irreversibly undermined.

We must now determine whether the model retained its validity after World War II. We have seen that toward the end of the 1940s African real wages began to rise and that Barber's interpretation of this phenomenon is no more satisfactory than his explanation of why wages did not rise in earlier times. The exceptionally rapid growth of the demand for African labor in the late 1940s and early 1950s (the number of Africans in wage employment rising at an average compound rate of almost 7 percent per year in the period 1946–1951) was certainly a major factor in pushing up real wages. Yet this was no new phenomenon: before World War II, also, large increases in the demand for labor, after periods of falling real wages, normally led to increases in the latter to restore them to the "single worker subsistence level." This was the case, for example, in 1908–1911 and 1924–1929. What was new in the postwar situation was that real wages continued to rise even when the rate of growth of the demand for labor fell—as it did in the mid-1950s—causing a decline in the proportion of indigenous African males in wage employment (see Table 5). This increase must obviously be traced to factors other than a situation of "quasi-full employment." [117]

Table 5

Trends in African Wage Earnings and Employment, 1946–1961

	1946	1951	1956	1961
1. Total number of Africans in wage employment (in thousands)	376	527	602	628
2. Proportion of indigenous African males in wage employment (percent)	48.0	61.0	57.5	55.5
3. Average annual earnings of African employees (£)	26	43	75	102
4. European cost of living index (Oct. 1949 = 100)	86	116	135	156
5. African real wages: (3)/(4)	30	38	56	65

Notes and sources: The European cost of living index is taken as a rough approximation to changes in the African cost of living, as no index of the latter is available prior to 1960. The data are derived from: *The National Income and Social Accounts of Southern Rhodesia, 1946–51; Economic and Statistical Bulletin of Southern Rhodesia* (February 7, 1952); *Monthly Digest of Statistics* (February 1966); *Censuses of the European Population; Reports of the Chief Native Commissioner and Secretary for Internal Affairs.*

Available evidence suggests that the rise in average African real wages, especially in the 1950s, was mainly due to the "upgrading" of a section of the African wage labor force. The rapid growth of secondary and tertiary industries, which had become the leading sectors of the Rhodesian economy, created a need for greater labor stabilization. For these sectors required a labor force with certain skills which, though simple, could not be imparted under conditions of high turnover.[118] The demand for semi-skilled labor was further enhanced by the spreading of mechanization and automation to the Rhodesian mining and manufacturing industries favored by technological development in the metropolitan countries as well as by rapidly increasing concentration of production in Rhodesia itself.[119] But stabilization of African labor presupposed the abandonment of the tradition of the subsistence wage (still obtaining after World War II) whereby the level of African wages was customarily fixed so as to allow only the subsistence of *single* men.[120] The persistence of this tradition meant that wage workers continued to rely on the tribal economy for the support of their families, and of themselves during their old age, sickness, and unemployment. Participation in the labor market thus left the worker's obligations and duties to his rural kinsmen and his general involvement in the tribal social system unchanged so as to retain his cultivation rights and to be able to claim support and succor when necessary.[121] The creation of a stabilized wage-labor force which would not periodically move to and from the peasant sector required, among other things, a level of African wages and living conditions in the capitalist sector that would provide Africans with some security not only during their working life but also during their old age, and above all that would enable them to support their families outside the peasant sector. That is to say, "stabilized labor" commanded a premium determined by the difference between the cost of the means of subsistence of single men during their working life in wage employment and the cost of the means of subsistence of the worker's family over his "life cycle."

Large enterprises—especially those operating in secondary and tertiary industries—which could introduce labor-saving methods of production began to find it profitable to pay the abovementioned premium because higher wages were more than compensated by the higher productivity of a stabilized labor force. It was in fact in those sectors in which stabilization mattered most (manufacturing, transport, and communication) that after 1954 most of the increase in real wages was concentrated (see Table 6). In agriculture, on the other hand, where stabilization mattered least, the increase in money wages was just sufficient to compensate for the rise in costs of living.

Table 6
Africans in Wage Employment (a), (in thousands)
and
Average Annual Earnings, 1954–1962 (b), (in £)

		1954	1956	1958	1960	1962	Average rate of growth 1954–62 (%)
Agriculture	(a)	218.0	228.0	230.0	240.0	243.9	
	(b)	48	52	57	59	61	3.1
Domestic service	(a)	76.1	85.4	90.9	94.1	95.2	
	(b)	71	81	88	94	102	4.6
Mining and quarrying	(a)	62.4	60.9	57.1	52.3	44.1	
	(b)	83	97	106	115	124	5.1
Transport and communications	(a)	12.1	13.7	15.1	16.0	16.6	
	(b)	94	114	148	166	209	10.5
Manufacturing	(a)	62.5	70.0	72.4	75.0	73.4	
	(b)	65	81	108	125	164	10.8
All sectors	(a)	555.0	602.0	628.0	640.0	616.0	
	(b)	64	75	88	94	109	6.9
European cost of living index (Jan. 1962 = 100)		80.6	85.5	91.2	96.0	100.8	2.8

Source: Monthly Digest of Statistics (February 1966).

The postwar trend of rising wages was not unrelated to the prewar trends in the economic position of the African population which we have analyzed in the previous sections. The "rush" for education of the late 1930s and early 1940s, for example, was certainly a factor which facilitated the subsequent politicization of the African masses. After the war, African workers showed an awareness of their increasingly proletarian status, something that led them to seek an improvement of their living conditions *within the capitalist sector,* i.e., *qua* proletarians rather than *qua* migrant peasants. With this new consciousness came a wave of strikes that made the late 1940s a period of African labor unrest of unprecedented intensity and scale. This phenomenon, developing at a time when a manufacturing capitalist class with an interest in labor stabilization and in the expansion of the internal market was temporarily playing a hegemonic role in Rhodesian society, induced the government to raise basic African wages and to introduce a system of grading in industry. And this contributed to the general increase in African real wages.

Our assumption that the main factors behind the postwar rise in real wages were the qualitatively new manpower requirements of capitalist production and, secondarily, the greater African militancy in wage bargaining does not of course exclude the possibility that mechanization, automation, and increased concentration of production might have been partly due to rising wages. This was in all likelihood the case in the gold-mining industry and among large-scale European maize producers. What the assumption does imply is that the qualitatively new manpower requirements of the capitalist sector (a factor largely exogenous to the situation in the Rhodesian labor market), rather than a shortage of African labor, was the *dominant* factor in the "rising wages–mechanization spiral" of the 1950s.

But if the relationship between shortage of labor, wages, and mechanization had changed with respect to the prewar period, the behavior of the demand for African labor had also changed. A comparison of such behavior during the slump of 1921–1923 and during the recession of the late 1950s and early 1960s will illustrate the change. During the 1921–1923 slump the growth of African wage employment proceeded at a sustained rate (see Figure 1). The main reason for this phenomenon was the predominance of competitive market structures in the Rhodesian economy of the time. For the presence of competitive pricing and investment behavior in most sectors ensured both a high "intersectoral mobility of capital" and a relative independence of the rate of investment from the current absorptive capacity of the market.

"Intersectoral mobility of capital" is here defined as the ease with which capital moves to and from branches of production in response to changes in relative profitabilities, and it is assumed to depend mainly on the financial and entrepreneurial "entrance requirements" of the various branches of production. In 1921–1923, the competitive pricing behavior of capitalist producers led to the drastic fall in grain and cattle prices referred to in Section 4. The relative profitability of farming geared to these chief staples was consequently reduced, and, given the smallness of the abovementioned "entrance requirements," there occurred the development of other branches of production which used (either as intermediary products or as foodstuffs for their labor force) these staples as inputs. In this way the slump led to the establishment or expansion of various industries (dairy industry, pig industry, tobacco cultivation, gold mining) which contributed to sustain the demand for labor.[122]

As noted, the other implication of the predominance of competitive market structures in the Rhodesian economy was the relative independence of the rate of accumulation from the current absorptive capacity of the market. Despite the Depression, European farmers showed

> a more than wanted activity in the way of permanent improvements and development. Labor was exceptionally abundant and the normal work being largely in abeyance, the opportunity was largely taken of making bricks, building houses, sheds, dipping tanks, kraals and stockyards, constructing roads, dams, canals and silos, fencing, sinking wells, clearing scrub, and in other ways preparing for the better seasons which are confidently awaited.[123]

That is to say, sanguine expectations, a desire to strengthen their long-term competitive position, and the exceptional abundance of labor (itself a result, as we have seen, of the slump in produce prices) induced European farmers to reallocate labor from current production to capital formation, thus sustaining the demand for African labor.

The essential characteristics of a self-regulating competitive capitalism were thus present in prewar Rhodesia, and this is an additional reason for taking the Lewis model as a rough approximation to the operation of the Rhodesian economy during the late 1920s and the 1930s.[124] By the late 1940s, however, the structure of the Rhodesian economy had altered radically. Foreign-controlled oligopolies, characterized by considerable "international mobility," had come to dominate important sectors of the economy (mining and secondary industries),[125] while the financial and entrepreneurial "entrance requirements" in most branches of production had greatly increased. As a consequence, prices had lost much of their downward flexibility and even when changes in relative profitabilities did occur, little intersectoral mobility of capital could be expected. Moreover, the greater calculating rationality of the large oligopolies relative to the atomistic producers of earlier times implied a greater dependence of the rate of accumulation upon the absorptive capacity of the market.[126] For these reasons the recession of the late 1950s did not lead to structural changes that could sustain the rate of accumulation and the demand for labor. It caused instead a fall in both rates and an acceleration in the outflow of investment income.[127]

Equally important was the fact that secondary industries *producing mainly for the internal market* had assumed a leading role in the Rhodesian economy, thus making the extremely unequal distribution of income a major constraint on accumulation in the capitalist sector. The acceleration in the growth of the demand for labor that was necessary for the absorption of a growing proportion of the African labor force into wage employment came, therefore, to depend not only on structural changes in the economy which, as we have seen, market forces were ill suited to promote, but also on changes in the power structure of Rhodesian society.[128]

The problems of capitalist accumulation which we have just discussed have no place in Lewis's theory of development. In his model all profits are automatically reinvested in productive capacity and, in addition, they are reinvested in such a way as to "widen" capital, i.e., to create new jobs rather than to increase the productivity of those who already have jobs. Neither assumption is, according to our observations, valid in the Rhodesian context of the 1950s and 1960s. Investment tended to "deepen" capital (largely irrespective of the situation in the labor market) and, as the limits of growth within the existing politico-economic framework were approached, reinvestable surpluses were either exported or absorbed unproductively or not produced at all.

In conclusion, the historical relevance of the Lewis model to the Rhodesian experience is limited to a period of roughly twenty years, i.e., from the mid-1920s to the mid-1940s: before the 1920s supplies of labor were in no sense "unlimited"; after World War II, though labor supplies could be said to be "unlimited" in Lewis's sense, the capitalist economy had become structurally incapable of absorbing them.

Before we close our discussion we may well ask how it was possible for Barber to misinterpret so utterly the process whereby an African wage-labor force was brought into being in Rhodesia. For Barber was not unaware of the two relationships which we have seen to be necessary for a proper understanding of the abovementioned process. Thus he recognized that:

1. Participation in the labor market depends not only on the level of real wages but also on the relative effort-price of participation in the produce market and that it is possible

> that population pressure may so intensify that the natural growth in numbers can no longer be absorbed on the land without reduction in per capita product. Should this occur, the African might be denied the option of dividing his time between the money and the indigenous economies. Instead he may be forced to accept whatever wage terms were offered in the money economy.

2. And that:

> If an African labor force is to be stabilized in wage employment and its productivity there increased, it may be necessary for the employer in the money economy to break from the traditional low-wage pattern of the past. The price which he must expect to pay for a stable labor force is a real wage sufficient to support the entire indigenous family at a standard which would make it attractive to grow roots in the money economy.[129]

Yet Barber makes no use of these assumptions in his analysis of the past and considers them as possibilities which may become relevant in the future. This arbitrary rejection of assumptions enables him to advance a mystifying picture of capitalist development in Rhodesia. In this, he exemplifies the ideological bent of the anti-historical approach which is the essence of modern economics. For in economics assumptions need not be historically relevant. In fact, they are often plainly untrue and recognized as such. Historical processes fall into the background and are summarized by statistical series of *ex-post* data, the "stylized facts" as they are sometimes called, which by themselves reveal nothing about causation. Thus, all that Barber takes from the complex historical process which we have been analyzing are a series of real wages and a series of rates of African participation in the labor market. Causal relations, on the other hand, are not derived from historical analysis, but are imposed from without, that is, through *a priori* analysis: and a set of assumptions which yields the "stylized facts" is held to have explanatory value, irrespective of its historical relevance. But since there will normally be many such sets, this methodology leaves room for considerable arbitrariness of choice and therefore for mystifications of all kinds. In view of this, the low scientific standards attained by modern "development economics" and, for that matter, by economics in general should surprise nobody.

Notes

1. W. A. Lewis, *Economic Development with Unlimited Supplies of Labour* (Manchester School, 1954).
2. The difference in real incomes is postulated to be necessary in order to overcome the "psychological costs" involved in the change to the more regimented environment of the capitalist sector and to offset differences in the cost of living.
3. W. L. Barber, *The Economy of British Central Africa* (London, 1961), p. 93.
4. Ibid.
5. Ibid.
6. Ibid., p. 46.
7. Ibid., pp. 212–14.
8. Ibid., p. 208.
9. Ibid., pp. 186–87.
10. Ibid., pp. 216–18.
11. The "prodding from the tax collector" quoted above is seen by Barber as a device necessary to induce the Africans to seek their own interest.
12. On the existence of such shortages official reports were unanimous and public debate was almost entirely focused on the problems created by them. See, for example, P. Mason, *The Birth of a Dilemma: The Conquest and Settlement of Rhodesia* (London, 1958), p. 219.
13. All available evidence suggests that, after the mid-1950s, the situation in the Rhodesian labor market, far from being one of "quasi-full employment," was for the first time becoming one of *open* African (and European) unemployment. The situation began to cause concern in 1958 (*Memorandum on Unemployment in Southern Rhodesia and Policy to Eliminate It,* by G. E. Stent, Adviser to the Labour Department, Salisbury, February 1959) and led to the passing of the Foreign Migratory Labour Act (1958), which made it illegal for labor from non-federal territories to seek employment in the main urban areas of Southern Rhodesia. This was the first time in the

history of Southern Rhodesia that the government took steps to discourage the inflow of foreign migrant workers.

14. In 1898 the administrator reported that African wages in mines had risen from 5s.–10s. to 15s.–30s. a month. In 1902 the average African wage rate in mines (rations apart) stood at 38s. 6d. and in 1903 it had further risen to 44s., the range of wages being 30s.–80s. Figures taken from *Ninth Annual Report of the Chamber of Mines of Rhodesia*, for the year ended March 31, 1904; *Report of the Chief Native Commissioner* (henceforth, CNC), *Matabeleland*, for the year ended March 31, 1904.

15. I shall discuss the consequences of the 1903–1904 crisis in a study, now in preparation, on Rhodesian economic development, 1890–1962. The best available account of the crisis and its implications is given in I. F. Hone, *Southern Rhodesia* (London, 1909).

16. In 1903 the Rhodesian Native Labour Board was established with the aid of government funds in order to centralize and coordinate the recruitment of labor. Competition among employers was further restricted by the promulgation of a Pass Law which regulated the mobility of African labor *within* the capitalist sector as well as between the capitalist and the peasant sectors.

17. "Factors in the Determination of Wage Rates in Central Africa," *Human Problems in British Central Africa* (December 1960).

18. The quotation is from M. Dobb, *Studies in the Development of Capitalism* (London, 1963), p. 274.

19. *Report of the Administrator*, for the two years ended March 31, 1904.

20. Hone, op. cit., ch. 12.

21. *Annual Report of the CNC* and *Annual Report of the Director of Agriculture*.

22. Ibid.

23. The Shona were cultivators rather than pastoralists. Their principal crop was finger millet *(Eleusine sp.)* and they grew many varieties of vegetables and fruit. Game and fish were also important items in their diet. Cattle were allegedly not killed for food (except in periods of necessity) but for ritual purposes. However, ritual did not prevent the people from enjoying their cattle as items of food as well as objects of ritual, and ritual killings were in all likelihood spaced out so that the people had a regular diet of beef. Nonagricultural productive activities included basket making, wood carving, weaving and net making from bark fiber, mat making, pottery, and iron work for the manufacture of agricultural implements, knives, and spears.

Social and economic differentiations were very limited compared to those obtaining in other African pre-colonial social formations. Every adult member was entitled to land (which was abundant) in amounts sufficient for his and his family's subsistence. Membership of a village also ensured emergency allotments of food from headmen and chiefs and gifts from kin in case of need. Division of labor was more developed *within* than *among* productive units (the families). All that is embraced in the term "housekeeping" were peculiarly feminine occupations. The building of houses and grain stores, weaving, net making, iron work, breaking up of new land, hunting, and the charge of livestock, came within a man's sphere of work. The cultivation of land, sowing, weeding, reaping and threshing were jointly performed by the two sexes, though with a probable predominance of female labor.

A significant share of the surplus produced by the Shona was appropriated by the Ndebele. The form of appropriation varied from those tribes who had been made subject to the Ndebele state and those who had not, but who were exposed to Ndebele raids: in the case of the former the appropriation was in the form of regular payments of tribute; in the case of the latter the appropriation had not been institutionalized and was made through raids. Some Shona tribes lay completely outside the Ndebele range of activities and were therefore subject neither to tribute nor to raids.

The Ndebele people had a much more differentiated system from both economic and social points of view, being divided into castes which arose as a result of the assimilation of conquered peoples. The ruler of the Ndebele state was primarily the commander of the armies and his authority depended upon the control of cattle and captives rather than on control of land, as was the case with the Shona chiefs. The basis of Ndebele social organization was military rather than territorial.

They derived their subsistence from animal husbandry, agriculture, tribute from subject tribes, and raiding parties. Cattle played a more significant political and economic role than among the Shona, and they were more frequently and admittedly killed for food. The division of labor was much more marked than among the Shona. Higher caste men concentrated their energies on hunting, raiding, and various martial pursuits, leaving many of the productive activities to the women. Cattle herding and the clearing and fencing of fields were masculine activities, but even in their performance most manual work was done by individuals of the lowest caste which consisted of the original inhabitants of the country. The latter, being of Shona stock, probably continued to organize production in a way not dissimilar from that of the Shona with the difference that part of their labor-time was used up in certain public works in which they were periodically called upon to perform.

The above characterization of Shona and Ndebele pre-colonial societies is based mainly on the following: T. O. Ranger, "The Nineteenth Century in Southern Rhodesia," in T. O. Ranger, ed., *Aspects of Central African History* (London, 1968); H. Kuper, A. J. B. Hughes, and J. van Velsen,

The Shona and Ndebele of Southern Rhodesia (London, 1955); F. W. Posselt, *Fact and Fiction: A Short Account of the Natives of Southern Rhodesia* (Salisbury, 1935); A. J. B. Hughes, "Kin, Caste, and Nation Among the Rhodesian Ndebele," *The Rhodes-Livingstone Papers*, no. 21 (Manchester, 1956); *Report of the Native Affairs Committee of Enquiry, 1911* (Salisbury, 1911); *Report of the Mangwende Reserve Commission of Enquiry, 1961* (Salisbury, 1961).

24. See note 23.

25. J. van Velsen, "Some Sociological Aspects of Community Development," unpublished manuscript (Salisbury, 1964).

26. That the Ndebele were more affected by expropriation from cattle is shown, among others, by Ranger, op. cit. That they were also more severely affected by expropriation from land was a consequence of their more concentrated settlement on the highveld, i.e., on those lands which most immediately attracted European settlement.

27. See notes 23 and 26.

28. The distinction between the two types of disguised unemployment is similar to that made by H. Myint in *The Economics of the Developing Countries* (London, 1964), pp. 44–45, in connection with his analysis of peasant production for the market.

29. By "cash income" we shall understand income derived from exchange, as opposed to "income" consisting of goods produced for auto-consumption. The category "effort-price" is the only possible category of cost for an economy in which there is no social phenomenon of wages. It is here defined as the quantity of labor-time of given drudgery necessary to obtain a unit (measured in real terms) of cash income. We shall use the short-hand expression "effort-price of participation in the labor market" and "effort-price of participation in the produce market" to indicate the effort-price of cash income obtainable through the sale of labor-time and through the production and sale of produce, respectively. On the concept of "drudgery" and on economic calculation in a peasant economy, see A. V. Chayanov, *The Theory of Peasant Economy* (Homewood, 1966).

30. *Report of the Inspector of Native Compounds*, for the year ended March 31, 1903. We have already seen that indigenous Africans received in 1903 an estimated £350,000 from the sale of produce. On the basis of wage rates and employment figures given in the *Annual Report of the Chamber of Mines of Rhodesia* and in the *Annual Report of the CNC* I have estimated that the total wage earnings of indigenous Africans were certainly less than £150,000 per annum and probably more than £100,000. It follows that at the beginning of the century sale of produce provided Africans with some 70 percent of their cash incomes.

31. An index of seasonal variations in indigenous African employment in Mata-

beleland mines, which I have calculated on the basis of data taken from the *Annual Report of the Chamber of Mines of Rhodesia* for the period 1903–1907, indicates that the supply of indigenous African labor probably doubled between November–December (the peak period in African agriculture) and May–June (the period of greatest underemployment). As for the discrepancy in Ndebele and Shona participation in the labor market, the *Annual Report of the CNC* stated that in 1902, for example, the proportion of able-bodied males in the age group 18–40 who spent at least three months in wage employment was 13 percent among the Shona and 48 percent among the Ndebele; in 1903 the corresponding figures were 20 percent and 50 percent respectively.

32. Though no marked increase in the L/Ni ratio during the period 1916–1919 is shown in Fig. 1, these years were characterized by an acute shortage of labor and must therefore be included in our analysis.

33. Owing to a lack of information on the European cost of living index, 1914 has been taken instead of 1915.

34. *Report of the Cost of Living Committee, 1921* (Salisbury, 1921) and *Report of the National Native Labour Board on its Enquiry into the Conditions of Employment in Industry and Within the Area of Jurisdiction of All Town Management Boards* (Salisbury, 1948).

35. See for example, J. C. Mitchell, "Wage Labour and African Population Movements in Central Africa," in K. M. Barbour and R. M. Prothers, eds., *Essays on African Population* (London, 1961), p. 199.

36. W. A. Lewis, op. cit.

37. L. H. Gann, *A History of Southern Rhodesia* (London, 1965), p. 124.

38. E. Tawse-Jollie, *The Real Rhodesia* (London, 1924), p. 148.

39. *Report of the CNC, Mashonaland*, for the year 1909; F. W. Witts, "The Native Labour Question in Southern Rhodesia," *The Empire Review* (December 1911), pp. 333–34.

40. Gann, op. cit., p. 123.

41. According to Hone (op. cit., p. 64), it was actually far easier to obtain labor from these distant areas than from villages situated within a day's journey of a mine or town. Given the scatteredness of gold mines in Rhodesia, it is not correct to assume, as P. Mason does in his already cited work, that only a small minority of the African population could participate in the money economy through the sale of produce. This assumption, as we shall see, became valid only after the development of capitalist agriculture which, on the one hand, made trade with the African population unprofitable and, on the other hand, occasioned widespread movements of Africans into the Reserves.

42. *Papers Relating to the Southern Rhodesia Native Reserves Commission, 1915* (London, 1917).

43. "The Division of Land Resources in Southern Rhodesia," *Annals of the Association of American Geographers* (March 1964), p. 51.

44. Around 1910 rents consisted of a charge of 20s. per annum per adult male on unalienated land and of a charge varying from 10s. to 40s. per adult male per annum on alienated land. In some cases an extra 10s. was charged for each wife exceeding one. (*Native Affairs Committee of Enquiry*, op. cit., p. 9.)

45. *Report of the CNC* for the year 1926. Similarly, the native commissioner of Belingwe was reported in the *Bulawayo Chronicle* of November 17, 1923, as follows: "Mr. Bullock instanced the case of a native paying 1d. per head a week for dipping. That was 4s. 4d. a year. The native beast was worth nominally 15s. so that the native was paying insurance at the rate of 30 percent per annum." He did not think any insurance company would have the audacity to ask such a rate.

46. An awareness of this relationship between the development of capitalist agriculture and the supply of labor is implicit in this passage taken from "The President's Address," *Seventh Report of the Chamber of Mines of Rhodesia*, for the year ended March 31, 1902:

"With this cheap form of labour [i.e., family labor] at his command, coupled with the fact that, provided he lives on Native Reserves, he has no rent to pay, and that his taxation is reduced to a minimum, the native is enabled year after year to produce a large amount of grain, which is in due course purchased from him by the trader, and eventually at an enhanced price by the mine owner, and in fact he continues year by year to become more affluent, less inclined to do any work himself, and to enter most successfully into competition with the white man in that most important of articles, namely, grain.

"I would suggest that a remedy can be found in two ways, namely, by taxation, and the adoption of a co-operative system of farming by the mine owners.

". . . Having the main factor, namely a soil sufficiently good to grow the grain, and in the majority of localities an unlimited supply of farm lands in proximity to our mines, I am certain that . . . grain could . . . be produced and delivered at the mines at a figure not exceeding 15s. per bag. If I am right in my contention, three most important points will be gained:

"1. It will be at once seen that grain at this price, coupled with the suggested special taxation, would enable us to successfully compete with the native, for it would practically leave no margin of profit to the middle man (the trader) . . . and, as a consequence, the main cause which at present enables a native to remain idle at his kraal would be removed.

"2. There would be an immediate saving to the mines for every bag of grain consumed during the year of from 10s. to 15s. . . .

"3. If this scheme of co-operative farming was adopted, it must mean the peopling of Rhodesia with a class of inhabitants which it requires more, perhaps, than any other class, namely, a settled farming population."

The *main* motivation for the administration's active encouragement of capitalist agriculture was not, however, that of solving the labor problem, but the desire of the B.S.A. Co. to recoup earlier heavy outlets in overhead capital. See Chapter 6 of this volume.

47. The shortage of labor was far more acute in capitalist agriculture than in the mining industry because the former's period of greatest demand coincided with the months of peak activity in the peasant sector *(Annual Reports of the CNC)*.

48. For example, owing to a low rainfall, difficulties of transport consequent upon a cattle plague, and a sharp increase in demand due to a spurt in the mining industry, a 200-lb. bag of mealies fetched 30s. The following year, on the other hand, owing to a large acreage of land having been put under cultivation by the white settlers, an extraordinarily favorable season, and a consequent large supply of African grain, the price per bag dropped to 10s. (Hone, op. cit., p. 200).

49. Tawse-Jollie, op. cit., pp. 131–36; Hone, op. cit., pp. 194–96. Tobacco cultivation, on a significant scale, was established only after the 1921–1923 crisis had created a situation of "unlimited" cheap labor supplies.

50. Calculated from estimates given in: *Report of the Administrator* for the year ended March 31, 1904; *Report of the CNC, Mashonaland*, for the year ended March 31, 1905; *Report of the CNC, Matabeleland* for the year ended March 31, 1905; *Report of the Secretary for Agriculture* for the year ended March 31, 1905; *Returns of the Census* held on April 17, 1904.

51. B.S.A. Co., *Directors' Reports and Accounts*, various years; *Annual Report of the Director of Agriculture*.

52. *Report of Cost of Living Committee* (Salisbury, 1913); B.S.A. Co., *Directors' Report and Accounts* for the two years ended March 31, 1914.

53. Cf. the discussion of the causes of low African participation in the labor market, above.

54. The concept of "subsistence" used here is in some ways similar to J. S. Duesenberry's "previous peak income" (*Income, Saving, and the Theory of Consumer Behavior* [Cambridge, Mass., 1949]) and T. E. Davis's "previous peak consumption" ("The Consumption Function as a Tool for Prediction," *Review of Economics and Statistics* [1952]). The main difference is that the period after which consumption becomes indispensable here is not specified. Moreover, the above authors discuss only the implications of the "incompressibility" of previous consumption on the propensity to save.

Here, on the other hand, the possibility that households may (in the face of a fall in income below "subsistence") increase their supply of labor or use more intensely the means of production (mainly land) under their control, is also taken into account.

55. *Report of the CNC, Matabeleland* for the year ended March 31, 1903.

56. *Report of the CNC, Matabeleland* for the year 1907.

57. *Report of the CNC, Matabeleland* for the year 1909.

58. *Report of the CNC, Matabeleland* for the year 1909.

59. *Report of the CNC, Matabeleland* for the year 1910.

60. B.S.A. Co., *Directors' Report and Accounts* for the year ended March 31, 1912.

61. *Report of the CNC, Mashonaland* for the year 1912; Tawse-Jollie, op. cit., p. 252; *Report of the Native Production and Trade Commission of Enquiry* (Salisbury, 1945).

62. E. A. G. Robinson, "The Economic Problem," in J. M. Davis, ed., *Modern Industry and the African* (London, 1933), p. 197.

63. *Notes on the Mining Industry of Southern Rhodesia*, compiled by N. H. Wilson (Salisbury, not dated); *Report of the CNC and Secretary for Internal Affairs* for the year 1943.

64. Tawse-Jollie, op. cit., p. 252.

65. *Mangwende Reserve Commission of Enquiry*, op. cit., p. 29.

66. Ibid.

67. Cf. M. Yudelman, *Africans on the Land* (Cambridge, Mass., 1964), pp. 236–37.

68. *Report of the CNC, Mashonaland* for the year 1909; *Southern Rhodesia Native Reserve Commission*, op. cit., p. 9; Gann, op. cit.

69. *Annual Report of the CNC.*

70. Broadly speaking we shall say that the productive absorption of the surplus is "efficient" when it takes into account existing scarcities of factors of production.

71. These forms of surplus absorption consisted of all labor-time directly or indirectly expended on religious and social activities whose main function was to foster social cohesion. There were, of course, many activities in traditional African societies whose main function was productive, or administrative, but which contributed to strengthen social cohesion. The empirical distinction between the two would often be problematic if not impossible.

72. *Annual Report of the CNC; Native Affairs Committee of Enquiry*, op. cit.; *Southern Rhodesia Native Reserve Commission*, op. cit.

73. *Annual Report of the CNC.*

74. The rate of consumption of cattle, and therefore their rate of accumulation,

was related to the size of the surplus. The ritual aspect of cattle played a crucial role in this relationship. In periods of adverse natural conditions there would be more "pretexts" for ritual killings, the rate of cattle consumption would increase, and the rate of accumulation decrease. Conversely, in periods of large yields the rate of accumulation would increase.

75. *Annual Report of the CNC; Native Affairs Committee of Enquiry*, op. cit.; *Report of the Director of Agriculture* for the year 1914.

76. *Annual Report of the CNC.*

77. By "land-consuming bias" we shall understand the tendency of an investment or innovation to lead to a greater use of land for a given output. Similarly, we shall talk of land saving, labor saving, labor intensive, and capital intensive biases. It goes without saying that these distinctions are not watertight and that an investment or innovation may have simultaneously two or more biases.

78. *Annual Report of the Director (or Department) of Agriculture.*

79. B.S.A. Co., *Directors' Report and Accounts* for the two years ended March 31, 1914.

80. "Statement of Case of Rhodesian Agriculture Union," in *Report by Brigadier General F. D. Hammond on the Railway System of Rhodesia*, vol. 2, Ann. "C" (Salisbury, 1925).

81. *Annual Report of the Director of (or Secretary for) Agriculture.*

82. *Report of the CNC, Matabeleland* for the year 1909; *Report of the CNC* for the year 1918.

83. *Report of the CNC* for the years 1920 and 1921.

84. *Report of the CNC* for the years 1918, 1919, and 1922.

85. Calculated from "The Economic Position of the Native," *Economic and Statistical Bulletin of Southern Rhodesia*, no. 8 (1933).

86. *Report of the CNC* for the years 1921, 1922, 1923, 1925, 1926, and 1931.

87. The amount paid in dog tax by Africans, "an unfailing barometer indicating the state of their cash holdings," as the CNC put it in his *Report* for the year 1932, fell by almost 33 percent between 1921 and 1923 and by over 43 percent between 1930 and 1934 (calculated from the *Annual Report of the CNC*).

88. *Report of the CNC* for the year 1926.

89. *Report of the CNC* for the year 1928.

90. *Report of the CNC* for the year 1932.

91. G. K. Garbett, "The Land Husbandry Act of Southern Rhodesia," in D. Biebuyck, ed., *African Agrarian Systems* (London, 1963), p. 190.

92. *Native Production and Trade Commission*, op. cit.

93. The number of grade bulls owned by Africans purchased through the Native Department, i.e., excluding those bought privately, increased from 918

in 1925 to 3,737 in 1930 (figures taken from the *Annual Report of the CNC*).

94. According to the estimates of the CNC, the number of African-owned wheeled vehicles more than doubled between 1926 and 1930.

95. *Report of the CNC* for the years 1934 and 1940.

96. According to all available evidence, i.e., that contained in the sources cited in Table 1, the fall in maize and cattle prices that occurred during the two slumps led to a drastic deterioration in the terms of trade of the peasant sector with the capitalist sector, notwithstanding the relatively moderate fall in money wages. In defining the concept of surplus (see above) we disregarded its relation to the terms of trade between the peasant and the capitalist sector. In the present context this relation has crucial importance and must be briefly discussed. A worsening in the terms of trade tends to reduce the real value of the surplus for two reasons: (1) because it increases the quantity of output that must be foregone in order to obtain those means of subsistence which are produced within the peasant economy; and (2) because it reduces the unitary value of the surplus in terms of the commodities against which it has to be exchanged in order to be realized. The negative impact of worsening terms of trade on the peasantry's surplus-generating capacity will therefore be the greater the more dependent are the peasants on exchange with the capitalist sector for their subsistence requirements and for the conversion of the surplus in its desired forms. It follows that the steady increase in such dependence which, as we have seen, took place in Rhodesia during the first two decades of this century had, among other things, the effect of magnifying the negative repercussion of the depressions of the early 1920s and 1930s on the surplus-generating capacity of the African peasantry.

97. Cf. Myint, op. cit., pp. 45–46. Myint deals with innovations in crops only, but his remarks obviously apply to most land-saving innovations such as green manuring, conservation works, etc.

98. *Report of the CNC, Matabeleland* for the year ended March 31, 1905, and for the year 1910; *Report of the CNC* for the year 1920.

99. *Mangwende Reserve Commission of Enquiry*, op. cit., p. 40.

100. Ibid.

101. *Native Production and Trade Commission*, op. cit., p. 26.

102. *Report of the CNC* for the year 1938; *Report of Commission to Enquire into the Preservation* (. . .) *of the Natural Resources of the Colony* (Salisbury, 1939), pp. 11–12.

103. The assumption of a changing role of the plough in peasant agriculture is consistent with the fact that, while before 1920 the acreage under cultivation increased rapidly (at an average rate of almost 5 percent per year be-

tween 1911 and 1920, according to the estimates of the CNC) and the proportion of indigenous males in wage employment remained constant (see Fig. 1), after 1920 the rate of increase in the acreage under cultivation slowed down (it averaged only 2.2 percent per year in the period 1920–1945) and the proportion of indigenous males in wage employment rose sharply. The assumption is also consistent with observations of the native commissioners: in 1908, for example, the CNC, Matabeleland, reported that the introduction of the plough tended to reduce the supply of labor because it induced greater involvement of male labor in the cultivation of land; in 1927, on the other hand, the plough began to be referred to as a "labor-saving device."

104. On this opinion the literature is unanimous. Cf., for example, A. Pendered and von Memerty, "The Land Husbandry Act of Southern Rhodesia," *Journal of African Administration*, no. 3 (1955); Barber, op. cit.; Yudelman, op. cit., pp. 132–33; G. Kay, "The Distribution of African Population in Southern Rhodesia: Some Preliminary Notes," *Rhodes-Livingstone Communication*, no. 28 (Lusaka, 1964).

105. *Report of the Native Education Enquiry Commission, 1951* (Salisbury, 1952).

106. Calculated from: *Annual Report of the Commissioner of Taxes; Annual Report of the CNC and Secretary for Internal Affairs;* and *Southern Rhodesia Statistical Yearbook* (Salisbury, 1947).

107. *Native Production and Trade Commission*, op. cit., p. 25. These fears were fully justified in view of the continuous curtailment of the *de facto* availability of land to Africans and also in view of official statements such as the following: "It is intended to develop the native reserves so as to enable them to carry a larger population, and so avoid, so far as possible, the necessity for acquisition of more land for native occupation. . . ." (*Report of the CNC* for the year 1932).

108. *Second Report of the Select Committee on the Resettlement of Natives* (Salisbury, 1960); and *Annual Report of the CNC and Secretary for Internal Affairs*.

109. R. W. M. Johnson, *African Agricultural Development in Southern Rhodesia* (Stanford, 1964), pp. 196–97; Yudelman, op. cit., p. 197.

110. *Interim Report on Livestock and Meat with Special Reference to Cattle and Beef* (Salisbury, 1936); Yudelman, op. cit., pp. 190–91.

111. *Native Production and Trade Commission*, op. cit., p. 50.

112. Cf. A. K. Sen, *Choice of Techniques* (Oxford, 1962), p. 30 and Appendix A in particular; see also Chayanov, op. cit., p. 7. This discrepancy in investment behavior is largely traceable to differences in "time horizons" in production and investment decisions. But the "time horizon" of the peas-

antry is itself a variable depending on the latter's surplus-generating capacity: the smaller such capacity, and therefore the more the peasants are struggling to maintain a certain level of subsistence consumption, the shorter their time horizon in reinvesting surpluses. It follows that the reduction in the African peasant's surplus-generating capacity that occurred in the 1920s and 1930s must have widened the gap between their "time horizon" and that of capitalist producers.

113. Thus, in the late 1950s the amount of *private* capital invested in European farms was estimated at £250 million (*Select Committee on the Resettlement of Natives*, op. cit., p. 49), while the gross value of *all* capital (i.e., including accumulated government investment in infrastructure) in African agriculture was roughly estimated at £90 million, over 35 percent of which was accounted for by livestock. (Yudelman, op. cit., p. 155.) At the time there were less than 4,500 European farms while the number of African holdings was estimated at about 380,000. It is, of course, impossible to assess the extent to which this huge difference in capital invested has been brought about by market forces rather than political mechanisms owing to the interaction of the two in the historical process.

114. In the 1950s it was reckoned that only 235,000 families could derive a sub sistence (as determined by a rather restrictive formula adopted by the government) from the land available for African use. This meant that probably more than half of the African population had to obtain the bulk of its means of subsistence from wage employment (*Select Committee on the Resettlement of Natives*, op. cit., p. 43). But even among the families who could derive a subsistence from agricultural production it was only a small minority that obtained its *cash* requirements from the sale of produce. In the Mangwende Reserve, for example, it was found that the so-called ordinary farmers, under which category fell 70 percent of all peasant holdings in the Reserve, had average net cash incomes (sales minus expenses) of only £3.5 per annum as against the £40 earned by the Master Farmers (rich peasants) who represented 4–5 percent of all peasant holdings (*Mangwende Reserve Commission of Enquiry*, op. cit., p. 32).

115. Cf. on this A. G. Frank's theses on Latin American underdevelopment in his *Capitalism and Underdevelopment in Latin America* (New York, 1967).

116. Lewis's reference to "primary accumulation" runs as follows: "[The capitalists] will not support proposals for land settlement, and are often instead to be found engaged in turning the peasants off their lands [see Marx on "Primary Accumulation"]. This is one of the worst features of imperialism, for instance."

117. Cf. p. 181 and note 13 above.

118. *First Interim Report of the Development Co-ordinating Commission of*

Southern Rhodesia (Salisbury, 1948); *Report of the Select Committee on the Subject of Native Industrial Workers' Union Bill* (Salisbury, 1956). The *Report of the National Native Labour Board,* op. cit., gives the following figure of labor turnover among the employees of the Bulawayo Municipality during the year ended March 31, 1948:

Number employed on April 1, 1947	3,059
Number engaged during the year ended March 31, 1948	3,448
Number discharged	3,426
Number employed at March 31, 1948	3,081

119. *Development Co-ordinating Commission,* op. cit.; *Censuses of Industrial Production, 1938–1953; Annual Report of the Chief Government Mining Engineer and Chief Inspector of Mines* for the year 1954.

120. *Report of the Urban African Affairs Commission* (Salisbury, 1958); D. G. Bettison, "The Poverty Datum Line in Central Africa," *Human Problems in British Central Africa* (June 1960).

121. Cf. Mitchell, op. cit., p. 223 also for references to the vast literature on the subject.

122. *Annual Report of the Director of Agriculture.*

123. *Annual Report of the Director of Agriculture* for the year 1922.

124. Throughout his article, Lewis implicitly assumes the operation of competitive forces in the capitalist sector.

125. See Chapter 6 of this volume.

126. I have discussed this problem more extensively in Chapter 3 of this volume.

127. The ratio of capital formation to GDP, which had averaged approximately 37 percent in the period 1951–1958, fell to 25.5 percent in 1959–1961 and to 15.4 percent in 1962–1964 (*National Accounts and Balance of Payments of Rhodesia, 1965* [Salisbury, 1966]).

128. See Chapter 7 of this volume.

129. "Economic Rationality and Behaviour Patterns in an Underdeveloped Area: A Case Study of African Economic Behaviour in the Rhodesias," *Economic Development and Cultural Change,* no. 3 (1960), p. 251.

Part III

Case Studies

6

African Socialism in One Country: Tanzania

John S. Saul

The evaluation of Tanzania's efforts at socialist construction provides a dilemma both for the indigenous radical and for the international socialist. Given the odds against the emergence of progressive initiatives in Tanzania under the objective conditions which characterize that country, what has been accomplished may seem significant. And this accomplishment becomes all the more important when it is compared with developments elsewhere on the continent or indeed with any immediately likely alternative regime within Tanzania itself.[1] At the same time, there are, not surprisingly, a number of features which would make any socialist uneasy. It is important, therefore, to avoid the uncritical enthusiasm of, say, Scandinavian social democrats who unself-consciously applaud shortcomings which parallel their own when they are clad in African dress. But there is also to be found on the left a wholesale rejection of Tanzania's efforts on militantly *a priori* grounds—Nyerere's Catholicism and his incomprehension of Marxism, for example, or the country's often mindlessly assertive "nonalignment"—which is almost equally misleading. For this "ultra-left" critique—at its most absurd in Robin Blackburn's recent *ex cathedra* characterization of Nyerere as a "tame African" (in his otherwise subtly argued analysis of contemporary Britain)[2]—is as insensitive to African reality and the range of possibility on the continent as the former, and opposite, error.

This essay was originally presented as a paper to the Dakar Symposium on Strategies for Development: Africa Compared with Latin America, sponsored by the African Institute for Economic Development and Planning in September 1972.

I am particularly grateful to two of my former colleagues at the University of Dar es Salaam, Fred Bienefeld and Peter Lawrence, for their critical encouragement and for their many valuable suggestions during my preparation of the paper.

1. Achievement

What are the crucial dimensions of Tanzania's achievement, then? At the most general level these can be grouped under three rubrics: those which relate to the articulation of the continental revolution in Africa, those which relate directly to the liberation of Southern Africa, and those which relate to the internal transformation of Tanzania itself. As regards the continent as a whole, it is scarcely profane knowledge that the sixties—the independence decade—have brought a striking defeat to the high hopes of nationalist assertion nurtured by the preceding decade. Fanon's most despairing imaginings—false decolonization, mere flag independence, the hegemony of a bankrupt petty bourgeoisie—have become the characteristic texture of contemporary Africa. Here and there brief but all too obviously blighted resistance has been offered, attempts made to stay such a collapse—Nkrumah's Ghana in the early sixties,[3] Touré's Guinée. From these experiences lessons, albeit many negative ones, were learned which will be of relevance to future generations of progressive Africans. When one realizes that Africa, especially black Africa, can only liberate itself continentally, not "nationally," the importance of this continental learning experience becomes all the more apparent. And in Tanzania, one can say quite unequivocally, the struggle for progressive solutions to Africa's development problems has been taken, in certain crucial spheres, a stage further than in any of its sister states. This is a point which will emerge more clearly as we proceed; suffice it to say here that, stand or fall, socialism in Tanzania has already made its contribution in this respect.

Equally noteworthy, though often underestimated, is the continuing importance of Tanzania's contribution to the struggle in Southern Africa. It may be that it is the latter struggle which will release, in time, the most potent revolutionary energies of relevance to the continent's future; the sociopolitical transformations which are taking place inside Guiné-Bissau and liberated Mozambique already suggest some ways in which this could prove to be the case. But the struggle is a long one and it is difficult to underestimate the crucial nature, at this stage, of the solidarity and support received from independent states on the border of the Southern Africa complex.

Here Tanzania's record is almost impeccable: constant critic of Britain, most vocal antagonist, in the OAU and elsewhere, of the "dialogue" with South Africa which is favored by many African states, staunch supporter of beleaguered Zambia, host and regular financial contributor (no small thing, unfortunately) to the OAU's Liberation Committee. Nor has it shown any sign of flinching in light of Portugal's invasion of Guinée, no closer to Bissau than Tanzania is to Mozambique; quite the contrary. For it is well known that Tanzania has provided facilities and much freedom of maneuver for Mozambique revolutionaries (among others) as they move south. Also important, though less well known, is the fact that Tanzania has increasingly been the guarantor of the emergence of the most progressive tendencies among the Mozambican revolutionaries themselves; even in this indirect manner, therefore, it has also contributed to the militancy of the struggle there.[4] No one knowledgeable about Southern Africa can overlook the centrality of such a diverse role, nor assume that this positive involvement is somehow automatically forthcoming merely because of Tanzania's geopolitical location. The examples of Zaire and Malawi provide ample warning against any such glib assumption. It is developments internal to Tanzania—in fact, the articulation of its own particular brand of socialism—which have helped sustain the stance vis-à-vis the South. For that reason alone these developments would have to be taken seriously.

Finally, within Tanzania itself: clearly a convincing assessment of the advances made in this respect should also provide the evidence which documents the other two areas of achievement staked out above. For this reason the argument cannot be neatly summarized in advance but must rather be proven in detail as we proceed. Here, in a prefatory manner, it can merely be suggested that, in terms of obtaining national control over surpluses and cutting the links of dependency, in terms of stemming the crystallization of reactionary privilege and power and providing the conscious and effective base for a further articulation of progressive policies, in terms of generating the cultural and ideological weapons necessary for resisting imperialist hegemony and underpinning such policies, significant breakthroughs have been made. Moreover, even though all of these advances are problematic (as we shall see), they do provide, at the same time, some promise of a further progressive transformation of the situation. This much having been said, we can now proceed to a concrete specification of the "achievement" which can thus be claimed for Tanzania by critically sympathetic analysts of the situation there.

The novel package of policies worked out in Tanzania since early

1967 (and referred to in the official rhetoric as the combination of "socialism and self-reliance") has found its most dramatic expression in the effort to restructure the country's inherited economy and, as noted, to redress the rigid dependence upon the international capitalist system which was inherited from the colonial period. As Nyerere argued at that time (1967):

> The question is not whether nations control their economy, but how they do so. The real ideological choice is between controlling the economy through domestic private enterprise, or doing so through some state or other collective institution.
>
> But although this is an ideological choice, it is extremely doubtful whether it is a practical choice for an African nationalist. The pragmatist in Africa . . . will find that the real choice is a different one. He will find that the choice is between foreign private ownership on the one hand, and local collective ownership on the other. For I do not think there is a free state in Africa where there is sufficient local capital, or a sufficient number of local entrepreneurs, for locally based capitalism to dominate the economy. Private investment in Africa means overwhelming foreign private investment. A capitalist economy means a foreign-dominated economy. These are the facts of Africa's situation. The only way in which national control of the economy can be achieved is through the economic institutions of socialism.[5]

Nationalization (with "full and fair" compensation) was the method adopted in the first instance to realize these goals of structural transformation; it was the mechanism which helped Tanzania turn "the large-scale manufacturing, commercial, and financial sectors from 90 percent foreign-owned in 1967 to 80 percent public-sector majority-owned in 1972."[6] But new public investment in various productive spheres has also been designed to reinforce this pattern of deep-cutting change. As we shall see, Tanzania has not avoided all of the more subtle dangers of sophisticated imperialist manipulation *within* the very framework of nationalization itself (management agreements, charges and patents, etc.), especially in the industrial sphere, nor taken every advantage of the further opportunities provided by its various initiatives. But real gains have been made nonetheless in terms of the availability of surpluses which would otherwise have slipped away,[7] and in terms of the access to levers of control over the economy without which any comprehensive and progressive planning would be impossible.[8] R. H. Green's summary is in fact a fair one, as far as it goes:

The investment plan can . . . be said to be characterized by primary reliance on domestic resource mobilization augmented by foreign borrowing. This is a pattern radically divergent from that of a majority of African states which combined government infrastructural investment progress largely financed from abroad with private sector directly productive investment ambitions which are seen as depending largely on foreign capital inflows, including reinvested local profits.[9]

Of course, the weakness of the Tanzanian economy at independence was expressed only in part by the fact of foreign ownership of trading, financial, and industrial sectors (the last named being in any case a minute one). For first and foremost was another structural reality imposed on Tanzania by the logic of colonialism: its agriculturally biased, export-oriented character. At independence, for example, 57 percent of the country's exports were provided by three main agricultural products (cotton, coffee, and sisal) and another 9 percent by diamonds from Mwadui, an important but rapidly depleting resource; this in turn represented 28 percent of monetary GDP at the time. This kind of bias in the economy has proven to be an even more difficult legacy to overcome, despite public investment activity in the "modern" sector, despite some efforts at agricultural diversification, and despite the constant reiteration of the slogan of "self-reliance." In the longer run, these latter emphases may begin to have more effect; equally significant could be the movement toward collectivization in the rural areas, the *ujamaa* villages program.[10] This effort to group farmers (where necessary) and gradually to shift their productive activities to a collective basis was first enunciated in 1967, but has gradually taken up an increasing proportion of government time and resources in the rural sector. The main locus of this policy's impact so far is still in those backward areas relatively untransformed by "possessive individualism"; there some massive population movements have already been realized. In more settled, longer established, cash-cropping areas the pace of change is considerably slower, but the intention is that in all parts of the country collective units will become the logical basis for improved production, technical innovation, agricultural diversification, and the improvement of the quality of rural life.

Intensified reliance on loans (and also on "aid"), though less dangerous than the reliance on direct capital investment which generally characterizes African countries, has also to be squared with the Tanzanian emphasis upon the rhetoric of self-reliance; ultimately it must be measured against the real rather than the rhetorical imperatives of an internally oriented, fully effective development effort as well. The government, for its part, has argued that in practice such loans and various forms of aid have positively serviced the realization of the country's broader goals, that these inflows, though a vital prop to Tanzania's investment plans,[11] have been chosen in such a way as to strengthen its efforts to shake free from the more obvious forms of dependence sketched above. Here one sees both change and continuity; at this point in the essay it is the changes which can be stressed. Thus the most dramatic innovation in the field of external economic relations has certainly been the importance attached to the establishment of links, of various sorts, with China. The latter has become an important partner in certain manufacturing spheres (textiles, farm implements) and in the Tanzania-Zambia railway project, an increasingly active partner in barter arrangements (tied, principally, to the railway project) that are beginning to shift the pattern of imports out of established grooves, and a potential partner in the designing of even more radical strategic departures.[12] Tanzanians would probably also want to place great emphasis on the fact that the other two sources which may provide (along with China) 20 to 25 percent each of the official capital and technical assistance inflows for the 1969–1974 plan period are the World Bank Group (a "multilateral" agency) and Sweden (a "neutral" country).[13] This is also a real part of Tanzania's diversification; how much structural, socialist change the latter two loan/aid sources will actually encourage is, of course, another question. This remains, in fact, a slippery area of Tanzanian practice to which we will return.

But even granting, for the moment, that the assertion of national, state, control is novel in scope and embodies formally, and increasingly in practice, real progressive potential, recognition of this fact alone does not take us far enough into the realities of contemporary Tanzania. For, significantly, the possibility that such an "étatist" approach to "economic independence" could degenerate into an exploitative system in its own right has not escaped the attention of the leadership. Indeed, an attack on the privileged access to the surplus enjoyed by the political and bureaucratic "elite," and on the bureaucratic and authoritarian methods of work which generally accompany such a reality, had begun even before the initiatives were taken to nationalize the "commanding heights." In the first instance, this took the form of an effort to democratize the *de facto* one-party state which had been created by TANU's (literally) overwhelming political successes; thus in 1965 an imaginative electoral system was constructed and put into effect which ensured a measure of genuine competition within the one-party framework and which reflected some real concern to institutionalize checks on the leadership from below.[14] In Africa this is striking enough; much more dramatic, however, was the "leadership code" lying at the core of the Arusha Declaration as passed by the National Executive Committee of the ruling party, TANU, in February 1967.[15] Under the terms of this ruling, "leaders" (defined to include all upper- and middle-level politicians and civil servants) were to be denied involvement in the private sector (with the exception of their ownership of small family farms). They were not to be allowed to employ labor, nor to receive rents or profits; furthermore, it was made impossible for such members of the elite to receive more than one salary within the public sector itself.

The intention which lay behind these innovations was stated quite explicitly: to preempt the possibility of leaders being "purchased" by private interests, foreign and domestic,[16] to forestall the emergence of the grossest forms of conflict of interest inherent in the overlapping of public and private realms (this latter pattern being a characteristic feature of recent developments on the continent), and to cut the gap, financial and psychological, between the elite and the mass of the population. Other changes have also been introduced in order to squeeze the petty bourgeoisie of the state apparatus. Thus there has been a particularly sharp attack on salary (and fringe benefit) differentials within the Tanzanian system in the period from independence to the present. Rough estimates of the range of real income differentials in the public sector wage and salary group for 1961 might place it at a level of 80 or 100 to 1. M. A. Bienefeld estimates that ten years later, after the introduction of various taxes, levies, and wage and salary adjustments, these ratios may have fallen to as low as 9 or 14 to 1.[17] This is not to say that the elite have been reduced to austerity levels, of course, but to point out a significant variation on a continental tendency merely to "Africanize" the received differentials. Slowly, slowly, other privileges have come under attack: the easy access to loans, the ready availability of various imported luxury items, including private automobiles,[18] and so on. To be sure, implementation of some of these measures could have been much tighter, much stiffer, but a distinctive trend can be seen to exist nonetheless.

As it has turned out, it was not the leadership's intention merely to seal off civil servants and politicians from the private sector in order to guarantee the preeminence of their personal concern for the "public interest." Going further, a sustained effort has been made to nip in the bud the emergence of *any* African entrepreneurial group whatsoever. Consider, for example, the trading sector. In Tanzania, nationalization and/or cooperativization of trade is the goal and has been pushed vigorously on a number of fronts; [19] at the same time, as long as the capacity fully to implement this program lags, Asians (who, in addition, are often noncitizens) continue to predominate within the substantial "breathing space" which is left for private entrepreneurial initiative. In nearby Kenya and Uganda, in sharp contrast, the African petty bourgeoisie has warped *all* policy in this sphere to service the replacing of the Asian group by themselves in their private capacities. Racist nationalism has thus become the tool of this rising African class to advance its own entrepreneurial aggrandizement, while in Tanzania strong efforts have been made precisely to defuse such tendencies in the interests of collective advance.

In a similar vein, 1971 saw the nationalization of all large private buildings used for rental purposes. In part this was to further dramatize, for public consumption, the fact that the Asian community, which provided the most prominent of such owners, was beginning to pay the price of collectivization. But, equally important, it was designed to close off another area of private profit to entrepreneurially inclined Africans.[20] Nor is the agricultural sector immune from such principled attack. The program of rural collectivization, mentioned above, has as its ultimate aim not just the raising of agricultural productivity but also, as an important goal in its own right, the displacement of differentiation in the rural areas:

> . . . as land becomes more scarce we shall find ourselves with a farmers' class and a labourers' class. . . . The latter will become a "rural proletariat" depending on the decisions of others for their existence, and subject in consequence to all the subservience, social and economic inequality, and insecurity, which such a position involves. . . . The present trend is away from extended family production and social unity, and towards the devel-

opment of a class system in the rural areas. It is this kind of development which would be inconsistent with the growth of a socialist Tanzania.[21]

Sealed off from the private sector (a private sector which may be, in any case, a declining proposition), other of their privileges being whittled away, the petty bourgeoisie who are in possession of the state apparatus in Tanzania are under great pressure either to reverse the trend *or* to commit themselves, increasingly, to its further extension and elaboration. Roger Murray has argued that those who inherit power from the colonial rulers in Africa are, at least temporarily, characterized by their "relative social autonomy and plasticity," [22] their lack of a decisive, structurally defined stake in the status quo. The Tanzanian leadership has, in effect, operated on this premise; as a result, moves to stem the consolidation of the elite's material stake in the system have also been complemented by the waging of some sort of *ideological struggle* for the commitment of this crucial stratum of Tanzanian society.

The educational system created by the colonialists was a crucial instrument in the genesis of the Tanzanian petty bourgeoisie:

. . . the educational system introduced into Tanzania by the colonialists was modelled on the British system, but with even heavier emphasis on subservient attitudes and on white-collar skills. Inevitably, too, it was based on the assumptions of a colonialist and capitalist society. It emphasized and encouraged the individualistic instincts of mankind, instead of his cooperative instincts. It led to the possession of individual material wealth being the major criterion of social merit and worth.

This meant that colonial education induced attitudes of human inequality, and in practice underpinned the domination of the weak by the strong, especially in the economic field.[23]

Not surprisingly, in light of Nyerere's own analysis, much of the effort to reclaim this class for national and for socialist development has been directed toward the ultimate transformation of that system. An early stimulus to the intensification of the socialist project in 1967 had been, in any case, the resistance offered by university students in 1966 to the introduction of a compulsory period of national service for all those who reached an advanced educational level (this service in turn having been designed to elicit a higher level of commitment from those who passed through it). In the aftermath of the expulsion of these students, other innovations, in syllabus and in the social life of educational institutions, were experimented with which have, to some extent, worked their way through the educational system.[24] The concept of education itself also began to broaden, with the idea of extending "political education" an increasingly ubiquitous one and involving, as far as the elite is concerned, participation in an increased number of seminars and sessions directed toward their enhanced understanding of novel policy initiatives. And, with the nationalization and further development of newspapers, as well as other measures to establish a communications network with a progressive tone, at least some of the ingredients necessary for realizing an ethos of information and discourse different from the hand-me-down, sub-European cultural milieu of most African capitals have been supplied.

In such an overall context, and with action on so many fronts, it can be affirmed that a real attempt is being made in Tanzania to cut back the privileges of the petty bourgeoisie, to forestall its becoming a quasi-capitalist class (even if a very dependent one), and to win over an increasing number of its members to a more progressive role. As Amilcar Cabral has phrased the point, "The petty bourgeoisie can either ally itself with imperialism and the reactionary strata in its own country to try and preserve itself as a petty bourgeoisie or ally itself with the workers and peasants who must themselves take power." [25] The most advanced sections of the Tanzanian leadership have, in effect, taken the first part of this proposition seriously; they have attempted to structure that choice for themselves and their colleagues and to encourage a socialist response. But it is equally significant to note their implicit agreement with the final, crucial clause of Cabral's formulation. For such leadership elements have realized that there are inherent limitations upon the extent to which a ruling class, even a nascent and fluid one, can be expected to commit altruistic suicide; the other side of the leadership coin has therefore been an attempt to find a *mass base* for Tanzanian socialism among those who have, objectively, a more immediate stake in the promise of socialist transformation. There is an attempt, in short, to invoke and to channel popular pressures and popular demands in such a manner as to underwrite Tanzania's progressive initiatives.

This attempt has, in turn, both ideological and organizational dimensions. Ideological struggle is not confined merely to the petty bourgeois stratum, for example. Progressive themes articulated in the course of that struggle have become part of the effort to raise the level of consciousness of the mass of the population, and this may well be of even more crucial long-run importance than intra-elite contestation. The vital contribution of such ideological clarification to mass involvement is, in fact, two-fold: it can defuse mystifying ideologies which confuse the masses on the one hand, and it can make available to them a positive understanding of the terms of their exploitation and the realities of their structural position within the system on the other. When seen in this light Nyerere's principled assaults, constantly reiterated, on "racism" and the cruder variants of Black Power are revealed as something more than mere moralizing.[26] They are part of a broader attack upon the ideological bases of elite aggrandizement and opposition to socialism (as noted above), and an attempt to free the ordinary citizen from the hegemony of biases which can provide, at best, only vicarious identification with the successes of newly privileged members of his own race and which are unlikely (partly for that very reason) to advance his own liberation.

The same can be said of the government's outspoken hostility to the politics of ethnicity and tribal confrontation. Though the dramatic mobilization and politicization of ethnic identity in contemporary Africa does have objective bases (colonially induced uneven development, for example), it is, under post-independence conditions, even more the creation of elite manipulation. Once stimulated it becomes a weapon by which individual members of the ruling group, as "ethnic spokesmen," strengthen their bargaining position vis-à-vis other elite contestants for power, and by which the class as a whole can neutralize any possibility of the mass of the population gaining consciousness of itself as a class in its own right, as the "losers" in a class structure whose logic cuts horizontally across tribal lines; such "tribalism" can readily be seen, in particularly flagrant form, in both nearby Uganda and Kenya. True, from the point of view of African elites there can be too much of a good thing—ethnic competition can get out of hand, threatening the disintegration of the whole system. To avert such dangers the worst excesses will be papered over, where possible, with a thin layer of nationalist rhetoric. But the real alternative to "tribalism" is to reject this pattern root and branch. And it is precisely this alternative that Tanzania has begun to choose. Far from seeking to so instrumentalize the mass of the population as to protect the elite, the Tanzanian leadership has chosen to discipline anyone who would seek to introduce such dimensions overtly into the political arena[27] and, even more fundamentally, has positively encouraged those in nonelite categories to think of themselves, first and foremost, as "workers and peasants"!

Framed within even a comparative East African perspective, therefore, the importance of the fact that these latter categories are consistently invoked in Tanzania may be sufficiently apparent (this despite the relative looseness in the usage of such terms upon occasion). But it can be noted further that the quasi-class perspective encouraged by such usage has taken its place alongside other elements in Tanzania's ideological formulations as merely one contribution to a distinctive overall pattern, a pattern which has come to possess, as it unfolds, increasingly broader and more progressive significance. For example, there can be few regimes in the world in which the populace is officially enjoined to distrust its leaders:

> President Nyerere has called on the people of Tanzania to have great confidence in themselves and safeguard the nation's hard-won freedom. He has warned the people against pinning all their hopes on the leadership who are apt to sell the people's freedom to meet their lusts.
>
> Mwalimu [i.e., Nyerere] warned that the people should not allow their freedom to be pawned as most of the leaders were purchasable. He warned further that in running the affairs of the nation the people should not look on their leaders as "saints or prophets."
>
> The President stated that the attainment of freedom in many cases resulted merely in the change of colours, white to black faces without ending exploitation and injustices, and above all without the betterment of the life of the masses.
>
> He said that while struggling for freedom the objective was clear but it was another thing when you have to remove your own people from the position of exploiters.[28]

Yet this is a theme often reiterated by the President of the United Republic of Tanzania. Certain closely related emphases also characterize *Mwongozo/The TANU Guidelines* of 1971: this document represents the most radical policy departure articulated by the ruling party since the promulgation of the Arusha Declaration itself. For a major theme of the *Guidelines* was a further extension of the concept of pervasive democratization and popular control, a concept which we saw to underlie the reshaping of the electoral system as early as 1965. In 1971, paragraph 15 of *Mwongozo* argues:

Together with the issue of involving the people in solving their problems, there is also the question of the habits of leaders in their work and in day-to-day life. There must be a deliberate effort to build equality between the leaders and those they lead. For a Tanzanian leader it must be forbidden to be arrogant, extravagant, contemptuous, and oppressive. The Tanzanian leader has to be a person who respects people, scorns ostentation, and is not a tyrant. . . . Similarly, the party has the responsibility to fight the vindictiveness of some of its agents. Such actions do not promote socialism but drive a wedge between the party and the government on the one side, and the people on the other.

And paragraph 28 concludes in a complementary vein:

The duty of the party is not to urge the people to implement plans which have been decided upon by a few experts or leaders. The duty of our party is to ensure that the leaders and experts implement the plans that have been agreed upon by the people themselves. When the people's decision requires information which is only available to the leaders and experts, it will be the duty of the leaders and experts to make such information available to the people. But it is not correct for leaders and experts to usurp the people's right to decide on an issue just because they have the expertise.[29]

Bland enough formulations in some ways, but there can be no mistaking their importance. In the months which followed their publication (and widespread distribution as a pocketsize booklet) aspects of the *Guidelines*, and paragraph 15 in particular, were avidly seized upon by workers, students, and others, and genuine assaults from below, in some instances overtly supported by senior leaders, were launched upon bureaucratic and authoritarian methods of work.[30]

Parenthetically, it can be noted that these fresh formulations have also had an important impact on Tanzania's emerging economic philosophy in ways which are complementary to the pattern of economic policy which we had begun to trace earlier in this section. For the nature of the yawning gap between the urban and rural areas has been much stressed in Tanzanian pronouncements; indeed, the felt need to close that gap was one of the most important (and most discussed) motives which underlay the various socialist initiatives of 1967.[31] This in turn has brought an increased emphasis upon rural development, broadly conceived: on *ujamaa vijijini* and on regional planning, including a radical decentralization of the decision-making process to which we will refer again below. Moreover, even the principle of a complementary decentralization from Dar es Salaam of industrial development—to regional centers and even, where possible, to the new collective villages themselves—is actively canvassed.[32] There is thus economic promise in Tanzania's recent moves: the promise of genuinely releasing the energies of the mass of the population, for example, and the further promise of placing the needs of the masses at the center of the economic development strategy.[33]

It will be apparent that *Mwongozo* has provided an ideological form and an ideological sanction for efforts to activate the necessary mass base of Tanzania's socialism. The parallel challenge is to meet the *organizational requirements* of realizing such a goal, and effectively to institutionalize the expression of popular power. Here, too, progress has been made. It is true that in the early post-independence period, the government's stance vis-à-vis the wage-earning section of the population had been tilted in the direction of control from above. Under African conditions this latter group is small and its better-organized members strategically well placed to bid up their wages. As the Tanzanian government expanded the state-owned sector of the economy and cut back certain elite privileges, its policy of tightly controlling the collective bargaining process, of undermining the relative autonomy of Tanzanian trade unions, and of bringing the latter into a government-sponsored and unified structure (the National Union of Tanzanian Workers—NUTA) could be to some extent justified (and certainly much more so than parallel government action in many other African countries) as satisfying the imperatives of a progressive development strategy.[34] Fortunately, however, the leadership chose not to let the matter rest there.

Worried, in any case, by the creeping apathy of the workers induced by such a structure,[35] and further stimulated by the growing general concern (which we have been tracing) to guarantee a base for socialism, great emphasis has recently been laid on the realization of "workers' participation" through the establishment of workers' councils in factories and offices.[36] And the *ujamaa* villages program has also had as one of its goals the growth from newly mobilized and conscious collectivities of more effective and coherent peasant pressures within various local and regional organizations, and within national institutions.[37] The most recent variation on this emphasis is equally important: a searching critique of the overcentralized planning system (with its attendant dangers of extensive bureaucratization) and concrete steps to significantly decentralize *and* democratize it:

> The purpose of both the Arusha Declaration and of *Mwongozo* was to give the people power over their own lives and their own development. We have made great progress in seizing power from the hands of the capitalists and the traditionalists, but we must face the fact that, to the mass of the people, power is still something wielded by others—even if on their behalf.
>
> Thus it has gradually become obvious that, in order to make a reality of our policies of socialism and self-reliance, the planning and control of development in this country must be exercised at the local level to a much greater extent than at present. . . . These proposals in fact follow logically from the Arusha Declaration and from *Mwongozo*, and from the basic principles of *Ujamaa*. For they imply putting trust in the people. And if we cannot do that, we have no claim to be socialists.[38]

One result of the success of such a program would be the further transformation of TANU, the ruling party, consolidating more securely its commitment to the cause of representing the needs of the masses. To say that it is already the best organized and most effective political party in independent Africa may perhaps seem faint praise, considering the pattern of development elsewhere on the continent. But it is vitally important nonetheless to have such a relatively firm political prop for the system. At the minimum, the corporate strength of the party has had the virtue of smothering many of the more mindless forms of factionalism and divisiveness which have confused developments elsewhere; thus Kambona, a consummate opportunist and the most prominent dissident yet produced by the system,[39] sank without much trace after 1967 in spite of his previously elevated position in party and government. TANU has also had the more positive function, both before and after Arusha, of helping to mobilize popular forces. A nationwide cell system (designed to incorporate every household in the country into ten-house political units) was already in the process of formation by 1964, and took its place within a broad network of branches and congresses at various levels of the system.[40] Moreover, such a network has been available for the assignment of more crucial responsibilities with the passage of time: the elaboration of programs of "political education," the absorption of important aspects of the rural collectivization program, a recent brief to improve the effectiveness of agricultural production.[41] Finally, and most crucially, it is the party which has provided the official stimulus for most of the progressive initiatives which we have been tracing so far; it has been, in practice, the guarantor of ideological advance over and against the generally more "pragmatic" and technocratic (and therefore generally conservative) pronouncements of institutions manned by Tanzania's civil servants (local or expatriate).

It would be misleading to overstate this case; many of the roles assigned to the party are still not realized in practice. But its formal "supremacy" is one feature which does give promise of further progressive developments; it has enabled the significance of those development imperatives which may be summed up under the slogan "politics in command" to be more sharply focused upon in Tanzania than elsewhere in Africa. This was an additional feature of *Mwongozo*. For example:

> Paragraph 11. The responsibility of the party is to lead the masses and their various institutions, in the effort to safeguard national independence and to advance the liberation of the African. The duty of the socialist party is to guide all activities of the masses. The government, parastatals, national organizations, etc., are instruments for implementing the party's policies. Our short history of independence reveals problems that may arise when a party does not guide its instruments. The time has now come for the party to take the reins and lead all the people's activities.
>
> Paragraph 12. The first task of the leadership is to spell out the national goal. This is understood and the party has already fulfilled this duty. Our aim is to build socialism in Tanzania. But to attain this goal the party must offer policies and guidelines concerning different aspects of the people's activities. The party has already given guidelines on socialism in rural areas, education for self-reliance. There is still the need to clarify the party's policies on other matters, such as housing, workers, money and loans policies, etc.
>
> Paragraph 14. In addition to organizing the people, leadership involves supervising the implementation of the party's policy. Ways must be found to ensure that the party actively supervises the activities and the running of its implementing agencies. Leadership also entails reviewing the results of implementation. It is the party's duty to ensure that it assesses the effects of the policy implementation undertaken by its agencies. This is the only way to establish whether people participate in devising solutions to their problems in offices, institutions, the army, villages, industries.

With the introduction of "decentralization" related points were also to be made. In carrying through that policy, in fact, the task of local

TANU bodies has been conceived as coming even closer in form to that of the party's National Executive Committee at the national level; this means that they too must take on new, more active responsibilities, including "that of guarding policy" at the local level. And "in addition to their new formal responsibilities, the TANU branches throughout the rural areas could, and should, make themselves into the active arm of the people, so as to ensure that every advantage is taken of this increased local responsibility." [42] There was a further promise in this latest document: "The necessary strengthening of the relevant departments of TANU is now under consideration by the NEC." Taken together with the president's recent decision to hand over many of his governmental responsibilities to an executive prime minister (Rashidi Kawawa, who also continues as second vice-president) in order to "devote more attention to questions of party and national leadership," [43] it might be argued that a series of steps were now being taken firmly in the right direction.

Before leaving this point, one further indication that at least the minimum requirements for progressive advance are being realized in Tanzania may also be mentioned. For a party so functioning is one counterweight to the most powerful instrument that the conservative elements of the petty bourgeoisie have for reversing a positive direction in the development effort: the military. Faced with the debris of the mutiny in 1964 (a situation only salvaged at the time by the summoning of British troops!) Tanzania cleaned house, manning the army with a new rank and file drawn from the TANU Youth League and similar sources and revitalizing the officer corps. Since that time the latter group has been consistently coopted into official circles, on the one hand, and political commissars, political education, have been made features of the military structure on the other. In addition, a further feature of *Mwongozo* has been the beginnings of a people's militia:

> In order that they may be able to oppose our enemies, the people must know that it is they who are the nation's shield. This means that defense and security matters must be placed in the hands of the people themselves. . . . Therefore it is imperative to start training a militia for the whole country.

Perhaps Guiné's solution to the dilemmas presented to African politicians by the military, a solution which involves the rotation of military personnel with those in civilian assignments, is an even more radically effective one. But organizational niceties are probably less important to neutralizing the army, in any case, than guarding against the possible existence of a political and popular vacuum within the social system into which the soldiers might move. And it is just such a vacuum that the leadership's policies have generally been designed to avoid.[44]

The challenge of organizing politically for socialist advance will be a continuing one for Tanzania; much will depend upon the extent to which the various processes already set in motion—the internally oriented economy, the reclamation of the elite, the conjuring up of an effective base—become self-sustaining and cumulative. One additional point may be suggested, however: if further progress is to be made, the ongoing refinement of Tanzania's ideology will be as crucial to the country's development in the future as it has been in the past. For there can be little disputing the creative role played by "ideas"—the perspective on development which has emerged in Tanzania—in forcing the pace of Tanzanian advance thus far. This is, in fact, a point which will become much more clear when the emergence of Tanzania's socialist initiative is traced historically in the following section.

But enough evidence has been presented to document something of the nature of the "ideal" element which is so active an ingredient in the Tanzanian situation. On the international side, for example, an ongoing reinterpretation of the realities of the world arena has enabled Tanzania to understand more clearly the character of imperialism, to align itself more actively with broadly progressive forces, and to assess critically the exact importance of various continentwide organizations and initiatives. Despite some real anomalies, its record on this front is a strong one, while its sharpened reading of the nature of worldwide trends has provided much of the intellectual infrastracture necessary for sustaining and consolidating the domestic emphasis on "self-reliance." At the same time, it must be noted that an internationalist perspective on the development problem has been less important in stimulating Tanzanian action than has been the consolidation in ideological form of lessons learned in the domestic sphere.[45] We have noted in this section many features of the *definition* by the leadership of the country's problems which have in turn stimulated progressive action: a perception of the elite as a potential brake upon development, a perception of the essential importance of an active, conscious, popular base to the realization of the country's aspirations, a perception of the necessity to organize (and *reor-ganize*) for further advance. Moreover, the result of this process of defining an ideology to meet Tanzanian needs can be quite baldly stated: no other country in independent Africa has come so far.

There are contradictions, of course. Thus the "definitions" may not always be clear enough. Even where they are, the organizational capacity of the system may be inadequate to the task of acting on those definitions. More fundamentally, the "objective conditions" of Tanzania, especially those characteristics of the class structure most relevant to a successful move toward socialism, may be sufficiently unpromising as to compromise the ability of "ideology" and "organization" to advance the situation; a further evaluation of the dialectic which exists in Tanzania between ideology and organization on the one hand, and objective conditions on the other, is an obvious necessity. Indeed, we will have to return (in Section 3) to each of the spheres already explored in a preliminary manner in order to make a more fully considered judgment of the significance of Tanzanian achievement. At this point the intention has been merely to present to the most skeptical of observers an itemization of the diverse fronts upon which progress has been made; once having done so, one is further tempted to say to such skeptics, with Brecht's Galileo, "And yet, it moves." Whether it moves fast enough, far enough—that is another question, and one to which we must also return.

2. Conditioning Factors

In Africa, then, this pattern of politics is atypical, though, as suggested, the calculation of the precise extent of Tanzania's deviation from the norm provides a challenge of relevance to a subsequent section of this paper. Before proceeding to that exercise, however, we must pose a somewhat different question: how and why has Tanzania managed to come so far, to pose, seriously, quite so many questions, to tackle, with some effect, quite so many aspects of the African development problem? The beginnings of an answer to this query may be found by adopting a historical perspective, and tracing, however sketchily, the emergence from the past of the chief components of the present Tanzanian conjuncture. Moreover, as will become apparent, such an exercise reveals not only the positive factors which have facilitated the launching of

Tanzania's brand of socialism; it also reveals the elements which condition this project in a negative manner and which threaten, powerfully, to distort and undermine it.[46]

On the positive side, we will see that Tanzania's historical experience has buried it less deeply in the mire of "underdevelopment" than many other African countries. Tanzania does share with such countries the burdens of dependency and a consequent distortion of economic potential, does share the installation of domestic strata whose vested interests in the status quo help to guarantee such dependency, does share the cultural and ideological mystifications which deform the terms upon which newly mobilized masses participate in the sociopolitical system. All of these results are to a significant extent the logical legacy of the colonial situation and, as Andre Gunder Frank and others have argued, the further these processes have gone the more difficult it can be to get back to a starting point where the most rational exploitation of the country's potentialities remains a live option. At the same time, Tanzania did remain, for a variety of reasons, one of the African countries *least transformed* by international capitalism and also one of the world's most desperately poor countries.[47] Ironically, as regards its prospects for breaking out of the syndrome of underdevelopment, it thus experienced some of the benefits of being a *tabula rasa*—less distorted and therefore more open-ended.

This situation contained ambiguities of its own, of course. To begin with, the (relative) open-endedness of the Tanzania conjuncture merely provided conditions which were *permissive* of experimentation and the launching of radical development strategies. However, there was nothing automatic about such a possibility; the opportunities inherent in this aspect of the historical legacy had to be consolidated by the judicious use of ideology and organization. In fact, the latter has been a marked feature of the Tanzanian situation and it is for this reason that the bases of such a political source of creative initiative will also have to be clearly identified here. Secondly, as we have noted, even if Tanzania's conditions appear to be relatively "permissive" of radical creativity, most of the elements comprising the pattern of underdevelopment which is characteristic of independent Africa are present, ready to further fasten their grip upon Tanzania's future at every sign of faltering; this too is a reality which we must bear firmly in mind. Finally, there is a negative side even to the virtue of being, in certain respects, a *tabula rasa*. For the country remains, in absolute terms, extremely *undeveloped*. Thus even if the use to which productive forces are put is somewhat less distorted in Tanzania than in many other African countries, the overall level of those productive forces is very low. Even if the favored domestic classes which might resist socialist advance are less evolved and entrenched, the "cultural level" of the country is also low.[48] Even if the mass of the population is less confused by those mystifications which the workings of peripheral capitalism have stimulated in Africa, it is less mobilized and dislodged from traditional entanglements and to that extent less likely to become, with ease, an active force for socialist advance. These paradoxes, too, are part of Tanzania's complex historical legacy. And we must return to each of these points in this section.

With such a perspective in mind, we may look first at the most obvious feature of Tanzania's historical development: the growth of its dependence on the outside world and the shaping of its structural subordination to the international capitalist system. The beginnings of this trajectory can first be perceived at a very early point in the history of the area. As Abdul Sheriff has recently shown, the Indian Ocean trading powers had begun to bend the weaker economies of East Africa to suit their demands from the middle of the first millennium A.D. In East Africa it is therefore possible

> to trace the emergence of some form of international specialization, stultification of industrial development at the periphery, the resulting tendency to maximize international inequalities, the development of deformed and dependent economies and the expropriation of surplus even before capitalism.

The greater trade in slaves and ivory of later centuries merely intensified this process, and also served gradually to introduce a European and international capitalist presence which would encapsulate the initial Arab and Indian trading networks within its larger framework. Thus colonialism, when it came, was simply "a logical development to ensure, by administrative means, the structures of dependence and domination and exploitation." [49]

Colonial overrule did, however, intensify the process significantly. As John Iliffe has demonstrated in his able survey of Tanganyika's agricultural history,[50] the pattern established was a complex one. For under the Germans until 1918, and afterward as a British mandate, Tanganyika

witnessed the emergence of a mixture of economic forms—the system
as a whole thus resembling neither the settler-dominated economy of
nearby Kenya, nor the small-holder-based economy of Uganda. Certainly a plantation sector, which with time concentrated in sisal production but which witnessed company and settler participation in the development of other crops as well, was of great importance. Though this
agricultural group of foreign origin never reached the point of establishing total hegemony over the colonial situation,[51] much policy was
shaped to service its needs. In particular, many government efforts were
undertaken in order to ensure an adequate labor supply, and certain
areas of the country became reservoirs for semi-proletarianized migrant
workers. The emergence of this latter group is itself important, of
course, but it is also worth noting that, with substantial manpower resources thus absent from home for long periods, the areas from which
these workers came tended themselves to be drawn into a whole vicious
circle of involution and cumulative underdevelopment (this pattern
being reinforced in some cases by the remoteness of such areas from colonially designed communications networks).

The colonial government, for a variety of reasons, did encourage (by
judicious use of carrot and stick) other areas of the country to become
centers of small holder cash-cropping, however. It is true that in a manner characteristic of much African agricultural change, most such market-oriented production tended merely to be added on to the still central
subsistence orientation of existing agricultural systems. As a result, its
impact upon agricultural technology and relations of production in the
rural areas often fell far short of being revolutionary. But the disruptive
impact upon the internal functioning of preexisting African societies is
nonetheless undeniable, as we shall have occasion to emphasize shortly.
Here two additional features of this pattern may be noted. First, despite
real disruptions, these cash-cropping areas can be considered to have
been in some senses "favored" by the colonial impact; here lies one of
the most important seeds of the uneven development of various regions
in Tanzania. Secondly, and even more significantly, *both* African small
holder agriculture *and* European agriculture contributed to the territorial
pattern of dependency which we have been discussing. For both were
premised on the servicing, through agricultural export, of metropolitan
needs. Thus by the 1930s, as Iliffe notes, the territorial colonial government found many of its plans to ebb and flow with the fluctuations in

the price of sisal—a situation little different from that of the "independent" government of the early 1960s!

In addition. Tanzania's export-oriented colonial economy failed to develop even those features of significant light industrialization which can, under certain circumstances, emerge from such a situation. Unlike the cases of Kenya and Rhodesia, the settler presence was never sufficiently strong to allow that group to serve as a nonindigenous "national bourgeoisie" which might have liberated some further productive potential from the colonial straitjacket. At the same time, though some important features of socioeconomic differentiation did emerge among the African population, such a "national bourgeoisie" was even less likely to spring from that source. Local entrepreneurship outside agriculture was largely confined to trade and services and, in addition, featured prominently the activity of an intermediary community of Asians who were important to the functioning of the economy but no real challenge to the institutional dominance of the colonial power within it. As a result, there slowly built up a network of metropolitan-based banking and trading institutions which fattened on the export economy on the up-swings and did nothing to encourage its transformation; this was the heart of the "modern" sector! [52] A final aspect of the picture, and one of perhaps equal importance, has been the reality of Kenyan economic dominance *within* Eastern Africa. Not only had Kenya developed over the years a range of productive activities unknown in its neighboring countries, but that very fact had turned it, gradually, into a "peripheral center" in the area—an entrepôt for trade, a magnet for international corporations, a syphon for surpluses from the surrounding territories (often, up to the present, under the protective cover of various forms of "regional cooperation"). Given this fact, Tanzania found itself beggared twice over by the process of uneven development which characterized the capitalist intrusion into East Africa. [53]

The resulting picture is in many respects a familiar one to students of Africa. Though "production" per se had been increased by the end of the colonial period, many resources and potentialities remained untapped. Moreover, given the impact of international capitalist priorities and the pattern of the "modern" economy which was in consequence emerging—with its export and agricultural bias, its exploitative institutional structure, its communications network (mainly back and forth from the coast), its attendant cultural pattern of conventional wisdom concerning the parameters of the acceptable risk and "pragmatic" choice—it was difficult even for Tanzania to begin afresh the pursuit of a new, more internally oriented logic for its economy. Indeed, as pointed out in Section 1, post-independence ideologues and planners would find this aspect of Tanzania's inheritance the toughest nut of all to crack. But there was also some leeway here. The absence of a strategic mineral resource or of a significant build-up in the presence of the industrial off-shoots of the multinational corporations meant that Tanzania remained rather marginal to the calculations of international capitalism. Indeed, one factor in driving Tanzania leftward toward self-reliance in 1967 was the very lack of response by private investors (more drawn to the amenities and infrastructure of the open Kenyan economy, for example) to an invitation to them contained in the first Tanzanian Five Year Plan (1964–1969). As a result, certain kinds of international pressures toward conformity may have been less intense—and the new elite which was emerging also had less opportunity to be coopted into a dynamic private sector. It is true that when Tanzania nationalized, it could not nationalize much—we have already suggested that Tanzania's low level of productive forces is a fact which must be confronted squarely—but this also meant that, as it turned its hand to exercising control over the modern sector, many choices still remained open to it.

If the colonial situation bequeathed a dependent but still relatively *undeveloped* economy to Tanzania, it also bequeathed it newly privileged classes which were likely, if their emergence remained unchecked, to further consolidate the country's *underdevelopment*. First and foremost among these was the educated elite, a stratum in formation from as early as German times and brought into existence precisely to man the lower and intermediate echelons of the colonial and bureaucratic apparatus. This group could be expected to learn, at Tabora and other schools, many of the lessons of capitalist colonialism—possessive individualism, authoritarian style, numerous aspects of "conventional wisdom" concerning development—even while they were developing, oftentimes, a legitimate and profound distaste for the overlay of racial oppression and paternalism which also defined the British moment in Tanzanian history.[54] Such people would be among the inheritors of *Uhuru* and of the colonial structures, particularly in their roles as civil servants, teachers, and technicians of various descriptions; their control over the state apparatus and their consequent privileged access to surpluses generated by the Tanzanian economy would prove to be the key to their power in the post-colonial period. Nor were these the only actors near the top of the colonial pyramid. Iliffe and others have documented the extent to which the emergence of rural stratification—characterized by the novel self-assertion of large farmers and African traders—was a feature of the stimulation of small holder cash-cropping and the attendant disruption (within limits) of existing economic systems in many parts of the country; such "economic activists" of town and country also fed into the emerging stratification system.[55]

In fact, the main components of a conservative alliance of indigenous privileged classes (overlapping the public and private spheres and subordinate to imperialism) were in place by the end of the colonial era: the British granted independence as easily as they did partly for this reason. Again, however, its relative sluggishness may be as important a feature of this process of class formation in Tanzania as its actual existence. For Tanzania's lack of transformation did mean that the members of the elite were fewer in number, their privileges much more first-generational in character, than was the case in many other African countries. By the time of independence, for example, there were less than 150 university graduates, and in that year (1961), there were only 176 students in the sixth form of secondary school. Moreover, as we have already noted, the prizes which would have facilitated cooptation were not readily available from an undernourished capitalist sector; equally significant, the competition from the Asian business class vis-à-vis African entrepreneurial advance was quite fierce. When the president said that had he waited another eighteen months to take the Arusha initiatives of 1967 it would have been too late to assault these various citadels of power, he was not only commenting, negatively, upon the quality of these strata and the direction of their evolution, but also documenting the tortoise pace, comparatively, of their consolidation in power. In short, there were objective reasons why the dominant elements in Tanzania may have been more clearly characterized by a "relative social autonomy and plasticity" than elsewhere in Africa and why they were, as a result, less likely to resist with full effectiveness a radicalization of the situation.

This is a "permissive" condition, then, though again it is a permissive condition only to a certain degree, and to a degree which remains to be fully and adequately identified. Certainly deeply ingrained biases which characterize the outlook of such an elite are not automatically eliminated by some reduction of privilege, nor is socialist creativity ensured thereby. We will have occasion to return to such subjective aspects of the elite's situation subsequently. Here, however, we can note that the relative weakness of the elite, historically defined, helped to make the Tanzanian context permissive of socialist creativity in one additional respect. In Section 1 we commented on the manner in which the African elite can work to instrumentalize mass participation in its own interests through the manipulation of tribal and racial symbolism. With a less developed, self-conscious, and assertive elite to juggle ethnic arithmetic, with fewer African entrepreneurs to reduce nationalism to anti-Asian self-aggrandizement, the masses were to that extent less closed to the development of other forms of consciousness.

There were other factors which also helped to ensure a relatively unified front of the mass of the population, however. Despite the legacy of uneven development, unity was more easily guaranteed in Tanzania during both the nationalist and post-independence phases by such factors as the widespread use of the common Swahili language,[56] and the very multiplicity of tribes which prevented any one, or few, of the country's peoples from emerging as dominant or from being perceived as menacing by others. Unlike Kenya and Uganda, therefore, tribal identification was less readily available for political manipulation by regional "barons" in their jockeying for positions within the elite. Significantly, given all these factors, it was more likely that the broad mass of the population could come to identify itself first and foremost as "workers and peasants" vis-à-vis any aspirants to illegitimate privilege (or would at least be less hesitant to respond to an invitation so to identify itself!). In other words, the contrast between nascent class privilege and mass aspiration could be that much less readily obscured in the Tanzanian context by vicarious identification with tribal magnates or by the false drama of regional rivalries, and the class dimensions of the syndrome of underdevelopment brought more easily into focus when the president and other progressive elements began to press such a view.

One must guard against exaggeration here; this condition, too, is more of a permissive than a determining one. The rhetoric of Tanzanian socialism sometimes goes further, favoring the proposition that "workers and peasants" provide an active, militant, and conscious base for the progressive endeavors of the leadership. But this is almost certainly to overstate the case. It is true that broadly framed peasant grievances did fuel the anticolonial struggle in significant ways (if sometimes in rather ambiguous ones).[57] Moreover, peasants are major losers within the conventional syndrome of underdevelopment; the growth of a progressive peasant consciousness is therefore always conceivable. But such consciousness is something which must be obtained through hard and effective political work, a truth which the Tanzanian leadership has only gradually come to appreciate. Spared the direct and immediate impact of feudal structures, often not far distanced from the world of subsistence agriculture, the bulk of the Tanzanian peasantry still evinces a deadly parochialism not easily transcended by the stirrings of class consciousness vis-à-vis distant exploiting classes, domestic and international. Given the fact that Tanzania is underexploited and (in some respects) underpopulated, this is even more true here than in many other parts of Africa. Thus, even in Tanzania, the "economic activists" have too often been able to ride parochialism, to activate patron-client relationships, and to present themselves as spokesmen and organizers for the rural masses.[58] We here return to a familiar paradox of Tanzania's socialist moment. In important ways an undeveloped Tanzania makes the masses more available for socialist mobilization. Nonetheless, given their historically determined characteristics, they are still not all that easily converted into a fully active agency of socialist reconstruction.

Related ambiguities mark the likely contribution of that other repository of progressive hopes, the proletariat. A weak colonial capitalism was not an effective force for proletarianizing large numbers of Tanzanians.[59] Most labor migrants either faded back into the peasantry on the one hand or, if among the more stabilized, articulate, and organized members of the working class, often became more conscious of their own privileged positions over and against the peasantry than of any potential posture of solidarity with the latter against other, more privileged, strata. In addition, the number of wage earners remained small (387,000 in 1962 out of a total population of roughly ten to eleven million) and the number was in fact to fall after independence, largely because of the decline of the sisal industry. Politically, the workers did contribute markedly to the displacement of colonialism; various unions and, in particular, the Tanganyikan Federation of Labour meshed effectively with TANU in many of its activities during the period. It may even be argued that the government and party overreacted to a presumed threat from organized labor when it brought the trade unions to heel in the early post-independence years (though it is also true that careerism and demagoguery were common failings of the union leadership at that time). But one thing at least is apparent: with workers as with peasants, pressures from below have not been the most dramatic or defining elements in Tanzania's movement toward socialism.

An elite less compromised, the mass more available—these then are the additional permissive features of an undeveloped Tanzania. There is a further complication to this legacy to which we must return, however: the very lack of development which reduces distortions also means that the cultural level of Tanzania remains low.[60] This represents, in turn, both a constraint and an opportunity. It is a constraint, unequivocally, in the sense that the emergence of a ferment of left-wing intellectual activity has been correspondingly delayed, the wide range of active revolutionary intellectuals who might have been thrown up by more searching and disruptive change a missing feature of much of the effort to concretize in practice the socialist project. But the problem of "cultural level" is more apt to be seen as a constraint in quite another sense, a constraint arising from the fact that the accumulation of those skills necessary for handling the technical challenges of a full-fledged socialist development effort is not far advanced. In this reality are rooted, say some observers, serious limitations upon the capacity of the regime to follow through on its initiatives and a further danger that the dry-rot of inefficient performance will penetrate a widening circle of government activity as the state sector expands. This same weakness, evidenced in the paucity of skilled, high-level manpower, also creates a wedge for the entry of expatriate expertise into almost every field of quasi-technical endeavor in the post-colonial period. Generally favored by language (English), steeped in the most fashionable (and dubiously "neutral") of techniques, financed by the "munificence" of the Western aid apparatus, most such foreign experts all too easily become Trojan horses within the socialist camp (as much, it should be noted, by reinforcing elitist and conventional preconceptions among their African counterparts as by more underhanded preemptive methods).[61] Such underlying "cultural" weaknesses may also help explain the temptation to settle for management contracts or consultancy agreements which are not entirely serviceable to the end of structural transformation.

While some of the latter points focus legitimately on real dilemmas, considerable caution is in order here. For the very notion of "technical skills" must itself be critically assessed. Beyond a certain minimal level of "universal" skills (literacy, numeracy), the technical requirements of Tanzania's desire to develop a technological and managerial capacity geared to its own needs, rather than servicing an intensification of advanced capitalism's stranglehold in this sphere, will be met only by a training program very different from that which characterized the colonial education system. Similarly, insofar as effective performance is as dependent upon the development of the consciousness and commitment which releases significant human energies as it is upon the acquiring of narrowly defined skills per se (a blending of "redness" and "expertise," in the Maoist sense), this is also something which a very new kind of educational system is more likely to encourage than the inherited one.[62] Here lies the root of opportunity in this sphere, in fact. In undeveloped Tanzania there was not at hand quite the same corps of colonially trained personnel with irrelevant skills and dangerous attitudes as in some other territories. Educational reform might be expected both to better the quality of the system's output and also to place its new products more rapidly into positions of influence. We have already seen in Section 1 the extent to which the educational system has been seen to be a critical arena for socialist creativity by the Tanzanian leadership; the argument here serves to reinforce the wisdom of that position.

Permissive conditions, then, are important, and so are the continuing limitations upon advance. But where to locate the actual creativity which has been evidenced? We have already suggested that the key can be found in the realms of "organization" and "ideology"; it is now necessary to identify the historical roots of these features and to clarify the nature of their impact. Thus, briefly stated, the linchpin of Tanzania's atypicality in comparative, continental, terms is to be found in certain peculiarities of its political development, and in the (short-run) lack of fit between its political development and the "spontaneous" drift toward dependence and class formation in its socioeconomic system. TANU, growing out of a tradition of *centralized* political activity from an earlier period (the Tanganyikan Territorial African Civil Servants' Association—TTACSA—and the Tanganyika African Association—TAA) and actually taking over the institutional legacy of such organizations, was able to crystallize and appropriate those other features, mentioned above, which facilitated the realization of an exceptional degree of unity in Tanganyika.[63] Secondly, in the 1950s TANU's effective organization managed to incorporate within itself rural-based groups and leaders across the country, and in particular the party identified itself effectively with the widespread rural protests that swept the country at that time in response to the colonial government's intensified efforts to grandly transform, by its own lights, the agricultural sector.[64] A rather more grassroots leadership and some closer identification with popular forces than was the case with many similar organizations in Africa seems to have been the result. A more achieved nationalism, a more deeply populist movement—taken together these political accomplishments consolidated the room for maneuver provided by the permissive conditions previously discussed. TANU, unlike any other political party in East Africa, became a conductor of forces which could drive the system in an increasingly leftward direction.

Even then, this might not have been enough to stay socioeconomic tendencies from jelling into a reactionary mold or to prevent the elite from hijacking independence in the interests of the "peripheral capitalism" option. Fortunately, however, in President Nyerere, and in others who supported his tendency within the movement, there existed leaders who could use the breathing space thus permitted them by historical circumstance to redirect creatively the trajectory of the system.[65] Thus in the post-independence period Nyerere spearheaded the democratic ventilation of the system (as seen in Section 1), thereby moving to consolidate the logic of a closer link between leadership and people and also encouraging the latter to become more active and conscious agents in their own interests. Slowly, too, he could deepen the logic, carrying the party and elements of the bureaucracy with him, tentatively, cautiously, toward more structural considerations of an increasingly socialist character. But it is important to note that the exercise of such political creativity had already begun in the nationalist phase. Efforts to introduce competition between religious denominations into the political arena were vigorously disciplined, for example;[66] though chiefs, possible foci of ethnic consciousness, were enlisted where possible to the nationalist cause, their new status of equality was consistently reaffirmed and indeed one of the first post-independence acts of the new African government was the abolition of these posts. Most important, Nyerere fought a persistent guerrilla war even within TANU against the spokesmen of the cruder forms of "black nationalism" who would have manipulated racism in the service of their own interests and reduced both the struggle and the consciousness of the masses to a lowest common denominator in this way. The seriousness of this struggle can be gauged by the fact that it was the latter issue, crystallizing around such issues as the pace of Africanization and the terms of Asian citizenship, which triggered Nyerere's temporary resignation from the top government post in 1962 in order that he might work to further consolidate his position.[67] But Nyerere and others were not about to allow the new elite to get off the hook of popular expectations in this way and were quite prepared to seize the more progressive strands of nationalist consciousness and draw out their full implications.

Not that these creative efforts erased with ease all of the ambiguities of the nationalist legacy in Tanzania. Nyerere himself has been the most sharp-tongued critic of Tanzanian nationalism, in fact, pointing out quite specifically the weak foundations it laid for socialist construction:

> Everyone wants to be free, and the task of a nationalist is simply to rouse the people to a confidence in their own power of protest. But to build the real freedom which socialism represents is a very different thing. It demands a positive understanding and positive actions, not simply a rejection of colonialism and a willingness to cooperate in noncooperation. And the anticolonial struggle will almost certainly have intensified the difficulties.[68]

In this, one of the most trenchant and important of his writings, Nyerere goes on to identify clearly the tendency of the nationalist movement to overstress racist and narrowly nationalist demands which could mask the more self-interested goals of leaders and also confuse the people concerning the long-term prerequisites of their genuine emancipation; he also emphasizes the tendency for such a movement to deposit in a position of unquestioned preeminence a party which in structure as well as in ideology is ill adapted to the further tasks a socialist development effort must dictate. These are crucial points; in addition, it is appropriate to note here a further negative feature of Tanzania's smooth transition from colonial government to independent government. Thus the success of the independence struggle was too easily equated with the taking over of established bureaucratic institutions, TANU's formal control in the last instance being considered sufficient guarantee of the reliability of these institutions. Yet such an institutional inheritance tended to allow for a mere Africanization of the bureaucratic style of work, the conventional criteria of relevance, the elitist mentality, ingrained in colonial structures. The Tanzanian leadership rather uncritically attached its development aims to the cabinet and ministerial structure, the system of quasi-independent corporations, and other institutions, with the broader implications of such an inheritance only slowly becoming apparent.

These cautionary notes must not blind us to the political achievement already pinpointed, however. For a context was being created from the late colonial period within which the petty bourgeoisie might more easily come to commit altruistic "suicide"; it was also a context within which the mass of the population might more easily come to a consciousness of their stake in structural transformation and act in accordance with such a realization. Important aspects of the institutionalization of such possibilities were discussed in Section 1. But it will now be more apparent than it was in that section that this is precisely the point at which the "ideal" element in the Tanzanian development equation has asserted itself. In fact, it is the ideological evolution of the leadership which in Tanzania has enabled it to discern possibilities, to avail itself of permissive conditions, and to divert trends which would otherwise foreclose a progressive solution to the challenges of underdevelopment.

Moreover, the chief source of such ideological elaboration has without doubt been Julius Nyerere himself. An adequate history of Tanzania's socialist development would have to trace the skillful means by which the president placed himself at the center of the Tanganyikan political system from an early date and managed to build his own personal links with an extremely wide popular constituency. It would also have to trace the evolution of his own convictions about the values most central to a new Tanzania and about the steps most necessary to ensure the country's development.[69] For to a rather surprising degree Nyerere's ideas have become Tanzania's ideology. Thus from the very beginning of his political career in the 1950s, one can discern in his statements many of the characteristic components of his emerging position: a critical nationalism, a socialist morality, a pragmatic methodology. And one can also trace the extent to which the harsh realities of post-independence Tanzania and the learning experience provided by failures elsewhere on the continent (Ghana and Nigeria, for example) gradually sharpened his insight and his sense of urgency. Finally, one can see, as in

Section 1, the way this insight and sense of urgency, communicated to some leaders and sections of the population at large, became the stuff of concrete policy-making. Nyerere seems a necessary (though obviously not a sufficient) condition, the final link in the complicated chain of factors which have facilitated Tanzania's socialist experimentation.

Some observers would argue that an essential piece of the puzzle has been ignored in this scenario—Zanzibar. And indeed we have said little thus far about the off-shore islands (population only 300,000) which since 1964 have formed, along with mainland Tanganyika, the United Republic of Tanzania. Yet in 1964 Lucien Rey, writing of the Zanzibar revolution and union of that year, could hypothesize that

> in Zanzibar all that could have been achieved has been; in Tanganyika there is still much to be done. There is a good chance that the Union will lead to the "spreading" of the Zanzibar revolution in a much more effective way than could have been done by outside example or adventures. The revolution goes on, at a new level.[70]

Is this then another key to the further elaboration of the socialist project on the mainland since that date? It is not surprising that the idea has been entertained, certainly. Zanzibar's history has been much more flamboyant than Tanganyika's, and its revolution particularly subject to left-wing canonization. For while it was triggered by a coup d'état (Okello's) it also unleashed what became, in effect, a social revolution. The components for the latter had been building up over a century of Arab hegemony. The Arabs, often with Asian financing, had established an oligarchical stranglehold over the means of production (primarily clove plantations) and power (which they shared with the guardians of British colonial overrule until "independence" was attained in 1963).

Never quite degenerating into an entirely straightforward communal confrontation because of the Arab ability to win some electoral and other support from sections of the indigenous African population of the islands (Shirazis, as distinct from the mainland Africans many of whom had come originally as slaves and, later, as laborers), the political situation which grew out of this set of circumstances had in fact many of the components of a class struggle.[71] Workers in Zanzibar port provided much of the initiative for African nationalism (as distinct from the "Zanzibar nationalism" of the Arab-dominated group) and it was the most poverty-stricken African peasants who seized the opportunity of an attack on the Sultanate to take over plantations throughout the islands. The Afro-Shirazi Party, under Karume, was pitchforked into power and began to ride the social revolution. Excoriated by the Western press and forced to turn to Eastern Europe and China for assistance, Zanzibar consolidated its reputation for radicalism; and indeed the country did launch further land reforms and embark on an impressive range of welfare programs—in health, housing, education. Though an almost parodic example of an historically conditioned monoculture (cloves) and suffering for a time from that bias, more recently the buoyant clove market has floated these various programs with ease.[72]

Yet it is still far from easy to see this as some consistent program of socialist reconstruction. A different model seems more apropos. If many of the trends elsewhere in Africa suggest merely an Africanization of "peripheral capitalism," so Zanzibar, with its different history, has come ironically to resemble an Africanization of the Sultanate—not socialist democracy but a (somewhat) benevolent despotism, with welfarism as the main credential of that benevolence. How else to explain the peculiar authoritarianism and too familiar high-handedness of the regime, for example, or the victimization (unfortunately with the connivance of mainland authorities) of the Zanzibar left in the wake of Karume's assassination in early 1972.[73] It was not accidental that only Karume among Tanzanian leaders has had the temerity to question overtly the Arusha Declaration leadership code—arguing that it was unfair for Africans to be denied ownership of houses for renting and the like while Asians, in the private sector, could do so.[74] Moreover, the "family store" system in Zanzibar has proven to be one thinly disguised means by which leading families within the ruling circles can take over the non-African trading sector for their own enrichment—and at the expense of the spirit of the leadership code.

It is no more accidental that the Zanzibar leadership has recently begun to revise its links with the East, and establish curiously cordial relationships with Western countries.[75] Karume, before his death, had developed, independently, an equally interesting friendship with Kenya's Kenyatta; there were even some mutterings concerning Nyerere's fiery approach to General Amin after the latter's Uganda coup and initial return to the orthodox path of neocolonialism. Thus, even if it is the cultural-cum-institutional legacy of the Sultanate which has shaped the way in which authority is exercised in Zanzibar, the various developments here itemized suggest another, complementary, pattern. For it is the ambiguous (and manipulative) ideology of "black nationalism" pure and simple, an ideology whose weaknesses in an East African context have been often pinpointed by President Nyerere, which informs much of the policy-making. The union with the mainland is in any case a loose one: despite constant promises, the ASP and TANU have never merged and government structures are almost equally disparate; Zanzibar does not appear in Tanzania's planning documents; the military establishments seem to follow quite separate paths. Perhaps it is just as well. Far from being a prod to Tanganyika's radicalism, the Zanzibar example, the Zanzibar style, embody those elements which are in many ways its greatest threat.[76]

We can safely leave Zanzibar at this point. Whatever else may be true of the murky situation there, it is clear that Zanzibar and mainland Tanzania are still, in most important respects, following their own separate destinies, that each is defined by its own specific dialectic. Moreover, the chief focus of this essay will continue to be the events and developments on the mainland, for it is there that the more important and instructive experience is in train.[77] About this experience, in turn, we can now expect to speak more clearly. The achievement of Section 1 is more precisely located in relationship to its broader context—to the continuing threats posed by dependency and the consolidation of domestic privilege, to the continuing weaknesses evidenced by shortfalls in productive capacity and cultural requisites, to the continuing challenges inherent in the need for organizational and ideological creativity and for consolidation of a conscious mass base. As a result, we are in a better position to evaluate accurately in the section that follows the exact extent of that achievement, and to identify those contradictions which remain close to the heart of Tanzanian socialism.

3. Contradictions

We turn to what is in certain respects the most difficult task of this essay—an identification of the shortfalls which are evident in Tanzania's attempts to realize socialist development to date and, equally important, an interpretation of the reasons for such weaknesses as may be said to exist. The first of these is obviously a controversial undertaking, if only because the strategies most likely to yield development are not self-evident, even to those who are absolutely committed to finding and implementing them. In evaluating, briefly, Tanzania's practice we will therefore have to move over terrain much disputed among socialists and we will probably do so at too rapid a pace. But at least it may prove possible to clarify what are the most meaningful terms in which a critical discussion of Tanzania's efforts should be cast, and in so doing to deepen our understanding of the evidence already presented in Section 1. The second task is, in some ways, even more complicated, for it raises tortuous questions about the nature of social causality which reverberate far beyond the bounds of this piece. That certain shortcomings characterize Tanzania's efforts will be evident. But do these spring, inevitably, from the "objective conditions" (already touched upon) which must distort any such attempt in Tanzania at this time—dependence and the character of the class structure, the absolute level of the country's poverty and its "cultural backwardness"? Or do they spring primarily from "subjective" and superstructural failures—of organization and ideology—the redressing of which is theoretically both possible in itself and likely to guarantee forward advance? Phrased in this way this dichotomy may sound excessively crude and unpromising. The present section will attempt to further illuminate it, however, and also to clear the way for a brief assessment of the prospects which confront a Tanzanian socialism so defined.

DEPENDENCE AND DEVELOPMENT

Of primary importance to such an evaluation of Tanzanian practice is a careful analysis of its grand design for "socialism and self-reliance" as it finds expression in the country's concrete efforts to achieve economic development. Here several points may be stressed. First, as spelled out in Section 1, what Tanzania has already done to guarantee the prerequisites for exercise of effective control over its economic destiny is important. Moreover, by engaging in such practical and progressive action, the Tanzanian leadership has also demonstrated the ability to reject some elements of the fashionable but bankrupt theories which premise development on the intensification of dependence—more foreign investment, more aid, more exports. Instead, it has seized hold of the concepts of self-reliance and social ownership as keys to effective transformation in ways novel to the continent.

Secondly, beyond the ground consolidated in this way by the ideology and the practice of "socialism and self-reliance," the country's conceptualization of the further imperatives of socialist development has been much less sure. In fact, it is only by deepening the logic of "self-reliance"—of "socialism in one (African) country," as it were—that Tanzania could expect to realize the full promise of the path upon which it has already embarked. Without such a follow-through there is a strong possibility that the economy will merely bog down in the very first phase of significant reconstruction. These points have been attested to by socialist experience elsewhere;[78] there is also a growing body of literature upon which Tanzanians could draw in deepening their insight in this field. Recent work by Samir Amin, for example, provides a useful framework for the further evaluation of Tanzania's achievement.[79] Amin (himself drawing on other literature, notably by Latin American economists) establishes an illuminating distinction between two different models of capital accumulation: the "self-centered system" and the "peripheral model." The latter is characterized by the continuing centrality of primary exports and the dominance of luxury consumption, with such industrialization as takes place being signally constrained by this reality and with the mass of the population being on the margin of economic calculation. Amin's "self-centered system" is structured very differently, being premised on "the determining relationship" which is established between the production of "mass" consumption goods on the one hand, and the production of capital goods intended for the production of such mass consumption goods on the other. A self-conscious shift to the latter emphasis provides, under contemporary conditions of underdevelopment, the key to relevant strategy.

If we were to imagine, in turn, a continuum linking the two poles provided by Amin's models, Tanzania would have to be placed, as we have seen, at some distance from the "peripheral-dependent" pole. What is being noted in this section, however, is that the country still remains a long way from conceptualizing, let alone realizing in practice, the construction of a markedly "self-centered system." In fact, the missing link in the chain of Tanzania's socialism lies precisely here: the absence of a *strategy* which might guarantee that the newly established framework of state control over surpluses and over decisions be used to transform the economy significantly. In debate about Tanzania's policies, the conventional shorthand for pinpointing this shortcoming is to note the absence of an "industrial strategy," and certainly the apparent lack of systematic criteria which might guide advance in the industrial sector is a crucial aspect of strategic weakness in the economic field.[80]

But the point can probably be most effectively conceived when phrased more broadly, using as a touchstone precisely Amin's model of the "self-centered system" mentioned above. As will become immediately apparent, it is easier to document the absence of a strategy for more fully realized "self-reliance" than to *prescribe* its detailed implementation in a particular case. Nonetheless, the broad outlines of a progressive alternative against which to measure the distance Tanzania must still travel in this sphere are by no means unknown. An economist like Muhbub ul Haq, for example, has recently (and rather surprisingly, given his background) launched a sharp attack on received (Western) wisdom on development, an attack which is of immediate relevance:

> . . . the problem of development must be defined as a selective attack on the worst forms of poverty. Development goals must be defined in terms of progressive reduction and eventual elimination of malnutrition, disease, illiteracy, squalor, unemployment, and inequalities. We were taught to take care of our GNP as this will take care of poverty. Let us reverse this and take care of poverty as this will take care of GNP. In other words, let us worry about the content of GNP even more than its rate of increase.[81]

The corollary of this argument is that

> consumption planning should move to the center of the stage; production planning should be geared to it. And consumption planning should not be in financial terms but in physical terms, in terms of a minimum bundle of goods and services that must be provided to the common man to eliminate the worst manifestations of poverty. . . . We must get away from the tyranny of the demand concept, and replace it by the concept of minimum needs.

Once the concern for more production and for better distribution are brought together so as to define the pattern of development, the two elements will in fact reinforce each other.[82] Here lies Amin's market for "mass consumption goods," planned into existence, not breaking on the reef of "lack of effective demand."

Posing the problem in such terms suggests the *radical* nature of the break with convention and the past which may be necessary to give practical and positive meaning to "self-reliance." Other often cited components of a progressive development package also fit in more neatly when discussed in relationship to the general framework provided by some such "self-centered" emphasis. Needless to say, each component also has a critical significance in its own terms: the degree of linkage of industrial development to the agricultural sector (as well as to the exploitation of other local resources), for example, and the relationships (and priorities) to be established as between heavy and light industry. The technological question is extremely important as well, and not merely because the costs and benefits of choosing between labor and capital intensive techniques in various sectors may raise real issues. Even more crucial is the necessity of creating, over time, an indigenous technological capacity which can power sustained advance. Finally, changes in the mode of production in the rural areas, often central to socialist advance elsewhere and certainly considered to be so in Tanzania, must be coherently and carefully planned in their own right. A more comprehensive treatment than we can hope to attempt here is really necessary to measure Tanzania's progress in each of these spheres.[83] But the exact nature of the relationship of each to some more comprehensive design remains, nonetheless, the most vital measure of their significance.

And yet, in Tanzania it is the relative absence of a comprehensive design, of a strategy for forward movement, that continues to confront us in the economic sphere. Much too often, in fact, the rhetoric of self-reliance has been substituted for the concrete goal of a self-centered economic system and for a specification of the steps which must be taken, in the context of day-to-day planning, for its realization. Proponents of more coherent strategies are not absent. Abdulrahman M. Babu, while Minister of Economic Affairs and Development Planning (1971), proclaimed the need for "a new strategy of development" in Tanzania and prophesied the emergence of one; though very generally stated, his suggestion was to push toward the solution we have been discussing, a solution postulated, in his words, on the "basic premise" that "development stems from within and not from outside." [84] But it is impossible to say that this position has carried the day. Instead, many of the subtler realities of dependence continue to assert themselves. And the key to economic planning in Tanzania remains, to a surprising degree, that of response to "effective demand," both international and domestic.

It will be apparent, in any case, that the existing pattern of "effective demand" is merely the immediate and spontaneous economic expression of the historically conditioned situation of dependence which we have discussed. Of course, it was not surprising that in the early post-colonial years Tanzania embarked on a path familiar to many newly independent countries in the 1950s and 1960s—that of merely modifying and updating dependence (this being realized as much in response to the needs of a maturing international capitalism as to such countries' own economic calculations). In Tanzania, as elsewhere, an intensification in production of its viable export crops (and some minimal diversification), as well as the beginnings of a light industrial sector (primarily centered on production of that range of semi-luxury consumer goods most in demand by the better-off members of the community), lay at the heart of its early plans and programs. Nor could all this be expected to change overnight with the launching of the socialist-oriented program. Self-reliance cannot mean autarchy, and under Tanzanian circumstances a complete disruption of cash-crop production for the world market, for example, would be suicidal rather than progressive. Even some of the obvious achievements of light industrial import substitution may have a contribution to make. But again, in the absence of a strategy which promises, cumulatively, to power a real movement away from this inherited pattern in the foreseeable future, excessive preoccupation with such emphases represents the making of too many "soft choices." And such choices, in turn, eat up valuable time or divert crucial surpluses; they may also serve to deepen the pattern of development of underdevelopment, moving Tanzania too quickly away from the moment of maximum opportunity to renew itself with which history had provided it.

Writing in 1967, in the immediate aftermath of the Arusha Declaration and the issuing of other related policy documents concerning education and rural development, Arrighi and I argued that "it will be easier to assess the direction of [Tanzania's] course if and when a presidential paper is issued which concerns itself with policies for industrialization." [85] Today, five years later, this gap has not been closed; economic strategy, narrowly ("industrial strategy") or broadly (as above) conceived, is without a doubt the crucial missing term in Tanzania's socialist equation. Even the leadership itself has sometimes confessed as much. The Second Five Year Plan, issued in 1969, strongly urges that work begin on generating such a strategy, though it contributes relatively little to that exercise itself.[86] And there have been some desultory gestures in this direction in the subsequent period, though generally at the highest rhetorical plane. Of the strategy there is little sign.

The results are predictable: too many "soft choices" made, too many "potential" choices of importance preempted and foreclosed. Some of the former we have already mentioned. The growing emphasis in Tanzania on tourism is another example. As has been openly and forcefully argued by Tanzanian militants (who represent only a small, student-based fraction, however),[87] tourism has its costs when measured against the goal of socialist development. Broadly conceived, the "demonstration effect" of luxurious hotels and their grotesque clientele may do something to undermine the ethic of self-denial and the "mass line" politics to which Tanzania is ostensibly dedicated. More narrowly, it may lure the country into expensive mistakes, into costly and prestigious investment (e.g., the Kilimanjaro airport, the beach hotels) which literally cannot pay its way within the context of the cut-throat competition which characterizes the international tourism business. At the same time, the militants have not always recognized another fact: properly organized, a tourist industry linked to the country's northern game parks is undoubtedly a strong earner of foreign exchange. But even if this is true, it is not necessarily good enough; tourism retains many of the characteristics of a soft option, keyed to the "tyranny" of international demand and to the balance of payments, tying up important resources and capacity for initiatives, and thus making economic sense primarily within the framework of a riskless program which does not try to restructure the economy dramatically.[88]

Soft choices feed on a strategic vacuum, then; even more subtle is the *preemption* of choice which takes place under such circumstances. One aspect of this process has been identified by I. G. Shivji in his forceful critique of "management agreements" and "partnerships" with international capitalist concerns operating in Tanzania.[89] All too often a substantial flow of surpluses continues under such auspices in the form of profits, charges, invoice manipulation, and the like; similarly, the metropolitan-based partners' own criteria concerning necessary imports, choice of technique, and salary structure may freeze out the possibility of more coherently founded domestic criteria. And even the crucial element of choice regarding the exact industrial mix to be encouraged may become the prey of accident and "demand" in this way. Industrial "planning" for the Second Five Year Plan period became, in practice, the preparation of a shopping list of 385 projects, many more than could be undertaken during the period.[90] Mere care to safeguard "internal economies" on a project-by-project basis will not then be sufficient. Nor will the increasingly successful efforts (on the part of Treasury, the Planning Ministry and financial institutions) to coordinate activity and plug project planning into a broader framework.[91] Such efforts inevitably suffer from the lack of principle and absence of effective criteria which are necessary for the exercise of critical control. The final selection comes to be more the sport of outside response and false criteria than the result of any coherent domestic initiative.

"Aid" can be an additional preemptive factor when availability of resources and mere "movement" for its own sake displace strategy at the center of thinking about development. As P. R. Lawrence has recently observed in examining Tanzania's aid package for 1971, many of its

> agreements were concluded for projects which tended to reflect and buttress its dependence upon and integration into the centre. The World Bank loans for tobacco and tea, shs. 65 million and 73.5 million respectively, will produce no change in the agricultural export character of the economy, even if there is some vague attempt to link these developments to Ujamaa villages. The USAID loan of shs. 5.6 million is to be used to finance farm and heavy duty tractors and light aircraft for aerial spraying in order to help eradicate tsetse fly—an activity which does lend itself to labour-intensive bush clearing. The Canadian loan of shs. 7 million to build an automatic bakery in Dar es Salaam—already very well provided with bread from existing labour-intensive operations—is another example of aid which does not appear to conform to the policy standards.

He finds that similar features have characterized USAID and World Bank or IDA loans for "major infrastructural projects such as roads and power stations." Too often these are designed to avoid "projects which appear to be risky, such as rural electrification"; they finance, instead, "the bitumenization of the existing road network built for colonial trade" or reinforce "the continuing bias towards expansion of power provision to existing urban centres" which "is a proven moneyearner." In short, "the powerful 'external economy' argument is invoked to reinforce the existing structure and the aid donor's position thus matches that of the private investor." [92]

There are other levers which guarantee substantial international "orthodoxy" even within the framework of "socialism and self-reliance," though their influence is often tacit and difficult to measure. How best to characterize Tanzania's continued traffic with the International Monetary Fund or World Bank missions, for example? The former institution, in particular, makes its negative influence most dramatically felt only at moments of financial crisis, but its brooding presence cannot help but bolster conventional thinking over the longer haul.[93] Again, this is not merely, or even primarily, because of such graphic anomalies as the fact that the director-general of the Bank of Tanzania (presently a New Zealander) must be approved, even sponsored, by the Fund. It is more because one further link is thus forged in the chain of orthodoxy which entangles the elite, and seduces it from a sufficiently radical perspective. That this is equally the implication of Tanzania's sustained contact with smooth and "efficient" representatives of the World Bank and with the friendly purveyors of "pseudo-socialist" aid from the Nordic countries seems probable.

One must guard against overstatement here; the point made above that these influences enter into a strategic vacuum must be taken seriously. Thus there might continue to be a case for primary product export, even a case for some small emphasis upon tourism, within a more effective overall strategy. Similarly, it might well be possible to push Scandinavian aid donors a great deal harder; they have already made significant accommodations to the imperatives of Tanzanian socialism. Perhaps, at the extreme, even certain kinds of links with international capitalist concerns and the IMF could be features of the kind of nuanced and long-term transition to socialism which may be necessary in a country like Tanzania. Roger Murray has argued that "perhaps we should admit that the field of present alternatives is merely obscured by schemas of the 'socialism or neocolonialism' type." [94] His concern is with the need for a finer discrimination of the variant forms of "neocolonialism," but the quantum of socialist advance may have to be measured with similar subtlety. Perhaps it is unwise, therefore, to be too categoric on such matters.

But it is nonetheless true that any positive results which might spring from such contacts (or even from some carefully selected range of them) will only do so if Tanzania operates from a posture of growing economic strength and ideological clarity. Much of its success in the international arena to date has reflected such accomplishments in any case. As Hoskyns has argued:

> What really distinguishes the Tanzanian experience from that of Guinea, Ghana, and the Ivory Coast is the continual attempt to evolve a locally derived overall strategy for development and see foreign relations primarily from the perspective of what helps or hinders the furtherance of this policy.

Writing in 1968, she could conclude, accurately, that Tanzania has "established conditions which both give it a limited independence and the possibility of moving further. In an Africa where most states are falling into anarchy, inertia or outright dependence, this is already something of an achievement." [95] More recently, as we have been describing, subtle weaknesses have revealed themselves in this "locally derived overall strategy for development"; not surprisingly, certain weaknesses in Tanzania's international posture have, simultaneously, become more readily apparent.

There is an additional dimension of Tanzania's posture toward the outside world which is relevant here. Hoskyns emphasizes the prime importance of a regime's internal dynamic and domestic choices for structuring pragmatically its foreign policy; she documents the fact that such a pattern of causality has moved Tanzania to pursue, up to a certain point, progressive policies. But it must also be stressed that a regime's very definition of the external environment is a second, somewhat independent, causal factor which can either reinforce or work against the first. Moreover, this second factor has been important in Tanzania's case. Thus its ideological perspective on the world system has developed in many exemplary ways, thereby promoting an increasingly critical and incisive reading of international realities and a rather tougher policy line. But, at the same time, it has stopped well short of being a fully effective theory of imperialism. And this failing seems also to have been a costly one for the realization of the country's socialist intentions.

It is certainly true that, at the most general level, there exists in Tanzania a significant measure of suspicion of "the West." At its most profound, this finds expression in vigorous passages of *Mwongozo* and in such items as the striking official analysis (presented to the Lusaka nonaligned summit of 1970) of the international role of the multinational corporations:

. . . multi-national corporations are, by their nature, advocates of "free-trade." For "free-trade" has (with reason) normally been the policy of the strong; its practical meaning is freedom for the stronger economic unit to enter the sphere of weaker units without the hindrance of restrictive measures or serious competition. And multi-national corporations are, by definition, the strong element in any business competition; they have massive resources at their command in money, men, and—therefore—power. . . . Such investments will not normally make the economy of the Third World nation concerned any more self-reliant as long as the multi-national corporation retains its control. The satellite relationship will continue to exist while questions of output, markets, technology, research and management are determined by corporations which are basically North American, West European, Japanese and South African.[96]

On a number of occasions—the showdown with Britain over Rhodesia and with West Germany over the recognition of the GDR, for example—Tanzania has safeguarded its independence at the expense of considerable promised inflows of resources; the leadership has also been quick to trace the strength of the Southern African white regimes to their links with the wider imperialist system. Moreover—the other side of the coin—the country has increasingly aligned itself with progressive forces on most of the crucial issues of the day: recognition of the Provisional Revolutionary Government of Vietnam, very early and vigorous support for the admission of China to the UN, and so on. As *Mwongozo* notes:

The party must take the necessary steps to establish this revolutionary relationship with revolutionary movements of Africa, Asia, and Latin America. Similarly, it is our duty to establish fraternal and revolutionary relations with those American citizens fighting for justice and human equality. . . . At the United Nations and other international organizations there is need to stress cooperation with all friendly countries, socialist and revolutionary countries in Asia, Africa, and Latin America.[97]

Similarly, efforts have been made (albeit with modest success) to create links of trade and aid with the "socialist" countries of Eastern Europe and with the Soviet Union, and a full panoply of diplomatic relations has been established.

At the same time, it is not hard to perceive a certain coolness toward the Soviet Union, though the terms of this do Tanzania some credit. For it is only in small part to be explained by Nyerere's suspicions of Marxism per se; what he has reacted against are the effects of ritualized, "official" Marxism (though Nyerere himself tends not to make the distinction between this and other variants) and, especially, the authoritarian character of Soviet society. It is significant that his attitude toward China has been different. A statement made during his second visit there in 1968 sounds a note which is often heard in Tanzanian pronouncements:

> Since my previous visit to China in 1965 there have been many important developments both in China and in Tanzania. . . . All of the major changes Tanzania has introduced have been intended to secure or at least to further the supremacy of the people. As I understand it, that was also the purpose of the Cultural Revolution.[98]

China, and Korea as well, have been consistently seen as places which have much to teach Tanzania. At the very least, Tanzania's eclecticism at the international level has provided for a substantial shift to the left, which viewed, as it must be, in continental perspective, seems quite striking.

It is likely, however, that the sort of radical transformation we have suggested to be necessary in order to realize a genuine economic breakthrough would eventually require the establishment of even closer links with the socialist world (though one must also be careful not to grossly overestimate the amount of disinterested and useful trade and aid which is likely to be forthcoming from such a source).[99] And it cannot be doubted that there will be limitations upon any further shift, limitations which emerge precisely along the fault-line in Tanzania's perspective which has been mentioned. For at the heart of Tanzania's foreign policy there still lies the concept of "nonalignment" at its most mystifying: Tanzania is "suspicious" of socialist countries in ways that sometimes parallel all too closely its equivalent suspicions of the "imperialist" camp.[100] This latter point is the key to much else as well, for nationalist suspicion proves to be no substitute, as suggested earlier, for a theory of imperialism. Indeed, in the absence of the latter, the way is cleared for many of international capitalism's subtler intriguers to enter Tanzania relatively unnoticed.

Is the exact function of the World Bank and the IMF within the capitalist system fully appreciated by the Tanzanian leadership? And what of the country's exaggerated deference to Sweden's "social democracy" and, *mirabile dictu,* Canada's "independent" role? [101] Small wonder that Niblock has been able to document even the inordinate amount of soul-searching that went into several of Tanzania's most adventurous confrontations with the West, including the British and West German incidents referred to earlier.[102] This is not merely a matter of some residual nostalgia for Western liberalism—though, in the president's case at least, there may be something of this. The forcing through of a root-and-branch approach to the West is also undermined by failure to situate the technical dimension of international relationships and international assistance in their proper socioeconomic context. Thus the extent to which seemingly technical advice must inevitably carry with it the ideological overtones of its capitalist origins seems often to be missed altogether. As a result, McKinsey and Co. is charged with crucial responsibilities in the field of governmental reorganization and, most odious of all, Harvard's Development Advisory Service has recently arrived, under contract to help develop Tanzania's "industrial strategy"! [103]

Weakness of strategy, weakness of theory—this is a formidable combination, especially since the two elements tend to reinforce each other. At the same time they are not the whole picture. Perhaps, for example, more should be made of Tanzania's specific economic achievements, even if some of the shortcomings which have been discussed are taken as given. Perhaps, too, such weaknesses should be viewed more sympathetically—more, say, as being necessary *compromises* with the intractable and hard reality of Tanzania's lack of development. To take the first point first, it must be noted that there has been substantive accomplishment beyond even that measure of consolidation of the preconditions for planning "socialism and self-reliance" which was justly celebrated in Section 1. For the country is "beginning to set more store by industrialization, and especially industries which forge close links with agriculture: the manufacture of farm implements, fertilizers, insecticides, and, in the other direction, the processing of agricultural products." Even "the necessity of establishing a capital goods industry has begun to be accepted in Tanzania and plans to build up capital goods manufacturing capacity figure, albeit superficially, in the current Five Year Plan." [104] The meeting of National Development Corporation managers in Dodoma in 1971 heard the general-manager, Mr. Kahama, speak at length about the need to stimulate rural and cottage industries, an emphasis, still largely rhetorical, that might also lead toward a more finely shaded industrial policy;[105] the move toward decentralization to "nine towns," as sketched in the Five Year Plan, could also prove to be of importance. And, more generally, the whole emphasis on income redistribution has itself a number of implications in this sphere, implying a progressive undermining of the roots of "effective demand" for a luxurious line of goods and the basis for a shift in direction if a mass bias in production were to be pursued more vigorously.[106]

All these elements are important. Yet it remains the most significant attribute of these positive features that, under present conditions, their presence is more *randomly* than systematically achieved. Under such conditions the case of fertilizer capacity (referred to above) is not atypical. Linked closely to West German finance, it has been based on costly imported materials and expensive infrastructural development (a jetty) in Tanga harbor, with much too little note being taken of the possibility of developing phosphate deposits at Arusha in the interior.[107] Indeed, Seidman has queried, in forceful terms, a number of emphases in the current policy package along related lines: their capital intensity, their limited linkages, their questionable export bias (the very dubious—and expensive—sisal pulp plant, for example).[108] Moreover, the proof of this range of criticisms can begin to be seen in the results; there is no sign of a productive breakthrough in Tanzania. Quite the reverse is the case.

We have said little thus far about the rural sector per se. Perhaps this is the place at which to do so, for there has been real achievement in that sector, even if it is achievement of a necessarily controversial character. Thus opinions differ among progressive writers as to the degree of priority to be assigned to rural collectivization within a socialist program for contemporary Africa; Amin, Dumont, and others would seem, in fact, to give such a program very short shrift, preferring to rely on firm control over the "modern" sector while commodity production is allowed to smash through the traditional integument at the base.[109] Tanzanian socialists have chosen otherwise and have given good reasons for their preference. In areas of widely scattered population, it is argued, the larger units which emerge from the *ujamaa vijijini* (rural socialism) emphasis should provide the focus for the rationalized distribution of work and the more modern inputs which could begin, for the first time, genuinely to transform agricultural production. And in more densely populated areas, even some which are most transformed economically, a movement toward collectivism is seen as promising their rescue from creeping involution. More broadly conceived, the program is, as noted earlier, designed to stem class polarization, and this in part because such polarization is felt likely to choke off the release of energies of large sections of the more parochialized peasantry.[110] There is a distaste for rural class formation in Tanzania which is, in the best sense, moralistic, but it has its economic rationale as well. Moreover, certain successful socialist "villages" scattered across the country have begun to indicate some of the potential which can be liberated by this mechanism.

It is much too early to evaluate the program, of course. In addition, its substance ranges from individual villages and collective experiments in remote parts of the country to the massive movement and regrouping of population (forty to sixty thousand people in less than six months) which characterized "Operation Dodoma" in 1971. That there are real weaknesses in conceptualization in this sphere (another vacuum into which the World Bank has begun to rush, incidentally), and also in generating effective methods of political work through which to realize the goals, is also true.[111] The further development of the program will therefore merit careful scrutiny. Yet there is a more basic point, one consonant with the general emphasis of the subsection, which can be made here. For it is really only the overall restructuring of the economy, the keys to which Tanzania has not yet fully grasped, that can finally guarantee the material basis for rural transformation. The leadership's heartfelt concern for the rural areas and for the peasants has sometimes blurred the necessity to guarantee the effective material linkage of the peasants to a revolutionized "modern" sector. Once again, the mounting of controls has made more systematic development a possibility here. But it is precisely at this point that the strategic conundrum also enters the picture to affect fundamentally Tanzania's rural socialism.

It is now evident that even Tanzania's achievement must be situated within the context of what remains to be done. What of the second qualification introduced above, that such seeming weaknesses are merely necessary compromises imposed by the objective conditions of Tanzania's economic situation? Again, there is some truth in this. Tanzania's absolute lack of development has been noted on several occasions; some transfers of resources, transfers of expertise, transfers of technology, will seem to be imperative in such a situation, and full cognizance must be taken of such facts if the Tanzanian left is to avoid substituting mere militant-sounding phrases for the elaboration of viable and progressive programs. Under such circumstances "nonalignment" does have the virtue of maximizing the number of sources from which one can draw; a deferential attitude toward Scandinavian "socialism" has certainly had its pay-offs in the quantity of funds and personnel made available. And pursuit of the short-term earners of foreign exchange must seem similarly tempting. Tanzania is also a relatively small country. Theoretically, larger African units certainly make economic sense (assuming the policy which such units adopt reflects a genuine challenge to neocolonialism);[112] what seems at times to be a rather uncritical Tanzanian approach to East African unity (and even continental unity) may find some justification in this fact.[113] On all these fronts, a small weak country obviously has its range of choice narrowed.[114] Nevertheless, one must continue to repeat the point made earlier in this subsection: what Tanzania can (and must) do is to strengthen further its economic and ideological sinews even as it deals with an external environment which, paradoxically, is at once threatening and seductive. Then the hidden costs of various kinds of "aid" and the irrelevance of certain seemingly advanced techniques and skills to Tanzania's real needs will at least be more apparent. And the optimum utilization of local manpower resources and indigenous technological potential will be much more nearly realized than at present.

In the end, of course, one may wonder whether a halfway house to structural transformation is likely to be viable at all over the long haul, whether an economic revolution can really be brought to pass by means of quite so much reformism. Perhaps the die was really cast when Tanzania chose to compensate for its nationalizations in 1967. At the very least, valuable time has been lost. When surpluses were first available, too few radical risks were taken and not enough "self-reliance" tried. Then, with the productive system not transformed, such surpluses have tended to dry up. And the availability of foreign exchange becomes a "constraint" for the first time.[115] Under such circumstances, the illogical "logicality" of orthodoxy becomes the more potent. Short-term "profitability" and balance-of-payments effects sing their siren song; the IMF shows its teeth. And the clutching for further loans and aid becomes more desperate and less critical. There are recent signs that this may be beginning to happen to Tanzania. In the process, the country moves even further away from the threshold of radical risk.

Yet the alternative—a full-fledged economic revolution—is not easily mounted. Few socialist countries have in fact established a "self-centered" system in cold blood, as it were; often enforced isolation has given them little option but to mount the sort of siege economy from which effective reconstruction springs. That Tanzania should find itself too often opting for the relatively risk-free policy, refraining from pushing the logic of its socialism further, is therefore not surprising. The danger is that it may then come to reap the worst of both worlds: stagnation, with neither the volatility and exacerbation of contradictions which can characterize capitalism even in its most peripheral expressions on the one hand, nor a realization of the promise of full-fledged socialist reconstruction on the other. Obviously, in the struggle to avoid this denouement to "socialism and self-reliance," the developments of the next few years should prove crucial. We may leave the question of "dependence and development" on this note; certainly the fact that the scrutiny of the Tanzanian experience forces one to pose such searching questions is a measure of how far the country has yet to go. At the same time, that questions about development so basic to socialists are vitally relevant here is also a measure of just how far Tanzania has come!

THE CLASS STRUGGLE

There is a further complexity to the Tanzanian situation which we must confront more directly. For, in the preceding subsection, one set of actors has hovered uneasily in the wings: the national elite which mans, formally, the commanding heights of the bureaucratic decision-making apparatus. Though this group has generally comprised the home-grown guarantors of neocolonialism elsewhere in Africa, in Tanzania, as we have seen, a real struggle has been launched to commit a growing proportion of them to socialist goals. Moreover, in the course of that struggle some real sacrifices—in *amour-propre,* in privileged access to surpluses, and in private sector economic aggrandizement—have been exacted from the elite. Yet mere compliance with the more dramatic of the Arusha Declaration demands, while important in providing valuable leeway for the progressive leadership to assert itself, is not sufficient. The most vital core of this group may number no more than the 44,000 Resnick suggests,[116] but their role in the concrete articulation of Tanzania's socialism is, at least in the short run, absolutely crucial. And it must be affirmed that, by and large, the elite has yet to engage itself *fully and effectively* in the task of socialist construction; its continuing lack of a realized capacity for *socialist creativity* remains a major constraint in Tanzania. And, to repeat, it is the nature of this class—for such it is—which forces qualification of our earlier formulations.

It remains true, as we have phrased it, that gaps still existing in Tanzania's socialist formulations provide a vacuum into which soft choices and preemptive pressures enter; for certain purposes it is useful to emphasize the regime's commitment and to phrase the problem in this way. But in the present context we must feed in another aspect of the situation: the so-called vacuum is already partly filled by the brand of self-interest and cultural set which continues to mark many of Tanzania's own indigenous decision-makers and implementers even in the post-Arusha period. Since these attributes, as we shall see, tend to be inimical to socialism, it remains a fact that the members of Tanzania's ruling petty bourgeoisie too often act as saboteurs (whether conscious or unconscious) of socialist effort at precisely the point where the task of socialist development presents its most subtle and intricate challenges. Progressive sections of the petty bourgeoisie have managed to force the pace and have provided a framework for socialist advance. Spelling out the program in practice on a hundred different fronts, blending it with technical considerations, *making it work*—that can be quite a different thing.

This continuing problem of the elite's role presents itself in a number of ways. There are some who would question even the reality of the sacrifice which has been made, stating that privileged access to the national surplus provided by control over the levers of state power is still the attribute which defines the elite as being, in reality, a bureaucratic class. A case for this can be built up by citing a number of components, such as continuing income differentials between urban and rural areas and within each of those areas themselves,[117] or, more subtly, biased attributes of the service sector. On the latter point, for example, Malcolm Segall has recently launched a vigorous critique of Tanzania's health system. The conclusion is worth quoting at length:

> Neo-colonialism would not be so successful if it did not benefit someone. Sophisticated medical facilities are concentrated in the towns and they benefit the urban dwellers. In particular, the higher income urban groups have major expectations in medical care and they create the pressures to have their demand fulfilled. This is a class interest, which is in conflict with the interests of the peasants. The competitive demands of these two groups on the health budget is an example of class struggle.

The urban elite also want to feel on a par with the bourgeoisie of the capitalist world, with whom they identify. They reasonably want to demonstrate national "achievements," but these are seen in terms of prestige buildings and other material accoutrements of "modern medicine"; such interpretation is truly "bourgeois." A socialist achievement in health would be the maximum well-being of the mass of the people; this would be something to show the world. The demand of the urban elite, their bourgeois nationalism and neo-colonialism are the main determinants of the current health policy of the country.[118]

Moreover, when some change comes in such spheres, as it has begun to do in the health sector in recent months, it is too often only as a result of the president's personal intervention.[119]

Some observers would also stress evasion of such features as the "leadership code"—either by elite members dispersing holdings to relatives or by the more cautious manipulation of "collectivism" for personal profit (the urban-elite-dominated poultry "cooperative"—WAKUCO—which has moved toward a monopoly of egg distribution in Dar es Salaam, for example). The Kenyan model—unbridled "conflict of interest"—remains an attractive one to many such "leaders." But this cynicism can easily be overstated. The main thrust of continuing elite self-interest is much more subtle. From the standpoint of bureaucratic incumbents, the process of radical transformation is worrisome in other ways, particularly in its very unpredictability. Thus reference to the Chinese experience and the insights of "Maoist economics," or to a genuinely self-centered economy, conjures up for them images of a release of human energies which may not be easily channeled along established grooves; it seems much safer to ride the existing system unadventurously. Small wonder that to many members of the petty bourgeoisie, *Mwongozo* has seemed at least as threatening as the Arusha Declaration.

Two further features serve both to rationalize this bias, and at the same time exemplify it: the omnipresence of "conventional wisdom" about development which characterizes the elite's outlook, and the overlay of bureaucratic style and elitist attitude which dominates their methods of work. The ideological bent of much of the elite is particularly patent, a clear triumph for colonialism (and neocolonialism) in the cultural sphere, and crystallizes around such truisms as the "necessity" of aid, the (unequivocal and neutral) "superiority" of Western technology and management systems, the priority of "efficiency," narrowly and technocratically conceived, over radical risk and that release of human energies referred to as a possibility above. Excuses for the soft choice, then, but also a reflection of a predominantly Western educational system and a set of skills which is derivative therefrom. Ineluctably the elite faces the West not as masters of their own fate but as apprentices in search of models. Yet this is precisely the point at which "self-reliance" should most seriously begin to be pursued. It is not surprising that concrete socialist programs, of necessity the end product of creative but laborious day-to-day planning and implementation, only spring with difficulty from such infertile soil.

Style and attitude. Here too the dead hand of colonialism lies heavy upon socialist Tanzania. At its worst, the colonial system was oppressive and authoritarian, at its best merely paternalistic; the education system exemplified hierarchy and command in parallel ways. Moreover, when untransformed, the arrogance bred by educational attainment has an elitist impact in and of itself which is graphic, and complementary to the other aspects of the inherited pattern. A cadre of leaders which is also the by-product of these processes comes reluctantly to mass line politics and the democratizing logic of protracted struggle in the economic sphere; they are as likely in practice to have the effect of *demobilizing* the populace and inducing apathy and cynicism.

Such observations are not speculative. One can trace the costs of such features through various spheres of policy. The question of overall economic strategy, already discussed at length, is merely one such sphere, though it is perhaps the most important. We have already noted the elite's self-interest in the risk-free option; their reluctance to marry their technical skills to the search for more total solutions is also rooted in the cultural preconceptions we are now exploring. For adequate strategy springs from adequate theory. And a major roadblock to progress still appears at that point where technical calculation begins to shade over into divergent ideological preconceptions, into fundamentally different "problematics," as to the very nature of underdevelopment and the strategic imperatives which that reality suggests. It is in just such a situation that the difficulties of the elite formulating, say, a specific set of radical policies for the foreign trade sector become so overwhelming (this being an actual case neatly documented by I. N. Resnick in a recent paper).[120] And it is such a context which permits the following results, documented by Bienefeld in his important survey of manpower and educational planning at the University of Dar es Salaam:

> In this process [of laying the basis for a new educational structure] one might have expected the university to have played a leading role; to contribute to this conceptualization of the future and to take the lead in marshalling the knowledge of traditional disciplines to develop an analytical framework to transcend them. But such hopes are probably naive, for here too the past asserts itself. Professionals trained in certain well-defined disciplines cannot, as a group, be expected to be the agents of fundamental changes which would invalidate their own particular specialization. Where their own professional status (both local and international), as well as their intellectual and pedagogic competence and security, are threatened, they will not be anything but conservative. It is thus no surprise that the university's protracted discussions concerning a reorganization of all subject matter has culminated in a crescendo of anti-climax. There are many changes in labels, but traditional departments teaching traditional disciplines are fully in charge of the content. Meanwhile, a full-scale engineering school is taking shape; the very traditional medical school is seeking to establish post-graduate courses; and all the best students and future university teachers are sent abroad for "proper" training. Under these conditions the possibility of making the education system an agency of change, or of building up an education system in harmony with Tanzania's aspirations, is gravely in doubt.[121]

The rural sector has also felt the sting of the system's still prominent "elitist" attributes, despite the real progress in that sphere which must also be taken seriously. As Cliffe has phrased it:

> There are vestiges of "orthodox" thinking associated with particular institutions, which are in some degree still colonial, and these are reinforced by the narrow, project focus of a bourgeois economic planning technocracy and by the fact that most planners, whether expatriate or local, are culturally alienated from the peasant environment. There is a broader question of how far the bureaucrats as some sort of proto-class of their own or as individuals, often with kinship links with rural notables or "kulaks," are unconsciously or deliberately resistant to any genuine *ujamaa* efforts. In the party, too, at various levels up to the national there is a problem that some of the active, representative elements are better-off farmers who may be anxious about the personal implications of *ujamaa* policy.[122]

Such brakes upon rural transformation were seen at work most dramati-

cally during the drafting of the Second Five Year Plan when planners
only took seriously the *ujamaa* principle after the president and cabinet
rejected the completed first draft on the grounds of its omission. But in
day-to-day practice this has also meant that even when mobilized to action many bureaucrats have carried over much of the intellectual
baggage of the World Bank's disastrous "settlement scheme" approach
(recommended to Tanganyika in the early sixties) into the era of self-
reliant *ujamaa* villages; there has been a consequent overemphasis on infrastructure, services, and supervision, which encourages the growth of a
dependent attitude in many of the villages. And attention has tended, in
a related manner, to be diverted from the need to fundamentally recast
the established agricultural system in areas where such modification, not
resettlement, is the key to long-run collectivization.[123] Finally, it is perhaps in the rural areas that manifestations of the hectoring, bureaucratic
style of such a leadership are most likely to have the predicted effect of
demobilizing the mass of the population, thus choking off that release of
latent energies which is the program's ostensible aim.[124] But examples in
other policy spheres could easily be multiplied; here we must assess the
more general implications.

The achievements sketched in Section 1, the "sabotage" demonstrated in preceding paragraphs—both are the artifacts of Tanzania's
petty bourgeoisie. Their juxtaposition suggests something of the nature
of the struggle which is being waged among the various tendencies
within the petty bourgeoisie.[125] What, then, can be said broadly about
the role of this stratum in the Tanzanian situation? In the first place, certainly, that the struggle continues. And, beyond such an affirmation,
that there are a number of alternative possibilities—though just what the
range of those possibilities is remains a controversial question in itself. T.
Szentes, writing of Tanzania, has suggested that there are only two:
"The elite as it exists today will either merge with the bourgeoisie of an
unfolding capitalist system, or will dissolve, losing its elite character, in
the process of socialist development." [126] For in Szentes' terms the
"elite" can never be considered a "class": its members cannot themselves be owners of the means of production and, equally important to
his argument, the conditions for the elite's "reproduction as a class" can
never be stabilized—in his phrase, cannot be "objectively guaranteed."
The short-term importance of this stratum is therefore only a transitory
way station.

These two possibilities are real, of course. The first one, in particular, is a constant threat to any progressive African experiment, and is embodied, most graphically (even in Tanzania), in the ever present danger of absolute *reversal* by means of military coup. The second, the reclaiming of the elite for the task of socialist construction, is the end toward which Nyerere and other progressives in Tanzania are bending their efforts. But in making such a neat dichotomy, it appears that Szentes is being overly schematic. For he underestimates the extent to which a group whose control over the state gives them a crucial role in the production process can take on the solidity of a class even when their activity in the private sector is constrained or eaten away.[127] Given that this is a real possibility, it can be further argued that an intermediate type, located somewhere between Szentes' two models, is at the moment an equally real alternative to the deepening of the socialist project in Tanzania. It is a model of a social formation which corresponds to the stagnating, "halfway house" economy sketched in the preceding subsection. Within it, the petty bourgeoisie of the political and governmental bureaucracies becomes, in effect, the custodian of a stagnant kind of peripheral state capitalism—a regime with just enough nationalist fervor and direction to ward off some of the worst depredations of international capitalism but not enough commitment and clarity to push toward the full release of socialist potential.

Thus Nyerere and other Tanzanian progressives must guard against an outright reversal *and* a mere running-down and distortion of the system of social control over the means of production already established. How much can be done in these respects? Certainly there are limits to how hard the elite can be pushed, though quite what those limits are remains mere guesswork. There are those who criticize the president for not demanding more from the elite, who say that he has taken the argument that members of the petty bourgeoisie are reclaimable too far, using it as an excuse for sometimes blunting the edges of ideological struggle, and for adopting a kind of "moral rearmament" approach to this class, within which perspective *all* are equally reclaimable and equally serviceable.[128] They would also deprecate, in this connection, the reluctance of Nyerere and others to take seriously the symbiosis established between this group and the subtle lures of imperialism, and to move to defuse the latter in a more root-and-branch manner. His defenders would point to what he has demanded from the elite so far and what he has accomplished with them, and would further argue that to demand more at any one time would almost certainly alienate too many of the technical cadres (and political notables) whose skills are vital (thereby reinforcing any tendency for them to drag their feet) or, even worse, virtually guarantee reversal. The elite can be won, they argue, or at least a significant proportion of it—particularly the younger genera- tion of recruits—but only slowly, cautiously, deftly. Unfortunately, a judgment between two such persuasive lines of argument is obviously not one that an outside observer can make with any degree of con- fidence, even though the most crucial features of the Tanzanian expe- rience are probably to be illuminated by precisely such a judgment. In the final analysis, in fact, this judgment must be a matter of praxis, not of academic observation. *On s'engage, puis on voit.*

One can return to other of the evidence of Section 1, however, in order to reaffirm the seriousness of much of the leadership's activity with respect to such issues: the reclamation of the elite is to take place not in some idealist vacuum, but under pressure from the "workers and peas- ants"! The latter are to play an *essential* role in building their own social- ism—essential both because the extent of the elite's ability to commit al- truistic suicide has, over the long haul, inherent limitations which are obvious, and because the masses' material stake in transformation, in the promise of a self-centered system, is more real and potentially more ur- gent than that of even the most progressive of the petty bourgeoisie. But what of consciousness, of the actual *felt* urgency of such claims upon the system, and of the understanding of the means necessary for their reali- zation? How likely is it that such a necessary base will come into exist- ence and find effective expression under Tanzanian conditions?

Take the case of the workers. Workers' participation holds real promise as a program, despite the ambiguities of the workers' own posi- tion within the broader socioeconomic system and the dangers that workers might merely use their stronger voice to skim off surpluses at the expense of the rural areas.[129] Its positive expression is even more apt to be distorted by the bureaucratic apparatus which sets it in train; one of the most awkward facts about socialist construction in Tanzania is that initiative for mobilizing a somewhat sluggish mass base must gener- ally come from the very bureaucratic group whose enthusiasm for the exercise has not always been marked.[130] Thus, in the case of the work- ers, managers (broadly defined) have been suspicious of the implications of innovation and have sought to tame the concept.[131] And NUTA, the official trade union, has itself tended to lay a dead hand upon the workers, another instance of the bureaucracy demobilizing the mass of the population and conjuring up only cynicism and apathy.

An even more fundamental criticism of the whole program has recently been made by H. Mapolu: that there are crucial, systemic, ambiguities which lie even at the heart of its most progressive articulation. "Tanzania's strategy has not gone as far as to identify a 'working class' that can be viewed as the chief action agent of socialist development." As a result, "workers' participation" is too easily defused and coopted into "more efficient" management structures and not really encouraged to generalize its impact to the whole system.

> As a consequence of the absence of political strategy due to the lack of a class ideological position, there has been no conception of a bureaucracy as a structural phenomenon. The tendency has been to view workers' participation not as a structural mechanism for the control of certain strata by the class that should be the pillar of socialist construction, but principally as a wrong attitude which leads to wrong methods of work.
>
> It follows therefore that when one reaches the factory level, participation can only be minimal in substance. Essentially, the tasks of "management" belong to the managers and the workers can come in only occasionally to "help" in certain fields and to quench their thirst for information on what is going on in the factory as a whole. This seems to be the only explanation of the preponderance of the managers in the workers' council and the council's mere advisory powers.[132]

And yet workers' participation and the *Mwongozo* spirit, once set afoot, are not quite so easily controlled by the less progressive members of the petty bourgeoisie; indeed, these elements have begun to have a distinctive impact on the workers and on the system as a whole. Lawrence is surely correct when he summarizes the events of recent months by stating that

> armed with *Mwongozo*, the workers appear to have gone beyond the economism of wage demands (especially since the incomes policy makes them redundant) and have been paradoxically "side-tracked" into the more difficult but significant pursuit of workers' control. Their strikes have been about and against unsympathetic management, lack of consultation, "commandism" at the work place, the maltreatment of trade union leaders (or conversely the ineffectiveness of the same leaders).[133]

Such a class, and the cadres which this new brand of activity presses forward, could eventually begin to ask even broader questions about the need for strategy and planning, as the present absence of such elements comes increasingly to be understood as affecting their own futures. Already this range of initiatives has impinged upon the elite's actions and upon their conception of the workers and of the norms to which they themselves must conform; here one can catch a glimpse of the road forward. One can also expect various rearguard actions from such a quasi-ruling class, however.[134] But, in any case, this need not be a bad thing. Tanzanian socialism is unlikely to advance much further without some greater exposure and polarization of the society's contradictions.

In the rural areas, some similar seeds have been planted. Here there is also a real potential; in many ways the peasantry has an even more vital long-run stake in radical transformation than the workers (though it is also characterized by much mystification and parochialism). Where it has worked, the *ujamaa* approach to rural collectivization has in actual fact thrown up socialist-minded peasants and leaders of a new and questioning kind. Even before the Arusha Declaration period and the nationwide "socialism and rural development" emphasis, for example, the Ruvuma Development Association (an early prototype of the rural *ujamaa* approach, from which the president in particular seemed to draw inspiration) had demonstrated in the remote Songea region the reality of this potential, generating an impressive range of genuine cadres. Of course, we have already mentioned the extent to which convention has taken the edge off this program in many ways, demobilizing some of its promise. Moreover, the move by the party bureaucrats to smash the superstructure of the RDA itself in 1969 seems a good example of the contradictions that real rural democracy can and does bring into the open.

Certain weaknesses, of immediate relevance to the latter point, can also be identified in the policy's very formulation—such, at least, is Cliffe's observation. He has emphasized the extent to which the top leadership has shied away from identifying clearly the fact of existing class polarization in the countryside, and using its presence strategically as a lever for socialist advance. "Without such an approach," he concludes, "it is difficult to see whence the great social force necessary for transforming a fairly inert rural society and an elitist, conservative ruling stratum can conceivably come."[135] Nevertheless, it must be repeated that some progress has been made even using more frontist (and, in the opinion of some observers, less adventurist) methods. And in Ismani (an area of Tanzania where capitalist relations of production are the most advanced), when Dr. Wilbert Klerru, the regional commissioner, was killed (in late 1971) by a capitalist farmer while beginning to push a more aggressive brand of collectivization (including the use of expropriation), poorer peasants and rural workers apparently rallied to support the program. Bureaucrats, too, have begun, albeit painfully, to adapt their thinking to these new pressures and demands for a "mass bias" in the system (as, for example, recent shifts in the priorities of the Water Development Ministry may indicate). Again, the horizon of really dramatic, cumulative change remains a distant one, but there can be little doubt that in the rural areas the *ujamaa* policy has given a content and structure to the struggle for progress in a nonrevolutionary situation around which consciousness can crystallize and a popular base may form.[136]

A final, potentially active element in Tanzania's progressive wing is the youth—and particularly the younger recruits to Tanzania's intelligentsia. There are ambiguities in their position, of course. Though a lack of expansion of the economic system and a consequent foreclosing of privileged prospects might eventually give a more material basis to the criticisms of this group, at the moment they are merely junior recruits to the bureaucratic group, and many have begun to drop into the elitist mold even by the time they reach senior secondary school. Conflicts between this group and the incumbents in positions of authority, such as have begun to mark Tanzania's schools and universities, can easily degenerate into mere generational antagonisms. Yet it is also true that the stake of this group in the old status quo is less frozen than that of the earlier generation of the elite (who had already made various compromises with the spontaneous development of peripheral capitalism), and their "plasticity" is enhanced to that extent. To take up the progressive side in ideological struggle within the petty bourgeoisie, to respond to new norms, can thus come more easily to them. It is therefore no accident that many of the most articulate militants in Tanzania have begun to spring from such a group.

The fortunes of such militants document something more of the complexities of Tanzania's "silent class struggle." The president himself has seemed at times to take the lead in cutting these militants (still a rather small fraction of the student body) down to size—initiating the banning of the University Student African Revolutionary Front and the important student theoretical journal, *Cheche* (Spark), in 1969, among other things.[137] Moreover, when a critique of authoritarian methods of work at the university was taken up by a larger body of students in 1971, the bureaucracy was tacitly supported at the highest level in its efforts to stall and demobilize the students, this despite the fact that earlier in the year the president had said on campus, however lightly, that some sort of "cultural revolution" might be necessary at the Hill (as the university is referred to).[138] When the students, invoking *Mwongozo,* went further and sought to link their activities to developments in Dar es Salaam by forging the basis of dialogue with the workers, their initiative was crushed, in this case by the bureaucrats of TANU itself! A bleak picture, but as so often in Tanzania one relieved somewhat by other kinds of facts: that *Majimaji,* the successor to *Cheche,* has been allowed to carry on the same high standard of critical socialist debate; that Nyerere did eventually intervene to facilitate some sort of dialogue within the university; that a number of the more admirable militants from the Hill have been recruited, over the years, into important party and related posts. These latter "victories," too, are part of the contradictory world of Tanzanian socialism.

In conclusion, and by way of summary, we can assume that certain fundamental peculiarities of Tanzania's class struggle are by now apparent. Most important is that it is a struggle on two fronts: to expand the numbers and the efficacy of the progressive petty bourgeoisie, and to release the energies of a more conscious and vocal mass of workers and peasants. Under Tanzanian circumstances this is not a simple task. Total reversal of what has been achieved to date is a very real possibility, one which must inevitably help to determine the calculations and the tactics of any progressive tendency. A more likely danger in the short run, perhaps, is the creation of a vicious circle within which a petty bourgeoisie, on balance still relatively untransformed, demobilizes and instrumentalizes the mass of the population and guarantees, at best, a stagnant quasi-state capitalism, thereby checking further progress. And some features of such a possibility do begin to haunt the Tanzanian experience as we have described it. The alternative to such a vicious circle is to struggle effectively on *both* fronts and, even more important, to see that effort on one front is likely to fail without simultaneous effort on the other—to see, in short, that the two fronts are closely, indeed dialectically, interrelated. Effectively achieved, the interchange between a petty bourgeoisie which increasingly allows itself to be radicalized, and the mass of the peasants and workers whose consciousness is rising, must at some point become self-reinforcing: the petty bourgeoisie working not only to serve the masses but also to mobilize them and raise their level of consciousness (a necessity), even as the masses increasingly move to put pressure on the petty bourgeoisie and thereby guarantee the latter's further solidarity and commitment (equally a necessity). Indeed, it can now be more clearly grasped than in Section 1, that *the core of the Tanzanian achievement lies in the fact that the leadership, and especially President Nyerere, has sought to mount precisely this imaginative alternative.*[139.]

Has our evidence suggested that, nonetheless, basic contradictions remain unresolvable by means of such an effort? For example, one criticism might be that Tanzania's ideology does not permit a clear enough conceptualization of the class structure of Tanzanian society such as could facilitate effective "class struggle," even of the necessarily nuanced kind we have been discussing; this is the thrust of comments by Mapolu, Cliffe, and others recorded earlier in this subsection and is a point to which we must return. A second possible consideration raises even more fundamental issues, suggesting that the struggle, however effectively waged, may still be lost under present Tanzanian conditions and such a cumulatively fruitful dialectic never set in motion. Thus some might wish to apply Engels' deft and searching description of Thomas Münzer's plight to Nyerere:

> The worst thing that can befall the leader of an extreme party is to be compelled to take over a government at a time when society is not yet ripe for the domination of the class he represents and for the measures which that domination implies. What he *can* do depends not upon his will but upon the degree of antagonism between the various classes, and upon the level of development of the material means of existence, of the conditions of production and commerce upon which class contradictions always repose. What he *ought* to do, what his party demands of him, again depends not upon him or the stage of development of the class struggle and its conditions. He is bound to the doctrines and demands hitherto propounded which, again, do not proceed from the class relations of the moment, or from the more or less accidental level of production and commerce, but from his more or less penetrating insight into the general result of the social and political movement. Thus he necessarily finds himself in an unsolvable dilemma. What he *can* do contradicts all his previous actions and

principles, and the immediate interests of his party, and what he *ought* to do cannot be done. In a word, he is compelled to represent not his party or his class, but the class for whose domination the movement is then ripe. In the interests of the movement he is compelled to advance the interests of an alien class, and to feed his own class with talk and promises, and with the asseveration that the interests of that alien class are their own interests. He who is put into this awkward position is irrevocably lost.[140]

If for "alien class" one reads the African petty bourgeoisie, and for "his own class," the workers and peasants of Tanzania, it is immediately apparent that there is an uncomfortable measure of truth in this comparison.

Yet for Tanzania this still appears to overstate the case in important particulars. Even those who feel that the president might have done more to challenge the most conservative of the petty bourgeoisie could hardly claim that he has unequivocally advanced the interests of that group. And the workers and peasants have had, rather than "talk and promises," more of an invitation, and some real opportunity, to shape their own destinies. There is a conviction among some Tanzanians, as we noted much earlier in this essay, that ideology and organization can force the pace even amid relatively unpromising "objective conditions" and can wrench socialist advance out of a society which is, in certain respects, "not yet ripe." The president has sought, in effect, to make his "insight" more rather than less penetrating and to spread that insight to others by the most effective means he can conceive.

We can now turn to an evaluation of the instruments which are thus placed at the disposal of Tanzania's progressive "tendency" in seeking to consolidate this creative initiative.

ORGANIZATION AND IDEOLOGY

We have already emphasized the point, in Section 2, that much of Tanzania's institutional and administrative inheritance from colonialism was not well adapted to the task of socialist construction; this is true whether one considers the centrality (and tenacity) of the cabinet system,[141] the structure of the quasi-autonomous public corporations ("parastatals"), or the framework of regional administration. Such mechanisms in themselves facilitated neither the emergence of an effectively committed leadership nor the forthright expression of a highly conscious mass pressure within the system and, more important, blocked the establishment of that necessary dialectic between the two which alone could guarantee sustained progress. Slowly, adjustments within the bureaucratic structure have been made such as could allow for more coordinated planning. But we have noted the limitations upon these advances if they serve merely to guarantee more coherent application of misguided principles and the more forthright expression of conservative interest. The real key to linking leadership and mass in a progressive manner and to resolving any contradictions which may arise from the interaction between these two elements must rather lie with the party—TANU. Socialist experience elsewhere suggests that it alone can be expected to guarantee the prerequisites of advance: to focus the efforts of the progressive members of the petty bourgeoisie and ensure the primacy of the socialist ideology, to mobilize the masses and raise their level of consciousness, and to provide increasingly the conduit for pressure from the workers and peasants themselves as they find their voice and realize more profoundly their interests.

We need not reiterate the extent to which important advances have sprung from party institutions, in particular the National Executive Committee. Moreover, the formulations of *Mwongozo* suggest an increasing awareness that socialist reconstruction requires the party to do more than merely provide the vaguest of guidelines, these in turn to be fleshed out by "neutral" technocrats. A range of small initiatives suggests, when viewed together, a pattern which may ultimately take on even greater significance: the National Executive Committee's direct intervention to wind up a government credit program (Karadha) which had been designed to facilitate the purchase of private automobiles by civil servants is one example; another is the variety of party organs which lent their voices to the general outcry in 1972 against a bonus payment to civil servants employed by the National Bank of Commerce, leading to the withdrawal of such payments. The same growing insight would seem to underlie such progressive announcements of a more systematic approach as the following:

TANU is to extend its grip on the economic affairs and running of the various government institutions and other organizations now that the economic affairs subcommittee of the TANU Central Committee has vigorously begun the task it was charged with when it was established in 1969.

. . . In short, through this subcommittee TANU would be the watch dog of the country's economy.[142]

In a related vein, the party in 1969 claimed primary responsibility in the field of rural collectivization.

Much of this remains mere rhetoric, of course, and action is often much too little and too late. The historical legacy carried over from the nationalist movement into the post-colonial political party distorts potential here, as Nyerere himself has been among the first to argue:

> All the national party organization and education were geared to defeating colonialism and opposing people of another race who happened to be in positions of power. This means that once independence is achieved, and the key positions of power have been Africanized, there is a grave danger that the party will lose support and will atrophy.[143]

Moreover, it cannot be assumed that the party has been systematically manned by the most progressive members of the petty bourgeoisie; too often its functionaries have been more typical representatives of that class, and have reflected many of the class's conventional preoccupations and its authoritarian style. And at the local level it has not been unusual for a district or regional party to fall under the sway of local notables and "economic activists" who have a vested interest in the status quo. It was just such a reality which prompted the following initiative by the TANU Youth League when it advocated "purges" in TANU in 1970:

> Members or leaders of TANU who have capitalist connections or ideas should be expelled from the party in order to make TANU a vanguard party of the workers and peasants only, it was resolved this weekend by a seminar of the TANU Youth League in Dar es Salaam. . . . It was also resolved that all loopholes in the Arusha Declaration leadership code which can be used by leaders to hide away their capitalist connections should be done away with, and the party was called upon to enforce the code more stringently.[144]

The president's cautious response to this suggestion, while tacitly acknowledging the problem, is equally instructive:

> Mwalimu said at present he could not conceive any person who had the qualifications to purge the nonsocialists from the party and added that it was necessary to recruit many socialists into the party before "we thought of excommunicating the nonsocialists." [145]

Indeed, upon occasion, it has seemed to be the progressive elements who were in most danger of being purged! [146] Thus the struggle within the petty bourgeoisie continues inside the party—and the same difficult questions as were raised in the preceding subsection, including those which query whether the struggle is being waged vigorously enough, are applicable there as well. Certainly, even the party cannot always be taken for granted, in its day-to-day functioning, as an unequivocal force for socialism.[147]

This is a question of the extent to which the party has the *will* to push for across-the-board socialist solutions in the manner one might theoretically expect of it; it remains an open question to the present moment. What is more immediately obvious is that TANU has not the actual *capacity* to do so entirely effectively in any case.[148] For certain steps which would seem to be necessary to confirm the party in its leading role have not been forthcoming. Thus despite the vigorous assertions of *Mwongozo*, TANU is not yet granted the manpower necessary for undertaking crucial tasks. Its research establishment is grievously limited, for example, and the wedding of ideological perspective and technical calculation so necessary to the task of *concretizing* an ideology in a practical and readily applicable manner is therefore difficult to realize. The *Guidelines to the Annual Plan*, published shortly after *Mwongozo* in 1971, spoke only of shifting "high-level manpower" from government to the parastatals;[149] this is of a piece with the consistent trend in Tanzanian manpower allocations to concentrate graduates and other skilled personnel almost exclusively in the civil service and to seal off the party from such inputs.[150] How then to guarantee that blending of "redness" and "expertise" which would make TANU a fully realized socialist presence within the elite? At the moment, of course, TANU maps out much of the general direction, but in vast stretches of policymaking the civil service roams at will. And in consequence even a party "economic affairs subcommittee" finds its feet firmly planted in mid-air.

It is true that the party nonetheless provides an umbrella for the activity of the most militant elements which do exist in Tanzania; [151] the general ethos of TANU, for all its crosscurrents, is far and away the most progressive in the society. It is from within the party that further attempts to deepen the logic of socialism can be seen to stir, often springing, in particular, from the TANU Youth League, whose various annual conferences and seminars have regularly thrown up radical challenges to orthodoxy.[152] Indeed, the TYL's university branch has been responsible for an especially high level of commentary and analysis,[153] while a further source of such intellectual activity has been the TANU Study Group, significantly named despite the fact that it seems at times to inhabit something of a twilight zone within the system. Other militants prepared to ask a range of critical questions have found breathing space in the party press, the Tanzanian papers often providing a refreshingly lively contrast to the officially sponsored press in other socialist countries.[154] The juxtaposition of these latter realities with what has been said before should not be thought to provide some mere paradox, however. Rather, both positive and negative aspects of this picture reflect, once again, the contested nature of Tanzanian reality.

The latter comment also applies when one shifts the focus of attention to the party's organizational capacity at less elevated levels of the Tanzanian system. It can be argued (a fact revealing in itself) that TANU is the most effective political party in all of independent Africa. Moreover, it does retain much of its historical legitimacy, first earned, as we have seen, in the nationalist period as trusted spokesman for the mass of the population. Even those workers who are most suspicious of NUTA, the official trade union, will often retain confidence in an appeal to TANU, and similarly the slogan "TANU yajenga nchi" ("TANU builds the nation") has real meaning for a great many rural dwellers. As a result, if a much stronger class base for the system is beginning to form around such nuclei as workers' participation and *ujamaa* villages, it will in all likelihood find expression within the party; there it may be expected to reinforce that "tendency" of the party which has pressed initiatives like the Arusha Declaration and *Mwongozo* on the overall system. At the same time, the limitations upon "spontaneity" under Tanzanian conditions reassert their claim to our attention here; TANU must also *lead* in easing such a base into existence.

For this reason it is especially unfortunate that, as I have stated elsewhere,

> much discussion about the party has focused upon the misleading juxtaposition of two presumed alternatives—an "elite" or "vanguard" party on the one hand, a "mass" party on the other. . . . Such a way of structuring the problem of the party obscures precisely the crucial necessity that both control [i.e., leadership] and participation (vanguard and mass, in effect) coexist at the very heart of the party.[155]

Of course, the nature of the leadership-mass relationship which should instead be emphasized has already been identified in the preceding subsection. But, as noted, it is within the party that the "struggle on two fronts" finds its most crucial arena. Moreover, the key to reconciling the two elements in such a way as to facilitate the eventual emergence of an effectively socialist pattern of politics (this in turn to involve, when perfected, the interaction of an extremely committed leadership and a highly conscious mass base) must lie in the identification of *fully effective methods of political work.* TANU's growing emphasis upon programs of "political education"—for bureaucrats, party officials, workers, and peasants—seems an important step in working out such methods. The challenge of advancing rural collectivization and agricultural activity or forwarding workers' participation bears the promise of giving real content (rooted, crucially, in the production process) to the day-to-day activities of party officials at intermediate and lower levels which has been lacking in the past.[156] The recent decentralization may also, as the relevant party document quoted in Section 1 anticipates, expedite the emergence of such a trend toward resolving the (inevitable) contradiction between necessary vanguard and genuine participation in an increasingly progressive manner.

Yet here again the manpower problem can be seen to impose a severe constraint upon political creativity, a constraint not only in terms of sheer numbers available, but, more importantly, in terms of the quality of those who are so engaged. For the *cadre,* who could be expected to resolve in his own person and in his method of work the contradictions between redness and expertise, and between leadership and participation (thereby becoming a catalyst of consciousness), is still the scarcest of all commodities in Tanzania. It is impossible to affirm as yet that an effective effort to make him the building block of the party, rather than the mere functionary, has been set in train. Occasionally one does see the problem beginning to be faced, as witness a recent article by Nyelwa Kisenge, who makes a spirited plea for a cadre-based party, suggesting that

> socialist political cadres are the party activists, propagandists, agitators, motivators, persuaders, ideologists, interpreters and defenders of party ideology in all walks of life. . . . In short, cadres are a sort of multipurpose revolutionary vanguard, an inexhaustible source of party renovation, rejuvenation, and dynamism. A party backed by such a corps of dedicated

individuals can rest assured that it will maintain its revolutionary militancy and be able to carry out successfully any type of program. The one that has none risks sooner or later deteriorating into an apathetic, immobile, anachronistic bureaucracy. When this stage is reached, the party becomes just another government department being led by the government rather than the reverse. In fact, this has been the misfortune of many political parties in developing countries, where very good intentions of building socialism have completely failed to materialize. It is therefore important to note in this connection that TANU has not had to date any serious and systematic program for training cadres, though its intentions of building a socialist state have been known since 1962.

Kisenge does make a number of practical suggestions as to how such a program might be carried through and such cadres "carefully selected and thoroughly trained," though he also notes the disturbing precedent that "a modest attempt . . . made in 1967 to train *ujamaa* village cadres . . . ended in fiasco because of an alleged lack of funds." And his conclusion is an equally searching one:

> . . . the success or failure of the socialist cadres at the grassroots level will largely depend on our ability to provide their counterparts at various levels above. This is for the obvious reason that however good, hard-working, and dedicated the lower cadres may be, they will inevitably be frustrated [by] the crushing weight and immobility of the bureaucratic bourgeoisie above. In general terms, it might be said that the cadres require a right organizational framework within which to operate effectively [and that] such a framework does not exist at the moment. Without it cadres will simply be absorbed into the established system, and sandwiched in various layers of *bureaucratic hierarchy* they will be neutralized and rendered harmless. It would follow therefore that the whole proposal presupposes also the necessity of party reorganization to provide such a framework. The overhauling of the party machinery and radical changes in methods of work could provide a basis for creating a vanguard within a mass party.[157]

Nyerere's statement, cited above, as to the paucity of available socialists may provide a partial explanation of this continuing weakness in the cadre field, but it is not adequate to explain the extent of the shortfall and the snail's pace at which "overhauling of the party machinery and radical change in methods of work" proceeds.[158]

Moreover, some observers have argued the existence of a closely related failing: the hesitancy to clarify adequately, in theory and practice, the relationship which should exist between "party" and "class" under Tanzanian conditions.[159] Concretely, this has often meant the drifting of the party under the hegemony of managers, chief administrative officers, activist farmers, and local notables, rather than that of the workers and poorer peasants who, in terms of the rhetoric, should be expected to carry the day. It is true that the Arusha Declaration "leadership code" has had some impact on the range of candidates who offer themselves and, as noted earlier, the worst manipulations of the masses on tribal and religious lines are checked. In addition, changes in the composition of the NEC in 1970 to give it a distinctly rural bias, and the facilitating of a wide-ranging, sometimes quite searching, debate in the party's biennial conferences testify to the institutionalization of greater and more meaningful mass participation. But if the raising of *class consciousness* in a vigorous manner and the encouragement of leadership from the most exploited strata of the society were seen to be even more crucial organizational and ideological tasks than they are, some of the continuing anomalies might be avoided. It is striking, for example, that the election of 1970, mounted by the party and providing an opportunity for renewal and mobilization, merely confirmed (albeit usefully) the country's unity and the voter's "confidence" in the system. It did not itself produce the sort of consciousness which could be expected to weigh heavily upon the actions of holders of privilege and, indeed, it in some ways reinforced the parochialism of many rural constituents.[160] More militantly defined efforts to release progressive political energies might be expected to multiply those important popular assertions which do, nonetheless, break out in parliament (and elsewhere) from time to time: the rejection of an attempt to provide gratuities for ministers and regional commissioners in 1968, the smashing of steps to allow regional commissioners to retain their elected seats in parliament in 1972—both being bills which were strongly sponsored by the government.[161]

Thus, despite continued gains, the organizational input for socialist construction remains to be consolidated. Moreover, we begin to see the many ways in which its further consolidation is crucial to continued advance; one of them carries us into the ideological sphere, to which we can now turn directly. For, as noted, a more effective and creative party would have the effect of complementing Tanzania's "pure" ideology with a "practical" counterpart[162]—concretizing Tanzania's socialism on a day-to-day, issue-by-issue basis—and making ideology more an instrument for sustained transformation and continuous direction than a basis for occasional (though significant) *inspired intervention.* Then too, the burden of creativity might be expected to fall less heavily on the shoulders of one man. For it is worth reemphasizing that President Nyerere has played an absolutely essential role in shifting the center of gravity of Tanzania's objective conditions. It is striking how often it is his "suspicions" of imperialism, his contempt for the pretensions of the elite, his confidence in the creative potential of the mass of the African population, which have become the common currency of ideological elaboration in Tanzania. It is also sobering to contemplate how much of the drive behind the forward movement of Tanzania's experiment would be extinguished were Nyerere to pass from the scene in the near future and before many more of the objective bases for socialism have been further consolidated.

Nyerere's ideology, as in some sense it is: what has been its impact? what are its strengths and weaknesses? Fortunately we have accumulated much evidence concerning these questions in this essay already. Nonetheless, the first question must remain something of a conundrum. Even when one can pinpoint gaps in the formulations which have been put forward, and in the practice which seems to follow from them, the possibility arises that tactical considerations in what is, after all, a rather hostile environment have counseled moderation of ideological precision; certainly this excuse is often advanced by the president's most fervent progressive admirers and there is no doubt some truth in it. Would a more relentless approach to class struggle merely consolidate the resistance of the conservative wing of the petty bourgeoisie to further advance before an effective mass base is available to guarantee successful confrontation with that group? The crucial nature of such a query under Tanzanian circumstances should by now be apparent. And even where shallowness of formulation is more graphically apparent—in the conceptualization of imperialism, for instance—a similar question remains relevant. Would aggressive confrontation merely guarantee the baldest kind of intervention from outside before the system is prepared to cope with it? In short, were the ideology clearer, would that be likely to facilitate its ultimate realization or the reverse? Some would argue that Nyerere's eclectic approach to socialism is well adapted to the situation in which he finds himself; certainly there are many reasons for caution in so unlikely a home for socialism as Tanzania, so that here again the observer and the activist may be well advised to avoid categorical judgment and mindless militancy.

This much having been said, we may also reiterate another point. The combination of various perceptions outlined in Section 1 is a potent one; Nyerere's formulations, Tanzania's ideology, are, quite simply, the most advanced official doctrine to be found in independent Africa. Only on the basis of that recognition can the real shortcomings, also hinted at in Section 1, be viewed from a proper perspective. For weaknesses there certainly are, even on the ideological plane. And, all qualifications having been made, it is difficult not to regard these as costly: the absence of economic strategy, the confusion about imperialism, the tentative nature of the link which is conceived between party and class, even (though this is more arguable) the hesitancy to identify classes clearly and to polarize them, find some of their roots in such weaknesses. It is common among Tanzanian militants to trace these weaknesses, in turn, back to two sources: on the one hand, a nostalgia for a traditional kind of social solidarity—*ujamaa*—which is felt, vaguely, to have some present-day referent despite the depredations of colonialism and the new national scale upon which contemporary socialism must be built; and, on the other hand, a humane but insufficiently critical taste for the brighter side of the Western liberal heritage.[163] There is probably truth in these points.[164] Nevertheless, the main problem lies elsewhere.

For what is at stake is much more *a question of method*. The president's suspicions of Marxism are well known. Marxism is only relevant to the nineteenth century, Marxism is too categorically antagonistic to religion, Marxism has itself become a religion—these themes he has reiterated on a number of occasions.[165] The claims of Marxism to importance as a method of analysis and as a scientific approach to socialist struggle he seems never to have considered. And something broader than mere hostility to Marxism is at stake in any case. As I have phrased it elsewhere,

> . . . the president seems suspicious not merely of Marxism, but of *any theory*, conscious of the danger that a "sociology," broadly conceived, can degenerate into dogmatism. But . . . he overreacts to that danger; the alternative, after all, can be an even more dangerous excess of pragmatism, a pragmatism which is founded upon unconscious and unexamined premises and which can become, in practice, contradictory and self-defeating.[166]

And without a "sociology," a strategy emerges only with difficulty. It is little wonder that the major strengths of Tanzania, and of Nyerere, have lain at the level of the broadest kind of conceptualization of goals and direction of the country, on the one hand, and of dextrous and timely innovation in the tactical sphere, on the other. The crucial intermediate component—once again, "practical" ideology—has been a less prominent feature.

It is significant that a younger generation of Tanzanian militants has begun to find more sustenance in Marxism and in related strands of the international socialist and anti-imperialist traditions. They have started the work of adapting this heritage, quite self-consciously, to the concrete realities of Tanzania; here may be germinating one of the fruitful seeds of the future.[167] As noted, this kind of innovation has not been entirely discouraged within the party. But neither has its emergence been markedly facilitated, and on occasion, as with the banning of *Cheche*, it has been quite aggressively curbed.[168] Nor has so potentially central an institution as the university ever been actively shaped to become the sort of dedicated ideologically based institution which could engage in socialist intellectual work of a high order of insight and practicality; if anything it has been the most reactionary members of the university community who have been consistently rewarded.[169] Again, suspicion of Marxism is part of the reason for such occurrences, as are other of Nyerere's ideological predilections (a dangerous liberalism with respect to the university, for example).[170] In Nyerere's case, it is difficult to decide how to weigh up these shortcomings against the continuing positive impact of his intellectual growth and deepening understanding. There are other aspects which are relevant to the picture in any case. We must not lose sight of the fact that hostility to currents which threaten a further clarification of the ideological question in Tanzania can spring from very much less savory motives. Though deprived of some of their most potent tools of mystification (as spelled out in Section 1), many reactionary members of the petty bourgeoisie still attempt to manipulate "African socialism," to "nationalize" ideology, to quarantine Marxism, and to contain full-fledged radical debate, this with the quite self-conscious intention of blunting the edge of socialist advance and safeguarding their own class interests. Ironically, Nyerere sometimes finds himself in the company of such dubious allies.

Thus here too, and finally, there is both promise and problem. Tanzania has come a long way indeed on the basis of moral dedication and patriotism, of pragmatism, and of the president's almost uncanny intuitive insight into Tanzanian realities. It is possible that some further strides can be made on this basis. But it seems likely that the elaboration and dissemination of a more scientific method of analysis is a prerequisite for conceptualizing with increased effectiveness the nature of the task which lies ahead and for stimulating and institutionalizing creativity over a broader front and by a wider range of cadres. A prerequisite, in short, for further advance. Of course, this is only to make more concrete Cabral's challenge:

> The crisis of the African revolution . . . is not a crisis of growth, but a crisis of knowledge. In too many cases the struggle for liberation and our own plans for the future are not only without a theoretical base, but are also more or less cut off from the concrete situation in which we are working.[171]

And it suggests that the challenge remains a real one even in Tanzania. Struggle on the ideological plane must be a continuing aspect of the country's socialist project.

4. Prospects

> *Pessimism of the intelligence,*
> *optimism of the will.*
> —Antonio Gramsci

What final balance can be struck concerning such a complex situation? Perhaps none, for the necessary balance sheet can in any case only be drawn up by those engaged in significant *praxis* within the Tanzanian context. But for such cadres Engels' analysis, quoted above, must continue to hover ominously. How much "plasticity" really characterizes the petty bourgeoisie? How effectively (and quickly) will the mass base come to play its essential role? How likely are "pressures from the capitalist [international] environment [to be] relieved"?[172] Certainly it is difficult to be sanguine about the fate of a socialism which defies in so many evident ways the pull of objective conditions and whose weaknesses in organization and ideology are at the same time being only slowly overcome. Yet it is impossible not to conclude that it would be equally foolish, and very dangerous, to deny the considerable progressive content of the Tanzanian experience to date, or to deny that a significant struggle has been joined.

If we look for negative lessons, we can, of course, find them: in the need for the African revolution to face the hard challenge of specifying economic development strategies and defining concretely, rather than generally and rhetorically, the impact of imperialism on the continent; in the need to innovate ideologically; and in the need to strengthen the available political apparatus and to refine methods of political work. At the same time, that Tanzania has reached the point where the most serious questions about the actual construction of socialism are relevant is an important measure of its advance. Moreover, this instructive process continues: some members of the petty bourgeoisie are "commiting suicide" (in Cabral's suggestive phrase) and new cadres are emerging; there are fresh stirrings at the base. If the results in the short run are nonetheless in doubt, that should not be surprising. It does not blunt the fact that the struggle in Tanzania remains a qualitatively different one from most of the rest of independent Africa.[173] Indigenous radicals in Tanzania will decide their own fates. Yet the fact that almost all have chosen to work within the established structures and upon the regime is no accident. With whatever misgivings, one can only conclude that the Tanzanian experiment in "socialism and self-reliance" also deserves the solidarity—albeit the critical solidarity—of every international socialist.

Notes

1. A great deal of secondary literature of relevance to an evaluation of the Tanzanian experience has been included in Lionel Cliffe and John S. Saul, eds., *Socialism in Tanzania: Politics and Policies* (Nairobi: East African Publishing House, P.O. Box 30571, 1972), in two volumes. The first two essays of the present volume provide a continental perspective within which the Tanzanian case can be more readily assessed.
2. Robin Blackburn, "The Heath Government: A New Course for British Capitalism," *New Left Review* (November–December 1971), p. 14.
3. On this subject, see particularly, Roger Murray, "Second Thoughts on Ghana," *New Left Review* (March–April 1967).
4. For a further elaboration of this point, see Chapter 8 of this volume.
5. J. K. Nyerere, "Economic Nationalism" (speech of February 28, 1967) in

Nyerere, *Freedom and Socialism* (London, New York, Nairobi, 1968), p. 264. Nyerere completes the argument by adding: "To Tanzanians this inevitable choice is not unwelcome. We are socialists as well as nationalists. We are committed to the creation of a classless society in which every able-bodied citizen is contributing to the economy through work, and we believe that this can only be obtained when the major means of production are publicly owned and controlled. But the fact remains that our recent socialist measures were not taken out of a blind adherence to dogma. They are intended to serve our society."

6. R. H. Green, "Foreign Resources and the Parastatal Sector in a Transition to Socialism," paper presented to the Seminar on the Use of Foreign Funds in the Development of East African Countries, Dar es Salaam, April–May 1972 (mimeo), p. 7.

7. A. J. M. Van de Laar suggests a rough figure of between 170 and 250 million shillings as being the annual savings in formerly repatriated surpluses which is likely to accrue from nationalization; see his "Foreign Business and Capital Export from Developing Countries: The Tanzanian Experience," in Cliffe and Saul, op. cit., vol. I.

8. See J. Loxley, "Financial Planning and Control in Tanzania," in Uchumi Editorial Board, *Towards Socialist Planning* (Tanzanian Studies No. 1, Tanzania Publishing House, P.O. Box 2138, Dar es Salaam, 1972) for a useful perspective on this question. Indeed, a number of other essays in the latter volume are of relevance to the analysis advanced in this essay.

9. R. H. Green, "Political Independence and the National Economy: An Essay in the Political Economy of Decolonization," in C. Allen and R. W. Johnson, (eds.), *African Perspectives* (Cambridge, 1970), p. 315. Green goes further (p. 319), reckoning that, given this leverage, substantial progress in terms of "output, investible surplus generation, identification of viable projects, Tanzanianization and coordination of national and firm-level planning" is beginning to follow.

10. *"Ujamaa"* is, literally, the Swahili word for "familyhood." It is generally used as the proper translation of the English word "socialism." Its connotation can be variable, and its use is sometimes overlaid with the (generally confusing) quasi-traditionalism of various brands of "African socialism." On other occasions and in other contexts it comes closer to a universal definition.

11. Green noted that "the 1969–1974 Plan proposes to continue the 60:40 ratio in financing of the development budget proper and extend it to the mobilization of resources for para-statal investment. . . . The foreign 40 percent is to be secured from soft loans, World Bank and East African Development Bank borrowing, long-term loans, and equity contributions of foreign

partners in joint ventures, and a relatively limited amount of medium-term contractor or supplier credit." Green, "Political Independence," p. 315.

12. One thinks here primarily of the fields of technology (where China's emphasis upon labor intensive techniques may be relevant, but its emphasis, already exemplified in Tanzania, upon training and upon establishing an indigenous *technological capacity* is even more so) and workers' participation broadly defined (this being already a feature of methods adopted in organizing the large labor force along the Tanzania-Zambia line of rail).

13. These proportions are suggested in Green, ibid., p. 320.

14. This electoral system was in use in 1970. A further exploration of electoral politics in Tanzania can be found in Lionel Cliffe, ed., *One Party Democracy* (Nairobi, 1967) and in J. S. Saul, "The Nature of Tanzania's Political System: Some Issues Raised by the 1965 and 1970 Elections," *Journal of Commonwealth Political Studies*, nos. 2 and 3 (1972), and reprinted in Cliffe and Saul, op. cit., vol. I (under the title "Background to the Tanzanian Election 1970"). It should be noted, however, that the elected parliament is not as close to the heart of the political process in Tanzania as a number of other institutions (e.g., the various organs of the party).

15. Cf. *The Arusha Declaration: Socialism and Self-Reliance* (Dar es Salaam, 1967), reprinted in J. K. Nyerere, op. cit., pp. 231–50. One crucial passage of that document reads as follows (p. 248): "Since the party was founded we have put great emphasis on getting as many members as possible. This was the right policy during the independence struggle. But now the National Executive feels that the time has come when we should put more emphasis on the beliefs of our party and its policies of socialism."

16. In his pamphlet *Answers to Questions* (Dar es Salaam, 1967), Nyerere makes the following comment on this point (p. 7): "When we were struggling for independence how many of us did the capitalists invite to become directors? How many of us were able to borrow money to build houses for renting out? How many of us were lent money to buy large *shambas* [farms]? If we have acquired these things since independence most of us have done so because the capitalists want to involve us in their system of exploitation so that we shall become defenders of that system. The fact that question is asked shows that the technique has had some success."

17. M. A. Bienefeld, "Planning People," in Uchumi Editorial Board, op. cit.

18. This ban on the importation of private automobiles in early 1972 had a particularly dramatic symbolic effect, especially upon younger recruits to the "leadership group."

19. As the experience in Guinée has shown, this is an especially delicate and difficult sphere in which to consolidate collective advance; for an analysis of Tanzania's initial efforts in this regard, see John Loxley, "The Role of the

State Trading Corporation in Transforming the Commercial Sector," in Cliffe and Saul, op. cit., vol. II.

20. Collectivization has proceeded more slowly in the transport sector, another area of African entrepreneurial activity, and is almost nonexistent as regards investment in hotels and bars (with the exception of those large hotels designed primarily to service the tourist trade).

21. J. K. Nyerere, *Socialism and Rural Development* (Dar es Salaam, 1967), reprinted in Nyerere, op. cit., pp. 344, 346. It will be noted that the discussion here concerns the "small-holder" sector. We are leaving aside in this context the nationalizations carried out with respect to large-scale, largely foreign-owned, sisal estates. On the latter subject see the excellent analyses by Peter Lawrence: "Plantation Sisal: The Inherited Mode of Production" and "Sisal: The Case for Ujamaa Production," in Rural Development Research Committee, *Towards Rural Cooperation in Tanzania* (Dar es Salaam: Tanzania Publishing House, forthcoming).

22. R. Murray, op. cit., p. 34.

23. J. K. Nyerere, *Education for Self-Reliance* (1967), reprinted in Nyerere, op. cit., p. 269; this was a crucial document in structuring the discussion of Tanzania's education reform. See also I. N. Resnick, ed., *Tanzania: Revolution by Education* (Arusha and New York: Longman's, 1968) and the materials collected in Part VII of Cliffe and Saul, op. cit., vol. II.

24. It is also worth noting that Tanzania, like most African countries, has been particularly slow to gear education to the creation of an indigenous technological capacity. Recently some progress has been made in the field of scientific and technological education, though even then the formal rather than the "on-the-job," popular and applied side of this exercise still holds pride of place.

25. A. Cabral, "Brief Analysis of the Social Structure in Guinea," in Cabral, *Revolution in Guinea* (New York, 1970).

26. See J. K. Nyerere, "Socialism Is Not Racialism" (1967), in Nyerere, op. cit., pp. 257–61; and his Republic Day Speech of 1968, reported in *The Standard* (Tanzania), 10 December 1968, under the headline "No Room for Racialism."

27. Any attempt to make use of ethnic appeals (as well as any appeals based on race or religion) has been officially outlawed from the (closely supervised) electoral campaigns, for example.

28. *The Nationalist* (Dar es Salaam), 5 September 1967. On another occasion he was reported as saying that " 'African leaders had their prices these days. The moment one becomes a minister, his price also gets determined. The prices are not even big; some are bought only for £500, or a simple house.' Mwalimu said that although it was possible to buy ministers, there was one

section of Africa that could not be bought. 'The people,' he said, 'cannot be bought.' " *The Standard*, 8 July 1967.

29. *Mwongozo/The TANU Guidelines* (Dar es Salaam, 1971).

30. This is a theme to which we will revert in Section 3. But see Nick Asili, "Strikes in Tanzania," *Majimaji* (September 1971).

31. It was this theme (as expressed in *False Start in Africa*) which attracted the president to the ideas of René Dumont during this period, rather than anything Dumont had to say about development in the rural areas per se. Another document influential in setting the tone of the period was the Turner Report (Government Paper No. 3, 1967, "Report to the Government of the United Republic of Tanzania on Wages, Incomes, and Prices Policy by International Labour Office"), with its heavy emphasis on the negative features of rural-urban inequalities.

32. For a useful perspective on this subject see W. L. Luttrell, "Location Planning and Regional Development in Tanzania," in Uchumi Editorial Board, op. cit.

33. That this is an essential key to a strategy genuinely designed to realize economic development has been clearly argued by Samir Amin in his *L'Accumulation à l'échelle mondiale* (Paris, 1970), to be published in English by Monthly Review Press. We will return to this question at much greater length in Section 3.

34. A case which justifies such action under Tanzanian conditions has been presented in M. A. Bienefeld, "Labour in Tanzania," in Cliffe and Saul, op. cit., vol. I.

35. This trend was reported in *The Report of the Presidential Commission of Enquiry into the National Union of Tanganyikan Workers (NUTA)* (Dar es Salaam, 1967).

36. For an important evaluation of workers' participation in Tanzania during its initial phases, see Henry Mapolu, "The Organization and Participation of Workers in Tanzania," Economics Research Bureau Paper 72.1 (Dar es Salaam, 1972); the institutionalization of workers' participation was also to be accompanied by an intensified program of political education.

37. On this point, with specific reference to the cooperative movement, see Vice-President Kawawa's speech reported in *The Nationalist*, 15 June 1971, and, for a commentary, John S. Saul, "From Marketing Cooperative to Producer Cooperative," in Rural Development Research Committee, op. cit. This impact of rural collectivization has potentially rather broad implications, however, and certainly ones which reach beyond the confines of the cooperative movement.

38. The substance of these new policies is spelt out in the TANU paper, *Decentralization* (Dar es Salaam, 1972), which was reprinted in full in *Daily News* (Tanzania), 17 May 1972; the quotations in the text are taken from this

document. Significantly, one additional point which is made in the document is that "there is . . . one danger which must be guarded against. The transfer of power to the regions and districts must not also mean the transfer of a rigid and bureaucratic system from Dar es Salaam to lower levels. Nor is it the intention of these proposals to create new local tyrants in the persons of the regional and district development officers. . . . It is essential that this should be understood by everyone, for those who cause the new system to become enmeshed in bureaucratic procedures, will, as they are discovered, be treated as what they will be—saboteurs."

39. A leading advocate of the idea of a "vanguard" party in Tanzania during his period in power, he became a vigorous "liberal democrat" once in London in exile. Cf. his *The Crisis of Democracy in Tanzania* (London, 1967).

40. On the cell system see W. Klerruu, *The Systematic Creation and Operation of TANU Cells* (Dar es Salaam, 1966); K. Levine, "The TANU Ten-House Cell System," in Cliffe and Saul, op. cit., vol. I; H. Proctor, ed., *The Cell System of the Tanganyika African National Union* (Dar es Salaam, 1971).

41. "Politics Is Agriculture," the party document laying out the terms of this emphasis, was reprinted in *Sunday News* (Tanzania), 14 May 1972; for a perspective on the party's role in rural mobilization see L. Cliffe and John S. Saul, "The District Development Front in Tanzania," *The African Review* (Dar es Salaam), vol. II, no. 1 (1972) and reprinted in Cliffe and Saul, op. cit., vol. I.

42. As in note 38.

43. From the text of a radio address by President Nyerere, reprinted in *The Standard*, 18 February, 1972.

44. Since the mutiny of 1964 (more like a relatively apolitical strike, in any case) the army has been more or less quiescent; the Kambona-inspired coup attempt of 1969 appears to have been badly planned, easily broken, and isolated in very small pockets of the military apparatus. Similarly, widespread rumors of trouble with the military in late 1971 seem to have come to nothing. Needless to say, however, this is a notoriously treacherous sphere in which to indulge in prediction.

45. This is a theme to which we will return in Section 3. The most useful analysis of Tanzanian foreign policy is still C. Hoskyns, "Africa's Foreign Relations: The Case of Tanzania," *International Affairs* (July 1968), reprinted in Cliffe and Saul, op. cit., vol. I.

46. This section draws, to some extent, upon the themes and even the specific formulations of my earlier essay published in East Africa, "Planning for Socialism in Tanzania: The Socio-Political Context," the introductory essay to Uchumi Editorial Board, op. cit.

47. Many figures could be cited; perhaps those in the health sphere are most

graphic: a life expectation of thirty-eight years; infant mortality, 200–250 per 1000; only twelve Tanganyikan doctors (at independence). Leys suggests that "the value of Gross Domestic Product forecast for Tanganyika in 1961 was £186 million," only about £20–25 million accounted for by subsistence agriculture, in which most people are engaged. He estimates an average annual income of £18 for 1961, though even that distorts the fact that "the great majority of families do very much worse and are living extremely close to the hunger line." ("Tanganyika: The Realities of Independence," *International Journal* (Toronto) (1962–63), reprinted in Cliffe and Saul, op. cit., vol. I).

48. The reference here is to Lenin's formulation concerning post-revolutionary Russia: "Our opponents told us repeatedly that we were rash in undertaking to implant socialism in an insufficiently cultured country. But they were misled by our having started from the end opposite to that prescribed by theory (the theory of pedants of all kinds) because in our country the political and social revolution preceded the cultural revolution, the very cultural revolution which nevertheless now confronts us." (V. I. Lenin, "On Cooperation," in *Selected Works* [Moscow 1961], vol. III, p. 819.) In Lenin's sense, Tanzania is also "an insufficiently cultured country"; it is worth noting that Lenin's chief solution for such a shortfall is "educational work." For Africa, however, there is a paradox here, which lies in the fact that novel forms of education have heretofore been instruments crucial to the effectiveness of cultural imperialism and to the formation of privileged strata, *as well as* a source, within certain narrow limits, of "modernizing" enlightenment.

49. Abdul M. H. Sheriff, "Trade and Underdevelopment: A Survey of the Economic History of the East African Coast" (typescript, Dar es Salaam, 1972). John Iliffe, in his *Agricultural Change in Modern Tanganyika* (Historical Association of Tanzania Paper No. 10, Nairobi, 1971) also discusses the impact on mainland economic activity of the increase of demand for foodstuffs and labor generated from an early date by the Zanzibar plantation economy.

50. Iliffe, ibid.

51. The German settlers were in fact close to establishing such a position for themselves just as German rule came to an end; without the "accident" of World War I, Tanzanian history might have been very different. See J. Iliffe, *Tanganyika Under German Rule* (Cambridge, 1969).

52. For descriptions of Tanzania's colonial legacy which are of relevance here see A. Seidman, "The Inherited Dual Economies of East Africa," J. Loxley, "Structural Change in the Monetary System of Tanzania," and M. Yaffey, "Self-Reliance and Foreign Trade," all in Cliffe and Saul, op. cit.

53. Perhaps economic activity was also delayed in Tanzania because of other peculiarities of its colonial history and status: it experienced the disruption of a change in colonial masters in 1920, and its mandate status, together with some uncertainty about Hitler's intentions in the 1930s vis-à-vis Germany's ex-colonies, also made it more marginal to colonial calculation than other territories.

54. See, for example, Fiah's (an early Tanzanian populist) description of Martin Kayamba, in his turn an early prototype of this kind of Tanzanian elite-in-the-making: "Martin Kayamba will be remembered as the selfish African who rose to the highest rank . . . in government service but without being of any use to his race—the detached man whose history finished with poultry raising in the Tanga district. We are not bitter—all we mean is that he never bothered about his African brothers and knew very little about them . . . Many of us remember Kayamba as a man who was fond of singing his own praises, the man who had the opportunity to go to London on a political mission but spent his time . . . sightseeing and tea-partying." *Kwetu*, 29 June 1940, and quoted in J. Iliffe, "The Age of Improvement and Differentiation (1907–45)," in I. N. Kimambo and A. J. Temu, eds., *A History of Tanzania* [Nairobi, 1969].) As Iliffe further notes, "All the bitterness of the divisions created by improvement is contained in this passage."

55. Iliffe's article and pamphlet, cited above, provide important evidence on this point; for a striking case study of the results of this process of rural differentiation, based on intensive field research in Rungwe district, see H. U. E. Thoden van Velzen, "Staff, Kulak, and Peasants: A Study of a Political Field," in Cliffe and Saul, op. cit., vol. II.

56. Some students of Tanzania have phrased this point more broadly, arguing the importance of a distinctive "Swahili culture," linked, though not exclusively, to Islam, which absorbs tribesmen, guarantees unity, and even has an egalitarian impact. See, for example, John Lonsdale, "Some Origins of Nationalism in Tanzania," and M. Abdul-Aziz, "Tanzanian National Language Policy and the Rise of Swahili Political Culture," both in Cliffe and Saul, op. cit., vol. I.

57. Cf. L. Cliffe, "Nationalism and the Resistance to Enforced Agricultural Change in Tanganyika During the Colonial Period," in *Taamuli* (Dar es Salaam) (July 1970) and reprinted in Cliffe and Saul, op. cit., vol. I. The ambiguity lies in the fact that this rural resistance represented, in effect, a variety of historical moments in Tanzania, ranging from the grievances of "economic activists" in Sukumaland to the quasi-traditional resistance to any sort of change in certain less-developed parts of the country.

58. For a case study of this process, with reference to the emergence of the cooperative movement, see J. S. Saul, "Marketing Cooperatives in a Devel-

oping Country: The Tanzanian Case," in Peter Worsley, ed., *Two Blades of Grass: Agricultural Cooperation in Developing Societies* (Manchester, 1971), and reprinted in Cliffe and Saul, op. cit., vol. II. In that study the differentiation between "economic activist" and "parochial" is seen as a crucial determinant of the way in which Tanzanian cooperatives have heretofore functioned. For a broader overview, see R. Woods, "Peasants and Peasantries in Tanzania" in Rural Development Research Committee, op. cit.

59. This is the central theme in J. F. Rweyemamu, *Underdevelopment and Industrialization in Tanzania: A Study in Perverse Capitalist Industrial Development* (Nairobi, forthcoming).

60. See note 48 above.

61. For a further discussion of this point, see J. Loxley, "Technical Assistance, High Level Manpower Training, and Ideology in Tanzania," paper presented to the Conference on Comparative Administration in East Africa (Arusha, Tanzania, September 1971).

62. Whether there has been enough done to overcome the omnipresent colonial legacy within the educational system itself is, of course, another question, and one to which we will have to return.

63. See J. Iliffe, "The Role of the African Association in the Formation of Territorial Consciousness in Tanzania," paper presented to the University of East Africa Social Science Conference (Dar es Salaam, January 1968), mimeo.

64. Cliffe's paper, op. cit., is of vital importance in documenting this point.

65. Compare the parallel formulation in my earlier paper, "The Nature of Tanzania's Political System," op. cit., where it was argued that the "Arusha Declaration can be seen as an attempt to consolidate those progressive aspects of the Tanzanian balance of forces which its peculiar historical development has afforded it, and draw out their socialist logic, before that possibility was eclipsed in turn by the process of 'spontaneous' change and class formation."

66. For example, Harvey Glickman, in his paper "Traditional Pluralism and Democratic Processes in Mainland Tanzania," *African and Asian Studies* (Jerusalem), no. 5 (1969), and reprinted in Cliffe and Saul, op. cit., vol. I, cites the fact of the immediate expulsion from the party of Sheikh Takadir, first head of TANU's Elders' Section, for "inquiring about the absence of Muslims from the TANU election slate" in 1958.

67. For an interesting account of this phase of Tanganyikan political developments, see Leys, op. cit.

68. J. K. Nyerere, Introduction to *Freedom and Socialism*, especially the section entitled "On the Problem of Building Socialism in an Ex-Colonial Coun-

try," which is required reading for anyone interested in Tanzanian socialist development. For a related commentary, see my "Nationalism, Socialism, and Tanzanian History," in Cliffe and Saul, op. cit., vol. I.

69. For a sympathetic and informative account of Nyerere's intellectual development see A. Mohiddin, "Ujamaa na Kujitegemea," *Mawazo* (December 1967), and reprinted in Cliffe and Saul, op. cit., vol. I.

70. Lucien Rey, "The Revolution in Zanzibar," *New Left Review* (May-June 1964), and reprinted in Cliffe and Saul, op. cit., vol. I.

71. The racial dimensions of oppression and consequent tension were sufficiently marked, however, to make this one of the explanations for the "racialist" deviation in Zanzibar "socialism" in the post-revolutionary period.

72. Cf. D. Martin, "Tasting the Fruits of World Monopoly," *Financial Times* (London), 2 December 1971. Some efforts have been made to redirect the economy, but not striking ones; in fact, Zanzibar leaders point with pride to vast balances held in European banks (more than 400 million shillings, Karume announced in 1971) which, with any kind of coherent socialist planning, could better have been turned to the realization of genuine development.

73. Thus among the numerous victims of this round-up were A. M. Babu, a long-time progressive voice in Zanzibar politics and a former Tanzanian cabinet minister. Fortunately, at the time of writing, those arrested (including Babu) were still being held on the mainland. When Hanga (Zanzibar's first prime minister) and others were transferred back to the islands under similar circumstances in 1969, they were summarily executed. Karume's assassination itself may merely have been the result of private grievances against governmental high-handedness, although by the very nature of the case it is impossible to know for certain.

74. See the article "Ownership Code Is Wrong, Says Karume," *The Standard*, 17 March 1971. On that occasion, Karume stated that "barring people from holding property as advocated in the Declaration was not proper. . . . This must be amended, he declared."

75. For further details concerning these relationships and those with Kenya, see Martin Bailey, "Les Relations extérieures de Zanzibar," *Revue française d'études politiques africaines* (March 1972). Bailey notes that "The British High Commissioner, posted in Dar es Salaam, is one of the most welcome visitors on the island. He is grateful for this, since his fondest dream is to sell Zanzibar a television system worth 50 million shillings to the British electronics industry" (my translation). Ambassador Phillips has recently been successful in achieving this goal.

76. Rather than taking the opportunity fortuitously provided by Karume's assassination to tie Zanzibar more tightly to the mainland administratively and

ideologically (as some suspected they might), the Tanzanian authorities at first seem merely to have shored up the established system. Nonetheless, it is probably too early to indulge in any elaborate speculation about the shape of post-Karume Zanzibar.

77. For this reason, we will continue to use the term "Tanzania" primarily with reference to the mainland portions of the country (as indeed we have been doing up to this point).

78. An instructive comparative framework for evaluating Tanzanian economic policy is sketched in Peter Lawrence, "Socialism, Self-Reliance, and For- eign Aid in Tanzania: Some Lessons from the Socialist Experience," a paper presented to the UN-IDEP Seminar on the Use of Foreign Funds in the Development of the East African Countries, Dar es Salaam, April-May 1972 (mimeo).

79. This framework underlies Amin's major theoretical work, cited in note 33 above; it is succinctly summarized in S. Amin, "Underpopulated Africa," *Majimaji* (Dar es Salaam), no. 6 (June 1972).

80. This critique of Tanzanian policy finds its most sustained expression in the various writings of Ann Seidman, notably in her *Comparative Development Strategies in East Africa* (Nairobi, 1972) and "Some Comments on Plan- ning in East Africa," in Cliffe and Saul, op. cit., vol. II.

81. Muhbub ul Haq, "Employment in the 1970s: A New Perspective," *Interna- tional Development Review*, no. 4 (1971), pp. 9–13. Ul Haq, formerly chief economist of the Pakistan Planning Commission, is now with the World Bank. He explicitly recognizes that the Chinese experience embodies many of the positive elements of a more effective strategy, while hastening to add that lessons can be learned there "even when we do not subscribe to its po- litical system"!

82. Ul Haq also argues that within such a strategic frame, "employment should become a primary objective of planning and no longer be treated as only a secondary objective"; then, for example, "if physical capital is short, skill formation and organization can replace it in the short run." Certain related insights are available in John Gurley, "Marxist Economics," *Monthly Re- view* (February 1971).

83. Lawrence, "Socialism, Self-Reliance, and Foreign Aid in Tanzania," ex- plores some of these dimensions of Tanzanian policy briefly but usefully.

84. See, for example, A. M. Babu, "A New Strategy for Development," *Finan- cial Times* (London), 9 December 1971; Babu was to be ejected from the cabinet and, as noted above, subsequently imprisoned, ostensibly in connec- tion with the events surrounding Karume's assassination. Conservative ob- servers (and, apparently, other cabinet ministers) have been quick to reject any such distinction between "an outward-looking and an inward-looking"

path to development; see, for example, K. E. Svendsen, "Problems of Economic Policy in Tanzania," a discussion paper presented to the Economics Research Bureau Seminar in mid-1971. Significantly, Svendsen, a Dane, is a special advisor in the president's office, Dar es Salaam. See also the June 1971 Budget Speech of A. H. Jamal (then Minister of Finance), which argues the case for a much greater emphasis on primary product exports.

85. See Chapter 1 of this volume.

86. The plan states that "a central concern . . . will be the fashioning of a longer term industrial strategy through the identification and preparation of projects in new industries meeting the more complex requirements of the next stage of industrialization." See United Republic of Tanzania, *Second Five-Year Plan for Economic and Social Development* (Dar es Salaam, 1969), vol. I, p. 62.

87. The arguments of this group appeared in a series of articles in *The Standard* in mid-1970; they have been collected, with other material, in I. G. Shivji, ed., *Tourism and Socialist Development* (Dar es Salaam: Tanzania Publishing House, forthcoming).

88. "Whether the government should plan para-statal investment of about £10 million in promoting hotels and associated projects to expand tourism, mainly to be managed by foreign partners for a fee, appeared to be another possible issue for further study. This amount equalled a third of all funds which NDC was to invest for industrial development. Another £3.5 million was to be spent on an international airport at Arusha to attract tourists directly to Tanzania." (A. Seidman, "Tanzania's Industrial Strategy," in Cliffe and Saul, op. cit., vol. II.)

89. I. G. Shivji, "Tanzania: The Silent Class Struggle," *Cheche* (special issue, October 1970), and reprinted in Cliffe and Saul, op. cit., vol. II; for a useful comparative framework see also B. Van Arkadie, "The Role of the State Sector in the Context of Economic Dependence," *Institute of Development Studies Bulletin* (August 1971).

90. On related issues, see P. Packard, "Management and Control of Parastatal Organizations [in Tanzania]" in Uchumi Editorial Board, op. cit. He emphasizes, as have others, the excessive reliance upon narrowly conceived criteria of short-term, enterprise-level *profitability* in the state-controlled productive sector (and especially spheres controlled by the National Development Corporation).

91. Loxley's essay "Financial Planning and Control in Tanzania," cited earlier, is particularly useful in documenting both the strengths and the weaknesses of some of these new control devices.

92. Lawrence, "Socialism, Self-Reliance, and Foreign Aid in Tanzania."

93. For a general perspective on the role of the International Monetary Fund,

see Cheryl Payer, "The Perpetuation of Dependence: The IMF and the Third World," *Monthly Review* (September 1971); on the World Bank see T. Hayter, *Aid as Imperialism* (Harmondsworth, 1971).

94. Murray, op. cit., p. 39.

95. Hoskyns, op. cit.

96. *Cooperation Against Poverty* (1970), reprinted in *The Standard*, 9 September 1970.

97. *Mwongozo/The TANU Guidelines*, op. cit.

98. *Daily Nation* (Nairobi), 10 June 1968, cited in L. Cliffe, "Tanzania: Socialist Transformation and Party Development," *African Review* (Dar es Salaam) (January 1970) and reprinted in Cliffe and Saul, op. cit., vol. I.

99. A forceful, if somewhat oversimplified, argument concerning the necessity of establishing closer links with the "socialist" countries is presented, in the context of an interesting overview of Tanzanian economic policy, by B. Ngotyana, "The Strategy of Rural Development," *The African Communist* (1969) and reprinted in Cliffe and Saul, op. cit., vol. II. By 1967, exports and imports with the East had both levelled off at what was still something less than 10 percent of total trade.

100. Take, for example, the following statement: ". . . because we ourselves had to fight against Western imperialism we are very conscious of it, and very concerned to safeguard ourselves against its resurgence. We are less conscious of other forms of imperialism, and as a result some of our people are oversensitive and oversuspicious in one direction only, believing that they are safe-guarding their country provided they disagree with whatever the British, or the Americans, do. This attitude we must fight against, for we shall not be a mature state until we have grown out of it." (J. K. Nyerere, *Principles and Development* [Dar es Salaam, 1966]), and reprinted in Nyerere, *Freedom and Socialism*, op. cit. Though there is room for debate about the subject of "social imperialism," as a description of Tanzanian realities this is one of the few presidential formulations which bears no discernible relationship to the facts of the situation.

101. It is worth noting that Canada was, until recently, the major source of military assistance and military advisers in Tanzania, though at present the Chinese seem the most prominent in this sphere. Nyerere's speeches in Sweden and Canada during his visits there in 1969 make striking reading from a socialist perspective, going far beyond what was required by mere diplomatic *politesse* in extolling the "virtues" of these two countries.

102. T. Niblock, "Tanzania's Foreign Policy: An Analysis," *The African Review* (September 1971).

103. On the nature and outlook of the Development Advisory Service, and its role elsewhere, see F. Ackerman, "Who's Afraid of Development Eco-

nomics," *Upstart* (Cambridge, Mass.), no. 2 (1971). The negative influence of McKinsey's "expert" advice has been evidenced most dramatically in the work of the State Trading Corporation. It is also worth noting, parenthetically, that the STC probably demands much more attention than we have been able to grant it here. To date, it has been one of the least effective of the new arms of state activity, the general absence of socialist economic strategy showing up clearly in its often anomalous ordering policy, and its inefficiency affecting the performance of the whole economy and sometimes disenchanting the population.

104. Lawrence, "Socialism, Self-Reliance, and Foreign Aid in Tanzania."

105. See the papers by George Kahama, General Manager of the National Development Corporation, to the NDC company managers' seminar in Dodoma, October 1971: "Town and Country: Partners in Progress," reprinted in *The Standard*, 28 October 1971, and "Small Industries for Ujamaa Villages," reprinted in *The Standard*, 29 October 1971.

106. Tanzania's achievement, from a very low base line, in such fields as quantitative improvements in education and social services have also been significant, of course; they have been effectively documented in J. K. Nyerere, *Tanzania: Ten Years After Independence*, Report by the President of TANU to the National Conference, September 1971 (Dar es Salaam, 1971).

107. Tanzania's early efforts to develop a steel industry followed a similar pattern of predominantly external linkages; more recently, the construction of the Chinese-financed railway has stimulated greater concern to develop the coal and iron potential of southwestern Tanzania into an indigenous iron and steel complex.

108. A. Seidman, "Tanzania's Industrial Strategy," op. cit.

109. Cf. Anon. (Samir Amin), "The Class Struggle in Africa," *Révolution*, (Paris), no. 1, p. 9; René Dumont, *Tanzanian Agriculture After the Arusha Declaration* (Dar es Salaam, 1969).

110. Moreover, the grouping of peasants in such collective centers may be necessary precisely in order to guarantee the popular and political base for challenging the logic of peripheral capitalism even at the level of the "commanding heights." This is a point often overlooked by observers like Amin and Dumont, and one to which we will return.

111. See W. L. Luttrell, "Villagization, Cooperative Production, and Rural Cadres: Strategies and Tactics in Tanzanian Socialist Development," Economic Research Bureau Paper 71.11 (Dar es Salaam, 1971), as well as various essays in *Rural Development Research Committee*, op. cit., for documentation of these points.

112. This is a very big assumption, of course; the failure of progressive propo-

nents of African unity, including Nyerere, to face squarely the implications of the fact that such an assumption does not hold has been discussed
in Chapter 2 of this volume. Tanzania, confronted with such develop-
ments as the many African states which now contemplate "dialogue" with
South Africa, has begun to take a somewhat more critical approach toward
the OAU and toward unity; witness the useful government paper on
"The OAU and the Freedom Struggle," presented to the OAU Heads of
Government Meeting in Addis Ababa, June 1971, and reprinted in *The
Standard*, 19 June 1971; and the stinging reaction to Amin's coup in
Uganda earlier in that same year.

113. Nonetheless, it could still be argued that Tanzania, in its enthusiasm for
East African cooperation, has never really confronted the full reality of
Kenya's role as a "peripheral center" in the international capitalist system.
And the attempts, understandable though probably futile, to facilitate realization of the benefits of economic scale in East Africa may therefore become, under present circumstances, merely another factor delaying the
country's commitment to a more radically "self-centered" emphasis.

114. Nor can one ignore the possibility of the most dramatic forms of intervention, a possibility exemplified elsewhere in Portugal's invasion of Guinée
in 1971 and one open to more subtle variations of pressure and support for
dissidents if Tanzania were to become an even more vital target for imperialism. Already, for example, certain relatively unfettered activities of the
Rockefeller Foundation at the University of Dar es Salaam bear a haunting
resemblance to the creation of an alternative leadership cadre in Sukarno's
Indonesia; compare David Ransom, "The Berkeley Mafia and the Indone-
sian Massacre," *Ramparts* (October 1970). As Jim Peck has recently
phrased it, there are distortions in socialist experiments in less-developed
countries which are likely to be removed "only when the pressures on
them from the capitalist environment are removed, when radical changes
within the capitalist world draw back their overbearing weight." (Jim
Peck, "Why China 'Turned West,' " *Ramparts* [May 1972].)

115. Svendsen, op. cit., outlines, albeit in conventional terms, some of the specific detail of Tanzania's recent economic difficulties. A further, almost inevitable, difficulty of socialist transition in Tanzania, though one made
more complex than it might otherwise be because of the erratic and unpre-
dictable line of advance, is that it frightens off some sections of the Asian
community—whose capital and skills lie at the heart of various intermediate sectors of the economy—before the country is fully geared to making
good their loss.

116. I. N. Resnick, "Class, Foreign Trade, and Socialist Transformation in
Tanzania," paper presented to the Economic Research Bureau Seminar,

University of Dar es Salaam (mimeo, 1972), which argues that "out of the 350,000 persons employed in wage and salaried jobs in 1968, only 44,000 fall into the 'privileged' class, . . . that is, are in occupations classified as 'high- and middle-level' by manpower definitions." Even this may understate the problem, however, for those members of the "staff" who are placed lower in the political-cum-administrative hierarchy may exemplify in practice similar interests, attitudes, and methods of work which are equally counterproductive in terms of socialist development; see H. U. E. Thoden van Velzen, op. cit.

117. Despite the gains which have been made (and noted in Section 1), Bienefeld, in an unpublished manuscript entitled "Urban Wage Earners in Tanzania," estimates that the top 20 percent of the adult male wage earners still earn more than 50 percent of the total wage bill in Tanzania.

118. Malcolm Segall, "The Politics of Health in Tanzania," in Uchumi Editorial Board, op. cit. Dr. Segall is Professor of Child Health at the University of Dar es Salaam.

119. Another way for a bureaucratic class to skim off surpluses is by means of various forms of corruption. This phenomenon is relatively well controlled in Tanzania, certainly as compared with its parodic expression in Nkrumah's Ghana, but the auditor general's *Report* for 1972 (extracts from which appeared in various issues of the *Daily News* in early July) gives some ground for concern in this sphere as well.

120. I. N. Resnick, "Socialist Policy Analysis," paper presented to the Universities of East Africa Social Science Conference, Dar es Salaam, December 1970.

121. M. A. Bienefeld, "Planning People," in Uchumi Editorial Board, op. cit. In fact, in this paper Bienefeld effectively analyzes a number of areas within the general field of education and manpower development where lack of ability or inclination to conceive the radical future has paralyzed planners who should be seeking strategies for forward advance.

122. L. R. Cliffe, "Planning Rural Development," in Uchumi Editorial Board, op. cit.

123. This is one sphere where class formation and uneven development as between regions may overlap to distort policy and introduce a subtle variant on tribal politics. Many more senior civil servants come from the most prosperous areas of the country (Chaggaland, Bukoba) than elsewhere; these educated men also *tend* to be linked generationally and by kinship with the better-off farmers in these areas, or indeed have sizable *shambas* (farmsteads) themselves. This is proably one factor which accounts for the heavy preoccupation with "backward" areas in the collectivization program; it is interpreted by many civil servants, willfully or not, as a kind of

"outdoor relief" program for the people of Dodoma and Kigoma, and at the same time is kept well away from Kilimanjaro. Certainly, for whatever combination of reasons, a viable program for rural *ujamaa* is still a long way off in such "developed" areas.

124. For a favorable overview of *ujamaa* practice to date, see A. Ellmann, "The Development of the Ujamaa Programme in Tanzania," in Rural Development Research Committee, op. cit., and, for a more critical perspective, W. L. Luttrell, op. cit.

125. It is worth reminding ourselves that, as noted in Section 2, this is a struggle less foreclosed in Tanzania than elsewhere in Africa because of the nature of the country's concrete pattern of historical development. In fact, Walter Rodney, when discussing socialist strategy in Tanzania and in particular Shivji's formulations about the country's "silent class struggle," takes this point very far indeed: "It is not a question of revolutionary forces against the petty bourgeoisie but of a struggle within that social stratum which is called the petty bourgeoisie and which includes the economic and political bureaucracy, whose actions are most relevant to the question of disengagement from the imperialist economy." (W. Rodney, "Some Implications of the Question of Disengagement from Imperialism," *Majimaji* [January 1971], and reprinted in Cliffe and Saul, op. cit., vol. II.) However, his conclusion that Shivji's "emphasis on the refractory nature of the petty bourgeoisie obscures the fact that contradictions are helping to detach more and more individuals of petty bourgeois background from the imperialist camp, and as they blend into the working classes the situation is created not only for disengagement from imperialism but also for the ultimate objective of constructing a socialist society" seems, when phrased so strongly, excessively sanguine and, within the confines of his admittedly brief paper, not really supported.

126. T. Szentes, "Status Quo and Socialism," *Majimaji* (special issue, February 1971) and reprinted in Cliffe and Saul, op. cit., vol. II. Szentes is surely correct when he notes of Shivji's alternative formulation that "we can hardly bridge over the problem by placing the 'social basis' of an assumed class outside the country, outside the very society it belongs to, by referring—as Shivji does—to the alliance of bureaucratic elite with the international bourgeoisie, however strong this alliance may be in certain cases." I have criticized Shivji's formulation—"the fundamental and antagonistic contradiction . . . is between imperialism and the people. . . . Once the main contradiction is resolved, the secondary contradiction will become enormously weak for the social base of the bureaucracy would have been destroyed. Without a class base in the international bourgeoisie, the bureaucracy would be more easily humanized and made more amenable to

workers' control"—in my paper "Who Is the Immediate Enemy?", *Majimaji* (January 1971) and reprinted in Cliffe and Saul, op. cit., vol. II on somewhat different grounds than Szentes', arguing that Shivji under-emphasizes the questions of state power and of the role of the "neocolonial state" in the production process.

127. As for their "reproduction" as a class, the nature of the bureaucratic structure certainly permits this class to reproduce itself *functionally;* moreover, this can occur even generationally in Tanzania, for despite the real open-ness of the educational system there is little doubt that the children of the petty bourgeoisie do have certain advantages in educational competition. Of course, Szentes is correct in saying that educational mobility does pose dilemmas for such a system, particularly if the economy refuses to expand.

128. One might cite a number of examples here, though perhaps the president's reluctance, during the university crisis of 1971, to discipline the leaders of the university—both in the administration and in the council—despite their blatant thuggery in handling the situation provides a good case in point.

129. Indeed, recent (1972) dramatic advances in the level of the minimum wage, while leveling up intra-urban differentials, might suggest that some such process is at work.

130. This paradox defines much of the essential "problematic" of Tanzanian socialism, as will become clearer shortly.

131. Cf. George Kahama's paper (op. cit.) for NDC managers, which opens on the note that industrial relations in the "developed world" manifest "a spiral of escalating irresponsibility" (not any kind of class confrontation), and devotes almost all its attention to the need to "educate" the workers to exercise their participation "with discretion." In a speech to the same Dodoma Conference a senior *Eastern European adviser* to NDC, one Ferene Cszogoly, is even more blunt: discussing *Mwongozo* and workers' participation, he concludes that "the danger of confusion of rights and duties of management with that of social bodies is very real. I would strongly insist, therefore, on the basic principle that management's responsibility should remain full and intact in any respect, without mixing it with misty excuses." (Reprinted in *The Standard* 30 October 1971.)

132. Mapolu, op. cit., p. 30. Mapolu concludes: "It is obvious that these difficulties are a result of the ideological plane on which development policy in this country is based. Tanzania's *ujamaa* does not emanate from a dialectical *class* analysis of society—it is very much 'an attitude of mind' whose cultivation cannot be placed very easily on the pedestal of a strategy for the purpose of analysis and evaluation." Mapolu's own analysis, however,

suffers somewhat from not facing clearly the ambiguities of the workers' own position within the Tanzanian class structure.

133. Lawrence, op. cit. Another feature which begins to be exposed under such circumstances is the nature of continuing links with imperialism. A recent confrontation with management in the Robbialac Paints firm forced clearly into the public press the extent to which the manager considered himself exclusively responsible to the Nairobi office rather than to any principles laid down by the Tanzanian government.

134. "Workers' education," seen as complementary to "workers' participation," is a particularly two-edged sword. A shrill insistence upon its "necessity" (and upon the continued dominance of management *within* the workers' councils) can be used merely to diffuse threatening rumblings from the "irresponsible" workers below (see note 131). Or it can become the foundation stone of a politically motivated "method of work" designed to raise consciousness and consolidate progress. An as-yet-unresolved combination of both dimensions has characterized Tanzanian practice to date.

135. L. R. Cliffe, "The Strategy of *Ujamaa Vijijini* and the Class Struggle in Tanzania," in Cliffe and Saul, op. cit., vol. II.

136. It has been estimated that 10 percent of the rural population has so far been affected by the rural collectivization program. That the intention is to increase that number significantly can be gauged from the president's recent statement in West Kilimanjaro to the effect that " 'state and cooperative farming are the only two forms that agriculture can now take in Tanzania bound toward Socialism.' . . . Mwalimu said that there was no future for individual large-scale farmers in Tanzania. He said a bright future lay ahead for peasants who would be ready to adopt improved farm methods through *ujamaa*." ("No future for capitalist farmers, says Nyerere," *Sunday News* (4 June 1972.) As noted in Section 1, radical decentralization *may* have related progressive implications, despite some dangers of reinforcing regional consciousness.

137. Relevant references might include Y. Museveni, "My Three Years in Tanzania (The Struggle Between Revolution and Reaction)," *Cheche* (July 1970); Karim Hirji, "Militancy and the Hill," *Majimaji* (July 1971) and the same author's "Crisis on the Campus: Diagnosis and Implications," *Majimaji* (August 1971); Munene Njagi, "The Upheaval Against Bureaucratic Arrogance," *Majimaji* (August 1971). I have surveyed earlier developments at the university in my essay "Radicalism and the Hill," *East African Journal* (December 1970), and reprinted in Cliffe and Saul, op. cit., vol. II. Of related interest is Sixth Former, "Crisis at Pugu Secondary School," *Majimaji* (September 1971).

138. In the initial skirmish the Field Force Unit (a paramilitary, trouble-shoot-

ing wing of the police) was called onto the campus to seize the "rusti-cated" Student Union president and rush him to a waiting airplane for re-turn to his native Kenya. It is instructive to note that the most important casualties of this incident were precisely that middle group of students (lo-cated somewhere between the militants and the most unregenerately elit-ist) who were potential recruits to the ranks of the revolutionary petty bourgeoisie. When their worst suspicions concerning the nature of power in post-*Mwongozo* Tanzania were confirmed they tended to withdraw into cynicism and apathy. The university case has shown clearly the lead-ership's difficulties in defining an effective method of work for struggle within the petty bourgeoisie.

139. A more sustained attempt to define the nature of this dialectic can be found in J. S. Saul, "The Nature of Tanzania's Political System," op. cit., where it is argued that it represents "a contradiction which cannot be evaded or suppressed but is nonetheless one which can be continually resolved in a progressive manner by effective methods of political work."

140. F. Engels, *The Peasant War in Germany* (Moscow, 1956), p. 115.

141. This is graphically demonstrated in R. C. Pratt, "The Cabinet and Presi-dential Leadership in Tanzania, 1960–66," in Cliffe and Saul, op. cit., vol. I, though Pratt himself seems to see this as a strength rather than a weak-ness of the system.

142. "TANU Moves to Tighten Hold on Economy," *The Standard*, 17 June 1971.

143. J. K. Nyerere, Introduction to *Freedom and Socialism*, op. cit., p. 30.

144. *The Nationalist* (Dar es Salaam), 22 October 1970.

145. *The Nationalist*, 5 November 1970. Again, opinions will differ here as to the precise combination of (1) a correct assessment of objective conditions, (2) a lack of power to affect his will, (3) an absence of ideological clarity, and (4) a failure of nerve, which this argument of the president's demon-strates. The historical reasons for this absence of socialists in the party is among the subjects frankly explored by Nyerere in his Introduction to *Freedom and Socialism*.

146. The dropping of Babu from the cabinet and his subsequent arrest, along with other radical Zanzibaris, in early 1972 was a particularly disturbing precedent (though the extent to which it was linked to considerations more specific to Zanzibar remains a question). But some observers have suggested the existence of a strong right-wing backlash in the political sphere ever since the left's highwater mark at the time of the promulgation of *Mwongozo*. Much of this "analysis" is based on Dar es Salaam's own brand of "Kremlinology," of course, and often turns on gossipy specula-tions about the current standing of such figures as Kisumo (right) and

Ngombale-Mwiru (left). After Nyerere, Kawawa, the second vice-president and, since early 1972, prime minister, would seem to be the crucial figure; a no-nonsense administrator, fiercely patriotic and undoubtedly a Nyerere loyalist, he remains something of an unknown quantity ideologically.

147. Needless to say, this is a sensitive area in Tanzania and one that even radicals approach with caution; perhaps that is why Shivji (op. cit.), in his otherwise admirable survey of Tanzania's "silent class struggle," blandly suggests with respect to the changes he feels to be necessary in TANU that "the mechanics and tactics of doing this is really a matter of detail!"

148. Certain structural weaknesses of TANU have been explored in H. Bienen, *Tanzania: Party Transformation and Economic Development* (Princeton, 1967) and in a committed and theoretically more sophisticated manner by Lionel Cliffe in his "Tanzania: Socialist Transformation and Party Development," op. cit.

149. Cf. Ministry of Economic Afairs and Development Planning, *Guidelines to the Annual Development Plan 1971–1972* (Dar es Salaam, 1971).

150. Obviously it cannot be argued that an influx of university graduates, even if they were to be drawn from the most militant former students, would be some sort of universal panacea for overcoming the party's weaknesses; certainly it was no real solution to "correct the administrative chaos of the party" (in 1966) by transferring, in Pratt's words (op. cit.), "a senior, and very nonpolitical, civil servant to the party to be its *de facto* secretary-general," even though he was a graduate. Nonetheless, the relative absence of trained people is one small indication, among others, of the party's continuing lack of capacity to generate, on a day-to-day basis, a fully effective presence in (so-called) "technical" spheres. Thus in March 1972 well over a hundred fresh graduates were taken up for important roles in the new structure of decentralized administration and planning; only a very small handful were taken into the party.

151. In any case, it is worth recalling from Section 2 the cultural dynamics which have so far dictated the relative paucity of such "revolutionary intellectuals."

152. Cf. note 144, as well as such fairly typical articles in the Tanzanian newspapers as "Reorganize TANU Urges TYL: Crucial Stage of Development," *The Standard*, 11 November 1970, and "Industrial Policy Needed, Engineer Tells [TYL] Seminar," *The Standard*, 24 January 1971.

153. The branch's theoretical journals, *Cheche* and, subsequently, *Majimaji*, have made especially significant contributions in this respect, their output having included Shivji's notable analysis, cited earlier. A second extended analysis by Shivji, entitled, "Tanzania: The Class Struggle Continues" (in

preparation at the time of this writing), will be published by *Majimaji* sometime in 1972; it promises to carry the work of the *Cheche/Majimaji* socialists a considerable step forward.

154. The party newspapers have been *Uhuru* (Swahili) and, until recently, *The Nationalist* (English). In addition, *The Standard*, nationalized in early 1970, became at that time a government newspaper directly under the president; its contribution was an at least equally militant one, particularly under the short-lived editorship of Frene Ginwala. Something of all these traditions was carried over when the press was reorganized again in 1972.

155. J. S. Saul, "The Nature of Tanzania's Political System," op. cit.: "It is essential . . . that party cadres raise the level of mass consciousness even while feeling the prod of the masses' class interests; choice must be structured for the system even while any vested interests which lurk behind the premises of choice so structured are being exposed; and so on. These are not mere paradoxes; rather they are the grim necessities of Tanzania's present situation."

156. This potential also remains to be fully consolidated by political practice, though it suggests the possibility, touched upon in Section 1, of giving renewed meaning and vitality to the cell system. A detailed analysis of planning and popular mobilization at the local level has concluded that "the further *political* task remains the most crucial dimension of the local development effort." (Cliffe and Saul, "The District Development Front in Tanzania," op. cit.)

157. N. Kisenge, "The Party in Tanzania," *Majimaji* (September 1971). The author was, until recently, the deputy secretary-general of the TANU Youth League. Referring to the 1967 case, Kisenge suggests that "one may rightly wonder how a ruling party can fail to raise sufficient funds to finance such a necessity while large sums of public funds are channeled to such prestige projects as building jumbo airports, or dubious ones like the multimillion hotels . . ." In the event, "thirteen village cadres were trained." See also the stimulating exchange of articles and letters concerning TANU's role which appeared, periodically, in *The Nationalist* during October-November 1970 or, among other items, Guido Magome, "TANU: Its Militant Continuity," *The Nationalist*, 31 December 1971, which specifically raises the following questions: "Is TANU ideologically strong? Can it be a vanguard Party? What of its mass membership?"

158. Of course, as noted earlier, the main hope must be that many such cadres will begin to emerge and, in effect, *select themselves* in the context of advancing the programs of workers' participation and rural *ujamaa*. The recent transformation of Tabora school, with some North Korean assistance,

may also be a straw-in-the-wind, though that institution is still experiencing teething troubles.

159. The question of the relation between party and class is crucial to a Marxist analysis of political developments; for an interesting survey of the "classical" writings on the subject see Chris Harman, "Party and Class," *International Socialism* (Winter 1968/69).

160. This point is further explored in Saul, "The Nature of Tanzania's Political System," op. cit., where it is concluded that "for Nyerere . . . the most relevant information reaped from the election may be . . . a sense of how much more remains to be done to create the base for guaranteeing the eventual success of his exemplary initiatives."

161. H.U.E. Thoden van Velzen and J. J. Sterkenburg, "Stirrings in the Tanzanian National Assembly," *Kroniek van Afrika* (Leiden), no. 4 (1968), and reprinted in Cliffe and Saul, op. cit., vol. I.

162. This distinction is suggestively explored in Franz Schurmann, *Ideology and Organization in Communist China* (Berkeley and Los Angeles, 1966.).

163. The president's Roman Catholic background may be an additional factor accounting for his suspicion of Marxism.

164. The idealist overemphasis on socialism as being primarily an "attitude of mind," which has sometimes characterized Tanzanian formulations (see H. Mapolu, quoted in note 132), may owe something to this ahistorical invocation of a living tradition of *ujamaa*, though it must be stressed that many of the most mystifying elements of the "African socialism" approach, crudely manipulated to paper over class contradictions elsewhere on the continent, have been transcended in this country. As an example of his "liberalism," the president himself candidly confessed to an emergency meeting of university staff during the student crisis of 1966 the difficulties he was having in overcoming his respect for "academic freedom" even at a time when the university most obviously needed a firm reorientation and was already drifting, "freely," under the hegemony of the Rockefeller Foundation and other reactionary interests.

165. These assertions are presented in their most startling form in J. K. Nyerere, Introduction to *Freedom and Socialism*, op. cit., pp. 14–19, and his interview with Peter Enahoro, published under the title "African Socialism," *Africa* (London), no. 6 (1972), pp. 55–63.

166. J. S. Saul, "Nyerere on Socialism: A Review," *Cheche* (October 1970), and reprinted in Cliffe and Saul, op. cit., vol. I. Compare "the president's own methodological injunction to 'apply scientific methods of study in working out appropriate policies' and his observation that 'a scientist works on the basis of knowledge which has been accumulated empirically' [which] may not take us far beyond a dangerously oversimplified positiv-

ism which leaves significant methodological realms uncharted." It is tempting to find the key to this aspect of Nyerere's thought in his academic training in the (very British) Makerere University College of Uganda and at Edinburgh University, for the missing link is precisely that identified for British culture and intellectual work as a whole by Perry Anderson in his suggestive essay "Components of the National Culture," *New Left Review* (November-December 1969). Here, perhaps, is cultural imperialism operating in its most subtle manner.

167. Two essays written by K. Ngombale-Mwiru for *Mbioni* (Dar es Salaam) in the year of the Arusha Declaration itself and entitled "The Arusha Declaration and the Perspectives for Building Socialism" and "The Policy of Self-Reliance" (reprinted in Cliffe and Saul, op. cit., vol. II) provide cases in point, as does the work of the *Cheche/Majimaji* socialists mentioned above.

168. The various ups and downs of Ngombale-Mwiru's own career are also of interest in this respect. On a slightly different tack, S. Hadji's "An Open Letter to Comrade K. Ngombale-Mwiru," *Majimaji* (June 1972), presents a controversial view of the gap between radical theory and possible practice which is imposed upon such militants by their involvement in the governmental/party structure as presently constituted.

169. During the university crisis of 1971–1972, Nyerere told groups of Tanzanian students and staff who met with him (in early 1972) that he had hoped to build a "socialist university," particularly after 1970 when the Dar es Salaam campus became independent of the old University of East Africa, but that "the right" (his term) had managed instead to entrench itself!

170. One of the president's rare personal weaknesses may have some impact here as well, albeit in a minor way. Nyerere cherishes his (well earned) role at the intellectual center of Tanzanian life; his status as "ideas man" is also his political stock in trade. These factors may help to explain his occasionally schoolmasterly approach to intellectual and ideological disagreement when it debouches onto the most fundamental questions of socialist construction.

171. Amilcar Cabral, quoted in R. Ledda, "Social Classes and Political Struggle," *International Socialist Journal*, no. 4 (1967).

172. Peck, op. cit.

173. We must also remind ourselves here, referring back to the very beginning of this paper, of the crucial contribution made to the struggle in Southern Africa by a Tanzania which has *not* "fallen into anarchy, inertia, or outright dependence" (in Hoskyns' phrase).

7
The Political Economy of Rhodesia

Giovanni Arrighi

The most important single element determining the nature of economic and political development in Southern Rhodesia was the British South Africa Company's overestimation at the end of the nineteenth century of its mineral resources, and the persistence of this overestimation for roughly fifteen years. The reasons behind such a misconception can be partly detected in the political interruptions which characterized the early period of colonization (Jameson Raid, Matabele and Mashona rebellions, Boer War). The costs incurred in the meantime increased the stake of the Company in the country and led to additional heavy development investment, particularly in railways. The overvaluation became apparent when, eventually, the Rhodesian gold fields failed to yield deposits comparable to those of South Africa. For example, even in 1910 against a profit of close to £7 million from the eleven leading Johannesburg gold mines, the ten leading Rhodesian mines yielded a profit of only £614,000. Large-scale workings were uneconomic because the deposits were scattered and the ore itself often of a low quality.

The desire to recover the original heavy outlays induced the Chartered Company to foster the formation of a white rural bourgeoisie which, by developing the country, would raise the value of its assets in the area—viz., the railway system, the mine claims, and especially land.

Settlement gathered momentum after 1902 when small workings of mine claims on a royalty basis were extended.

This article was originally published by Mouton and Company, The Hague. Copyright © 1967 by Mouton & Co., N.V. A revised version was published in *New Left Review* (September–October 1966), copyright © 1966 by *New Left Review*. The version which appears here is a combination of the two, with a theoretical introduction to the Mouton edition omitted. Reprinted by permission.

The influx of peoples, European and African, to the mining camps brought about a derivative demand for other products. Between 1901 and 1911 the European population doubled from 11,000 to over 23,000. Farmers began to settle and to feed the growing population and commercial undertakings became established in the growing towns of Salisbury and Bulawayo.[1]

Thus a cumulative process was started leading to a class structure which crystallized during the depression of the 1930s.

Within this class structure the white rural bourgeoisie was the foundation of the capitalist sector of the economy. This bourgeoisie consisted largely of both owner-workers of small- and medium-sized mines and farmers who were economically committed to the development of the country. This *national* character of the white rural bourgeoisie, even at that time, distinguished Southern Rhodesia from practically all other African colonial territories north of the Limpopo and south of the Sahara, where exploitation of resources was carried out by large-scale *international* capitalism. In these other territories, where exploitation was based on large-scale mining or plantation or monopoly trade, capitalist interests in the economy were not permanent but lasted until, for example, deposits were exhausted or the raw material was substituted in the industrial process overseas or some more economic source of supply was found. In inter-war Rhodesia about a third of the Europeans gainfully occupied belonged to the rural bourgeoisie, but to assess the full strength of this class it is important to take into account the would-be agriculturalists. In fact, "even the civil servant, business and professional man, miner or railway employee looked forward to retiring to a plot of land."[2] International capitalism was represented mainly by the British South Africa Company which, apart from its control over the railways, the bulk of gold production, and coal mining, also owned land in part exploited for productive purposes (maize, cattle, citrus, etc.). In accordance with its interest in encouraging the growth of the white rural bourgeoisie, it also experimented with new crops.

Large estates had been given to companies and syndicates for certain interests acquired by the British South Africa Company.[3] Other big companies were already dominating asbestos and chrome mining.[4] Control over tobacco production was exercised indirectly through monopsonistic practices by the United Tobacco Company which, in Huggins' view, "was aiming at becoming the country's sole tobacco buyer, and

managed to draw the best experts out of the government service." A
third class consisted of craftsmen engaged in manufacturing, whose activity was totally dependent on the rural bourgeoisie and big international capital, mainly the British South Africa Company. It was typically a petty bourgeoisie and, indeed, the colony's official yearbook of
1932 does not even mention the manufacturing industry.

Much more significant was the class of white wage workers formed
of artisans, semi-skilled workers, foremen, clerical workers, administrative employees, etc. Demand for their labor was concentrated in mining,
transport (mainly railways), and service activities (civil service especially). It is important to notice that, unlike South Africa or Algeria,
their settlement was *a consequence of,* and did not precede, capitalist development in the country. Therefore they had to be attracted by the
offer of high wages, and with their skills they brought union organizing
abilities. This phasing of white settlement and capitalist development is
at the root of the absence of "poor-white-ism" in Southern Rhodesia.
This class of white wage worker, together with the white petty bourgeoisie, i.e., handicraftsmen, shopkeepers, and small employers in agriculture and mining, already in the prewar period constituted the bulk of
the European population in Southern Rhodesia.

The Africans were still essentially a class of self-employed rural cultivators. The African wage workers, the African middle class, and the
petty bourgeoisie were merely appendages of the peasantry rather than
independent classes.[5] Land was not a salable commodity, but each adult
had rights to its use. The system of cultivation involved a form of land
rotation whereby land was used until its fertility was diminished and
was then abandoned and left to recover until its fertility was restored.
Within the peasantry some division and hence specialization of labor
could be observed.[6] The role of men was to regulate the community's
relationship with animals (tending cattle and hunting) and to provide
development works, such as bush clearance and building huts. The
women's role, on the other hand, consisted of routine tasks: sowing,
weeding, threshing, fetching water, preparing food, and making beer.
Communal ties were very strong,[7] and when the peasant left to seek
wage employment he left his family behind and kept close links
(through a flow of goods, cash, or occasional labor) with the peasantry
to which he belonged and meant to return, even after several years absence. At the same time the size and number of holdings under cultiva-

tion within the rural areas contracted and expanded as the wage laborers left or returned to their wards. Thus, given this security in land tenure, we cannot strictly speaking refer to the African wage workers of the 1930s as a proletariat.[8]

On the other hand, the African middle class and rural (petty) bourgeoisie were numerically and economically insignificant. For example, by 1930,—i.e., before the Land Apportionment Act was introduced—Africans had managed to acquire only 45,000 acres in the open market while Europeans had purchased about 31,000,000 acres.[9] The reasons for the failure of these classes to emerge are a consequence of the class structure itself and therefore they will be dealt with later.

To sum up: we can discern five main classes in prewar Rhodesia. There were (1) the white rural bourgeoisie operating in mining and agriculture, national in character; (2) large-scale international capitalism controlling transport (railways) and power (coal) and engaged in primary production and speculation in land; (3) the white wage workers whose entrance into the economy followed and did not precede the capitalist development of the country; (4) the white petty bourgeoisie operating in all sectors of the economy but especially trade; (5) the African peasantry and wage earners.

To assess the class interests of the white rural bourgeoisie, we must consider gains from both production and from appreciation of land values. This double function of land as a factor of production and as an object of speculation meant that more land was to be appropriated than was needed for productive purposes, i.e., land had to be set aside for both production and speculation. Since the appreciation of land depended to a great extent on the profitability of its productive use, let us focus our attention on this profitability. It essentially involved a continuous expansion of the demand for its produce and of the factors of production entering in combination with it in the productive process. Land was in fact practically in unlimited supply, whereas labor and overhead capital were not.[10] The expansion of the demand for the produce of the white agrarian bourgeoisie depended on the growth of the internal market and the reduction of competition (in both internal and export markets) from the peasantry or from a potential African rural bourgeoisie.[11] In fact, given the identity of outlets for African and European agricultural produce, the white agrarian bourgeoisie could not expect the indigenous population to provide an internal market for its production, as might have been the case if the white bourgeoisie had been a manufacturing or trading class. What it had rather to expect was competition in both internal and external markets. The expansion of the internal market thus implied the development of complementary sectors, i.e., sectors which would not compete with, but would rather increase, the demand for European agricultural produce. Hence the interest of the white agrarian bourgeoisie in the industrialization of the country.

It follows that the expansion of overhead capital mentioned above was needed not only in view of direct cost benefits for agricultural production, but also because by fostering industrialization it would have directly stimulated demand for agricultural produce. In this respect, therefore, the interests of the white rural bourgeoisie lay in an expansionist policy preceding and not following economic development.

Turning now to labor supply, there were essentially three ways in which it could be expanded: (1) through a system of forced labor; (2) by lowering the opportunity cost of the peasantry, i.e., by progressively reducing its overall productivity; and (3) by means of the proletarianization of the peasants. Alternative (3), however, runs against the other interest in limiting competition from Africans, since the proletarianization of the peasantry would bring about the emergence of a black agrarian bourgeoisie bound to compete in the markets of produce and of factors of production. Probably more important is the consideration that by preserving the traditional system of land tenure, wages could be kept lower in the long run, since part of the real cost of the means for the subsistence of the migrant workers' families would be borne by the peasantry.

I have dwelt on the interests of the white agrarian bourgeoisie because, as mentioned earlier, the Rhodesian prewar capitalist economy was geared around this class. The discussion of the interests of other classes has thus been simplified. International capitalism, and within its fold the Chartered Company in particular, had to rely on the development of a national white bourgeoisie in order to recover its initial investment in the territory. Hence the interests of these two classes basically coincided. Nevertheless, with regard to mining activities the coincidence of interests was limited to the necessity of expanding the overall labor supply. In fact, a too rapid growth of the national bourgeoisie through industrialization might have endangered the supplies of African labor (also and especially from neighboring territories) required by operations outside the country, i.e., in South Africa, Katanga, and later Zambia. This represents the inconsistency inherent in the relations between international and national capitalism in pre-World War II Rhodesia. The speculative interests of the former implied the expansion of the latter, but such an expansion might have threatened its more important productive interests.

A more manifest conflict of interest was centered around investment in overhead capital. As we saw, the national bourgeoisie had an interest in the expansion of overhead capital to foster the economic development of the country. On the other hand, the British South Africa Company, which controlled the railways and power, had an interest in restrictive policies, i.e., in increasing investment in response to, and not to induce, greater demand. This is the well-known shortcoming of private enterprise, where investment decisions taken individually tend to follow market demand rather than lead it, while market demand itself depends largely on aggregate investment decisions. When the capitalist system is highly competitive, or using a Keynesian expression, when the entrepreneur's "animal spirit" is very high, the situation is different because investment is almost entirely autonomous, i.e., does not depend on demand. But if capitalist production is highly concentrated, as in the case under discussion, the "animal spirit" is likely to be very low and investment is almost wholly induced. Hence the conflict of interests between the British South Africa Company and the national bourgeoisie.

The white wage workers were employed mainly in service activities and big mining companies. Since their settlement followed and did not precede local capitalist development, they enjoyed wage premiums over South Africa and consequently United Kingdom wage levels. In fact, given the lack of a stable African urban population and of adequate government expenditure on African primary education, it was in all likelihood cheaper for the private employers to import skilled and semi-skilled workers than to train local African labor for skilled positions. In other words, the white working class had not emerged out of a local dispossessed class (like the poor whites in South Africa) but came to fill specific jobs so that no "reserve army of white labor" existed in the country. There were two implications: a very strong bargaining power of the white workers vis-à-vis their employers; and the fact that white workers could be organized effectively. Bearing this in mind, the class interests of white wage workers are easily identified. They consisted of making use of their strength to obtain economic concessions from the employers, and to perpetuate those conditions on which their strength was based, i.e., the lack of (1) a reserve army of white labor, (2) a stable urban African population and, above all, (3) an effective educational and training system for the Africans. We may thus assume a conflict of interest between this class and international capitalism (its main employer), which has an interest in resisting economic concessions and in fostering greater competition on the market of those skills it employs.

No such conflict existed between the white working class and the national bourgeoisie, which was a minor employer of white labor. Rather, the interests of these two classes coincided on the issue of industrialization since development would bring greater opportunities of employment and thus strengthen further its bargaining power. Similar also were the main class interests of the white petty bourgeoisie (whatever its branch of activity), which can be summed up as (1) limitations on actual and potential African competition, and (2) growth of the domestic market.

We are thus left with the mass of the Africans. In the first place their interests lay in being drawn into the money economy not because of decreasing productivity in the traditional system, but rather because of increasing productivity which would have strengthened their bargaining power. In fact, the wage rates to be paid in the capitalist sector to labor outflowing the traditional sector is a function, among other things, of the opportunity cost of the peasant in the latter sector. That is, the greater the opportunities for earning a living outside the capitalist sector the higher must be wage rates in order to attract labor. A first conflict can thus be assumed between the peasantry (wage workers included) and white capitalists, be they national or international in character. Such a conflict was reinforced in the case of the agrarian bourgeoisie, which not only was the employer of African migrant labor, but also competed in the market with peasant produce.

A similar conflict existed with the white workers and petty bourgeoisie. To the interest of these classes in limiting racial competition corresponded that of the Africans in eliminating those conditions on which differentials in the standard of living were based. It can thus be assumed that in this particular respect there was a coincidence of the interests of the Africans and international capitalism since both would benefit from greater racial competition in the skilled labor market.

The Political Implications of the
Pre-World War II Economic Base

The key to understanding the outcome of the struggle for political power in the period under discussion is the different degree of class consciousness—that is, the awareness of their own interests displayed by the various classes. While the classes within the European section of the population were characterized by a remarkable degree of class consciousness, particularly in periods of economic depression, the Africans were not. In a scattered peasantry whose economic conditions had not yet notably worsened, and one which still used the traditional mode of production based on kinship relations, rather than impersonal market relations, class loyalty could not possibly be substituted for tribal loyalty.

> In Mashonaland . . . the small and broken tribes, scattered and restricted to their separate and distant reserves, were prevented from developing any cohesion or a wider outlook, while in Matabeleland the only rallying point of national feeling—the family of Lobengula—was becoming . . . more a family and sentimental affair than a national aspiration.[12]

At the same time the wage workers still belonged to the peasantry, and furthermore their incessant movements "from job to job, from location to kraal, from the Protectorates to the Union" prevented them from "developing, as a community, any corporate independence, initiative and self-respect." [13] It is true that protest movements were already appearing in the 1920s, but either they were concerned with the status of the negligible nucleus of educated Africans, or they were vague and illdirected and disappeared as soon as they were faced with official repression. In consequence, the African masses were politically inert, passive, and hence virtually powerless. The only signs of a class struggle were therefore to be seen within the European section of the population. The rather mild character of such a struggle can be ascribed precisely to the political inertia and passiveness of the large majority of the population which created the possibility of a deal between the different interests of the white classes.

The class structure sketched above obviously could lead to a coalition of all white classes, national in character (i.e., rural bourgeoisie, wage workers, and petty bourgeoisie, whose interests were compatible, if not identical) in opposition to international capitalism; the conflict being

mainly focused on the issues of overhead capital expansion and monopsonistic practices. This is, in fact, what happened. Two stages of political evolution can be discerned. At first the community of interests of the
Chartered Company and the rural bourgeoisie materialized in an ambi-
tious program of investment and in legislation aimed at obtaining labor
from the indigenous population. The latter included (1) expropriating
land while encouraging the dispossessed peasantry to remain where they
were as tenants, their rent being commuted for labor; (2) a hut tax
which virtually compelled the adult African males to spend between one
and three months a year in wage employment, and (3) a Pass Law intended to direct labor where it was wanted.[14] Of the three ways, mentioned above, in which the supply of labor could be expanded, "forced
labor" was thus the one relied upon at this stage.

With World War I the economic power of the national bourgeoisie
and white wage workers vis-à-vis international capitalism had grown
stronger. Hostilities and their aftermath had produced a widespread
shortage of skilled white labor and of world supplies of raw materials.
This relative strength lasted throughout the 1920s and by the time the
depression of the 1930s had set in, the coalition of the white national
classes had managed to obtain a good share of political power. A decisive
step toward greater national control was the achievement of responsible
government as opposed to amalgamation with the Union of South Africa. This latter course was, according to Gann and Gelfand, favored by
international capitalism because of the reliability of Smuts as an upholder
of imperial interests.

Responsible government merely meant a greater share of power for
the national white classes and by no means their undisputed rule. Economic dependence on foreign capital forced the settlers' government to
adopt middle-of-the-road policies, compromising between the interests
of the national bourgeoisie and white workers on the one hand, and of
international capitalism on the other. The result was that these conflicts
fell into the background and that greater national control over legislative
power found expression in an institutional framework strongly biased in
favor of the interests of the white national classes, which would regulate
future class relations. This is reflected in the legislation passed before
World War II (especially in the 1930s, when the Depression stiffened
the class consciousness of the white classes) to regulate the supply of

labor, the reservation of produce markets, government expenditure, monopsonistic practices, and the expansion of overhead capital.

Though the railway system and coal supply remained under the control of the British South Africa Company, the government took important steps in other spheres to provide basic facilities for the economic development of the country in line with the class interests of the national bourgeoisie and white workers. Government intervention increased remarkably and moved in two directions; expansion of overhead capital and strengthening of the bargaining power of the national bourgeoisie in the raw materials market. Public works, especially road building, were carried out on a large scale; several state enterprises were founded in the 1930s and early 1940s, including the Electricity Supply Commission power stations, the Rhodesian Iron and Steel Commission foundries and mills, and the Cotton Industry Board mills. Raw material processing plants (e.g., a roasting plant for processing low-grade ores and the establishment of a Sugar Industry Board) and marketing organizations were also set up. A side effect of these developments was a reduced economic dependence on international monopolistic interests. More direct steps were, however, taken to strengthen the bargaining power of the white farmers vis-à-vis the United Tobacco Company. The Tobacco Marketing Act (1936), by limiting competition among growers, attempted to replace the monopsonistic market with a kind of bilateral monopoly. Whether the attempt was successful is another matter. It is interesting that in 1943, seven years after the implementation of the act, the Southern Rhodesian finance minister still maintained that the price of leaf was controlled by powerful interests outside the colony.[15]

More significant was the legislation passed to ensure an expanding supply of labor and to divide the economy into noncompeting racial groups. This was achieved by a series of legislative measures and finally by the Land Apportionment Act. This act put a definite limit to the land available for permanent African settlement and in consequence made necessary the transformation of the traditional system of cultivation from shifting to continuous cultivation. The change was also encouraged by the government, which "centralized" the African rural areas, i.e., divided them up into permanent arable and permanent grazing land. Given the techniques employed by the peasantry and the type of soil allocated to them, this move from shifting to continuous cultivation produced progressive soil erosion, thus decreasing the productivity of African land.[16] However, since the criteria employed for allocating land to Africans was an average acreage per family rather than the income off that acreage, the progressive decrease in the productivity of land was tantamount to a progressive decrease in the overall productivity of the peasantry. Thus a built-in trend of decreasing peasant productivity was established, which would ensure an expanding supply of labor. Apart from these long-term implications, the Land Apportionment Act provided the European farmers with a pool of labor straight away. This was achieved by allowing a European farmer to enter into an agreement "whereupon a native or his family shall be permitted to occupy a portion of such land under condition that he supply labor to such owner or occupier." Similarly, the hut tax guaranteed a steady flow of labor from the tribal areas. Furthermore, as time went by and contacts with the money economy increased, new needs were felt (especially for education and clothes), altering the means of subsistence.[17] In consequence, the demand for cash was itself growing and, given the limitations on the production of cash crops, a further element was at work to expand labor supply.

The distribution of the total African labor supply between the different capitalist sectors was not left to the law of supply and demand but was also legislated for, mainly through the Native Registration Act (1936). This act tightened up the Pass Law and effectively contributed to the maintenance of a wage structure whereby the white farmers constantly paid unskilled labor lower wage rates than did other employers.[18]

The second implication of land apportionment was to be the division of the economy into noncompeting racial groups. Racial competition could potentially take place between (1) white agrarian bourgeoisie and African peasantry; (2) white and black bourgeoisie in both the produce and the labor markets; (3) white and black petty bourgeoisie in retail trade; and (4) white and black wage workers in the skilled labor market. In restricting competition in these markets, the Land Apportionment Act drew the general lines whereas more specialized legislation tightened the restrictions in the individual spheres.

The competitiveness of the peasantry on the produce markets was restricted in a number of ways. In the first place, the Africans were confined to the poorer land resources of the country. Secondly, the conversion of part of the peasantry into tenant-laborers inevitably reduced the marketable surplus. Thirdly, the same effect resulted from the decreasing productivity of African agriculture. Fourthly, the clear separation of land between Africans and Europeans made it possible to direct capital expenditure in roads, dams, etc., so as to widen the differential in overall productivity of European and African agriculture. These were indirect checks on African competition. At the same time, more direct steps were taken in order to discourage African sales through discriminatory price policy (e.g., the Maize Control Act of 1931).

Competition from an African rural bourgeoisie was potentially much more dangerous. Its emergence was accordingly prevented or at least contained within well-defined limits. This was achieved by preserving the traditional system, whereby land was not a salable commodity in the African areas. Native Purchase Areas, where Africans could hold land in individual right, were set aside, but the African rural bourgeoisie was nevertheless bound to remain negligible, for land in the Native Purchase Areas was to be allocated by the government and thus the formation and growth of the African bourgeoisie could be indirectly controlled by the very class which feared its competition. However, the total land to be allocated constituted only 8 percent of the total land areas of the country and it was generally located even farther away from markets, railway lines, and main roads than that of the traditional peasantry. Furthermore, though land, once allocated, was owned individually, there were many limitations to its transferability, such as maximum size of holdings and sales to Europeans. Among other things this meant that the extension of credit (which could possibly come only from European sources) to African farmers was hampered and therefore a constant lack of financing was bound to hold back their development. In other words, quite apart from direct discriminatory practices in granting credit, the preservation of the traditional system of land tenure prevented the consolidation of land holdings so that administrative difficulties made credit extension to Africans impracticable.

Interracial competition was also prevented in trading activities since the Land Apportionment Act, by prohibiting African ownership or lease of premises in the European areas (which included all towns and cities), banished African traders to the poorest markets, implicitly preventing their growth. Furthermore, under the Native Registration Act, even hawkers were restricted to the African locations: only sales of curios, baskets, and similar articles were allowed in the towns, whereas sale of such goods as chicken, eggs, butter, etc., was prohibited.[19]

The greater political power achieved by the white wage workers, through their coalition with the national bourgeoisie, also found expression in a number of acts and policies which aimed at improving their social and economic condition, and at perpetuating the scarcity of skills on which their bargaining and political strength was based. Under the Industrial Conciliation Act (1934) and its Amendment of 1937, machinery was set up for settling disputes in practically all industries employing white labor. Agreements between employers and employees in the Industrial Councils were to become legally binding in the industry concerned. The act explicitly excluded African workers from its definition of employee, but all the same wage rates and conditions of employment negotiated by the Industrial Councils were applicable to skilled white and black workers alike. In practice this meant that Africans were debarred from climbing the industrial ladder since no white employer would have employed an African if, for the same wage, he could obtain a European. Even more significant was the provision which empowered the Industrial Councils to regulate the conditions of apprenticeship. This provision created a situation strikingly similar to that governing competition between the white and black agrarian bourgeoisies. In other words, here too, remarkable power was given to a white class (wage workers) to control the rise of African competition. Thus the white workers came to control the scarcity of their own skills. This scarcity was also guaranteed by the government immigration policy which was, especially in the 1930s, highly selective and against any large-scale immigration of whites.

This body of legislation and policies was well summed up in the prevailing ideology of the period: the doctrine of "parallel development" or the "two-pyramids policy," according to which interracial competition ought to be prevented. Having shown how the economic base has produced a certain superstructure, we now turn to deal with the effects of the superstructure on the economic base.

War and Postwar Economic Development

The desire for industrialization and the progressive decrease of the peasant's productivity, implicit in the institutional framework produced by the class structure of the 1930s, were inconsistent with each other. A necessary condition of industrialization was an expanding internal demand, whereas the deterioration of peasant productive capacity inevitably led to the opposite—an internal demand which, if not stagnant, grew at a negligible rate. In fact, a growing population combined with constant per capita income in the subsistence sector simply means greater subsistence output rather than expanding aggregate demand for capitalist production. Thus, notwithstanding increased government intervention to foster economic growth, the system lacked an *internal* force sufficient to start development. The result was stagnation, and in fact in the 1930s, after nearly two decades of self-government, the country still had a typically colonial economy with no industrial sector apart from the railway workshop and small firms engaged in wholly subsidiary activities.

There was a second inherent contradiction in the institutional framework. The preservation of the traditional African system of land tenure was meant to prevent the emergence of a proletariat which, nonetheless, was an inevitable consequence of the decreasing productivity of the peasants combined with labor migration.

Once the process of deterioration of African agriculture had started it became cumulative, since the lowered and continuously decreasing opportunity cost of the peasantry in the traditional sector was bound to force an ever growing number of men into wage employment. This was true even though the average per capita income in the traditional sector remained constant, for two reasons: (1) the "effort-price" of that constant income increased, by extension of the acreage under cultivation; (2) a constant average conceals important variations from area to area. Furthermore, the process was accelerated by the fact that cattle was the most important of the few forms of investment open to Africans, so that the population explosion was accompanied by remarkable increases in the cattle population which worsened pressure on the land.

Thus in the long run to the savings of the wage workers there would not correspond, in the traditional sector, an increased productivity of the peasantry that would make the production of a surplus above subsistence possible. Therefore when the limits of land available had been reached, the attempt by wage laborers to realize their "savings" would be frustrated, their security would be lost, and a proletariat would arise.

The upshot of this was that the institutional framework established in the 1930s, while it could not lead endogenously to economic growth, was unable to prevent the formation of a proletariat.

The lack of internal demand represented a brake on industrialization and development, and the progressive decrease of overall peasant productivity increasingly worsened this obstacle. World War II was the external stimulant which more than offset the hindrance and started economic growth in Southern Rhodesia after the stagnation of the 1930s. Goods previously imported became practically unavailable, thus creating a demand for local industries; chrome and asbestos assumed strategic importance; world shortage of agricultural produce provided a rapidly growing outlet for farm output. More specifically, an air training scheme was implemented in the country, in association with the British government, whereby Southern Rhodesia had to supply air stations, quarters, land, and buildings.

> The air training scheme proved a major economic boom. Farmers and industrial firms suddenly found an almost insatiable market, and Guest calculated that Imperial expenditure on the scheme alone almost equalled the indirect benefit which the country derived from its entire gold-mining industry.[20]

This explosion in demand could have led *merely* to inflation as it did in many other underdeveloped countries. Instead, it was under these circumstances that the *national* character of the white bourgeoisie and white workers who controlled the government became important. Contrary to what happened in the economies of the "enclave" type, controlled by *international* capitalism with no interest in the development of the country, the government in Southern Rhodesia could intervene both through direct anti-inflationary controls and by setting up actual iron and steel production and cotton spinning plants which made the growth of secondary industry possible. Though the shortage of manpower and especially of capital goods prevented the capitalist sector of the economy from taking full advantage of the high war demand, it was during this time that overhead capital was developed and resources were being accumulated which could finance future developments.[21]

By the end of the war the limitations on the expansion of the internal market (the institutional framework) had not been removed and therefore a slump would have ensued had it not been for new external stimulants. The world shortage of raw materials which followed the war was accompanied by a dollar shortage. Asbestos and chrome were both dollar-savers and demand for them increased considerably. More important still was the role played by tobacco production which, after the war, was greatly stimulated by the limitation of dollar expenditure by the United Kingdom: the amount of tobacco produced tripled between 1945 and 1958, its value rising fourfold. This remarkable increase in production was accomplished through an increase in the same period in the number of producers from just over 1,000 to 2,669,[22] and was the main factor behind the high rate of immigration in the postwar years.[23] The influx of Europeans in turn created demand for goods and services, particularly housing, and the number of Africans in wage employment rose from 254,000 in 1936 and 377,000 in 1946 to more than 600,000 in 1956, thus keeping up internal demand for manufactured and agricultural products. These effects, induced by the increased demand for tobacco and other raw materials, account for the permanence of a sustained rate of growth between the end of the war and the late 1940s. By then an additional external stimulant came into operation: the outflow of capital from the Union of South Africa and the United Kingdom.[24] In the Union the *national* bourgeoisie and white workers had seized power in 1948 and *international* capitalism, scared by the possibilities of nationalization of means of production in the interests of the new ruling classes, reacted by looking for alternative outlets for its investment. In fact, "the City . . . from about 1947, was increasingly inclined to channel money directly into Rhodesia instead of routing funds via Johannesburg" [25] and "considerable sums formerly earmarked for investment in the Union have been placed in Southern Rhodesia . . . to escape extremist Nationalist policies, or . . . hedging against the possibility of later migration under conditions where capital movements might prove more difficult.[26] Southern Rhodesia, with its developed overhead capital, growing industries, and European immigration could provide the alternative outlet for international capitalist investment. Thus, foreign investment in Southern Rhodesia, which amounted to £13.5 million in 1947, was more than double that amount in 1949 and reached £50.7 million by 1951.[27]

The overall results of this remarkable war and postwar economic development of Rhodesia can be gauged by the fact that the net domestic product at current prices had risen more than ninefold, from £27.4 million in 1939 to £251.1 million in 1961, and that fixed capital formation in the period 1946–1961 was at a yearly average of more than £50 million.[28] However, even more significant changes occurred in the class structure of the economy, which we must now discuss.

Changes in the Economic Base Since World War II

From 1901 to 1950 the productivity of the peasantry had been constantly declining so that the "effort-price" of maintaining a constant subsistence income had been continuously growing. This helps to explain why the volume of African employment continued to expand between 1930 and 1945, notwithstanding the fact that real wages steadily declined, as shown for example by Barber. The formation of a proletariat, implicit in this trend, was accelerated by the active implementation of the Land Apportionment Act. This was started as soon as the squatting of the African peasantry on unalienated land encroached upon European cultivation, but especially when more land had to be provided for the postwar white settlement and tobacco cultivation. In 1948 close to 300,000 Africans were either residing on European land or were occupying land within the areas marked for European use, and in the postwar years 85,000 African families were shifted in organized expulsions.[29] This settlement was accompanied by large destocking programs which curtailed the main form of investment open to Africans.

Declining real wages, deterioration of peasant productivity, restriction of land available for African use, curtailment of African investment —all these combined to make the wage workers realize not only that their living conditions were constantly worsening but also that their savings were illusory and so was their "old-age insurance." Frustration and insecurity ensued, and with them the consciousness of being wage workers for good—that is, of forming a proletariat. "I have grown up under the white people. . . . My wish is that . . . we get *better treatment in the way of wages.* Today I am getting older and I have nothing. *I have not saved anything.* I might die and not know how my children are going to manage." [30] With this new consciousness came a wave of strikes and political activities on a completely new scale.[31] The emergence of a proletariat did not mean that the solidarity between wage workers and peasants was diminishing. On the contrary, the interests of the two classes largely overlapped, for the decreasing productivity of the peasantry was at the root of the impoverishment of both classes. Unrest spread from the towns to the rural areas where grievances over destocking and the organized expulsions provided a ready demand for political leadership.[32] This solidarity of interests stemmed also from the fact that the transformation into proletarians was gradual and did not involve *all* wage workers. In fact, when in the early 1950s the government, now pursuing a policy of labor stabilization, tried to implement the Land Husbandry Act, the class consciousness of both peasants and proletarians gathered momentum.[33]

A second major change in the class structure was the emergence of a manufacturing as opposed to a rural capitalist class. The contribution of manufacturing to national income rose from 9 percent in the late 1930s to about 15 percent in the early 1950s to over 18 percent in the early 1960s. Even more important was the fact that the growth was matched by the concentration of production as the industry passed from the small family-shop stage to the large-scale, mechanized, corporate-owned factory. The proportion of firms whose gross output exceeded £50,000 was more than a third in 1957 but accounted for less than 8 percent in 1938, and "while the typical industrial unit is growing in size, there is also a growing concentration of industrial output in the largest units, as experienced by the fact that 85 firms with gross outputs of £250,000 and over, comprising only 9 percent of the total number, accounted for 67.8 percent of the gross values of manufacturing output in the territory."[34]   The labor requirements, both qualitative and quantitative, of this sector came to differ sharply not only from those of prewar manufacturing but also of mining and agriculture. With mass production and mechanical aids, complex jobs could be divided into simple operations. Hence new possibilities of substituting relatively unskilled labor for artisans arose. On the other hand, with greater capitalization of production, specialization and hence stability of labor became relatively more important than large supplies of cheap migrant labor. Demand for nonmanual labor increased more rapidly than demand for manual labor.

In order to gauge the interests of the manufacturing class, the outlets for its production must also be considered. As we should expect, the bulk of manufacturing has been concentrated in heavy construction materials, processing of local food production, and low quality consumer goods. Production of heavy construction materials was stimulated by large expenditure in overhead capital and housing. Production of low quality consumer goods has increasingly come to depend on the *growth of the purchasing power of the African peasants and wage workers*. Its development can be explained by import substitution, European immigration, and the increases in African wage employment, but its long-run prospects are being hampered mainly by the institutional framework which has led to a continuous decrease in the peasantry's productivity. Processing of local farm production was stimulated by the expansion of the European market brought about by postwar immigration and import substitutions. The stabilization of the European population since 1960 (the natural increase has hardly offset net emigration), and especially the low income elasticity of demand for food, has been seriously limiting expansion in this field. African food consumption, on the other hand, "is dominated by the cheapest foodstuffs: mealie meal, low quality meat, dried and fresh fish, bread and sugar, account for roughly 80 percent of the food outlays of African families." [35] Hence, for this sector too, the *growth of the purchasing power of the Africans* and their rapid proletarianization, and especially urbanization, became a condition for expansion.

Though the emergence of a proletariat and of manufacturing capitalism represent the major changes in the prewar class structure, important changes *within* mining and agrarian capitalism have also occurred. Three main changes can be observed: the relative decline and increased concentration of the mining industry; the economic strengthening of the agrarian bourgeoisie; the shift of emphasis from the internal to the external market for agricultural produce.

The contribution of mining to national income declined from over 25 percent in 1938 to about 10 percent in the early 1950s and about 5 percent in the early 1960s. This general trend conceals significant internal variations. Gold output has decreased, mainly "because of the static dollar price of gold in relation to rising cost of production," [36] while production of asbestos, chrome, and coal has shown a steady rise since the war. The fact that mining of these three minerals has been dominated by four large firms by itself accounts for the increased concentration of mining in general. Furthermore, in gold production the "small workers" were eliminated by rising mining costs so that the total number of gold workings dropped from over 1,750 in 1935 to 700 in 1947 and 300 in 1956. This greater concentration was accompanied by the employment of more modern techniques and greater capitalization which reduced the dependence of the industry on a growing supply of labor.

Opposite trends appeared in European agriculture, where the total value of output (at current prices) in 1958 was ten times that of 1937.

As mentioned earlier, wartime production and increased export of tobacco was the decisive factor behind this spectacular increase. Tobacco has become since the late 1940s Southern Rhodesia's most important single export commodity and therefore the major foreign exchange earner. Since the growth of the tobacco industry was accomplished through an influx of new producers, the number of firms increased.

The other significant change has been the shift from maize to tobacco as the main crop. Two important implications of this change must be made explicit. In the first place, the emphasis was shifted from internal to external market, thus reducing the agrarian bourgeoisie's dependence on, and interest in, the industrialization of the country. In the second place, mechanization has been held back by the fact that tobacco growing demands more labor intensive methods than maize, so that agrarian capitalism remained on the whole more dependent on unskilled labor than mining and manufacturing.

Significant changes have also occurred in the relationships between national and international capitalism in Rhodesia. Before World War II the main foreign interests were centered around the appreciation of land values, the mineral rights, and the railway. The mineral rights were bought by the government in 1933, and the railway line in 1949. On the other hand, in the postwar period the interests of international capitalism came to involve practically every sector of the Rhodesian economy, nonagricultural industries in particular.

Within foreign capital, three main interests may be singled out: (1) interests connected with the Anglo American Corporation (AAC); (2) interests in primary production of large-scale foreign companies other than Anglo-American; and (3) interests of manufacturing firms.

1. The interests connected with AAC are centered around four "giant" corporations (Tanganyika Concessions, De Beers, British South Africa Company, and AAC itself) which are united by interlocking holdings and directorships.[37] The wealth and power of the group is based on the exploitation of the mineral riches of South Africa, the Zambian Copperbelt, and Katanga. Its interests in Rhodesia are subordinated to those of these other areas. It is probably right to assume that Anglo-American depends neither on British nor South African capitalism but is rather an "independent superstate," an economic empire centered in Southern and Central Africa (this is the reason for dealing with the group separately). Apart from the group's control over the extremely

important coal supplies of the country, the Rhodesian economy has offered, particularly since the late 1940s, an outlet for investing the profits reaped in Zambia and to a certain extent (and for certain periods) in South Africa. In Rhodesia the group dominates coal and iron pyrites mining, the ferro-chrome and cement industries, and, together with RST, controls iron and steel production (formerly a government-controlled enterprise) and the Argus Group which has practically the monopoly of the Rhodesian daily press.[38] Other major investments include citrus and sugar estates, forests, clay products, financial houses, etc.

2. The other giant companies engaged in primary production in Southern Rhodesia are not locally based (i.e., in Southern Africa as a whole) and therefore their interests in the economy are less diversified and their profits generally flow overseas in a greater proportion. The Rhodesian (now Roan) Selection Trust (RST) is controlled by the American Metal Climax Co. and has no significant mining interests in Southern Rhodesia. The Trust operates in the Copperbelt and its participation with AAC in certain sectors of the economy is subsidiary.

Production of asbestos is dominated by a British company, Turner & Newall, which controls approximately 90 percent of the territory's output and also dominates the asbestos cement product industry.[39] Other examples of big foreign interests in primary production are Lonrho (gold mining, cattle, and ownership of the oil pipe line) and Forestal Land, Timber, and Railways Company, one of the world's largest producers of tanning extracts, which through its subsidiary Rhodesian Wattle Company owns nearly all of the wattle acreage.[40] When account is taken of the monopsonistic practices in the purchase of tobacco, the general picture which emerges is one of a highly concentrated and to a great extent foreign-controlled primary production sector.

3. The situation in manufacturing is similar. Well over one-third of the fifty largest British manufacturers have direct interests (subsidiaries and not merely sales organizations) in Rhodesia.[41] As a result, the presence of "giant corporations" can be observed in practically every sector of the Rhodesian manufacturing industry, with a relatively greater concentration of British capital in the first stages of production and South African capital at the other stages (including distribution).[42]

The overall control of foreign interests over the Rhodesian economy can to a certain extent be gauged by examining the results of a questionnaire sent to companies operating in the Federation in 1960. The results from Southern Rhodesia (which covered over 65 percent of the total profits earned in the country) show that two-thirds of the total recorded net operating profits accrued to companies not domestically controlled.[43]

Meanwhile, economic development shifted the "center of gravity" within the *white* community from the petty bourgeoisie to the wage worker. the concentration of ownership over mining and manufacturing resulted in the elimination of the craftsmen and "small workers," which was only partially compensated for by the increased number of shop-keepers.[44] On the other hand, the wages and general welfare of the white wage workers have improved considerably since the 1930s. This class has become one of the better paid working classes of the world, with average annual earnings well above £1,000 in the late 1950s. The main factor behind the trend has been the high rate of development and capital accumulation maintained in Rhodesia during the war and post-war period, which kept the economy in a perennial state of over-full-employment in the nonmanual and skilled-manual occupations. The result was the strong bargaining power of the white workers, which put them in a position not only to obtain economic concessions, but also to resist any infringement, let alone the repeal, of the legislation passed in the 1930s. The entrance of Africans into skilled occupations was consequently hampered, and the growth of an African petty bourgeoisie was prevented both by the institutional framework of the 1930s and by the increasing concentration of production in mining and industry, which was thus ill-suited to bring about the rise of an African artisan class. In agriculture, on the other hand, though the decreasing importance of maize production reduced the resistance of European farmers to African sales in the home market, the African petty bourgeoisie of the Native Purchase Areas was blocked from taking advantage of the boom in export crops. Furthermore, their numerical increase was held back by the government, the pretext being the lack of surveyors.[45]

Given these changes in the class structure, what interests can be attributed to each class?

In the first place, there occurred the growth of an African proletariat and a greater political consciousness in the African population at large. This had many consequences. The pressure for higher wages, better working conditions, and greater investment in industrial training and

African education increased; the opposition to an institutional framework, which meant a decreasing productivity of the peasantry, grew stronger; the loss of security of land tenure was resisted; etc.

Secondly, this phase saw the rise of manufacturing capitalism (induced by a series of exogenous "shocks"), the growth of which was hampered by the decreasing productivity of the African peasantry.

Mass production and the high capital intensity of operations in this new sector meant a dwindling demand for unskilled migrant labor and a growing interest in a more stable labor force. The substitution of the traditional system of cultivation by African agrarian capitalism, which would bring about both greater productivity of African agriculture and stabilization of the labor force, thus suited the interests of manufacturing capitalism. *Greater competition* between African and European agriculture would inevitably follow such a substitution. The greater degree of capital intensity also meant that high-level manpower has become important in the cost structure of manufacturing; hence an interest in fostering *competition* between European and African skilled and nonmanual labor, i.e., an interest in a growing African middle class and consequent weakening of the white workers' bargaining position. At the same time, the manufacturing sector of the economy was still dependent on the market of the white Rhodesians. In other words, manufacturing capitalism required for its expansion the relative worsening of living conditions of the very classes on which it still heavily depended.

Thirdly, the white agrarian bourgeoisie, having shifted from maize to tobacco production, had lost interest in industrialization and continued to require large supplies of cheap unskilled migrant labor. This further emphasizes the conflict of interests between white manufacturing and white agrarian capitalism.

Fourthly, there was a greater diversification and penetration of international capitalism in Southern Rhodesia. The interests of the giant foreign manufacturing companies overlap with those of manufacturing capitalism in general, but some important differences distinguished them from the interests of the corresponding national capitalist class. The big foreign companies engaged in primary production were even less interested in the country's industrialization than the agrarian national bourgeoisie. These big companies are specialized on a world scale in the exploitation of certain raw materials, so that what matters for their expansion is the growth of world demand for their products and this growth does not in any way depend on local development. Since they employ or can easily adopt more modern techniques and greater mechanization, their expansion is less dependent on migrant labor than in the case of the national agrarian capitalists. The interests of AAC and related companies, given their "unique" position, lie somewhere between those of the other two categories of international capitalism, manufacturers and primary producers.

Lastly, there are some features which characterize foreign capitalists in general (whatever the nature of their activities) vis-à-vis the national bourgeoisie. Other things being equal, given their financial power, greater capital intensity, and scale of operations, they are much less vulnerable to local competition. Secondly, their size and concentration give them a stronger bargaining position at government level. Thirdly, their common and all-pervading interest is to prevent "nationalist" policies which might tamper with their local operations, irrespective of whether these policies are in favor of a national bourgeoisie, or a racial minority, or the majority of the population.

In conclusion, we can say that there is a certain coincidence of class interests between African middle class and African bourgeoisie on the one side and manufacturing capitalism on the other. But much more evident is the community of interests of the white agrarian (and petty) bourgeoisie and white wage workers, focused on preventing racial competition. On the other hand, the interests of foreign capitalism engaged in primary production were drawn nearer to those of the manufacturing class by the emergence of the African proletariat and its external manifestations, which acquired a broader political significance from the rise of African nationalism throughout the continent.

The Political Implications of the Changes
in the Economic Base

The changes in the superstructure resulting from the altered class structure were epitomized by the shift from the ideology of the "two pyramids," or separate development, to one of "racial partnership"; i.e., from noncompeting racial groups to the "color blind" law of supply and demand. Competition was to concern mainly the African middle class and bourgeoisie, since peasantry and proletariat were too weak to be able to compete with anybody but themselves. The African middle class and bourgeoisie, as we have seen, had interests coincident with those of manufacturing capitalism and therefore their rise was to be fostered as industrialization proceeded.

As early as 1948, at the time of the African strikes and the emergence of the African proletariat, Huggins was led to think that "we shall never do much with these people until we have established a native middle class." [46] Later, in 1952, "*under the pressure of industrialization* . . . [he] quite deliberately thought of power in terms of social class, and aimed at a working alliance between the European ruling strata and the more prosperous Africans, bus-owners and master farmers, building contractors and senior employees. . . ." [47] We can trace two complementary interests underlying these passages: the need for an African middle class and bourgeoisie, both as a *requirement* for industrialization and as an "insurance against the mass of Africans." As a matter of fact, the constant factor noticeable in government policies during the 1950s was the creation of an African middle class and bourgeoisie by inducing more interracial competition.

The institutional framework established in the 1930s no longer reflected the underlying class interests, and in consequence a series of reforms were attempted by the government.

Since the early 1950s, under Huggins but especially under Todd[48] and later Whitehead, there was a reversal of policies, whereby all restrictions on competition were increasingly questioned. In 1954 a bill was introduced by the government to give recognition to African trade unions; the bill was referred to a select committee which after two years recommended an amendment to the Industrial Conciliation Act so as to include Africans in the definition of employee. Since the recommendation did not discriminate between the voting power of Europeans and Africans and sought to make all unions "vertical" (i.e., a single union covering a whole industry), African-controlled unionism could become a possibility.[49]

In African education the "whole emphasis had changed from the slow, steady uplift of the villages . . . to the rapid creation and training of an *elite*." [50] The number of teachers and pupils increased between 1956 and 1959 by about 10 percent each year; between 1954 and 1960 the number of pupils doubled and multiracial university education was introduced.

Similarly, reforms were attempted in order to increase competition between European and African agriculture. In the 1950s expenditure on African agriculture increased remarkably:

In the nine years from 1941 to 1949 inclusive, expenditure on agriculture development is estimated to have been close to £2.5 million. In the following nine-year period, 1950–1958 inclusive, the level of expenditure increased very rapidly, totalling £18.8 million, a sixfold increase over the preceding nine years.[51]

Between 1948 and 1958 the first serious effort was made to introduce purely cash crops, such as cotton and Turkish tobacco.[52] Though a differential between the prices paid to Europeans and Africans remained, the lower prices were now paid in order to accumulate funds for the improvement of African agriculture. In 1961 a select committee recommended some purchase of European land for African use and the establishment of small unreserved areas where farmers of both races could buy land; and finally, at the congress of the United Federal Party in October 1962, Whitehead pledged himself to repeal the Land Apportionment Act in case of electoral victory for his party.

These attempts to accelerate the promotion of an African middle class and bourgeoisie were matched by reforms of the electoral system to enfranchise these classes. This enfranchisement had a double purpose: In the first place, it aimed at compensating the loss of votes by the white classes whose interests were bound to be encroached upon by the very emergence of the African middle class and bourgeoisie.[53] Secondly, it aimed at preventing the latter from becoming "agitators" by siding with the peasantry and the proletariat.[54]

It remains to examine the political implications of the formation of the African proletariat. The problem here was the stabilization of the proletariat, because the high rate of turnover associated with migratory labor retarded specialization within the manufacturing sector. This stabilization, which as early as 1943 was deemed necessary by "several industrialists," [55] had an urban and a rural aspect. In fact it implied the severing of the ties linking peasantry and proletariat, something which, in turn, had two implications. In the first place, a rise in the minimum wage in urban areas and mining locations would become necessary in order to put the workers in a position to support, even at bare subsistence, their families in the towns. However, such a policy ran against the interests of the white agrarian bourgeoisie; in 1943 a senior official of the

Native Affairs Department warned the Howman Committee, inquiring into the matter, that if a minimum wage was introduced in the towns "you are bound to have repercussions amongst the farming community and today the farming community rules this country, so that flattens out the minimum wage straight away." [56]

The second implication of urban stabilization was that the traditional system of land tenure in the rural areas ought to be abandoned in order to remove the right of free access to land for urban Africans. Here too, the interests of manufacturing and white agrarian bourgeoisies conflicted. The interests of the former were voiced in the Legislative Assembly by Todd (at the time a government backbencher): "We do not want native peasants. We want the bulk of them working in the mines and farms and in the European areas and we could absorb them and their families." If 100,000 families moved from the rural areas, "we can begin to cope with what is left . . . and give each family 150 or 200 acres on a 99-year lease." [57] In other words, it was necessary to substitute an African agrarian bourgeoisie and proletariat for the peasantry but the change was bound to bring about greater competition for the European farmers and therefore conflicted with their class interests. The Land Husbandry Act (1951) represents a compromise between these conflicting interests. A money value was attached to farming rights which were granted to all individuals who were cultivators at the time. The rights expired on the individual's death and their transferability was limited. Thus the privilege of free access to land for urban Africans was removed, but at the same time the growth of an African agrarian bourgeoisie was prevented.

This wave of "capitalist reforms" failed conspicuously. The amendment of the Industrial Conciliation Act recommended by the select committee was not accepted, and the bill which was finally enacted was much less "revolutionary"; neither were the recommendations of the 1961 select committee on land apportionment accepted. Though progress was made in African education, it fell short of expectations and, particularly, of what was being done for Europeans. In agriculture more competition between Europeans and Africans had been introduced, but this was done in the less profitable markets.[58] Similarly, though government expenditure in African agriculture had grown, a dual standard was still applied to the two racial communities.

The ruling United Federal Party (UFP) lost the December 1962 election and the Land Apportionment Act was therefore never repealed. This electoral defeat of the UFP was itself the consequence of another, possibly the major, failure of the reformist program, the failure to achieve the aims pursued with the enfranchisement of the African middle class and petty bourgeoisie.

At the root of this total failure were a number of inconsistencies inherent in the reforms themselves. First and foremost was the fact that the new policies encroached upon the interests of those very classes on which manufacturing capitalism and its political counterpart still relied heavily, both economically and politically. As a consequence, government actions were continuously hampered by its dependence on the ruling party's rank and file and on the electorate. Such a dependence explains the abortive nature of the reforms which, in turn, accounts for the failure to encourage the growth of a sizable African middle class and bourgeoisie. The ensuing frustration induced these classes, condemned to remain a negligible economic force, to side with the peasantry and the proletariat whose grievances were also fostered by the contradictory policies of the 1950s.

A compromise between the conflicting interests of the white classes (of manufacturing and agrarian capitalism in particular) was attempted, as in the 1930s, at the expense of the Africans. The main example of this compromise is certainly the Land Husbandry Act. Labor stabilization was pursued through the stabilization of the peasantry, but no urban counterpart of the policy (such as guaranteeing the subsistence of the *family* of the workers in the towns) was envisaged to guarantee the interests of the white farmers and workers. The "deal" which might have been possible in the 1930s was bound, in the 1950s, to set up strong reactions on the part of the Africans whose political consciousness had greatly increased. In fact the reaction was such as to make the government discontinue the implementation of the act. On the other hand, the resistance to the implementation of the act strengthened the African nationalist movement, which was joined by the African bourgeoisie and middle class frustrated in their growth.[59]

These developments within African ranks brought about firm acts of suppression on the part of the government, and at the same time brought even closer the interests of manufacturing and international capitalism in accelerating the formation of an African middle class and bourgeoisie. When this "acceleration" was attempted in the early 1960s, the result was a polarization of white workers, agrarian and petty bourgeoisie, around the reactionary Rhodesian Front Party which obtained power with the elections of December 1962.

Recent Political Developments

We have seen that in the 1930s a class structure which had its center of gravity in a *national* agrarian bourgeoisie found expression in an institutional framework which meant (1) the division of the economy into largely noncompeting racial groups, (2) the continuously decreasing productivity of the African peasantry, and (3) government intervention to foster economic development through industrialization. The framework was internally inconsistent since a stagnant home demand for manufactures could not foster industrialization. It was also "unstable" because of the formation of a proletariat which would alter the class structure.

World War II, the postwar shortage of dollars and the increasing demand for raw materials, the outflow of capital from the United Kingdom and South Africa, and the creation of the Federation, continuously increased external demand. This tendency, which could have led merely to inflation, was instead exploited by the government to foster economic growth. Development accelerated the rise of the African proletariat, altered the pattern of foreign investment in the country, and, above all, brought about the emergence of manufacturing capitalism which became the new "center of gravity" of the class structure. These changes resulted in strong pressures to remove the institutional framework of the 1930s. Greater interracial competition, stabilization of the proletariat, and creation of an African middle class constituted the new ideology. A wave of reforms ensued. But these reforms failed because they set up "centrifugal reactions" which culminated in the seizure of power by the white workers, the *national* agrarian capitalists and petty bourgeoisie, who all rallied around the Rhodesian Front Party. These developments of the 1950s and early 1960s in Rhodesia were strikingly similar to what happened south of the Limpopo roughly a decade earlier.

Today there are three fundamental political questions to be asked:

1. Is a neocolonial solution possible in Rhodesia?
2. How can the seemingly absurd attempt of seizing independence unilaterally be explained?

3. Whither Rhodesia?

But before we turn to answer these questions, we need to adopt some interpretation of the behavior of the United Kingdom government *in colonial situations in general and in the Rhodesian situation in particular.* It seems a good working hypothesis to trace the rationale of its behavior in the interest of *large-scale international capitalism* (or British capitalism whenever a conflict of interests arises). If this assumption is accepted, the granting of independence to African territories can be explained as a strategy to retain economic power (i.e., to guarantee the interests of foreign capital) by concessions, in the political sphere, to the indigenous middle classes. This is the so-called neocolonial policy, the failures and successes of which need not be examined here. The creation of conditions favorable to the formation of an indigenous middle class has undoubtedly been one of the most general characteristics of the pre-independence periods in colonial countries. In the Rhodesian context, as we have illustrated in previous sections, the affinity of the interests of the African middle class and those of large-scale capitalism can explain the series of reforms attempted during the Federal period, a corollary of which was the development of the African middle class itself. This affinity of interests, however, is not absolute. If the advantages to be derived from the development of an African middle class are offset by the reactions of other classes, then the interest of large-scale capitalism in such development fades away and a policy of "second best" will probably emerge. The meaning of this will emerge in our discussion of prospects for a "neocolonial" solution to the Rhodesian problem.

In other African countries the development of an indigenous middle class was and is relatively easy, either because no class with an interest in resisting its emergence existed, or because those classes that had such an interest had no sufficient political and/or economic power to organize themselves successfully and because the economic and political role to be played by the nascent class was to varying extents unsophisticated. In Rhodesia this was and is problematic. Here there is a vicious circle stemming from the cause-effect relationship between control of political power by the white settler and insignificance of the African middle class. The former induces the latter which in turn prevents the growth of a nationalist movement suitable for a solution of the "neocolonialist" type. Hence large-scale capitalism (and the British government) are in a weak position vis-à-vis the white workers and petty bourgeoisie, who are thus enabled to consolidate their power position in the political as well as economic sphere. The circle is closed.

This vicious circle explains the fading away of the reformist attitude of large-scale capitalism and the British government in the three years between the end of 1962 and the end of 1965. During this period a series of political setbacks (the advent to power of the RF at the end of 1962, Field's resignation in April 1964, Welensky's electoral defeat in October 1964, the referendum on independence in November 1964, the general election of May 1965) marked the retreat of the upholders of reform and the consolidation in power of the Rhodesian Front and the classes it represents. The advent to power of the Rhodesian Front can be interpreted as an attempt to halt the wave of reforms of the Federal period, and, in particular, the process of constitutional advancement which was a necessary condition for such reforms. After a period of transition (ending in April 1964 when Smith became prime minister) the long-drawn-out *threat* of UDI and the tightening of the repressive machinery against the African nationalist movement proved to be most effective in reversing the political evolution from reforms to reaction. There was a return of the ideology and policies of the pre-Federal period. By means of mass arrests and restrictions the government was able to wipe the leadership of the African nationalist movement from the political scene. The relative ease with which the Rhodesian Front government succeeded in disrupting (at least temporarily) the organization of the nationalist movement cannot be explained as is often done, especially by leaders of other African countries and in "liberal" circles, in terms of some inherent shortcoming of the Rhodesian African leadership as compared with the leadership of other African movements. A far more realistic explanation can be provided by the observation that the organization of the movement had, in the late 1950s and early 1960s, been shaped on the same pattern as that generally adopted in other African nationalist movements. This pattern showed a general bias in favor of securing power either by constitutional means (participation in elections, agitation and propaganda, lobbying and pressure group activities, etc.) or, if unconstitutional means were adopted, by nonviolent action (refusal to pay taxes, strikes, etc.). This type of strategy and related party structure and organization have undoubtedly proved successful in most African countries where, as suggested above, the socioeconomic formation (i.e., economic base and superstructure) was such that the groups controlling political power were willing and able to transfer it to the African middle class. In these countries the granting of independence was as much, if not more, the outcome of external circumstances as it was the result of the independence struggle waged by the nationalist movements. We have seen, on the other hand, that the classes controlling power in Rhodesia have altogether different class interests, i.e., the prevention of the growth of an African middle class and of a "neocolonialist" solution is the very objective of their rule. *It was the inadequacy of the African nationalist party as an underground revolutionary movement suitable to cope with this kind of superstructure that contributed to its repression.* The Rhodesian Front government, in the year preceding UDI, set up an effective repressive machinery and thereby hampered considerably the functioning of the African nationalist party as a nonviolent movement. The significance of this achievement is that *it deprived the British government and the reformist groups of an alternative to the settlers' rule* and, what is even more important, *it hampered the growth of an African threat* which might have counterbalanced the UDI threat that accompanied the repression of the African nationalist movement.

UDI obviously expresses, in the ideological sphere, the interests of the classes represented by the ruling party. These interests were threatened by a possible political alliance of large-scale foreign capitalism and of the African middle class and petty bourgeoisie. UDI was brandished as the only way to eliminate the possibility of such an alliance. It was, therefore, directed as much against large-scale capitalism as against the Africans. The populist undertones of the UDI campaign were very noticeable. The effect of the UDI threat was to force the British government to realize that in *Rhodesia,* as opposed to the normal colonial territory, it had no viable substitute solution for settlers' rule. UDI, in other words, was a threat to bring the issue of "settlers" government versus neocolonialist solution into the open. In this sense the issue both crystallized the class consciousness of the majority of the white population, clinching the political power of the RF, and intimidated the British government and related interests into renouncing the reformist program and constitutional advancement up to 1965.

But if it is true that the *threat* of UDI, combined with the repression of the African nationalist movement, was enough to consolidate the status quo and to divert the possibility of reforms, what induced the RF government actually to *implement* UDI?

Many reasons can be found, but at the present stage of documentation none is per se convincing. All we can do is to list a number of possible motives; any attempt to assign weights to these possibilities may be misleading.

A first reason may be traced in the African unrest in the rural areas adduced by Lardner-Burke (the Rhodesian Minister of Law and Order) in order to justify the declaration of a state of emergency over the whole country, which was the prelude to UDI. It is not possible to judge to what extent African unrest really threatened a breakdown of law and order since too little of what has been happening over the last year or two in the African rural areas and townships has leaked out through the Rhodesian and foreign press. But if sufficiently widespread unrest had persisted within the African population it is quite possible that the RF government feared that, notwithstanding the strict security measures, the internal situation might explode, upsetting the delicate balance of threats and counterthreats upon which the preservation of the status quo rested.

A second reason is that the threat of UDI was wearing out both as a catalyst of class solidarity and as an instrument of intimidation. Some African leaders north of the Zambezi were already voicing (for example at the Commonwealth Prime Ministers' Conference in London at the end of June 1965) the idea that UDI was merely a device to divert attention from more fundamental issues, viz., African constitutional advancement. It may be, therefore, that in want of a substitute for the UDI threat, which was becoming an empty one, the RF government decided to implement it.

The relationship between economic base and superstructure is always one of mutual interdependence. The superstructure can influence the economic base by conditioning the behavior of the members of the various classes. If this is accepted, it is possible that UDI, having been embodied in the ideology of the ruling classes, came to be regarded by the rank and file of the RF not as an instrument of intimidation vis-à-vis the reformist groups, and of propaganda in fostering class solidarity within the white population, but as a real solution of the contradictions inherent in the Rhodesian society. Remembering the high degree of control exercised by the rank and file of the RF over the ruling elite, it is reasonable to conclude that the pressure exercised by the former probably represented a powerful spur for the latter to declare independence unilaterally.

The realism of these three assumptions increases once they are seen in the light of yet another possible explanation. That is, the RF government may have considered that conditions were particularly favorable for the success of the operation. There were no alternatives to white settlers' rule acceptable to the British government and related interests; class consciousness of the white classes was high; and both conditions had been reinforced by the Rhodesian government's policies. In order to assess whether or not the expectations of the RF government were misplaced we must discuss the nature and the chances of success of the retaliatory action undertaken by the British government. But, whether UDI succeeds or not (in the sense to be discussed below), it is difficult to deny that it was a "fair bet."

Let us first examine the chances of success of the retaliatory action undertaken by the British government. In assessing the success of this action what really matters is not so much *the extent to which economic sanctions will hit the Rhodesian economy* but rather *the existence of a mechanism whereby economic hardship (whatever its intensity) can induce the emergence of a political alternative* acceptable to those classes or groups which directly or indirectly share political power in Rhodesia, namely the settlers and the British government. What is acceptable to the British government is determined by a set of circumstances which are largely exterior to the Rhodesian situation; they concern British domestic politics and Britain's international relations in general and in Africa in particular. At any event, we may assume in the first place that what is acceptable to the British government is some program of reforms aimed at the development of an African middle class to whom power could *ultimately* (say, in five to six years' time) be transferred according to the traditional pattern followed in granting independence to colonial territories. For the white Rhodesians, on the other hand, UDI has represented an attempt to perpetuate those restrictions on competition which are at the root of their privileged economic and political position. Reforms aimed at promoting the development of an African middle class will lead to increased African competition in the produce, retail, and skilled labor markets. African advancement would mean a progressive erosion of their social status and of the premium they enjoy over wages and general

working conditions in Britain, South Africa, and other white Commonwealth countries—because it would induce substitution of African for
white workers and/or because it would eliminate those restrictions on
the supply of their (real or imaginary) skills from which that premium
originates. White workers, petty bourgeoisie, and most of the agrarian
capitalists are aware that their socioeconomic position *as classes* is based
on their control of the political machinery. If and when they think that
such control cannot be maintained indefinitely (that is, under present
circumstances, that UDI has failed) they will prepare themselves to
leave the country.

It is unrealistic to expect the majority of the white Rhodesians to cooperate in bringing about those conditions which would force them to
relinquish their present political and economic power. Thus if white unemployment is induced by these sanctions, all the white unemployed
can be expected to do is either to emigrate or to put pressure on the
party leadership to step up unproductive activities (army, police, civil
service, etc.) in order to absorb them, and to subsidize or force capitalists
to keep them in employment. (Of course, such a situation would be un-
tenable in the long run, but as argued below, the long-run effects of
sanctions are to a large extent irrelevant.) Other classes within the white
population—manufacturing capitalists, some professional groups, and in
general all those who are not vulnerable to African competition—are
not directly opposed to African advancement. These classes, however,
cannot possibly be organized politically in opposition to the present rulers for two main reasons.

In the first place they are numerically insignificant and, though they
retain a crucial position in the economic structure of society, their *economic* power cannot be translated into *political* opposition because of the
high degree of class consciousness of the overwhelming majority of the
electorate. The second reason is probably more fundamental. Though
these classes are not directly threatened by African competition, their
economic functions are tied to a certain economic base in the sense that
the possibility of finding an outlet for their products and services is
highly dependent on the given composition and level of demand, which,
in turn, is determined by the existing class structure. Though a gradual
removal of the shackles on competition would benefit them by improving market conditions in both factors and products market, any major
and especially any *sudden* change in the economic base would seriously

endanger their economic position. Under conditions of fast economic development such as obtained in the 1950s, relatively minor reforms were easily smuggled into the superstructure and manufacturing capitalism (and related interests) could play an important political role. As economic growth slowed down, population growth outstripping the growth of production, class conflicts hardened, and reforms became impracticable. Under these new circumstances the alternative to the status quo became a radical, revolutionary change of the superstructure but, for the reasons just mentioned, the former was and is preferable to the latter for those groups who had attempted the reformist programs. It follows that a solution of this type cannot be implemented without the prior removal from political power of the white settlers (which can only be achieved through military intervention and subsequent direct rule), since it cannot be expected to be brought about from within the system.

If military intervention and subsequent direct rule are not considered viable in London, then we must assume that, provided some face-saving device is available, the British government is prepared to meet the "minimum" acceptable to the ruling classes in Rhodesia. This "minimum" is the indefinite continuation of their control over the political machinery, which can be brought about essentially in two ways. In the first place, there can be a gradual consolidation of the regime in the political sphere, even though the economic hardship caused by sanctions increases—at least temporarily. Irrespective of the degree of contraction of the economy, what matters most from the regime's point of view is to last long enough, say a year or two after the declaration, to consolidate itself politically to such an extent that, even if sanctions have not been formally relaxed, loopholes will be more easily found. Furthermore, one can also assume that given a long enough period, a certain readjustment in the pattern of trade and production would take place. One can expect a switch (at least partial) in productive processes which would lessen the economic dependence on Britain and other "hostile" countries, increasing the economy's self-sufficiency and/or dependence on the South African economy. Given the absence within the system of any mechanism that can translate *economic* hardship into *political* opposition to UDI, only British military intervention can stop this consolidation. A commitment against such intervention can only mean its tacit acceptance.

The acceptance may even be negotiated. It is clear that the Rhodesian rulers are prepared to make concessions (constitutional or otherwise) provided they are left in control of the political machinery. Whatever the constitutional arrangements, it would then be possible to control administratively, economically, and socially, the political evolution of the system—ultimately reverting to an apartheid system of one sort or another consistent with the class interests of white workers, petty bourgeoisie, and agrarian capitalists. Any sign of success of the "talks about talks" between British and Rhodesian civil servants, at present (June 1966) being held in Salisbury, would therefore seem to point to a negotiated, rather than tacit, acceptance of the trend toward apartheid in Rhodesia.

To sum up, the ability of sanctions to impose economic hardship on the white population should not be denied. Given sufficient determination on the part of the British and Zambian governments, such hardship can be increased at will; there is a limit, of course, determined by the resilience of the economy and the determination—difficult to assess correctly—of the South African government to keep Rhodesia under white settlers' control. What must be questioned is the belief that such hardship will bring about political change in the sense of accepting ultimate African rule. Since it ignores the economic base and superstructure (and especially their interdependence) of the Rhodesian social system, this belief is based on naive analysis. On the other hand, if it is accepted that political change in the desired direction cannot be produced from within the Rhodesian social system, ultimately the British government will have either to intervene militarily in order to produce the change from without, or gradually to accept the status quo. If the first alternative is chosen, it is not clear why military intervention was not carried out in the first place when UDI was declared. Even if the main obstacle was British public opinion, there is no reason to expect this obstacle to disappear. What is more important is that the passing of time is not going to improve the prospects of a bloodless intervention, and this for two main reasons. In the first place a certain confusion of interests was bound to exist in the top and middle ranks of the army, police, judiciary, and civil service when UDI was declared. These were in fact inherited by the RF government from the Federal period and to some extent must have retained the "liberal" characteristics of the previous rule. At the time of UDI the presence of a British armed force could have made the choice between "treason" and "loyalty" a real and not merely a theoretical one, as in effect it became. In the absence of such force the crucial choice was, and is, between supporting the status quo and resigning. As a result of delaying action on the part of the British government, these groups will be increasingly committed to the Smith regime, both through increased commitment of the individuals and through a process of selection and substitution which inevitably accompanies promotions, recruitment, and resignations. From this point of view, therefore, the increased commitment to the regime of the administrative and military apparatus can only reduce the chances of a swift, and possibly bloodless, seizure of power by Britain. Moreover, of course, anti-British feelings among white Rhodesians have hardened since UDI and the introduction of sanctions. These feelings are an expression, in the ideological sphere, of the class consciousness of white Rhodesians. As such they have perfectly rational roots, but they may easily develop emotionally into an autonomous element capable in itself of influencing the behavior of the party's rank and file, the ruling elite and the white population at large.

If the assumption of naivete on the part of the British government is not thought to be satisfactory, then the conclusion must be drawn that British government and related interests accept the prospect of Rhodesia ultimately resorting to apartheid.

One crucial question has been left out of the discussion so far: the prospects for an African revolution. Can we expect an African revolution to halt the trend toward an apartheid society—which, as we have seen, may be the result of the British government's Rhodesian policy? There are two problems here. What are the chances that an insurrectionary movement will gather momentum? If it did, how would it influence the trend of events outlined above?

Notwithstanding the severe security measures taken by the government, outbursts of violence have already occurred in Salisbury and in some rural areas in the northern and eastern parts of the country. The regime, while disclosing acts of violence due to infiltrators from outside the country, has tried its best, often successfully, to conceal any violent activity originating within the country. Whether these activities will gather momentum is difficult to say. The disproportion of forces—in weapons, organization, training, etc.—between the two sides is enormous, being itself a reflection of the class structure of the system. Geographically the country is land-locked and except in the north is surrounded by countries more or less sympathetic to the regime.[60] There are no jungles or mountainous areas except on the borders (the region being a plateau, generally from 4,000 to 5,000 feet, above sea level, enclosed by the Lowveld of the Zambezi and Limpopo valleys to the north and south respectively). What is more important, the Land Apportionment Act, besides its political-economic effects, has segregated the Africans in such a way that they can be "sealed-off" from the white communities in the urban areas, enhancing the security of the latter. All these factors are handicaps in the organization of revolutionary activity in Rhodesia. Furthermore Rhodesia (with South Africa) represents the unique situation of a society where, almost literally, all the top and middle ranks of the army, police, civil service, etc., are occupied by the ruling classes who are easily identified by the color of their skin. Moreover, some units of the armed forces consist exclusively of members of the dominant classes. This factor rules out the possibility of the ruling classes being ousted by any form of coup d'état and makes protracted guerrilla warfare of the traditional type unlikely to succeed in directly toppling the regime.

Presumably this is consciously or subconsciously realized by the African population. Unless it lapses into resignation, its widespread discontent will be channeled into terrorist activities.[61] Assuming that the organization of the nationalist movement is being restructured in this sense, a *tendency* for widespread terrorism will most certainly develop with the steady increase (worsened by sanctions) of unemployment.

It is of course possible that such activities could come just at the "right time," adding insecurity to economic hardship, transforming the "creeping" emigration of whites into a "galloping" one, and then setting up a cumulative process of violence and economic hardship the outcome of which is uncertain: intervention from the south, intervention from the north, British or U.N. intervention, a combination of these—or no intervention at all.

Notes

1. *Report of the Urban African Affairs Commission* (Salisbury, 1958), p. 4.
2. R. Gray, *The Two Nations* (London, 1960), p. 13.
3. M. Yudelman, *Africans on the Land* (London, 1964), p. 141.

4. W. J. Barber, *The Economy of British Central Africa* (London, 1961), pp. 119–22, and L. H. Gann and M. Gelfand, *Huggins of Rhodesia* (London, 1964), p. 175.

5. Middle class and bourgeoisie (or capitalist class) are distinguished by the fact that the former consists of white-collar employees or self-employed professional men, whereas the latter is formed by employers of labor for the purpose of profit. The members of the petty bourgeoisie are characterized by the fact that though employers of labor they themselves provide part of the manual labor.

6. M. Yudelman, op. cit., pp. 12–13, 132–33; Barber, op. cit., p. 46.

7. *Report of the Mangwende Reserve Commission of Enquiry* (Salisbury, 1961), pp. 18, 37.

8. By proletariat is here understood the class of modern wage laborers who, having no means of production of their own, are reduced to selling their labor-power in order to live. This definition is, however, too broad and must be qualified to exclude the middle class. Such a distinction is unnecessary, and indeed impossible, at a high level of abstraction when labor is defined as a homogeneous quantity, i.e., as abstract labor. In the present analysis, however, this would be an oversimplification preventing a correct assessment of the class structure. The proletariat will therefore include only manual and semi-skilled labor. The distinction has its rationale in the fact that the middle class sells its labor in a seller's market, or at any rate in conditions less unfavorable to the seller than is the case for the proletariat.

9. Gann and Gelfand, op. cit., p. 79.

10. By overhead capital will be understood such basic economic facilities as transport and communications, water, power, marketing facilities, and (stretching the definition a little) heavy industry.

11. The conditions of demand on the export markets as opposed to the sales on such markets (which depend also on the supply conditions within the system) were (and are) exogenous to the system and as such irrelevant to our present purpose.

12. Gray, op. cit., p. 159.

13. Ibid., p. 269.

14. C. Leys, *European Politics in Southern Rhodesia* (Oxford, 1959), p. 10.

15. Gann and Gelfand, op. cit., pp. 175–76.

16. For the effects of continuous cultivation over African agriculture, see K. Brown, *Land in Southern Rhodesia* (London, 1959), pp. 6–10. Also *Second Report of the Select Committee on Resettlement of Natives*.

17. It is therefore assumed that a historical and social element (besides a physical element) enters into the determination of what is socially accepted as subsistence income and consumption. For a discussion of the meaning of "subsistence," see Maurice Dobb, *Wages* (Cambridge, 1959).

18. Recruitment of labor outside Southern Rhodesia was certainly one of the major factors in determining both the rise and distribution among sectors of the total African labor force.

19. Gray, op. cit., p. 154.

20. Guest was the head of the Department of Air, set up in 1940. Gann and Gelfand, op. cit., p. 153.

21. C. H. Thompson and H. W. Woodruff, *Economic Development in Rhodesia and Nyasaland* (London, 1954), p. 20.

22. Barber, op. cit., p. 131.

23. The yearly average of European net immigration, which was less than 800 between 1921 and 1946, shot up to more than 7,000 in 1946–1956.

24. For the reasons for, and characteristics of, the outflow of capital from the United Kingdom see M. Barratt-Brown, *After Imperialism* (London, 1963), chs. 7–8.

25. Gann and Gelfand, op. cit., p. 212.

26. L. Tow, *The Manufacturing Economy of Southern Rhodesia* (mimeo, Washington, 1960).

27. Thompson and Woodruff, op. cit., p. 173.

28. Central Statistical Office, *Report on the Results of the National Income and Balance of Payments of Northern Rhodesia, Nyasaland and Southern Rhodesia, 1954–63* (Salisbury, 1964). Also Thompson and Woodruff, op. cit., p. 173.

29. *Second Report*, op. cit., pp. 13, 51.

30. Evidence to the Howman Committee (1943). My italics.

31. Gray, op. cit., pp. 283–90.

32. J. van Velsen, "Trends in African Nationalism in Southern Rhodesia," in *Kroniek van Afrika* (Universitaire Pers Leiden, June 1964), pp. 146–47.

33. A leader of the African nationalist movement, G. Nyandoro, is reported to have said that the act had become "the best recruiter the African nationalists ever had."

34. Tow, op. cit., p. 17.

35. Barber, op. cit., p. 171.

36. Thompson and Woodruff, op. cit., p. 154.

37. *The Economist*, 7 October 1966, p. 55. Also J. Ziegler, *La Contre-révolution en Afrique* (Paris, 1963).

38. Tow, op. cit., p. 124; Ziegler, op. cit., p. 34. Also O. Guitand, *Les Rhodésies et le Nyasaland* (Paris, 1964), p. 60.

39. Tow, op. cit., p. 50.

40. *The Rhodesia Herald,* July 8, 1964.

41. The proportion of those who have direct *and* indirect interests (through South African subsidiaries) is certainly greater, but not easily ascertainable.

42. These are the conclusions I have tentatively reached from an examination of published material.

43. *Report on the Results*, op. cit., Table 4.
44. For the pattern of the European employment in 1951 see Leys, op. cit., pp. 81–82.
45. Barber, op. cit., p. 27, and pp. 23–24.
46. Gray, op. cit., p. 314.
47. Gann and Gelfand, op. cit., pp. 224–25. My italics.
48. It is significant that Todd obtained the premiership with the support of the "Action Group" formed by business and professional men.
49. Leys, op. cit., pp. 116–18.
50. Gray, op. cit., p. 207.
51. Yudelman, op. cit., p. 159.
52. Ibid., p. 240.
53. Leys, op. cit., pp. 225–29.
54. Ibid., p. 246.
55. Gray, op. cit., p. 227.
56. Ibid., p. 228.
57. Ibid., p. 299.
58. As mentioned earlier, African producers were almost completely prevented from taking advantage of the boom in tobacco exports.
59. For the political polarization of the 1950s in Southern Rhodesia, see van Velsen, op. cit., pp. 143–54.
60. The Zambian government, however, has so far impeded the flow of arms through its country.
61. The distinction between terrorism and guerrilla warfare is based on the fact that the latter is *mainly* directed against regular forces while the former is mainly directed against the civilian population.

8
FRELIMO and the
Mozambique Revolution

John S. Saul

The presentation of a fully adequate account of the nature of the Mozambique liberation struggle, and of the revolution which has sprung from that struggle, would be a major undertaking. It would require an analysis of how the present situation has emerged from the complex history of the area. It would also require that the struggle in Mozambique be set clearly in its broader context—both the immediate context of the Southern African complex taken as a whole, as well as that of the worldwide balance of forces. And considerable attention would have to be paid to the logistics of the military confrontation and to a more precise delineation of the considerable progress being made in that sphere by Mozambican freedom fighters. To present such an account is not the intention of this brief essay; its more modest objective is to attempt to learn something significant about Mozambique by focusing on the recent development of the Mozambique Liberation Front (FRELIMO), the movement which leads the resistance to Portuguese colonialism. This is important because the politics of FRELIMO have been much misunderstood: as I shall argue, the leadership crisis which surfaced in FRELIMO after Mondlane's untimely assassination in 1969 was a mark of the movement's *growing strength,* not of its weakness, as unsympathetic or uninformed observers have sometimes tended to assume. This focus is also important because the developments which have taken place inside FRELIMO—and, more broadly, within liberated Mozambique as a whole—have implications which must be taken seriously by all who are committed to the liberation of Southern Africa.

An earlier version of this essay was presented as a public lecture at the University of Lund, Sweden, in April 1970. It was substantially revised in 1972 for publication in this volume.

1. Nationalism and Revolution

The denouement of the African nationalism which came to power in the late 1950s and early 1960s has almost invariably been a mere Africanization of the existing colonial structures. A distinctive pattern of external dependence and domestic hierarchy has emerged in post-colonial Africa which has served to choke off development rather than to liberate productive forces and release human energies. The domestic attributes of this syndrome are by now familiar:

1. An educated elite, or petty bourgeoisie, controls the state, using it both to guarantee the neocolonial presence of international corporations and to gain privileged access to surpluses for themselves. Moreover, this group overlaps with a class of commercial Africans who are rising within the middle levels of the private sector (the "commanding heights" being the preserve of the international giants).

2. The mass of the population is, at worst, terrorized and repressed; at best, demobilized and manipulated with the sideshow of tribal, communal, and religious competition.

3. Political structures, whether they be those of one-party dominant systems or of outright military-cum-bureaucratic regimes, are primarily designed as instruments to facilitate such repression and/or manipulation in the interests of the newly dominant classes.

4. Official ideologies—the vaguest of "nationalisms," the most meaningless of "African socialisms"—serve primarily to rationalize and legitimatize just such exploitative relations within the system.[1]

These results were already prefigured in the nationalist movements themselves, as Fanon and Nyerere, among others, have emphasized. Fanon's analysis of "the pitfalls of national consciousness" and of "false decolonization" are, of course, well known. But Nyerere's less familiar approach to this reality is almost equally instructive, for he summarizes precisely those aspects of the inheritance from the nationalist phase which have had negative implications for post-colonial Africa: leaders who desired, first and foremost, to occupy the privileged positions of the former exploiters; masses sufficiently confused by the more simplistic nostrums of nationalism to see such Africanization as a significant accomplishment, and yet very soon to become disillusioned and apathetic; political organizations too exclusively geared to the straightforward demands of nationalism and therefore destined to "lose support and . . .

atrophy"; ideologies which easily degenerated into "racialism" (Nyerere's term) and mere black nationalism, providing no real defense against the underlying structures of capitalist exploitation. Being thus as aware of the ambiguities of nationalist assertion as of its very real achievements, Nyerere can only conclude:

> It is comparatively easy to get independence from a colonial power—especially one which claims to base its national morality on the principles of freedom and democracy. Everyone wants to be free, and the task of the nationalist is simply to rouse the people to a confidence in their own power of protest. But to build the real freedom which socialism represents is a very different thing. It demands a positive understanding and positive actions, not simply a rejection of colonialism and a willingness to cooperate in non-cooperation. *And the anti-colonial struggle will almost certainly have intensified the difficulties.*[2]

Here and there in independent Africa steps are being taken to challenge this pattern. In Tanzania, for example, Nyerere and his colleagues have made some real effort to break out of the impasse of conventional nationalism and increasingly to expose and remedy the contradictions which are masked by this inheritance; it is a difficult task, as Nyerere is well aware and as I have had occasion to document elsewhere,[3] though it is not perhaps an impossible one. In any case, the problems of post-colonial Africa are not the immediate subject matter of this essay. Rather our focus is upon the nature of insurgent nationalism as it finds expression in the struggle to liberate Mozambique. And here we enter a world very different from that described by Nyerere, whose descriptions are in fact applicable to most of the rest of Africa. Of course, the struggle in Mozambique (as elsewhere in Southern Africa) is immediately distinguished by the nature of the colonial resistance to nationalist aspirations there, and by the strategies of sustained military confrontation which must, of necessity, be adopted. But this kind of struggle also detonates other processes which reshape the pattern of nationalism into a new mold and dictate, *in the nationalist phase itself,* an attempt to restructure social, economic, and political relationships in a fundamental way. This is what is happening in Mozambique; the conventional denouement of African nationalism becomes increasingly unthinkable as more and more fundamental choices are forced upon the people in the very course of waging their struggle. The result, in all likelihood, will be not merely national liberation, but a social revolution.

2. *The Logic of Protracted Struggle*

One crucial point must be made at the outset: all those features characteristic of the brand of nationalism which has facilitated false decolonization elsewhere on the continent have been present in the Mozambican context. Take, first, the danger of elitist and entrepreneurial dominance both of the institutional expressions of nationalism and of the structures of the newly independent country (in this case, within the liberated areas of Mozambique). Inside FRELIMO there has been a continuing problem of coping with the demands of educated elements. Many educated Mozambicans abroad have been reluctant to return to take up positions in the ranks of a people's struggle, and have preferred instead to snipe at the organization from outside. Closer to home, the "educated" have often been equally intransigent about integrating themselves effectively with the masses, lured by inflated expectations of reward for their services and the example of their privileged counterparts in independent Africa. Such reactionary members of the petty bourgeoisie have been the backbone of the conservative line within the movement from the outset. And they have been joined by others who saw independence primarily as an opportunity for mere entrepreneurial aggrandizement and the consolidation of their own personal power. We shall observe this group in action in the new Mozambique in the following section.

The mass of the Mozambican population has suffered from many of the same disabilities, for revolutionary purposes, which characterize the African peasantry generally: a profound parochialism, for example, and an only slowly dawning awareness of the broader meaning of exploitation. Of course, the particularly brutal nature of Portuguese colonialism over the centuries, and of the repression of recent years, has rendered exploitation more graphic than in many other parts of the continent. But the danger that resistance to a vaguely perceived exploitation may take on a merely ethnic or regionalist expression remains real. Moreover, Mozambique has been no exception to the rule that to a significant degree the politicization of ethnicity in Africa springs from the manipulations of opportunistic elements of the leadership who thus turn ethnic competition to their own uses.

The latter is, in any case, only one way in which a conservative petty bourgeoisie can seek to instrumentalize and demobilize the masses in the service of its own self-aggrandizement. In fact, a liberation movement can provide its own particular variation on this theme. FRELIMO's experience demonstrates that such elements will find themselves much more at ease with the intra-elite infighting of exile politics than with trusting their political fates to the less predictable and less easily controlled will of the newly mobilized masses in the liberated areas. The military line of such a group parallels this preference; when combined with nostalgia for the relatively easy ride to power of petty-bourgeois leaderships elsewhere in Africa, the basic distrust of the masses and of a genuine release of energies leads to a putschist approach to the necessary armed confrontation with intransigent colonialism. Finally, a familiar ideological construct locks all these components into place: thus certain elements within FRELIMO have advanced a nationalism which asks no basic structural questions about the nature of the society being brought into being, and a racialism which ignores the broader meaning of exploitation in the interests of a mere Africanization of existing structures.

From the point of view of conservative members of the petty-bourgeois leadership of the Mozambican independence struggle there has been just one flaw in all this: in the context of a genuine liberation struggle this kind of nationalism, quite literally, *does not work* as it did for African leadership groups elsewhere on the continent. On the contrary, for such a struggle to be waged successfully the energies of the masses *must* be released in a new way, the leadership *must* link its fortunes to the masses more effectively, and the imperialist enemy *must* be defined and confronted more meaningfully. In fact, once set in motion the reality of protracted struggle has increasingly imposed its own logic upon the Mozambican liberation movement.

What are the crucial dimensions of this "logic" of protracted struggle in Mozambique? We will sketch them only briefly here, though they are attested to in the publications of FRELIMO and, even more convincingly perhaps, in the eyewitness accounts of a number of visitors to the liberated areas of Mozambique in recent years.[4] Most important has been the need to close the gap between the leadership—a potential elite —and the mass of the peasantry, the need to evolve methods of work which render the contradiction between these two elements nonantagonistic and which promise to resolve it in a cumulatively progressive manner.

A number of items are relevant here. First, given the fact of Portugal's reprisals and its calculated destruction of much of the established infrastructure of economic and social life in areas where its military hold has faltered, entirely new institutions and programs have had to be begun in the liberated areas in the spheres of health, education, trade, and the like. Even day-to-day village life has been reorganized when villages were regrouped in more sheltered areas to minimize the dangers of direct attack, great efforts being made to render agricultural activities, in particular, safe and secure. Moreover, in the classic manner of guerrillas, FRELIMO combatants must be able to move freely from village to village without fear of betrayal; under such circumstances the peasantry has had to become the military units' active partners in struggle. As the existence of a secure military backdrop for penetration further south has become imperative, so the population has also been reorganized into an actual militia behind the front lines—this in spite of the severe constraint represented by a continuing shortage of firearms. A growing body of evidence suggests that each of these advances has begun to be effected as FRELIMO has consolidated its military advance. The most important implication of such a pattern is equally clear: that such advances involve something much more than "a rejection of colonialism and a willingness to cooperate in non-cooperation." On the contrary, they demand from the people "a positive understanding and positive actions." The knot of neocolonialism is being untied even at this very early stage.

Secondly, such a struggle has forced a deepening of national consciousness. What has been stated earlier concerning the inadequacy of certain varieties of "nationalisms" in Africa should not be taken to imply that national consciousness is unimportant: quite the opposite is the case. As noted, there is a potential for self-defeating divisiveness inherent in the realities of ethnic and cultural diversity which characterize every African territory. In addition, one of the main instruments of colonial oppression, not least in Portuguese Africa, was to "divide and rule" by means of intensifying such divisions. Under these circumstances, an achieved national identity represents a considerable accomplishment. It is therefore particularly important to affirm that a struggle like that in Mozambique actually *deepens* the meaning of such a national identity; it does not in any way by-pass it. Cadres and guerrillas must be able to move easily into regions very far from their homes; tribesmen in one region must continue to appreciate that theirs is an involvement in a more long-range, territory-wide struggle even after their own immediate geographical corner has been liberated; others, beyond the front lines, must see that the struggle in the far north is more than just the tribal outburst the Portuguese would have them believe it to be. Such a nationalism cannot be some lowest common denominator masking a transitory alliance of tribally based notables. Not surprisingly, therefore, the spokesmen for the most militant line among the Mozambican leadership have responded with alacrity to this imperative; they have been increasingly firm about distinguishing *revolutionary nationalism* from its less savory look-alikes, and communicating this distinction to the populace.

To do this is also to deprive the least progressive members of the petty bourgeoisie of one of their trumpcards—their manipulation of ethnic consciousness under the very umbrella of a vague and sloganized nationalism. Moreover the elite, *qua* elite, has been undermined in other ways by the dynamics of the struggle. Thus both the carving out of liberated areas and the concomitant involvement of the populace introduce dimensions which slowly but surely displace the world of exile politics. Those politicians who have based their power upon links with the notables of host governments or with fellow exiles in Dar es Salaam and Lusaka must transform their practice or find their preeminence passing to others more closely linked to novel political forces within the contested territory itself. The military also yields to this logic of guerrilla warfare. A military apparatus dependent upon its ties to a mass base must develop methods of work which ensure its popular touch even while it provides leadership and raises the level of consciousness of the masses; those who cannot make the transition to being members of a real people's army are quickly spotted. As a direct result, the style and commitment which characterize cadres, rather than mere functionaries, become the order of the day both in the political and the military spheres.

In Mozambique, FRELIMO has slowly adjusted to these imperatives, though not without certain very real difficulties and tensions to which we will return in the following section. As it has done so, its further practice has tended both to consolidate these advances and even to push their logic further. If the people have, in effect, demanded cadres rather than functionaries (and new exploiters) from a movement which lays claim to their "positive understanding and positive actions," so too the movement has taken concrete steps to forestall its own possible degeneration. As a *line,* we have seen this to involve a deepening of the connotations of nationalism. It has also meant a conscious assault on the seeds of privilege—an assault most dramatically exemplified in the restructuring of the educational system. After dismal experience with the first products of a quasi-liberated secondary school system at the Mozambique Institute in Dar es Salaam, the new school at Bagamoyo (in Tanzania) has provided an entirely different (and extremely impressive) model, as fundamentally work- and military-oriented as it is academic, with a selection and promotion system stressing both political and more formal criteria. The Bagamoyo school is in any case merely the further extension of a progressive primary school system which is mushrooming in the liberated areas. This system is quite specifically designed to fend off alienation and to turn skills to the service of the community; it is every bit as impressive as the Bagamoyo experiment (if equally constrained by lack of funds and equipment). In addition, what can only be described as a people's health system—again in sharp contrast to the standard postcolonial pattern of Africa—is being generated in these same liberated areas.

Other possible gaps between "leadership" and mass which arise in the economic sphere have also begun to be quite self-consciously preempted, the solution being collective economic structures like a cooperative-based, "state trading" network, and even the beginnings of some cooperative productive activities at the village level (e.g., the "FRELIMO fields"). Finally, and fundamentally, the institutionalization of structures of participation and genuine self-assertion by the mass of the population has proceeded apace, at the levels of the *cercle,* the locality, the district, and the province—this too in the interests of consolidating a people's struggle. Such developments are crucial to the effectiveness of the drive for liberation, of course, but it is worth noting that they have important implications as well for the kind of Mozambique which is emerging ineluctably from such a struggle.

Such a protracted struggle has an important educative impact as regards the international posture of a new Mozambique, and of the new Mozambicans. As the confrontation continues, the leadership as well as the mass of the population have had that much greater opportunity to become aware of the complicated network of imperialist forces which lock Portuguese hegemony into place; it is no accident that Museveni and others have found many peasants in Mozambique fully conversant with the intrigues of the NATO countries, for example.[5] Similarly, when arms and military advice, as well as other kinds of aid, are seen to come primarily from the socialist countries—and from those few progressive forces in the advanced capitalist countries that are committed to Southern African liberation—further stimulus is given to the crystallization of an anti-imperialist ideology in Mozambique. Indeed, it is on the ideological plane that one can see many of the advances we have discussed being registered. For the ideology of the progressive members of the petty bourgeoisie who have come to dominate FRELIMO is not merely anti-imperialist; in fact, it is, at least implicitly, increasingly socialist. Unlike their more conservative counterparts, such leaders have begun to cut through to the realities of exploitation per se in their formulations, and this awareness is also communicated to the people. Here, at the level of consciousness, is emerging a final guarantee that in Mozambique the nationalist struggle will be carried through to its "logical" conclusion.

These, then, are the terms of progress in Mozambique which have been witnessed and confirmed by a number of close observers of Mozambican realities. Obviously, further first-hand observation of the life of the liberated areas would make for an even more convincing analysis, but this is not something which, under the circumstances, can be easily realized. Fortunately, however, we need not leave the matter here, for there is a range of additional evidence which is much more immediately accessible. I refer to the most visible aspects of Mozambican politics as they have publicly revealed themselves. If one looks carefully at the tensions within FRELIMO itself in recent years, one can see clearly documented the record of a sea-change in the nature of the Mozambican struggle. These tensions are most readily explained in terms of the underlying pattern which we have been tracing, and, at the same time, they confirm that such a dramatic shift from conventional nationalism to revolutionary nationalism has in fact been taking place.

3. The Politics of FRELIMO

It will now be apparent that the relationship between the objective imperatives defined by the waging of such a successful liberation struggle and the political movement which comes to give institutional form to that struggle is a dialectical one of some complexity. As has happened in Zimbabwe, most members of the petty bourgeoisie can fail to make the leap from nationalist to revolutionary politics and in consequence the struggle is momentarily stalled, the dialectic is not set in motion.[6] Elsewhere, as in Mozambique, the logic of the struggle—of mass-line politics, social reconstruction, protracted warfare—imposes itself upon a growing number of the petty bourgeoisie, who feel no other choice is open to them but to commit "suicide as a class in order to be reborn as revolutionary workers, completely identified with the deepest aspirations of the people to which they belong." [7] Simultaneously, that group consolidates this advance organizationally and ideologically and is thus able to give further shape and direction to the positive forces unleashed by revolutionary struggle. Such a reciprocal process can then become a self-reinforcing one.

This advanced stage is not reached easily. For a movement like FRELIMO is, in reality, two entities for much of the early period of its existence: a conventional nationalist movement frustrated in achieving any easy transition to power, and a revolutionary movement struggling to be born. In the short run, this dichotomy between the two finds concrete expression in a struggle within the petty bourgeoisie, increasingly pitting those who are and those who are not prepared to make the transition to revolutionary practice against one another. Of course, as the struggle develops, and in the longer run, the masses themselves come to an ever greater degree to be the arbiters of this conflict; this too is one of the "benefits" of the horrors of guerrilla warfare. We shall see that both of these latter aspects have been present in Mozambique and that the political patterns of Mozambique and of FRELIMO reflect them clearly.

Ironically, the seeds of the subsequent division within the nationalist forces were already present at the very first moment of effective unity, the founding of FRELIMO in June 1962. The convention which brought together the then existing nationalist groupings—MANU, UDENAMO, UNAMI—was a reluctant marriage in many respects, in part the result of demands made by younger militants with more recent activist experience within Mozambique itself, in part of pressures from the Tanzanian government, host to several of these organizations. Indeed, it was the younger group which took the major initiative in drafting an initial and already quite progressive program for the new front in September 1962, "at the very moment when the established organizations were hesitating to place even their existing material possessions in a common pool for the benefit of the new movement." Small wonder that, as FRELIMO has recently admitted, "the causes which kept these organizations separate in the past—namely, tribalism, regionalism, lack of a clear and detailed set of goals and of agreed and relevant strategies —continued to exist" and that "the early days of FRELIMO were marred by mutual recriminations, expulsion, withdrawal, as between exile politicians who refused to give up the dead, futile in-fighting of an irrelevant brand of nationalist politics."[8]

Fortunately, the most obviously opportunist and irrelevant elements were the ones who split off, reconstituting in the process many of the organizations which had gone to make up FRELIMO, as well as several more. From this bewildering array of micro-parties there eventually emerged a second front, COREMO, based in Lusaka, which has been distinguished since its inception by its token membership and its almost total lack of activity. Not surprisingly, it has never been granted recognition as a meaningful liberation movement by the OAU Liberation Committee. On the other hand, FRELIMO, under the leadership of Eduardo Mondlane—a returned Mozambican academic of some distinction who was elected at the first congress as president primarily with the support of the younger, more militant elements referred to above—managed to strengthen its position, as much as a result of the various defections which characterized the first few years as in spite of them. By September 1964, when its first military units crossed the Ruvuma from Tanzania, FRELIMO was ready to launch armed struggle; the socio-military process described in the preceding section was thus set in motion.

The least adaptable elements within the original nationalist coalition had been cast aside, but this did not by any means ensure clear sailing for FRELIMO. In fact, the struggle within the petty bourgeoisie merely became more subtle in the succeeding period as, from 1964 to 1969, a fresh wave of tension built up. As hinted earlier, one aspect of this centered on the question of education broadly conceived, and particularly on the role of the proto-elite within the institutions of a free Mozambique. Confrontation with overseas graduates arose early and led, among other things, to the movement's instructing certain sources of American-based scholarships to cut off support for Mozambicans who were proceeding to second and third degrees; it was hoped in this way to force skilled nationals back into the struggle, after mere persuasion had failed. Such exemplary initiatives were not particularly successful, but it is the fact of these and other initiatives having been launched which helps account for the (quite unrepresentative) hostility of many elitist Mozambicans in the United States toward the FRELIMO leadership. However, the most important arenas of confrontation, as also noted earlier, were closer to home—and particularly at the Mozambique Institute, FRELIMO's center for post-primary education.

A key actor in this particular drama was a Mozambican Roman Catholic priest, Father Gwenjere. Many people now believe him to have been an agent provocateur acting on behalf of the Portuguese, and certainly he came to nationalism rather precipitately after an orthodox early career inside Mozambique itself. What is more clear is that, from mid-1967 when he left the territory and linked his fortunes to FRE-LIMO in Dar es Salaam, he inflamed elitist sentiments, particularly within the Mozambique Institute, encouraging students to expect scholarships for further studies and quite specifically advising that they resist the 1966 decision of FRELIMO's Central Committee that all such students spend at least a year inside Mozambique actively participating in the struggle after completing secondary school. To this was added the demand that the medium of instruction be English not Portuguese (English being, in effect, the language of scholarships!) and, manipulated equally demagogically, the demand that certain progressive white teachers at the Institute be sacked. This conflict escalated to the point of forcing temporary closure of the school. However, it also brought the censure of Gwenjere by FRELIMO in March 1968, and his eventual removal from the movement (though not before he had stirred up members of the long-standing community of non-FRELIMO Mozambicans in Dar es Salaam to stage a raid on the office of FRELIMO during which a Central Committee member was killed). Even more importantly, perhaps, these events stimulated an intensification of those efforts, referred to in the preceding section, to restructure the education system of the new Mozambique. Meanwhile the political reverberations of these incidents continued to be felt within the movement well into the following year.

A second arena of tension developed during this period which also involved the broadest kinds of structural implications, though it too centered most graphically around the person of a single man, Mzee Lazaro Kavandame. Kavandame had been an active leader among the Makonde of Cabo Delgado Province (in MANU and in the cooperative movement) for many years, and soon became the most prominent of FRE-LIMO politicians with a base in the area (being, for a period, the

Secretary of the Province and a member of the Central Committee). But the limitations of his particular kind of leadership soon revealed themselves: such leadership was self-serving economically, divisive politically, incoherent militarily,[9] reflecting, in short, a style and substance very much after the fashion exemplified by regional political "barons" in a country like Kenya. Most negatively, he sought to turn the new commercial structures of the liberated areas to his own use, skimming off large surpluses for himself and his immediate supporters. As he came under increasing pressure from FRELIMO leaders, and from more committed militants within his own area, he quite predictably began to play the tribal card, seeking to crystallize "Makonde consciousness" around his own person. He also actively sought support for his intrigues among certain of the less progressive but strategically placed elements in the Tanzanian leadership. By 1968 he was even prepared to make an (abortive) bid for separatist independence for his province, to actively sabotage FRELIMO's military efforts,[10] and, when finally balked and expelled from the movement in early 1969, to go over to the Portuguese and make public pronouncements on their behalf. It is important to note that long before this latter move it was perfectly clear that Kavandame had forfeited any claim to enjoying popular support, even among his own tribesmen. Just as the logic of the struggle had transcended Gwenjere and his elitism, so too it was moving beyond the familiar politico-economic royalism and Africanized exploitation of such men as Kavandame and others.

By 1969 the existence of two different "lines," as FRELIMO periodicals came increasingly to refer to the elements of contestation within the movement, was readily apparent. But the final scenes of this particular phase of the Mozambican drama were not to be acted out until after the assassination of Mondlane in February 1969. It is impossible to say what the pattern of FRELIMO's development might have been had that assassination, by an unknown hand, not occurred—probably much the same, with minor variations. What is clear, however, is that Mondlane's role had been crucial to *guaranteeing* the kind of shift within FRELIMO and within liberated Mozambique which was taking place during his presidency. If Gwenjere, Kavandame, and (as we shall see shortly) Vice-President Uria Simango represented a wholly petty-bourgeois nationalism, and if a handful of others represented a quite developed revolutionary position from a very early date, then Mondlane stood closer to the center of the FRELIMO political spectrum. And, so situated, he came to epitomize those absolutely crucial members of the Mozambican petty bourgeoisie who were prepared to accept more and more of "the logic of protracted struggle," to contemplate "committing suicide" in the interest of a revolutionary politics.

Thus it was impossible to talk with Mondlane, or to hear him speak over the years, without observing the growth of his own understanding and practice. Some observers have insisted, nonetheless, that aspects of his accustomed life style and political approach would have imposed a severe limitation upon how far he could have continued to move in this direction. Again, it is unnecessary to speculate about such matters. The fact remains that by using his powerful presence within the movement to guarantee the necessary minimum of organizational unity, while also swimming with the tide of revolutionary nationalism and accepting more and more its logic, he did preside over the build-up of the prerequisites for further progress. By the time of his death the struggle was sufficiently advanced to have shifted the center of political gravity to within the territory. The Second Congress, held, significantly, inside the liberated areas in 1968, had already moved to increase markedly the presence in the Central Committee of direct representatives from the political and military institutions of the interior. The new mass basis of Mozambican politics was beginning, strikingly, to assert itself. Similarly, a cadre of revolutionary petty bourgeois, adapting, like Mondlane, and often even less equivocally, to the new imperatives had by then emerged within the political and military spheres and could hope to consolidate its hold on the leadership positions. In fact, Samora Machel, who was to become president in 1970, can be seen as being fully representative of this group. When the showdown came inside FRELIMO, as it inevitably had to after the cancelling out of Mondlane's dominant role, it was these popular and progressive forces which were able to carry the day.

The result did not take place without a struggle, a struggle which racked FRELIMO in 1969. For the "tendency" toward conservative, petty-bourgeois nationalism ran right through the movement and very far up the apparatus. Indeed, it became increasingly clear that this tendency found its ultimate focus in no less important a personage than Reverend Uria Simango, the vice-president of FRELIMO under Mondlane. Simango, a powerful figure within FRELIMO from the outset (he was Mondlane's closest rival for the presidency in the earliest days, for example) staked out a position which consistently tilted in that direction, tending to reduce the complex nature of the struggle to its most baldly racial dimensions and the question of military tactics to its most adventurist (and self-defeating) formulae. Not surprisingly, it also began to be apparent in the last few years before Mondlane's death that Simango was giving tacit support to the deviations represented by both Gwenjere and Kavandame, despite his having taken an active hand in the Central Committee decisions which expelled them both; indeed, his involvement with Mozambique Institute students appears to have been particularly overt and was in any case only one of many indications of his identification with such elitist pretensions. Still other aspects of the syndrome of conventional nationalism were to characterize his position in a quite predictable manner—notably the use of ethnic and regional counters as a means of consolidating his power base. In this case Simango tried to light the spark by setting his fellow "northerners" against the specter of "southern dominance."

Enough of this was clear by 1969 for spokesmen of the progressive tendency to move to block Simango's "automatic" ascendance to the presidency in the wake of Mondlane's assassination. When the Central Committee did meet in April 1969, the ground rules of post-Mondlane politics were staked out by means of a fierce and effective attack on the many conservative elements which continued to be prominent within the organization (Nungu, for example); not coincidentally, a number of such men were known to be close associates of Simango. In such an atmosphere it was also possible to organize the succession in a manner more favorable to the progressive group: a Presidential Council—consisting of Simango, Marcellino dos Santos (a man of the left within FRELIMO for a long time), and Samora Machel, the head of the army —was formed. In this way certain formalities were observed; FRELIMO statements could even conclude at the time that:

> Almost from the very beginning of FRELIMO there had been comrades with . . . erroneous conceptions. Some of them had deserted in the course of the Revolution . . . Gradually, therefore, it was seen that "the Revolution itself ensures the rejection of the impure load it carries." But other elements remained among us carrying their mistaken ideas. It was on the latter that the last meeting of the Central Committee had a decisive influence, bringing them back again to the revolutionary path. This action was the work of a group of comrades who had always kept themselves

faithful to the interests of the masses, respecting collective values and fighting individualism and personal ambition that foment opportunism, comrades linked with the concrete reality and immersed in the realization of the principal tasks of the struggle.[11]

Yet, as very soon became apparent, what really happened was that "in that meeting we finally identified the existence of two ideological lines":

After this, the division became more acute. A struggle began between the groups representing the two lines. And all the problems, all the difficulties we have had since then are the result of this division.[12]

The stage had merely been set for the final act of the struggle for succession between these two tendencies.

As noted earlier, however, the die had been already cast. Samora, after all, represented the army, a powerful base in its own right, but all the more so when one considered that this was an army with an ever increasing number of the attributes of a people's military force and one rooted in a vital political process now established *within* Mozambique itself. Thus it was no accident that when Kavandame held back the "Cabo Delgado delegation," representative of his own clique, to the FRELIMO Conference of 1969, Cabo Delgado was effectively represented by military delegates from that province; no accident, either, that it was the "military," and not Kavandame, who could claim the effective allegiance of the people in Cabo Delgado, as events were to prove very soon thereafter. We have also observed the way in which the Central Committee, after the conference, reflected these new facts of political life in its composition. Simango himself must have realized that time was running out, that the days of exile politics and exile politicians, of nonrevolutionary nationalism and simple racialist pieties, were drawing to a close. He chose to stake all on one last, desperate gamble: the publication of his document "Gloomy Situation in FRELIMO." [13]

This text, a *locus classicus* for students of the disintegration of conventional African nationalism in the context of truly revolutionary conditions, made entirely clear what could only be suspected prior to its circulation. In addition to many shrill and reckless accusations of murder and assassination made against the "Samora group," Simango's document publicly revealed the latter's close identification with each of those reactionary aspects of Mozambican nationalism against which the more progressive tendency of the leadership had set itself. The mobilization of tribal sentiment for factional advantage is one aspect of this. Simango's document several times manages to identify his opponents—albeit mis-leadingly—as "southerners": "Since 1966 there has been a tendency of a group, unfortunately composed of people from the south which in-cluded the late president of FRELIMO, to meet and take decisions by themselves and impose them on the people through maneuver." Simi-larly, the attack on Janet Mondlane, which is also premised on a totally false picture of the degree of autonomy the Mozambique Institute has had from Central Committee scrutiny, comes across clearly as an at-tempt to substitute emotive and racial arguments for substantive argu-ments concerning policy.

Equally significant are Simango's expressions of solidarity with ele-ments which were, by the time of his document's publication, wholly discredited. Now for Simango, "the participation of Father Gwenjere in the Mozambique Institute problem and in other affairs of FRELIMO was an expression of sympathy and solidarity with his own people." Yet Simango had participated fully and without dissent in the decision to expel Gwenjere from FRELIMO. Exactly the same was true for the case of Kavandame, but in his document Simango's picture of the Cabo Delgado situation is a blurred one, and Kavandame emerges as much sinned against as sinning. Needless to say, nothing is noted in his analy-sis about the economic aggrandizement and exploitation indulged in by the Kavandame group, though that had been the heart of the issue. In a parallel manner, other sections of the document seem quite specifically designed to flatter the elitist pretensions of the Mozambican student group, in Tanzania and abroad; moreover, immediately after his subse-quent expulsion from FRELIMO in December 1969, Simango wrote to Mozambican students in the United States assuring them that in any movement of his own which was subsequently established, their accom-plishments would be scrupulously recognized. As noted above, FRE-LIMO responsibles had suspected at the time that Simango was more linked with the initiatives of Gwenjere and Kavandame than he had cared to state openly; now his declining fortunes had forced him to re-veal his hand in an open bid for what remained of their constituencies.

Predictably, this package was cemented ideologically: by means of the disarming rejection of the necessity for any ideological clarification!

There is a swing to say that we are divided on ideology. This can only mean difference on economic, religious, social policies (class), etc. I agree that ideology is very important but it should never be considered as a uniting or dividing factor of the nationalist liberation force at this stage, if all agree and accept fundamental principles: (a) liberate Mozambique from the Portuguese colonial domination and (b) through the armed struggle.

Of course, many others who have continued to play an active role in the FRELIMO leadership would agree, up to a point, with this sentiment—agree that it is premature to speak too overtly and aggressively about the tasks of "socialist construction," agree that a broad-based national liberation front characterizes the essential nature of the movement at the present time. But in Simango's case such sentiments have to be interpreted in the light of the particular kind of faction he was attempting to put together and of the particular kinds of quasi-class interests he was objectively representing. Only then can this kind of "negative ideology" be understood for what it is in practice: a shield for the sorts of "internal" exploitation, inimical to the further development of the struggle, which we have been describing.

It also represented an appeal to a particular kind of external constituency—in Tanzania, and in Africa in general—whose support Simango now sought. There were elements within the Tanzanian leadership, for example, which could be attracted by this brand of "anti-ideological" (and effectively self-serving) black nationalism; indeed, such men had actually attempted to facilitate the strengthening of this sort of tendency within FRELIMO in the immediately preceding period. Simango may have hoped that similar elements, themselves more strongly entrenched in African countries other than Tanzania, would rally to the support of this kind of line. But Tanzania was the key, and there such leaders were being themselves outflanked by the development of Tanzania's own brand of socialism; with the issue already settled in that country, at least for the time being, Nyerere could make clear his unambiguous preference for the more progressive wing of FRELIMO. Moreover, the essential opportunism of Simango's own shifts of position soon became graphically apparent. By the time of his issuing a second, even more desperate, document at a meeting of the OAU Liberation Committee only a few months later Simango's description of the "gloomy situation" in FRELIMO had been turned more or less upside down. Whereas before it had been the Samora/dos Santos group which had been prematurely introducing "the question of scientific socialism and capitalism in Mozambique" ("Gloomy Situation in FRELIMO," p. 4), now the same group stood accused of the opposite vice: "Talks about replacement of people and necessity *to purge the organization of Communist elements were frequent.* Precisely it is these people the propaganda was directed against who have been removed in one way or another." [14] One could only speculate that Simango, having failed in Tanzania with his black nationalist ploy, was now laying the basis for a possible (though equally unsuccessful) "ultra-left" appeal to Chinese sources of aid.

For Simango, effectively blocked within FRELIMO by the strength of the organization and the new reality of its popular character, and deprived, as well, of any Tanzanian support, had in mind the launching of a new movement; suspended from FRELIMO (November 1969), he tried to mount just such an alternative. This in turn was the last straw for the Tanzanian authorities, and in February 1970 he was ordered from the country. He drifted to Cairo, with occasional forays into Zambia and the United States, and before long, like others before him who could not keep pace with the Mozambican revolution, he had entered COREMO. From that resting place his ineffective sniping action has continued.

The volte-face of some of his closest confidants is even more striking. Murupa, an erstwhile Central Committee member, went over to the Portuguese side not long afterward, becoming in time a senior official in the colonial apparatus with responsibility for implementing the strategic hamlet program. To give him his due, Simango has to date publicly resisted Portuguese blandishments designed to lure him to their side. But the links which continue to exist between him and Murupa, for example, remain unknown and, in any case, the objective result of his apostasy can only be to strengthen the ability of the Portuguese to confuse the issue at stake in Mozambique.

Fortunately, the creation of such a possibility is not the most important result of the series of events we have been tracing. More significant is the fact that this process has, on balance, helped to *strengthen* the movement. Indeed, FRELIMO's own conclusion seems to be substantially accurate:

> The spirit which prevailed at the latest meeting of the Central Committee
> revealed that we have already reached an advanced phase in that process of
> purifying our ranks. Frankness reigned—there was friendship and revolu-

tionary fraternity among all members. The climate that we felt was the result of the ideological unity that existed among us. For the first time in the history of FRELIMO, there were no discordant voices on the Central Committee which were opposed to the revolutionary positions; it constituted a solid and united block.

We consider that a great victory has been achieved, one that must be preserved and defended at all costs. The Central Committee itself recommended continuous vigilance; in order that that vigilance may be efficiently exercised, the Central Committee clarified certain concepts. Thus, the Central Committee stressed its definition of the enemy. The enemy has two faces: the principal and direct enemy, i.e., Portuguese colonialism and imperialism, which are open enemies we confront daily in the battlefield, and in relation to whom no doubt or confusion is possible. The other face is that of the indirect or secondary enemy, who presents himself under the cover of a nationalist and even a revolutionary, thus making it difficult to identify him. The Central Committee reaffirmed that the characterization of the enemy for us will never be derived from color, nationality, race, or religion. On the other hand, our enemy is that one who exploits or creates conditions for the exploitation of our people, whatever his color, race, nationality, or religion.

Within the same intention of providing ideological weapons to our comrades so that they may be able to better defend our revolution, the Central Committee defined the qualities which every FRELIMO militant must build or develop in himself: continuously fighting ambition, opportunism, tribalism, and corruption. The existence of a high level of these qualities will be the condition for a militant to be appointed for positions of responsibility in our organization. . . .

Thus, a new period is being opened in the life of FRELIMO. We took an important step forward in the consolidation of our unity, we elected a truly revolutionary leadership, we clarified our political line, we came nearer our final victory.[15]

It may be that some potential contradictions remain beneath the surface. The terms of the emerging ideology are still left somewhat undefined. "Exploitation" and "imperialism" characteristically join "Portuguese colonialism" and "ambition, opportunism, tribalism, and corruption" in the list of FRELIMO's enemies, but any public hint that the movement has "socialist" intentions is systematically avoided. It is therefore possible that there remains ground for tension within FRELIMO ranks between the varying claims of "socialism" and "nationalism" (albeit "revolutionary nationalism") at some subsequent stage of development, and particularly in the post-independence period. But even if this possibility exists, it is, for the time being, a fairly remote one. Moreover, all our evidence suggests that the trend of events may work, in the future as in the past, to resolve this potential contradiction and to fuse the meanings of social- ism and revolutionary nationalism in Mozambique. For FRELIMO's *practice* continues to be an increasingly progressive one. And with the most overt sources of tension within the movement removed, the cadre who remain are primarily those who can be expected to move still fur- ther with the logic of protracted struggle. Mozambican advances since 1969—both in military terms and in terms of national reconstruction— would seem to bear out this supposition in impressive fashion.

4. Prospects

It can be concluded that the triumph of this line within FRELIMO both reflects the emergence of a popular base and a progressive infra- structure for the Mozambican liberation struggle *and* gives promise of further mobilizing and consolidating these crucial features. The positive impact of these developments upon the military struggle can scarcely be overemphasized. Experience elsewhere suggests that liberated areas of the sort which are being firmed up politically and economically in northern Mozambique are the *sine qua non* of further advance. It is sig- nificant that in both 1970 and 1971 the Portuguese launched what were heralded, in advance, as final mop-up campaigns in Cabo Delgado and Niassa provinces, throwing vast numbers of soldiers and much matériel into the fray. On both occasions they were forced to draw back beyond the Zambezi in disarray, leaving only the few fortified posts which they already held and a population largely undismayed by the outbursts of Portuguese terrorism and intimidation witnessed during the offensives. A local population increasingly conscious, organized, and self-reliant also frees many more full-time militants for further advance; the dra- matic successes during the past two years in Tete, where guerrillas have pushed south of the Zambezi and into the vicinity of the Cabora Bassa dam, are testimony to the accomplishments which lie behind. Moreover, such successes tend to have a snow-ball effect. Certainly, progressive forces in the world at large have come to recognize the vigor and com- mitment of FRELIMO's efforts ever more decisively. Thus the Chi- nese, somewhat loath in the past to commit themselves to movements which already enjoy Soviet and Eastern European assistance, have continued to intensify their support for FRELIMO and their overt manifestations of solidarity. Even liberal forces in the advanced capitalist world (e.g., the World Council of Churches, the governments of the Scandinavian countries) have had to come to terms with the reality of FRELIMO advance and begin to examine critically their previous indifference to, or even tacit support of, Portuguese colonialism.

Equally important, these developments in liberated Mozambique have slowly but surely begun to foreclose the possibility of a false decolonization along lines hitherto quite predictable in much of Africa. Nothing can be said with certainty in this respect, of course, but there can be little doubt that the process of continually weeding out from the leadership the least progressive of the petty bourgeoisie has done a great deal to ensure the continuity of the social revolution already in train in the liberated areas. Moreover, we have noted the extent to which the army, a threat to revolutionary decolonization even under conditions which seem quite promising, has also been linked with popular aspirations and activities in ways that differ markedly from the situation in Algeria, for example. Finally, to the (considerable) extent that the mass of the peasantry is becoming an organized and active ingredient in the decolonization equation under Mozambican conditions, this too is a surety of continuity; Museveni's findings as to the growing peasant understanding of the nature of imperialism and the increasingly progressive character of their identification with the Mozambican nation suggest attributes of consciousness that are not likely to be easily shed in the aftermath of colonialism.

Of course, there are vast stretches of Mozambique which have not been directly touched by the full logic of the liberated areas, including so large an urban conglomerate as Lourenço Marques, which is the home of a significant proletariat *and* of a potentially conservative African bureaucratic group whose fortunes have heretofore been linked to the Portuguese but whose skills may have to be accommodated, albeit with great caution, within an independent Mozambique. The timing and the terms of the full integration of such parts of the country into the Mozambican revolution will have their influence on the shape of the postcolonial nation. At the same time, it is apparent that FRELIMO is quite active clandestinely far beyond the front lines of its own military advance and the promise of the liberated areas is already well known and increasingly well understood in most parts of the country. The time is long past, if it ever existed, when any safe and manageable "neocolonial solution" was a serious option for the Portuguese; the Portuguese, for very good reasons of their own,[16] eschewed it at the earliest stages, and now FRELIMO, as we have seen, has long since outgrown it. But there are tame Mozambicans; some of them, like Kavandame and Murupa, have already been on display. Simango's brand of nationalism may eventually make him easy prey for slightly more subtle blandishments; then COREMO, or some other structure altogether, could become the vehicle for a last, desperate, preemptive move by imperialism as the Portuguese falter even more dramatically. FRELIMO would not be fooled by any such elevation of a Mozambican Hastings Banda to formal authority; in all likelihood the movement would go on fighting. What the response of African states, even the most committed of them, would be to this kind of "victory" for African nationalism is more problematic. Certainly supporters of Mozambican nationalism would be wise to inform themselves of what is really at stake well in advance of such an eventuality.

Yet it must be emphasized that even this is not the most probable path of the continuing struggle in Mozambique; in fact, an even more desperate, much less equivocal, confrontation seems to be in the cards. As noted, the time may well be past when any very straightforward brand of "neocolonialism" is a live option there. Moreover, the response to the conflict inside Mozambique on the part of racist and imperialist powers which lie beyond the territory's borders seems increasingly less likely to be such a measured one. The possible contagion of Mozambican (as well as Angolan) military success is sufficiently threatening to South Africa and Rhodesia to have already forced such actors to intervene more menacingly: South African troops have been at the ready around the Cabora Bassa dam site for months and Rhodesian soldiers and airplanes have been very active militarily in Tete Province, south of the Zambezi; the police and military commanders of the three white redoubts exchanged regular visits most recently, South African mercenaries (with at least tacit South African government connivance) were identified as carrying out defoliation missions over the fields of northern Mozambique.[17] This trend is bound to continue. Nor has the existence of this broader threat to the whole of Southern Africa been overlooked by the forces of international capitalism, who have noted with alarm the intensification of FRELIMO's revolutionary and anti-imperialist line (in itself vital to the movement's military success, as we have seen).[18] The hardening American position, first under Johnson and later under Nixon, which culminated in the Azores Agreement of 1971,[19] has no doubt been partly a response to the specter of a future, FRELIMO-ruled, militant Mozambique (a Mozambique which gets some support, need one add, from the "Communists" !). Thus the increasingly successful Mozambican revolution is one of the chief sparks which is lighting the fuse for all of Southern Africa; in all probability, therefore, the struggle will be less easily compartmentalized along territorial lines in the future than it has been in the past. This fact does not make the liberation of Mozambique any less important in itself, of course, but it does widen the field of relevant considerations for both Mozambican revolutionaries and for their supporters abroad.

5. Implications for Metropolitan Radicals

This pattern of development in Mozambique has implications for the practice of progressives in the advanced capitalist countries. Since Southern Africa could become, from the mid-seventies, the sort of crucial zone of confrontation that Southeast Asia has been since the mid-sixties, it is well to state these precisely, albeit too briefly, here.

1. Take, first, the case of the liberal sympathizer. We have seen the extent to which the Mozambican liberation struggle has given rise to a social revolution and an anti-imperialist movement. In Africa this is the logic of genuine liberation. Yet if one reads between the lines of many liberal treatises on Southern Africa, this is precisely the denouement that most liberals seek to avoid; too often they advise, say, American support for liberation before "extremists" profit from a "deteriorating" situation.[20] Of course, most such spokesmen are in any case mere apologists for the corporate structure, but the most sincere (if confused) of them must be encouraged to face squarely the necessity of backing socialist and revolutionary solutions to liberation struggles. It seems inevitable that, as the Southern African situation escalates, FRELIMO will find its aims and its accomplishments distorted in the Western press; a firm understanding of the realities of the anti-imperialist struggle may be some inoculation against any attendant hysteria. Liberals may also draw their own brand of solace from the fact that FRELIMO is not so "aligned" as the NLF/PRG and that it sternly safeguards its independence from for-

eign ideology and foreign influence of any sort. But in important respects the Vietnamese and Mozambican situations are similar. Left-liberals—of all colors—who seek some (nonexistent) middle ground in Mozambique (as in Vietnam) will be objectively lending their support to the worst barbarisms of imperialism.

2. A closely related point should also be considered by those most sympathetic toward *nationalist* aspirations in contemporary Africa. Here one thinks most immediately of black nationalists in the metropoles who are, inevitably, deeply concerned with the Southern African situation; it is clear, for example, that in the United States the black community is becoming an increasingly vital force pressing for progressive solutions in Southern Africa, one whose views and likely reactions must be taken into careful account in the strategic and tactical calculations of wielders of state and corporate power. But the relevance of the cautionary note which must be sounded here is by no means confined to black groups. All those who commit themselves to the cause of African nationalism will have to make subtle discriminations in the course of the coming struggle, discriminations for which the analytical tools made available by a nationalist perspective pure and simple will not prove fully adequate.

It is true that a preemptive "neocolonial solution" may not be the most likely outcome of this phase of the Mozambican revolution, but it is not beyond the realm of possibility. If this should happen, it would be tragic if many uncritical militants in the metropolitan countries were to be caught with a Mozambican General Thieu (or even another Hastings Banda) on their hands and on their consciences. At the very least it can be safely predicted that the diverse brands of nationalism in Mozambique are to be played off against one another by the Portuguese and their mentors in order to maximize confusion in the advanced capitalist centers. Careful scrutiny of the claims of movements will therefore be necessary, as well as an awareness that under African conditions the most black-sounding of nationalisms can become the most easily coopted and the least serviceable to the mass of the African population. Not all nationalisms are equivalent; it is the revolutionary nationalism of a movement like FRELIMO which guarantees that "real freedom" to which Nyerere was referring at the outset of this paper.

3. However, as we have seen, the importance of these latter considerations should not at present be exaggerated. Even were the Portuguese to become so inclined, they could not conjure away the fact that FRE-

LIMO already has more than 10,000 men under arms, is in effective control of vast tracts of territory, and is moving forward. Nor in the foreseeable future could imperialism really hope to breathe effective life into any shadowy, African-based hypothetical alternative to FRELIMO. Thus there is no need for any confusion as to where the responsibility of international socialists of all colors lies.

The matter cannot be allowed merely to rest with this bland affirmation, however. The fact remains that the struggle in Mozambique must be granted a much higher priority by metropolitan activists than it has been heretofore. As noted, the Southern African white regimes and many of their allies are aware that tension is beginning to escalate markedly within their gates; they will undoubtedly continue to act firmly and brutally. At the same time, the Left's response has been as yet scarcely an adequate one, in spite of the fact that revolutionary advances in Portuguese Africa are the major force which is placing the whole ugly question of Southern Africa ever more firmly on the historical agenda. Valuable time was lost in Vietnam—five or ten years at least—because the Left failed to take seriously what was happening there. The same thing must not be allowed to happen in South Africa in general, or in Mozambique in particular. To be sure, some progressive elements in the West are already engaged in concrete manifestations of solidarity. But it is imperative that many more international socialists treat this struggle with the seriousness it deserves.

Postscript, September 1972

Shortly after completing the preceding essay (in mid-1972) I was invited by FRELIMO to accompany a column of combatants on a march into the liberated areas of Tete Province. I was thus afforded the opportunity to spend sixteen days during the latter part of August 1972 observing at first hand some of the events and structures which I had been able to investigate up to then only from a distance. I hope to recount this experience at greater length elsewhere, but it seems relevant to note here that the evidence I was able to collect inside Mozambique bore out, even more fully than I had anticipated, the argument advanced in this paper. In addition, the recent announcement that in September FRELIMO opened up military activities in Manica and Sofala Province is further dramatic proof of continued FRELIMO success *and* of the continued escalation of the confrontation—with all the implications to which I have referred.

Notes

1. For a relevant perspective on continental developments see Chapters 1 and 2 of this volume.
2. J. K. Nyerere, "Introduction," pp. 26–32 (section subtitled "The Problems of Building Socialism in an Ex-Colonial Country") in *Freedom and Socialism* (London, New York, Nairobi, 1968); emphasis added. See also Frantz Fanon, *The Wretched of the Earth* (New York, 1966).
3. See Chapter 6 of this volume.
4. See, for example, Y. Museveni, "Fanon's Theory of Violence: Its Verification in Liberated Mozambique" in N. Shamuyarira, ed., *Essays on the Liberation of Southern Africa* (Dar es Salaam, 1971), and the series of articles by F. Ruhinda entitled "My Long March," which appeared in *The Nationalist* (Dar es Salaam) in six installments between 14 June and 25 June 1971. It has been estimated that already well over a million Mozambicans live within the framework of FRELIMO-sponsored institutions, and that the liberation forces control from one-quarter to one-third of the land area, including most of the three northern provinces, Cabo Delgado, Niassa, and Tete.
5. Y. Museveni, op. cit.
6. Of course, there are other variables, logistical ones in particular, which affect the differential pace of development of the struggle as between territories in Southern Africa.
7. Amilcar Cabral, "The Weapon of Theory," in his *Revolution in Guinea* (New York, 1970), p. 110; see also his "Brief Analysis of the Social Structure in Guinea" in the same volume.
8. Editorial, "25th of June—The Starting Point" in *Mozambique Revolution* (Dar es Salaam), no. 51 (April-June 1972).
9. Nor is it accidental that in the military sphere Kavandame was one of those attracted to the most adventurist of lines, arguing (prematurely) for such strategies as the direct assault on large towns (e.g., Beira).
10. Among other things, he appears to have been very directly involved in the assassination of the FRELIMO military commander, Kankhomba, on the Tanzanian border in late 1968.
11. Editorial in *Mozambique Revolution*, no. 38 (March-April 1969).
12. Editorial in *Mozambique Revolution*, no. 41 (October-December 1969).

13. Uria T. Simango, "Gloomy Situation in FRELIMO" (mimeographed, n.d.). The quotations which follow in the text are taken from this document.

14. Uria. T. Simango, "The reason why I issued a document on the situation in FRELIMO" (mimeographed, n.d.); emphasis added.

15. Editorial in *Mozambique Revolution*, no. 43 (April-June 1970). By the time of the Central Committee meeting described in this editorial (May 1970), the expedient of establishing a presidential triumvirate in the preceding year had served its purpose; now Samora Machel was elected president of FRELIMO in his own right, and Marcellino dos Santos became vice-president.

16. This point, among others, is discussed in Chapter 2 of this volume.

17. See Cal McCrystal, "Portugal Wages Chemical War to Starve Rebels," *The Sunday Times* (London), 9 July 1972.

18. Of course, from the early 1960s Portugal reversed its long-standing policy of fending off non-Portuguese investments in the colonies precisely with an eye to guaranteeing this kind of long-term support.

19. See Africa Research Group, "Le Pacte des Açores: des dollars contre les africains," in *Africasia* (Paris), 7 February 1972.

20. Cf. Waldemar Nielsen, *The Great Powers and Africa* (New York, 1969); for a critique, see Africa Research Group, "Southern Africa," in the *Guardian* (New York), 18 April 1970.

Appendix:
African Peasantries

John S. Saul and Roger Woods

The terms "peasant" and "peasantry," in addition to their popular and political usages, have been used in the social sciences for the description and analysis of types of rural society with reference to a wide range of geographical settings and historical periods; unfortunately, despite considerable usage, there has been no consistent definition of the term. This conceptual inconsistency has had the consequence that analyses of "peasant society" are by no means readily comparable in either their scope or their theoretical underpinnings. There have been, it is true, some recent attempts at a more systematic categorization in which peasants have been differentiated from "primitive agriculturalists" on the one hand and from "farmers" or "agricultural entrepreneurs" on the other.[1] Yet what appears to be a successful way of specifically differentiating "peasants" from other agriculturalists and nonagriculturalists in any particular area often presents difficulties when applied to another. Thus the variety of peasant types and the variety of approaches to them by social scientists promises to provide sufficient fuel for a virtually endless debate on the appropriate dimensions of the concept. There is a danger, however, that the definitional exercise will obscure the real point at issue. For the value of any concept lies in its ability to illuminate and explain empirical data when used in a theoretical argument. Thus the proper questions to ask before trying to define the "peasant" in an African context are: what are we trying to explain, and will a concept defined in a particular way do justice to the empirical data and be logically appropriate to the argument?

This article originally appeared in T. Shanin, ed., *Peasants and Peasant Societies* (London, 1971), pp. 103–13. Copyright © 1971 by Penguin Books Ltd. Reprinted by permission.

Our interest lies in identifying and explaining the patterns of change and development in contemporary Africa, and we are therefore concerned to use terms such as "peasantry" and "peasant" as effective concepts within an analytical framework which does usefully structure such an explanation. A precise identification of the phases of social evolution and world economic history during which the peasant may become an important actor on the African stage and his role a crucial one in the understanding of the process of historical change thus becomes of central importance in pinpointing this category. Moreover, as we shall in fact see, the changing African social structure has thrown up, during certain periods, strata which may be usefully so identified in structural terms.

It should also be stressed, however, that any definition must not aggregate together uncritically all peasants under a monolithic category, for the peasantry may also be differentiated internally in terms of certain structurally significant variables. This becomes all the more important an emphasis in light of our focus upon the changing context within which the peasantry operates, for the category will of necessity remain fluid at the margins as various segments of society pass in and out of the relevant range of social involvements which it epitomizes and at different rates. Not surprisingly, under certain circumstances different segments of the peasantry can come to play diverse historical roles with important consequences for the pattern of historical development. In brief, there can be among the peasants *different peasantries*—differentiated according to their structural position at a specified moment of time.

This much having been said, we must still specify some criteria for differentiating peasants from other rural people. Our emphasis here is twofold and highlights economic characteristics. Firstly, our concern with the structural position of the peasantry suggests that it must be seen as being a certain stratum within some wider political and economic system. A second dimension centers on the importance to the peasantry of the family economy.[2] Thus peasants are *those whose ultimate security and subsistence lies in their having certain rights in land and in the labor of family members on the land, but who are involved, through rights and obligations, in a wider economic system which includes the participation of non-peasants.*[3] The fact that for peasants ultimate security and subsistence rests upon maintaining rights in land and rights in family labor will be seen to be an important determinant shaping and restricting their social action. It is also the characteristic which peasants share with "primitive agriculturalists," though not with capitalist farmers. For while the capitalist farmer may *appear* to depend upon his land and even upon family labor in some cases, he is not *forced* to rely solely upon these in the last instance; he has alternative potential sources of security and investment. What the peasant does share, in general terms, with the capitalist farmer (though not with the primitive agriculturalist) is his integration into a complex social structure characterized by stratification and economic differentiation. In fact, it is precisely the characterization of the peasantry in terms of its position relative to other groups in the wider social system which has particularly important explanatory value in the analysis of development.

The work of elaborating upon such criteria can only be begun here, but it is certainly possible to carry the discussion beyond the point reached by Fallers, for example, in his article entitled "Are African Cultivators to Be Called Peasants?" [4] Confining himself to the discussion of "traditional" social systems rather abstractly conceived and working partly in the anthropological tradition of Kroeber and Redfield, he defined peasant society as being a society "whose primary constituent units are semi-autonomous local communities with semi-autonomous cultures." This semi-autonomy he broke down further into economic, political, and "cultural" dimensions. He demonstrated the involvement of many Africans in the trade and exchange of agricultural produce and even the existence, albeit more limited in scope, of political states which in some areas allowed for the emergence of many political attributes of a peasantry. But crucial to his argument was the nonexistence, as he saw it, of any juxtaposition between high and low cultures even in those African societies which had, in effect, economic and political proto-peasantries. Fallers concludes, in fact, with the suggestion "that one of the reasons why Christianity, Islam and their accompanying high cultures have been so readily accepted in many parts of Africa is that many African societies were structurally 'ready' to receive peasant cultures"!

Yet such a conclusion graphically demonstrates the dangers of looking for cultural aspects of peasant societies within the framework of an abstract and ahistorical approach.[5] For the history of colonial Africa shows, on the contrary, not any structural readiness to accept, and consequent acceptance of, a "high culture," but rather a clash between different types of social systems in which the resulting system, independent of its cultural content, was the product of the interaction of the two systems. Moreover, despite the existence of some prefigurings of a peasant class in earlier periods, it is more fruitful to view both the creation of an African peasantry, as well as the creation of the present differentiation among African peasantries, as being primarily the result of the interaction between an international capitalist economic system and traditional socioeconomic systems, within the context of territorially defined colonial political systems.

Sub-Saharan Africa viewed in continental perspective is still predominantly rural in its population, but the ubiquitous reach of colonialism has ensured that no significant numbers of the primitive agriculturalists who previously comprised the vast majority of the population have remained outside the framework of a wider economic system. Under our usage, most of this rural population has thus been transformed into a peasantry. Of course, in certain areas, not only have non-African immigrants established themselves as capitalist farmers, but a significant number of African cultivators have moved out of the peasant category and must also be called capitalist farmers. In addition, as the logic of capitalist development has worked itself out in Africa, other peasants have lost their land rights and have been *proletarianized* either in the rural or industrial sectors of the economy. In other words, the further development of capitalism has begun to phase out the very peasantry it first defined and created. Moreover, in most of the continent it is a capitalist route to development that is favored and insofar as capitalism does have the inherent strength to fully transform African societies, the existence of a peasantry could be viewed all the more as a transitional phenomenon. The possibility of a realization of this kind of transformation is of course most problematic[6] and, in any event, remains a very long-term proposition. The identification of a continental bias toward the further encouragement of this possibility may therefore help to explain the fluidity at the margins of the peasant category referred to earlier; it does not relieve one of the necessity of analyzing the contemporary characteristics of that peasantry itself or of suggesting its likely response to the social structures which are emerging and serving to reshape it.

The colonial situation was everywhere one in which the local populations were both exposed to new goods and services and, in many cases, subjected to specific government-enforced economic or labor demands with the result that new needs were generated which could only be met by participation in the cash-based market economy. Two ways of participating were open to them: sale of their labor or sale of their agricultural produce. Within this broad process four variables have been of particular importance in defining the nature of the "participation" in the overall system by primitive agriculturalists through which they acquired, in effect, their peasant characteristics.[7] These variables are:

1. The presence, or otherwise, of centers of labor demand, such as mines, plantations, industries, and the like.

2. The presence, or otherwise, of a suitable local environment for the production of agricultural crops for sale, combined with the degree of availability of marketing opportunities for these crops.

3. The presence, or otherwise, of an immigrant settler group of capitalist farmers who would be competitors with African producers.

4. And, at a later stage, the presence, or otherwise, of an indigenous elite (basing themselves upon educational attainment and, in some cases, upon political skills) which under certain circumstances (notably the absence of an immigrant settler group) could take over formal political power from the colonial regime. This new stratum might be complemented and reinforced in its exercise of authority by a newly emergent, indigenous "national bourgeoisie," to be found in trade and in agriculture itself.

Equally important, it must be remembered that these variables have operated upon a pre-colonial Africa that was itself characterized by a large number of ethnic and political groups at different levels of political and economic organization. By taking full cognizance of such a wide variety of factors, it may be easier to get a clear idea of the full range of permutations and actual consequences possible within the overall process of "peasantization."

It is perhaps worth extending briefly the discussion as to the importance of environmental potential, a factor which helps to define both the character of the traditional agro-economic systems as well as their subsequent responses. For the extent to which labor-exporting peasantries developed was not only a function of the labor demand/economic need dimension introduced by an absence of readily available cash crops. It also reflected in some instances the degree to which adult men were underemployed in the traditional agricultural system and hence the extent to which they could be absent without threatening the security of minimal subsistence production. Similarly, the extent to which a peasantry could respond to cash-cropping also depended on the adaptability of the traditional agricultural system to the incorporation of new crops or the expanded production of established crops *without threatening the security of minimal subsistence production.* Of course, these complexities further contribute to the process whereby a number of "African peasantries" are tending to be created, rather than a single monolithic stratum. But the reiteration of the italicized phrase is equally significant, for we are reminded of the second of the general characteristics of the peasantry mentioned earlier. Insofar as particular African cultivators can continue to be identified as peasants, one will observe such a calculation to be central to the defining of their existence and to the grounding of their activities.

A distinctive African peasantry exists, therefore, though it may find itself involved in broader national systems which can have a range of possible characteristics—societies in which the dominant elements will be a variable combination of international corporations, immigrant settlers and immigrant trading groups, indigenous elites and indigenous national bourgeoisies. Secondly, in each territory we can distinguish a number of peasantries who are differentiated according to locality— some localities being labor exporting, some food-crop exporting, some cash-crop exporting and some with varying proportions of each. In addition, these differentiations will often coincide with, and be reinforced by, localized cultural identifications, often of an ethnic or tribal nature. Of course, the pattern will not be a static one, but rather one changing over time as the system develops. Thirdly, the dynamic of capitalist development tends to introduce a further element which cuts across the differentiation of peasants by locality with a differentiation based on the degree of involvement in the cash economy. This involves, as we have seen, the possible movements toward proletarianization of migrant laborers on the one hand and toward capitalist agriculture on the other, and these two can chip away at the peasantry, pulling it in different directions.

It will be apparent that these complexities make any attempt to identify the historical role which the African peasantry is likely to define for itself a most treacherous one. For even were "peasants," under certain circumstances, to become conscious of their common interests and act politically on the basis of that awareness, the likely results are not readily predictable. Upon occasion, for example, one might find that the bulk of the peasantry in a given territory was available for an attempt to press its demands upon the other classes and interests in the society—where abuses by an alien authority or a highly compromised indigenous urban elite become so unbearable as to override consciousness of other fissures. More often, perhaps, localisms of various sorts (e.g., tribal consciousness) will prevail, to the point where even those aspects of the peasantry's economic and social grievances which might be generalized onto a territorial scale become obscured.[8] Similarly, where it is nascent horizontal dimensions which define a variety of peasantries, these may become the overriding determinant of peasant intervention in the historical process. Thus wealthy peasantries may move merely to open their own paths to capitalist farming (thereby altering the options for other peasants, some of whose passage to the agrarian proletariat may be correspondingly accelerated).[9] Or the "lower" peasantries may awaken to the burden of their condition and the quality of their likely fate before the latter is in fact sealed, and act on that awareness. For the latter, the means of their gaining consciousness, much less power, are particularly circumscribed, and as yet this is perhaps the most speculative of the alternatives which we have thrown up.

But in any case, such a discussion cannot be taken far in the abstract. Continental trends may be fruitfully discussed, of course, but cumulative insight into the peasant's role is more likely to be gained by bringing together an analysis of the nature of a particular national social system (situated within the context of the world economy) with a characterization of the internal dynamics of its peasantry. And this can be done satisfactorily only through case studies of actual historical experiences. We will therefore conclude with some brief reference to three such experiences, not under any pretense of exhausting their complexity but merely in order to *begin* the task of exemplifying the various criteria which we have presented and of underscoring the range of historical possibilities which we have hinted at.

In the context of Southern Rhodesia, where the capitalist framework of colonialism was characterized by the existence of a significant settler farming community able to establish political dominance over the various forces contending for control, the ability of the local African population to develop cash-crop agriculture on a scale that would have allowed the growth of a class of non-peasant capitalist farmers was checked.[10] In this specific situation only the development of tightly controlled small-scale cash farming has been permitted. The involvement of the peasantry has been forced into a pattern of subsistence agriculture with only small cash sales of agricultural produce on the one hand, and periods of paid employment for most males of working age as a means of meeting cash needs on the other. An attempt to stratify the peasantry by allowing the acquisition of small holdings with individual tenure through what was termed "native purchase" has been on too small a scale to have significant structural effects. As population pressure on impoverished land increases and circular patterns of labor migration become more difficult to sustain, almost all African agriculturalists within Rhodesia have therefore to accept the fate of increased proletarianization for at least some among their number, as well as a declining standard of living.[11] The alternative to this situation is a growth in consciousness about their class position and a revolutionary response to it.

In Ghana where, by contrast, there was no large-scale European farming community and hence a very different economic and political cast to the colonial situation, other patterns among the peasantry emerged. Thus in certain regions the cultivation of cocoa allowed the growth of large-scale cocoa farming by Ghanaian farmers. The peasants who developed these cocoa plantations were largely migrant farmers who quickly became capitalist farmers—to them we can hardly apply the term peasant.[12] But their emergence profoundly affected the position of other peasants in the Ghanaian political economy. Certain areas not well endowed with agricultural resources now developed labor-exporting peasantries, these traveling not only to some mines and to the cities, but also to the cocoa farming areas. A group of tenant farmers or debt farmers also emerged, and these can properly be seen as a peasantry, with a distinct class position.

Historically the capitalist cocoa farmers and wealthier peasants have been a politically conservative force, underpinning right-wing political parties as well as the post-Nkrumah military regime. In contrast, however, the lower peasantry was never fully and effectively enlisted into Nkrumah's movement, for the latter retained too many of the characteristics of a parasitic urban group to effectively mobilize their support. Market forces have therefore continued to chip away at the peasantry, albeit indecisively, for a deteriorating international market situation has sapped the power of cocoa to transform the rural economy and neither the Nkrumah regime nor its successor has developed strategies for industrialization which would provide an effective substitute. The peasantry's place has not therefore been eliminated by capitalist development, but neither have the abuses of incumbent elites proven a sufficient prod to generate its active intervention in the political arena.[13]

By contrast, Tanzania has not seen the development of one sizable and homogeneous group of cash-crop farmers from its peasant ranks. In many different areas (in accordance with the environmental potential that existed) annual or perennial crops have been developed as marketable cash crops, and in each such area some degree of differentiation has emerged among farmers. This differentiation is expressed not simply in terms of economic status, but by differential involvement in cooperative organizations and other modern institutions and privileged access to the advantages which they make available.[14] Increasingly there have been for the early movers paths leading out of the peasantry into the farmer class. But once again the economic mobility of some agriculturalists changes the nature of the system in which others begin to move. Thus, the unhindered play of this process promises to result in a complex pattern of stratification, one marked by a number of strata of agriculturalists stretching all the way from capitalist farmer to landless laborer. In addition, regional differences which spring in part from the realities of different agro-ecological environments and marketing opportunities may give rise, as has happened elsewhere, to "local" peasantries (sometimes wearing the cloak of tribalism) which have different structural positions, and conflicting interests, in the total system.

The Tanzanian government has been aware of the first stirrings of these possibilities and—almost alone among governments in sub-Saharan Africa—has chosen to confront the tasks of *preempting* them. So far this has involved only the tentative beginnings of that radicalization of the political structure which might enlist the support and involvement of the mass of the rural population. But the leadership does argue for the possibility of a *socialist transformation* of the peasantries and has embarked upon a search for the modern collective forms appropriate to that end.[15] There has been some parallel attempt to redefine the nature of the country's relations with the international capitalist system and by so doing to effect a basic change in the peasants' structural position. Whether this attempt will withstand the opposition of those non-peasants (and advanced peasants) whose positions are threatened by such a strategy remains to be seen.

It is hoped that such "case studies," though derisory in their brevity, will at least have indicated the importance of continuing the study of the African peasantry along some of the lines which we have indicated. It scarcely requires stating that a great deal of additional work in the spheres of conceptualization and historico-sociological investigation remains to be done.

Notes

1. E. R. Wolf, *Peasants* (Englewood Cliffs, N.J., 1966), p. 2.
2. Chayanov's theory of the peasant economy with its emphasis on the dual role of the peasant *household* as both a productive and a consumptive group is a valuable conceptual tool in any study of peasants. In much of Africa the concept needs to be extended to that of a *homestead* economy as a basic unit of analysis. The homestead, which is based on the joint property rights of an extended family, frequently has rights to farm land rather than rights to a particular farm. (A. V. Chayanov, *The Theory of Peasant Economy* [1925; Chicago, 1966].)
3. Pastoralists are an important category of the rural population in a number of African countries. Since these predominantly pastoral people are subject to the same kinds of political and economic forces as their predominantly agricultural brethren and since their productive economy (in as much as it involves rights to, and control over, the family herds) is based on a similar kind of "homestead" principle, they would fulfill our own limited criteria for peasants. We would thus include them in any study of African peasantries, however much this might offend "peasant purists."
4. L. A. Fallers, "Are African Cultivators to Be Called 'Peasants'?", *Current Anthropology*, no. 2 (1961), pp. 108–10.
5. See A. G. Frank, *Capitalism and Underdevelopment in Latin America* (New York, 1967), and M. Harris, *Patterns of Race in the Americas* (New York, 1964) for two very different but illuminating studies which situate Latin American peasantries in historical and structural terms.
6. See Chapter 1 of this volume, which assesses the socioeconomic patterns to be found in the "modern sector" of African countries in terms of their ability to transform the rural economy.
7. Our attention was drawn to the importance of seeing peasant aggregates in certain of these terms by an unpublished paper of D. L. Barnett, "Three Types of African Peasantry," mimeo (n.d.).
8. On this point as well as for further discussion of the likely range of political

roles for the peasantry in contemporary Africa see Chapter 2 of this volume.

9. An important variable which we have not been able to explore here is the pressure of population upon the land. Taken as a whole African land resources are considerable but areas of "population pressure" do exist and in these areas the options open to individual peasants are much more limited. There the growth of a farmer class tends to mean the proletarianization of others.

10. See Chapter 7 of this volume.

11. A forthcoming study by Roger Woods on the "Native Purchase Areas of Rhodesia" will elaborate upon these and related points.

12. P. Hill, *Migrant Cocoa Farmers of Southern Ghana* (London, 1963).

13. B. Fitch and M. Oppenheimer, *Ghana: End of an Illusion* (New York, 1966).

14. J. S. Saul, "Marketing Cooperatives in a Developing Country," in P. Worsley, ed., *Two Blades of Grass* (Manchester, 1971).

15. J. K. Nyerere, *Socialism and Rural Development* (1967), reprinted in Nyerere, *Freedom and Socialism* (Oxford, 1968).